Constitutional Reform
and
Effective Government

About Brookings

The Brookings Institution is a private nonprofit organization devoted to research, education, and publication on important issues of domestic and foreign policy. Its principal purpose is to bring knowledge to bear on the current and emerging policy problems facing the American people.

A board of trustees is responsible for general supervision of the Institution and safeguarding of its independence. The president is the chief administrative officer and bears final responsibility for the decision to publish a manuscript as a Brookings book. In reaching this judgment, the president is advised by a panel of expert readers who report in confidence on the quality of the work. Publication of a work signifies that it is deemed a competent treatment worthy of public consideration but does not imply endorsement of conclusions or recommendations. The Institution itself does not take positions on policy issues.

JAMES L. SUNDQUIST

Constitutional Reform and Effective Government

Revised Edition

THE BROOKINGS INSTITUTION
Washington, D.C.

Copyright © 1992

THE BROOKINGS INSTITUTION

1775 Massachusetts Avenue, N.W., Washington, D.C. 20036

Library of Congress Cataloging-in-Publication data:

Sundquist, James L.
    Constitutional reform and effective government / James L.
Sundquist.—Rev. ed.
        p.   cm.
    Includes bibliographical references and index.
    ISBN 0-8157-8230-6 (cloth)
    ISBN 0-8157-8229-2 (pbk.)
    1. Presidents—United States.   2. United States Congress.
3. Separation of powers—United States.   4. United States—
Constitutional history.   I. Title.
JK585.S86   1992
342.73'04—dc20
[347.3024]   92-30775
                                                             CIP

9 8 7 6 5 4 3 2 1

The paper used in this publication meets the minimum requirements of the
American National Standard for Information Sciences—Permanence of paper
for Printed Library Materials, ANSI Z39.48-1984.

Foreword

That the structure of the U.S. government, designed in the great convention of 1787, has survived virtually intact through two centuries of turmoil, growth, and change is testimony to the wisdom of the framers and the basic soundness of the governmental system they created.

Yet the framers themselves, when they adjourned after that hot summer in Philadelphia, were the first to acknowledge that their handiwork was less than perfect and that, as the nation gained experience under the Constitution, it would have to reexamine its provisions and, as necessary, modify them. Nevertheless, although the Constitution has been amended twenty-seven times, not one of those changes has altered the fundamental institutional structure.

In the original edition of *Constitutional Reform and Effective Government*, published by Brookings in 1986, James L. Sundquist reviewed the framers' rationale for the governmental structure they created, the successful and unsuccessful efforts to modify it during the ensuing two centuries, and the arguments for and against specific alterations that have been discussed. In the end, he developed his own recommendations for constitutional reform.

The favorable response to that book prompted Brookings to encourage the author to undertake this revised edition. As in the first version, he organizes his critique around five questions: First, does the recent tendency of the voters to divide control of the executive and legislative branches of the government between the major parties exacerbate conflict between the branches and lead to stalemate and deadlock? Second, does the short interval of only two years between national elections tend to preoccupy presidents and legislators alike with the always-imminent next election, and therefore limit to only a few months each four years the "window of opportunity" for dealing with pressing matters? Third, is there need for a workable mechanism

v

for replacing a government that has palpably failed, for any of a wide range of possible reasons, without waiting for what may be a dangerously long time until the next regularly scheduled election? Fourth, can collaboration between the branches be improved, particularly by strengthening political parties as unifying instruments? Fifth, should the system of checks and balances designed two hundred years ago be altered by, for example, giving the president the item veto, restoring the legislative veto that has been declared unconstitutional, or reducing the two-thirds requirement for Senate approval of treaties?

Within this context, he has added discussion of two constitutional issues that have become topics of lively public discussion since 1986: whether the number of terms a member of Congress may serve should be limited, and whether the election process that assigns the choice of the president to an electoral college (and, if that body produces no majority, to the House of Representatives) should be altered.

In refining and sharpening his analysis of the pros and cons of various possible constitutional amendments, Sundquist has benefited from the intensive discussion of the Constitution during the bicentennial celebration of that document in 1987; from the outpouring of scholarly research and commentary in the last six years, stimulated especially by the recognition that a government divided between the parties has become the norm instead of the exception; and from participation in the work of the Committee on the Constitutional System, an organization of present and former government executives and legislators, scholars, and other observers who have been meeting since 1981 to consider issues of constitutional reform and who issued a report in 1987.

The author acknowledges once again the encouragement and assistance he received in the original work from Paul E. Peterson, then director of the Brookings Governmental Studies program; the constructive comments of James W. Fesler, Nathan Tarcov, and Aaron B. Wildavsky; and the aid of Diane Hodges, Pamela D. Harris, Nancy K. Kintner, Judith H. Newman, and Joel M. Ostrow. In preparing this edition, he thanks Robert L. Faherty, director of Publications, for making the original suggestion; Thomas E. Mann, currently director of Governmental Studies, for advice and guidance; his associates in the Committee on the Constitutional System—particularly Douglas Dillon, Lloyd N. Cutler, James MacGregor Burns, Donald L. Robinson, and Peter P. Schauffler—for inspiration and stimulation; Antoi-

nette T. Williams, Susan J. Thompson, and Elizabeth O. Toy for sec-
retarial assistance; Jane Foxon Maddocks for preparing the index; and
Nancy D. Davidson for patient and skillful editing. He and all of her
other associates at Brookings also take this occasion to honor the
memory of Alice M. Carroll, who edited the original edition as well
as four of Sundquist's other Brookings books.

The Brookings Institution is grateful for the financial support
granted for the original study by the American Express Foundation,
the Dillon Fund, the Ford Foundation, the William and Flora Hewlett
Foundation, and the Rockefeller Foundation. The views expressed in
the book are the author's own and should not be attributed to financial
donors, the officers or members of the Committee on the Constitutional System, or the trustees, officers, or other staff members of the
Brookings Institution.

BRUCE K. MAC LAURY
President

August 1992
Washington, D.C.

Contents

For
Gerry

CHAPTER ONE

The Constitutional Dilemma

"Nothing human can be perfect," wrote Gouverneur Morris, looking back at the work of the Constitutional Convention twenty-eight years afterward. "Surrounded by difficulties, we did the best we could; leaving it with those who should come after us to take counsel from experience, and exercise prudently the power of amendment, which we had provided."[1] Thus did the one among the founding fathers who contributed most to the style and arrangement of the Constitution agree with the one who contributed most to its substance, James Madison. "I am not one of the number if there be any such," wrote Madison after eleven of the thirteen states had approved the document, "who think the Constitution lately adopted a faultless work."[2]

The Constitution achieved two purposes. First, it created a structure of government for the new republic; it defined the unique American tripartite system of independent yet interdependent branches (executive, legislative, and judicial), prescribed how those holding national office should be chosen, and sought to draw a boundary between the powers of the national government and those of the states. Second, it provided a limited body of fundamental substantive law, relating to such subjects of controversy at the time as slavery,

1. Letter to W. H. Wells, February 24, 1815, in Max Farrand, ed., *The Records of the Federal Convention of 1787*, 1937 rev. ed., 4 vols. (Yale University Press, 1966), vol. 3, pp. 421–22.
2. Letter to G. L. Turberville, November 2, 1788, in ibid., p. 354.

civil liberties, the public debt, taxation, regulation of commerce, and titles of nobility.

When Madison was writing, public dissatisfaction centered on the second of these elements of the Constitution, its substantive provisions—specifically on the absence of a bill of rights. That omission was corrected when the First Congress proposed the ten amendments that the states ratified by 1791. Since then, the Constitution has been amended only seventeen times in two centuries, and most of those amendments have pertained also to substantive matters. Two of them—the Eighteenth, which prohibited alcoholic beverages, and the Twenty-first, which repealed the prohibition—left the document substantively unchanged. Of the remaining fifteen, seven further expanded the guarantees of civil rights. The Thirteenth outlawed slavery, and the Fourteenth guaranteed the rights of blacks and other citizens as well; four extended the right to vote, to blacks (the Fifteenth), to women (the Nineteenth), to young people at the age of eighteen (the Twenty-sixth), and to residents of the District of Columbia in presidential elections (the Twenty-third); and the Twenty-fourth Amendment abolished the poll tax as a requirement for voting. Two of the remaining amendments concerned the powers of the federal government: the Eleventh imposed a minor limitation on the jurisdiction of the federal courts, and the Sixteenth removed the constitutional prohibition against a graduated income tax. And the Twenty-seventh Amendment, proposed by the Congress in 1789 as part of its bill-of-rights package but not ratified until its rediscovery two centuries later, in 1992, attended to an administrative detail; it requires the Congress, whenever it raises the pay of its members, to postpone the effective date until after the next congressional election.

Only five of the twenty-seven amendments, then, dealt with the structure of the government created by the Constitution—which is the concern of this book—as distinct from the scope of its authority and the rights and liberties of U.S. citizens. And of those five, three can be considered technical or peripheral; they corrected flaws in the design of the structure or adapted it to new circumstances without altering the nature or relationships of the institutions as the framers had conceived them. The Twelfth Amendment, ratified in 1804, separated the balloting for president and vice president in the electoral college and thus accommodated to the age of parties the rather anomalous—from a modern perspective—nonpartisan presidential selection system conceived by the founders. The Twentieth Amendment, adopted in 1933, established the present January dates for the inauguration of presidents and the convening of Congresses, thus belatedly adjusting the political calendar to the development of steam transportation. The Twenty-fifth Amendment, approved in 1967, finally filled two gaps in the constitutional system that the founders had neglected to close. One provision established a procedure for the vice president to become acting president when the president is disabled. The second set up a process for the selection of a new vice president when that office becomes vacant—the process that was promptly used twice, when Gerald R. Ford was chosen to succeed Spiro T. Agnew and when Nelson A. Rockefeller was approved to replace Ford on the latter's advancement to the presidency.

That leaves only two amendments that have affected in any way the character of the institutions that were bequeathed to the twentieth century by the eighteenth. One was the Seventeenth Amendment, ratified in 1913, which provided that senators would be directly elected by the people rather than appointed by state legislatures. That action not only altered the constitutional balance between the federal government and the states but changed the nature of the Senate by introducing into its membership men and women of new political styles. The other was the Twenty-second Amendment, ratified in 1951, which limited presidents to two four-year terms and so decreed that each reelected president would enter his second term as a "lame duck," with whatever consequences that status might have on his relations with the Congress.

Even these two amendments influenced the institutions only indirectly, by affecting the selection or retention of the occupants of offices, not by adding to or subtracting from the constellation of institutions established by the Constitution or altering the formal distribution of power among them. The country's governmental architecture has proved, then, to be amazingly durable in a world of change. While some nations have shifted from monarchies to democracies to dictatorships and back again, while some have adopted and discarded and redesigned entire constitutions, the structure that was designed for the United States government in one eighteenth century summer remains in force essentially unchanged.

Does this mean that this human document was, after all, perfect in its basic design, despite the modest disclaimer of Gouverneur Morris? Many have thought so. It was William Ewart Gladstone, the British prime minister, who described the Constitution in a moment of ecstasy as "the most wonderful work ever struck off at a given time by the brain and purpose of man."[3] Surely the durability of the constitutional structure and the growth and prosperity of the country governed by it are a testament to the wisdom and inspiration of the framers. Had the system they designed verged at any time on outright failure, serious and sustained movements to alter its basic features would have been born. Yet in two centuries, the only two significant movements for structural change were those that produced the Seventeenth and Twenty-second amendments, and even those alterations did not reach to the fundamentals of the institutional system. In all that time, no failed movement of any consequence can be added to the short list of reform efforts.[4]

The Current Constitutional Debate

If the constitutional structure has served the country so well for so long, the question is appropriate: Why discuss reform at all? The cliché "If it ain't broke, don't fix it" makes a valid point. Trying to improve something that is working reasonably well can sometimes make things worse.

Yet that counsel is too negative. Its message is that breakdown must be awaited, not averted. Moreover, breakdown is not usually

3. "Kin Beyond the Sea," *North American Review* (September 1878).

4. As of the summer of 1992, the only proposed constitutional amendment with significant momentum is one that would write into the Constitution, with one or another form of escape clause, a requirement that the federal budget be balanced. Thirty-two state legislatures had by then joined in proposing a constitutional convention to consider such an amendment—just two short of the number (two-thirds of the states) that would compel the Congress, under the Constitution, to call the convention. Responding to this pressure, both houses debated balanced budget amendments in June 1992, but defeated them—the House by a favorable vote of 280 to 153, 9 short of the necessary two-thirds, and the Senate by failing to muster the 60 votes required to close debate. In any event, a balanced budget amendment would fall into the category of a substantive change that would not affect the institutional structure with which this book is concerned. Therefore, like other substantive amendments, such as those concerning abortion, school prayer, and equal rights for women, it is not discussed further.

an absolute but a matter of degree. Weaknesses in a governmental system can debilitate and devitalize a government, short of outright collapse. Should a partial breakdown, reflected in simple inefficiency and ineffectiveness, be tolerated on the supposition that the cure will be worse than the ailment? After all, most of the world's great inventions, in technology and social affairs alike, have sprung from somebody's urge to make better what, at the time, most people undoubtedly considered good.

Inefficiency: Both Safeguard and Danger

Few would deny that the American governmental system, in its two centuries, has shown weaknesses and inefficiencies. Defenders of the status quo respond simply that this is as it was meant to be and should be. Writing just before his retirement in 1984, Barber Conable, the veteran Republican representative from New York, acknowledged "the well-known mess which at any given time clutters up the Washington landscape" and the "laggard" character of the American government, but argued that the system was intended to work that way and "we are better for it." "The Founding Fathers," wrote Conable, "didn't want efficient, adventurous governments, fearing they would intrude on our individual liberties. I think they were right, and I offer our freedom, stability, and prosperity as evidence."[5]

The danger lies in the fact that a government has objectives that all will agree are good and necessary—national security and economic prosperity, to name but two—in addition to whatever objectives some may deem unworthy. And the good and bad cannot be separated. A government too inefficient to embark on adventurous efforts to change society is also liable to be, by necessity, too inefficient to meet its inescapable, imperative responsibilities. U.S. history abounds with illustrations of governmental failures that, if they did not destroy "freedom, stability, and prosperity," at least threatened and sometimes impaired them. What constitutes failure may, of course, be disputed, but contemporary popular opinion as well as the retrospective judgment of history may be called on to help in identifying some examples.

---

5. *Roll Call*, April 19, 1984; reprinted in *This Constitution: A Bicentennial Chronicle* (Winter 1984), pp. 42–43.

The most indisputable of all the instances of failure—secession and civil war—perhaps could not have been averted by any American government, however structured. Maybe the same can be said of the crash of 1929 that precipitated the Great Depression. But the paralysis of the government for more than three years after that crash, in the face of increasing and intolerable suffering, is harder to explain away as reflecting virtue in the system. The constitutional structure provided no mechanism by which the people, when it was clear they had lost confidence in their leaders, could place in office new ones, with a fresh mandate to use the powers of government vigorously to alleviate suffering and restore prosperity. They could replace only a part of the government, in 1930, and that only intensified the policy deadlock that prevailed until the presidential election two years later.

The country's foreign affairs, in this century, offer innumerable examples of ineffective policy, brought about by the inability of leaders to harmonize all of the institutional elements that, under the Constitution, must act in concert before any decisive policy can be carried out. The country could participate in the sacrifices of World War I, by the will of the majority, but it could not join in the League of Nations that its president helped to design to construct and maintain the peace—not because the majority did not similarly will it, but because the constitutional system that requires a two-thirds majority of the Senate to approve treaties empowered the minority to rule. In Vietnam, the United States lost its first war—surely a failure by any objective standard—because it could not muster sufficient unity either to do whatever was necessary for victory or to disengage and withdraw cleanly at an early stage. Since then, conflict between the president and the Congress has rendered American policy ineffective—most conspicuously, in the 1980s, in the case of Nicaragua, where neither the president's policy of assisting the contra forces to overthrow the Sandinista government nor the congressional opposition's policy to withdraw support altogether could be pursued with firmness and decision. One consequence of that executive-legislative conflict was the so-called Iran-contra scandal uncovered in 1987–88, in which high administrative officials were convicted of taking illegal action to circumvent congressional prohibitions against assistance to the contras. President George Bush's success in obtaining the support of a majority in Congress for his intervention to free Kuwait in 1990–91 is more atypical than typical of interbranch relationships during the past quarter century.[6]

In retrospect, the country clearly approves of social security, unemployment compensation, medicare, civil rights, and federal efforts to alleviate poverty and raise standards of education, housing, and nutrition. During the Reagan administration, the national commitment to some programs in these areas was scaled back but few were eliminated; the structure of the welfare state that remains in place reflects a genuine national consensus. But the welfare state came late to the United States; most of its major elements were adopted here decades later than in the industrial democracies of Europe, and in some of the essential elements that make up the welfare state, the United States still lags. Health care is the most conspicuous example; despite the almost universal recognition that the roughly 35 million Americans unprotected by medical insurance represent an urgent national problem, the instruments of government have been immobilized to deal with it. They are equally ineffective in providing, or influencing the market to provide, housing within the reach of low-income families. And in instances where effective policies are now in place, the process of pushing legislation to enactment has often been excruciatingly slow and painful. Civil rights legislation was stalled for years, even decades, until the logjam was broken by the televised images of law enforcement officers using police dogs and fire hoses on peaceful demonstrators. The social legislation that is deemed necessary and useful now would have been equally useful earlier, and the national

6. Interbranch conflicts over foreign policy in recent years are reviewed in a series of case studies in Thomas E. Mann, ed., *A Question of Balance: The President, the Congress, and Foreign Policy* (Brookings, 1990). Earlier issues, from the mid-1960s to the mid-1970s, are discussed in my *The Decline and Resurgence of Congress* (Brookings, 1981), chaps. 9, 10. Foreign statesmen have often complained of the difficulty of dealing with the divided U.S. government on urgent matters of common concern. Typical is the plaint of Peter Smithers, former member of the British Parliament, minister in Conservative cabinets, and secretary-general of the Council of Europe: "The decision-making mechanism in the U.S. is, in the literal sense of the word, incoherent. The president is elected with a program he considers himself obligated to carry through. Congress is elected separately and its composition will not necessarily correspond with the president's wishes. . . . The president has no power to dissolve Congress. . . . The result, inevitably, is a conflict of wills and a dangerous paralysis of government. . . . The effect of this paralysis of government on U.S. interests and the outside world is devastating. . . . In foreign policy those institutions are uncertain and vacillating. Will the policy of the president or that of the Congress prevail? Or will we get a lame compromise between incompatibles?" "Of Presidential Paralysis and Constitutions," *Wall Street Journal*, December 29, 1987.

consensus in support of most of the measures—civil rights is a conspicuous example—had formed two or three decades before they were
eventually enacted. Failure to translate consensus into policy with
reasonable promptness can be attributed in considerable measure to
the multiple veto points that exist in a system of separate and coequal
branches, which enabled minority interests in these cases to thwart, in
the name of individual liberty, the will of the majority. The consequences
of America's constitutional structure became the nation's loss.

In 1973 and 1974, the country witnessed the collapse of an administration mired in crime, but lacked the means to place a new leader
in the White House—until by lucky accident an Oval Office tape
recording was finally discovered that implicated the president in criminal activity beyond a reasonable doubt. President Richard M. Nixon's
resignation restored the government, but only partially. The deadlock
between the Republican president and the Democratic Congress that
had rendered the government immobile in the Nixon period continued under Gerald Ford, with incessant quarreling between the
branches over the whole range of foreign and domestic policy.

Throughout the 1980s and into the 1990s, the country's gravest
domestic problem was universally adjudged to be its unprecedented
peacetime budgetary deficit. This averaged over $200 billion during the
nine-year period beginning with President Ronald Reagan's first full fiscal
year (which began October 1, 1981) and ending with the fiscal year
1990, rose to $287 billion in 1991, and was officially projected to reach
$399 billion in 1992 and $352 billion in 1993, even using highly optimistic
assumptions about the state of the national economy. The estimated
1992 deficit will amount to 6.7 percent of the gross domestic product
(GDP), a proportion higher even than the deficits of the Great Depression years and exceeded only during World War II.[7] In 1992, the total
national debt stood at $4,000 billion (more than quadrupled since 1981)
and was officially projected to reach $6,000 billion by 1997—or more
than six times the 1981 level. As a proportion of GDP, the debt had
been brought steadily down from 127 percent in 1946 to 33 percent
in 1981, but has risen each year since, passing the 70 percent mark
in 1992.[8]

---

7. *Budget of the United States Government, Fiscal Year 1993*, tables 2-3, 2-9.
8. *Budget of the United States Government, Fiscal Year 1992*, table 7-1, and *Budget of
the United States Government, Fiscal Year 1993*, chart 2-2. The percentages for 1946–81

All this, too, represented an alarming failure of governmental institutions to translate a clear national consensus into policy: both Presidents Reagan and Bush, the leaders and majorities of both parties in both houses of Congress, virtually every serious candidate for national leadership during the decade, and the preponderance of expert opinion inside and outside the government (including the governors of the Federal Reserve System) all agreed that the ballooning national deficit imperiled the economy, limited the government's ability to respond to any recession that might occur (as one did in 1990–92), and represented a moral default by thrusting on future generations the burden of paying for this generation's profligacy. Yet the competing branches of the government could not arrive at a common policy. Indeed, until the decade's end they did not even engage in good faith negotiations. President Reagan resisted overtures from the Democratic leadership for formal discussions; during most of his term, it could truly be said that it was easier for the Soviet Union's president, Mikhail Gorbachev, to arrange a "summit" meeting with the president of the United States than it was for the Speaker of the U.S. House of Representatives. After a stock market crash late in 1987, Reagan did accede to a meeting with congressional leaders, and an agreement was reached. In 1990 President Bush negotiated a further agreement with the legislators. But the budget ceilings and tax increases that were agreed to will, at best, only slowly reduce the magnitude of the annual deficit. The forceful measures that would have been necessary to even approach the balanced budget that the leaders of both parties proclaimed as their goal would have required more unity and decisiveness than a government divided between opposing parties showed any promise of attaining.

The Recurrent Questions

Whenever the people sense that their government is failing, their tendency is to blame the individuals who hold elective office. Sometimes the condemnation falls on politicians as a class, as shown in the anti-incumbent mood that seemed to sweep the country in the early 1990s. But usually it has come to center upon the most con-

---

are calculated from the gross national product (GNP) rather than GDP, but the differences are not significant.

spicuous and powerful of all officeholders, the one who occupies the
White House. It was not the system that failed, in the public view,
but Herbert Hoover, or Lyndon Johnson, or Richard Nixon, or
whoever. The process by which leaders are selected is a crucial part
of any governmental system, of course, and some selection methods
may produce better results than others. But granting that none of
them can assure that ideal leaders will be chosen, the American constitutional system places extraordinary obstacles in the path of any
leader. A president is expected to lead the Congress, but its two
houses are independent institutions, and, most of the time of late,
one or both are controlled by the political opposition. And when a
president fails as leader—whether because the Congress chooses not
to follow or because of any of the many possible forms of personal
inadequacy—the system has no safeguard. The government cannot
be reconstituted until the calendar announces that the day of the next
presidential election has arrived. Unless one contends that all of the
historical episodes cited here as examples of governmental failure
were in fact successes, one is impelled to ask whether the constitutional system inherited from the eighteenth century is indeed ade-
quate for the twenty-first. Specifically, five questions recur.

Would an electoral system that encouraged unified party control of
the three centers of decisionmaking—presidency, Senate, and
House—make for more effective, responsible, and accountable government?

Would longer terms for the president or for legislators, and a longer
span between elections, enable leaders to rise to a higher level of
statesmanship in confronting crucial issues, permit the resolution of
issues that now go unresolved because of the short two-year life of
each successive Congress, and allow greater deliberation and care in
the legislative process?

Can a better solution be devised to deal with the immobility of government brought about by leadership failure, or deadlock and quarreling between the president and the Congress, than simply waiting
helplessly until the next presidential election comes around?

Can harmonious collaboration between the executive and legislative
branches be induced through formal interlocking of the branches or
through strengthening the political parties that are the web that binds
administrators and legislators to a common purpose?

Should any of the constitutional checks and balances by which the executive and legislative branches are enabled to thwart each other be modified to permit one or the other branch to prevail more readily and thus facilitate decisions?

Questions such as these (which are the subjects of chapters 4 through 8 of this book) are being asked more insistently now, by more national leaders of experience and stature, than probably at any time in history. This is evidenced by the founding early in 1981, of the Committee on the Constitutional System (CCS), cochaired after its incorporation by a former cabinet member (Douglas Dillon, secretary of the treasury in the John F. Kennedy administration), a former White House counsel (Lloyd N. Cutler, counsel to President Jimmy Carter), and an incumbent senator (Nancy Landon Kassebaum, Republican of Kansas) and enrolling in its membership a significant number of current and former members of Congress and high officials of the executive branch, as well as constitutional scholars, journalist observers of the Washington scene, and others.

"Our governmental problems do not lie with the quality or character of our elected representatives," contended Dillon at the time he joined in founding the CCS. "Rather they lie with a system which promotes divisiveness and makes it difficult, if not impossible, to develop truly national policies." The division of power between the president and Congress makes "stalemate" inevitable, and "no one can place the blame," continues Dillon. "The President blames the Congress, the Congress blames the President, and the public remains confused and disgusted with government in Washington." The country cannot speak with "one, clear voice" in foreign affairs, and it lacks ability "to act promptly and energetically in the face of a crisis."[9] Cutler put it in similar language. "In parliamentary terms," he wrote, "one might say that under the U.S. Constitution it is not now feasible to 'form a Government,' " one made up of an elected majority that is "able to carry out an overall program, and is held accountable for its success or failure."[10]

9. Douglas Dillon, address at Tufts University, May 30, 1982; reprinted in Donald L. Robinson, ed., *Reforming American Government: The Bicentennial Papers of the Committee on the Constitutional System* (Westview Press, 1985), pp. 24–29.

10. Lloyd N. Cutler, "To Form a Government," *Foreign Affairs*, vol. 59 (Fall 1980), pp. 127, 132; reprinted in Robinson, ed., *Reforming American Government*, pp. 11–23.

In its report, issued in January 1987, the Committee on the Constitutional System struck an alarmist tone in analyzing what it called "the failures and weaknesses in governmental performance." "The signs of strain in our governing processes," it concluded, "are unmistakable." It found the "mounting national debt" to be perhaps "the most alarming evidence," and emphasized also that "consistency in our foreign and national security policies is . . . frustrated by an institutional contest of wills between Presidents and shifting, cross-party coalitions within the Congress." Frustration and "leaks" have in turn "led Presidents and their staffs to launch important diplomatic, military and covert activities in secret and without consulting Congress." While the separation of powers "has served us well in preventing tyranny and the abuse of high office," it has done so "by encouraging confrontation, indecision and deadlock, and by diffusing accountability for the results." Particularly in times when the executive branch and the Congress are controlled by opposing parties—80 percent of the time since 1968—the consequence is "inconsistency, incoherence and even stagnation in national policy." The report appeared, by coincidence, at what should have been an auspicious moment—the beginning of the bicentennial of the framing of the Constitution—but the nationwide commemoration during that year was conceived as a celebration of the wisdom of the framers and the merits of the 1787 Constitution, and the year passed with no significant discussion, outside an occasional academic conference, of what may be the "failures and weaknesses" of the governmental structure then entering its third century.[11]

Ideology and Reform

The words *stalemate* and *deadlock*—or, in their latest variation, *gridlock*—recur as a constant theme in the critiques of the reformers. The historian and political scientist James MacGregor Burns, a founder of

11. The recommendations in the CCS report, entitled "A Bicentennial Analysis of the American Political Structure" (Washington: January 1987), are summarized in chapter 3 and further discussed in the sections of later chapters that analyze particular problems and proposed remedies. The decision to form the CCS was taken at a meeting in Washington in January 1981. I joined in founding the CCS and have been a member of its board of directors since the beginning, but my own views were developed independently and were incorporated initially in the first edition of this book, published by Brookings in 1986, a year before the CCS report was issued.

the CCS, described in 1963 what he called *The Deadlock of Democracy:* a "somber and inexorable cycle" that leads this country's public affairs from "deadlock" to "drift" to the enactment of "bits and pieces" of an election mandate during a "short honeymoon" between the president and the Congress, then back once more to "the old cycle of deadlock and drift."[12] Burns was writing then of the failure of the Congress to enact the liberal program of John F. Kennedy, just as supporters of Franklin Roosevelt's New Deal had complained of the legislators' "obstruction" of their hero's legislative proposals a quarter century before. One source of constitutional reform sentiment, then, has been the frustration of activists with a government that, because of the division of policymaking authority, has so often proven incapable of moving boldly and decisively in dealing with domestic problems.

To the conservatives, of course, the relative sluggishness of the U.S. government in intervening in domestic matters is a merit of the Constitution rather than a fault. They agree that the American system has an endemic tendency to deadlock, stalemate, delay, and indecision. But, they contend, with Barber Conable, that the founding fathers were right to contrive just such a system, to check impulsive, demagogic, and egalitarian legislation. James Q. Wilson, in a well-argued summary of the case against constitutional change, is frank to emphasize that one of the merits of the existing constitutional system is that it serves to advance the conservative political agenda: "Political change is slower, and so the growth of new programs and public spending is slower."[13] And while the system requires an extraordinarily high degree of consensus for action to be taken, conservatives argue, that is a necessary foundation for enforceable legislation anyway. Contending forces must compromise, and minority views must be accommodated, and that confers legitimacy on the policies ultimately adopted.

To a degree, then, constitutional reform has been a debate between liberals and conservatives, between those who see the separation of powers as a barrier to governmental activism, and those who see it as a protection against excess. That debate is essentially unresolvable,

12. *The Deadlock of Democracy: Four Party Politics in America* (Prentice-Hall, 1963), p. 2.

13. James Q. Wilson, "Does the Separation of Powers Still Work?" *The Public Interest*, no. 86 (Winter 1987), p. 49.

for the two sides are influenced heavily by value judgments relating
to the ends and role of government. Would a government capable of
translating an election "mandate" into quick, decisive action do more
good than harm? The activists say it would, but that is because they
have been traditionally optimistic about the beneficence of governmental intervention. The conservatives have been generally less san-
guine about the wisdom of politicians and the competence of administrative agencies. Beyond that, the two sides can never agree on what
is truly beneficial. All of the constituent programs of the welfare
state—social security, education, health, housing, and all the rest—
redistribute resources from taxpayers to the recipients of the governmental benefits, which usually means from the upper to the lower
ranges of the income scale. Whether one regards the redistribution
as "beneficial" depends largely on whether one views the transaction
from the top or from the bottom, on where one's sympathies lie.

   Yet there are other themes in the constitutional debate beyond the
liberal-conservative argument over domestic policy, and these provide
the basis for a broader, less partisan and ideological, discussion. A
second impulse toward constitutional reform has come from those
who have helped to conduct the nation's foreign affairs, and here the
liberal-conservative split is less apparent. The liberal Woodrow Wilson
was defeated when the Senate rejected the Versailles treaty, and the
liberal-backed Strategic Arms Limitation Treaty (SALT II) negotiated
by Jimmy Carter had to be withdrawn, but conservatives Richard
Nixon, Gerald Ford, and Ronald Reagan found their foreign policies
undercut by congressional liberals, often leaving the country with no
clear foreign policy at all.

   In the Reagan years, the country witnessed an unprecedented political configuration—an activist conservative president determined to
roll back the welfare state encountering increasing resistance from a
moderate Congress more disposed to defend the status quo. It was
the conservatives' turn to experience the frustration of the separate
powers. Nevertheless, not many Reaganites identified the constitutional structure as a problem to be concerned about; perhaps the
phenomenal success of their president in 1981 in mobilizing the Congress—including even the Democratic-controlled House—to enact
the essential features of his program was still too fresh a memory.
Yet his inability, after the 1981 success, to lead the government significantly further in the direction he had set did arouse some alarm

on the conservative side of the ideological divide. "We're learning that our worst fears about the inability of our institutions to function are turning out to be right," warned Alan Greenspan, then chairman of President Ford's Council of Economic Advisers, commenting on the government's failure to come to grips with "the real long-term budget problem." [14] Earlier, David A. Stockman, about to retire as President Reagan's budget director, had deplored the "political division and policy conflict within our governmental institutions" that had "reached such an extreme and intense state that it is nearly impossible to see where the political will and consensus will come from that is necessary to enact any plan big enough to balance the books—or even substantially close the gap." [15] Decrying congressional conduct during the Iran-contra scandal in 1987, Jeane Kirkpatrick, the former Reagan ambassador to the United Nations, concluded that "maybe we ought to have some congressional hearings on the problem of divided government." [16] Five years later, House Minority Leader Robert H. Michel, Republican of Illinois, was urging President Bush to campaign on the issue that "divided government doesn't work." [17]

If the conservatives continue to elect presidents, and then find themselves confronting the same deadlocks that liberal presidents experienced most of the time in their years in power during the past half century, conservatives and liberals may some day find constitutional reform, for the first time, a common cause. But perhaps not. If conservatives begin to decry obstacles in the constitutional structure

14. "Waiting for the Crisis: An Interview with Alan Greenspan," *Washington Post*, August 4, 1985, p. B8. Greenspan was appointed chairman of the Federal Reserve Board in 1987.

15. Speech, June 5, 1985, reported in *New York Times*, June 29, 1985, p. 37. While not questioning the basic constitutional structure, conservatives, including President Reagan, were rallying behind the item veto as one reform they considered necessary, but their main effort was directed at accomplishing the change by statute rather than through constitutional amendment. (This issue is discussed in chapter 8.) They also supported the proposal for an amendment to require a balanced federal budget except in certain circumstances and to limit the growth of spending.

16. Jeane Kirkpatrick, "Abrams and the Strange Workings of Divided Government," *Washington Post*, July 6, 1987, p. 11. (The reference is to Assistant Secretary of State Elliot Abrams, who admitted misleading Congress by withholding information.)

17. David S. Broder, "GOP's Michel Calls Perot 'Demagogue,' " *Washington Post*, May 22, 1992, p. A20. (Michel was discussing the independent presidential candidacy of Ross Perot.)

because they hamper Republican presidents just as they blocked Franklin Roosevelt or John Kennedy, liberals may find new merit in those same obstacles, for the same reason.

That is the constitutional dilemma. An institutional structure that enables the government to move decisively to do good things will also enable it to move with dispatch to do bad things, whatever one's definition of those terms. To support constitutional reform, the political players would have to be prepared to gamble. The liberal and conservative sides would each have to be ready to wager that they could win most elections and so make their policy views prevail most of the time. On less partisan issues—foreign policy in particular, but also the many elements of domestic fiscal policy—a national consensus would have to arise that a government able to concert its powers and act decisively will, most of the time, take the right action, that its positive achievements will outnumber its mistakes, that when it speaks with the authority that flows from unity it will speak mostly wisdom and not folly, and that, when it does err, a government capable of decisive action is best able to correct mistakes.

The Barriers to Constitutional Reform

If the founders wanted those who came after them to "exercise prudently the power of amendment," as Morris suggested, they still erected enormous barriers to that exercise—obstacles that proved to be greater, undoubtedly, than they anticipated. Approval of each amendment by two-thirds of both houses of the Congress, followed by its ratification by three-fourths of the states, can on occasion be attained, as the twenty-seven successful efforts attest. But this is more easily accomplished on a substantive matter, such as prohibition of alcoholic beverages or the repeal thereof, when waves of popular enthusiasm can be aroused. Issues pertaining to the structure of government do not stir mass excitement in the absence of outright governmental collapse. Such questions are examined closely by few except officeholders and politicians, and they are apt to appraise each proposal from the standpoint of its direct and immediate consequences to themselves, the offices they hold, and the parties they belong to.[18]

18. The Constitution provides an alternative to Congress as the initiator of amendments—a constitutional convention called on petition of two-thirds of the state leg-

Within the political elite, for an amendment to clear the barriers to passage, its acceptance must come close to unanimity, because it can be killed by one-third plus one of those voting in either the Senate or the House, or, if it survives those hurdles, one-fourth plus one of the states—today, thirteen of fifty. Yet the approval level in the states must usually be even higher than that, for with one exception the states have two-house legislatures. Thus as few as thirteen of ninety-nine state legislative bodies can defeat the ratification of a congressionally approved amendment; stated in reverse, as many as eighty-six of the ninety-nine—or 87 percent—may still be insufficient, which amounts to a requirement for virtual national unanimity. The Constitution does provide a unicameral alternative to ratification by bicameral state legislatures; the Congress may specify that the states shall act through conventions, as they did in ratifying the Constitution itself. But only one of the twenty-seven amendments—repeal of Prohibition—was adopted through that procedure.

The requirement for such extraordinary majorities means that, in the case of structural amendments, any significant political bloc possesses an effective veto. To succeed, a proposed amendment either must have no measurable adverse effect on anybody—as, say, the amendment that rescheduled inauguration days and congressional sessions—or must distribute its adverse effects so nearly neutrally that no substantial interest is offended. It must be neutral in its impact on the president and Congress, for either one can probably block it (while the president is not part of the approval process, his influence and that of past presidents and former executive branch officials who defend presidential prerogatives would usually be sufficient to give supporters of the presidency an effective veto). It must be neutral in its impact on Republicans and Democrats, on incumbent officeholders and challengers, on liberals and conservatives, on professional politicians and amateurs, or on any other of the dichotomous groups between which the political world can be divided. And structural amendments, by their very nature, are rarely neutral. Altering an institutional structure inevitably redistributes power, taking from some and giving to others. In the long run, the country as a whole, and both parties, may be better off by a redistribution. But it is in the

islatures—but this method (discussed further in chapter 9) has never been employed. As noted in footnote 4, it is currently being attempted by backers of the balanced budget amendment.

short run that politicians plan their careers. In the absence of a manifest collapse of government, the power losers can be counted on to exercise their veto. Those who worry about the shortcomings of their government, then, have traditionally sought remedies that do not involve the obstacle-strewn route of constitutional reform. Laws can be changed more readily, with simple majorities in both houses; political party rules and institutions can be altered; and politicians can be exhorted to change their ways.

But if these remedies are exhausted and the deficiencies of government remain, then there is no recourse but to reexamine the constitutional structure itself.

The Parliamentary Model—and Incrementalism

Those who have been frustrated with the stalemates of the American system over the years have looked longingly across the Atlantic and northward toward Canada and admired the streamlined unity of other democratic governments. In the parliamentary democracies, the legislative majority is sovereign, and a committee of that majority— the cabinet—both leads the legislature and directs the executive branch. Power is unified. Responsibility is clearly fixed. Strong party discipline assures prime ministers and their cabinets that they normally can act quickly and decisively without fear of being repudiated by their legislatures. Yet the leaders are held accountable by the requirement that, to remain in power, they must maintain the confidence of the parliamentary majority that chose them. In two-party parliamentary systems, of which Great Britain is the prototype, votes of nonconfidence are rare, but on occasion the majority has forced a prime minister in which it has lost confidence to resign—as when Neville Chamberlain was compelled to give way to Winston Churchill early in World War II and Margaret Thatcher to John Major in 1990. In the multiparty parliamentary systems of the European continent, governments are usually formed by coalitions, and they collapse when the parties making up a government fall into conflict. As long as they can resolve disagreements—or postpone or evade issues—within their cabinets, however, they are as certain of legislative support as are the governments of Britain. Under any of these parliamentary systems, governments can be formed, in Lloyd Cutler's phrase. They can act. They can speak to the world with a single, clear voice.

Douglas Dillon, for one, has suggested that the answer to this country's governmental stalemate "could well be some form of parliamentary democracy."[19] Former Senator J. William Fulbright of Arkansas, from the perspective of more than thirty years in Congress—sixteen of those years as chairman of the Senate Foreign Relations committee—finds that the separation of powers "obstructs accountability . . . promotes the spread of adversarial conflict throughout the political process . . . leads to indecision and stalemate," and "is growing inadequate for the formulation of a coherent, rational foreign policy." He commends the parliamentary system, with its unification of executive and legislature, as in many ways "a superior form of democracy."[20] Cutler, on the other hand, suggests that "the most one can hope for is a set of modest changes that would make our structure work somewhat more in the manner of a parliamentary system, with somewhat less separation between the executive and the legislature than now exists."[21] Many of the specific changes that are discussed in this book and that have been under consideration by the CCS are adapted from parliamentary systems, but for most constitutional reformers the parliamentary system represents only a source of ideas for incremental steps that might bring more unity to the American government, each such step to be con-

19. Tufts University address, May 30, 1982.

20. J. William Fulbright with Seth P. Tillman, *The Price of Empire* (Pantheon Books, 1989), p. 45. As a member of the board of directors of the Committee on the Constitutional System, Fulbright deplored that body's refusal to consider even recommending that the desirability of adopting the parliamentary system be seriously studied. "With the exception of a few members, they were no more willing to question the validity of the principle of separation of powers than to discuss the virginity of the Virgin Mary," he recalled. *Price of Empire*, pp. 45–46. Fulbright's advocacy of parliamentary government has been consistent throughout his career; after the 1946 election had given the Republicans control of both houses of Congress, Fulbright was bold enough—and indiscreet enough—to propose that Democratic President Truman appoint a Republican as secretary of state (who would, in the absence of a vice president, be next in line for the presidency) and then resign in order to give the Republicans full control of the government and full accountability. As he recounts (*Price of Empire*, pp. 46–48), President Truman never fully forgave his audacity. Faithful to the principle, Fulbright made a corresponding proposal to Republican President Eisenhower when the Democrats captured control of Congress in 1954, midway in Eisenhower's first term.

21. "To Form a Government," p. 139.

sidered on its own merits in terms of its adaptability to American tradition and institutions. Parliamentary democracy is not a model to be adopted in its entirety, supplanting the entire U.S. constitutional structure with something new and alien. Reformers should be "careful," in the words of the CCS report, "to preserve" the Constitution's "enduring virtues."[22]

What Changes Might Work?

The purpose of this book is to examine what some of the incremental steps might be, if it turns out at some point that the Dillon-Cutler-Fulbright-CCS diagnosis is the correct one and something must indeed be done. It does not attempt to make the general case for constitutional reform, beyond what has been said already. And, accepting the premise that incremental change is all that is feasible or desirable, it does not attempt comparative analysis of the relative merits and disadvantages of presidential and parliamentary systems or hybrid systems that combine features of the two.[23] The book is directed primarily toward those who are already persuaded that the tripartite constitutional design has evident and serious weaknesses and the question is not so much *whether* constitutional change is needed as *what* changes might work best. My object is to contribute to practical thinking about what might best be attempted, if one day a national consensus emerges that the U.S. government is indeed too congenitally divided, too prone to stalemate, too conflict-ridden to meet its immense responsibilities.

The next chapter presents the rationale for the structure of government designed two hundred years ago, as expressed by the more articulate among the fifty-five men who met in Philadelphia to create it. That is followed by an account of the few serious attempts made

22. CCS, "A Bicentennial Analysis," p. 8.
23. For a current and thorough comparative analysis of the entire range of constitutional systems found in the world, see Matthew Soberg Shugart and John M. Carey, *Presidents and Assemblies: Constitutional Design and Electoral Dynamics* (Cambridge University Press, 1992). A series of case studies directly comparing the effectiveness of the American presidential system with various parliamentary systems in coping with specific governmental problems is analyzed in R. Kent Weaver and Bert A. Rockman, eds., *Do Institutions Matter? Government Capabilities in the United States and Abroad* (Brookings, forthcoming).

in two centuries to alter that structure. The next five chapters analyze the principal proposals that have been advanced for incremental change in the constitutional system (including not only constitutional amendments but statutes and changes in political party rules and processes). A final chapter summarizes what appear to be the more constructive and feasible of the array of possible changes and then reviews the difficulties that must be overcome to accomplish any change at all.

CHAPTER TWO

Origins of the Constitutional Structure

The men who made up the Federal Convention of 1787 wavered during the course of their deliberations on most of the specific features of the constitutional structure they evolved, but they never vacillated on its central principle. That was the doctrine that the powers of government must be separated into independent branches—legislative, executive, and judicial. Nearly all the delegates arrived in Philadelphia clearly committed to that objective.

And so, clearly, were the constituents of the delegates. In the *Federalist* papers that explained the new Constitution to the country, James Madison of Virginia referred to the separation of powers as "the sacred maxim of free government,"[1] and during the intense debates over ratification nobody disputed that precept. The opponents of the Constitution did not take their stand on the ground that the new charter separated the powers of government too cleanly, that a more unified government would serve the country better. They attacked, rather, from the other side, charging that the new charter did not separate the powers of government cleanly enough, that the branches were not sufficiently protected against encroachment of one on another. The British government was cited as the model, but not today's British government. It was the government that existed—or was understood to exist—at that time, which was a government of separated powers.

1. *The Federalist*, no. 47 (New American Library, 1961), p. 308.

22

Nobody advocated the kind of unified government that has since evolved in Britain, the one that current critics of the U.S. Constitution often put forward as a model. Insofar as the framers of the Constitution foresaw the coming rise to supremacy of the House of Commons, they were mostly alarmed by the prospect. The overwhelming majority of them wanted no single group, legislative or executive, to be supreme in the new republic on this side of the Atlantic.

For the men of 1787 lived in the fear of despotism. Their generation in Europe and America was emerging from a long era of rule by monarchs, sometimes benevolent but too often tyrannical. And the philosophers who spoke for that generation were those who heralded the rights of man. When the framers turned to designing a new government, then, they sought "vigor" and "dispatch" and "strength" and "efficiency"—characteristics the Continental Congress had so conspicuously lacked—but they also were determined to erect safeguards to protect the citizenry from abuse of power by the invigorated organs of the state. To that end, power would have to be dispersed among branches of government capable of checking and controlling one another. Madison turned to "the celebrated Montesquieu" as the "oracle who is always consulted and cited" on the principle of separation of powers, and that philosopher had said, "There can be no liberty where the legislative and executive powers are united in the same person, or body of magistrates" or "if the power of judging be not separated" also.[2] Under the Articles of Confederation, the powers had been united in the Continental Congress with no loss of liberty, but that body was devoid of any final power, being wholly dependent on the consent of the states to all its actions. And, in any case, it was no model to be copied; its failure was the reason that the convention had been assembled in the first place to propose amendments to the articles that would give the new nation a better and a stronger central government.

The delegates had had experience, however, with other and more potent governments that verged on unity—those of the new states during the interval between 1776 and 1787. And they were the proximate cause of the framers' fear of despotism. King George III and the concentrated executive power that he represented were more than a decade in the past; the new state legislatures were very much in the present. "Our chief danger arises from the democratic parts of

2. Ibid., pp. 301–02.

our constitutions," Governor Edmund Randolph of Virginia said in introducing the Virginia plan that became the basis of the convention's deliberations. "It is a maxim which I hold incontrovertible, that the powers of government exercised by the people swallows up the other branches. None of the constitutions have provided sufficient checks against the democracy."[3] Expanding on this theme in the next few days, Randolph attributed "the evils under which the U.S. laboured" to "the turbulence and follies of democracy."[4] Elbridge Gerry of Massachusetts agreed: "The evils we experience flow from the excess of democracy," he declared, citing the "most baneful measures" enacted in his state in response to "popular clamour"; he was still a republican, but "had been taught by experience the danger of the levilling spirit."[5] In *The Federalist*, Madison specified the nature of the leveling: "A rage for paper money, for an abolition of debts, for an equal division of property, or for any other improper or wicked project."[6] In the processes by which the states chose their delegations to the convention, the dread levelers had somehow been effectively excluded, so there was none to take issue with Madison and defend such acts, and the Randolph-Gerry-Madison view as to the prime source of danger to the public liberty prevailed. James Wilson of Pennsylvania even observed that the colonists had revolted not against the king but against Parliament, "not against an unity but a corrupt multitude."[7]

If the legislative branch was omnipotent in the states, if it was "everywhere extending the sphere of its activity and drawing all power into its impetuous vortex," as Madison claimed, then the other branches of the new government had to be protected against legislative usurpations. As Madison put it, "It is against the enterprising ambition of this department that the people ought to indulge all their jealousy and exhaust all their precautions."[8] Much of the intellectual

3. Max Farrand, ed., *The Records of the Federal Convention of 1787*, 1937 rev. ed., 4 vols. (Yale University Press, 1966), vol. 1, pp. 26–27, proceedings of May 29, notes of James McHenry.

4. Ibid., p. 51, May 31, notes of James Madison. Unless otherwise indicated, quotations from the convention records are from Madison's notes.

5. Ibid., p. 48, May 31.

6. *Federalist*, no. 10, p. 84.

7. Farrand, *Records*, vol. 1, p. 71, June 1, notes of Rufus King. The same observation is attributed to King himself in ibid., vol. 3, p. 466, T. H. Benton on King's retiring from the Senate.

8. Ibid., vol. 2, p. 36, July 17; *Federalist*, no. 48, p. 309.

energy of the convention was accordingly devoted to considering how best to check the ambition of the legislature.

Yet not everyone at Philadelphia would go so far as Madison in asserting that *all* the jealousy of the people ought to be directed toward the ambition of the legislative branch. While fear of democratic demagogues was a dominant theme in the convention, dread of tyrannous executives was a secondary one. The venerable Benjamin Franklin of Pennsylvania expressed from time to time his foreboding that the new republic would inevitably drift to monarchy, seeing a "natural inclination in mankind to Kingly Government." George Mason of Virginia rose repeatedly to warn against establishing in the new presidency "a more dangerous monarchy, an elective one," and at the close he declined to sign the Constitution because, among other reasons, "it would end either in monarchy, or a tyrannical aristocracy; which, he was in doubt, but one or the other, he was sure." And men like Randolph, even as they denounced the excesses of popular legislatures, could wax equally eloquent against the "foetus of monarchy," as Randolph termed it, whenever they sensed that the structure of government was overbalanced in favor of the executive. "He will be an elective King, and will feel the spirit of one," warned Hugh Williamson of North Carolina. During debate on the executive's veto power, Pierce Butler of South Carolina observed that "Gentlemen seemed to think that we had nothing to fear from an abuse of the Executive power. But why might not a Cataline or a Cromwell arise in this country as in others."[9]

The concerns of both groups—or the concerns of individual delegates about both dangers—merged naturally into a general theory of "checks and balances," by which all three branches would be protected against encroachments by one another. The system to be evolved would be one in which "ambition must be made to counteract ambition."[10]

Checks on the Congress

In the founders' plan, the all-powerful legislative branch would be checked in two ways. First, it would be weakened by dividing its own

9. Farrand, *Records*, vol. 1, p. 83, June 2, and p. 101, June 4; vol. 2, p. 632, September 15; vol. 1, p. 66, June 1; vol. 2, p. 101, July 24; vol. 1, p. 100, June 4.
10. Madison, *Federalist*, no. 51, p. 322.

powers between two branches. Second, the executive and judicial branches would be provided means of self-protection. For the judiciary, that means would be its power to declare unconstitutional any laws that it found invaded the judicial powers.[11] For the executive the most important safeguards would be the independent election of the president and his right to veto legislation that encroached on his powers.

Bicameralism

Dividing the legislature into two branches, wrote Madison in the *Federalist*, "doubles the security to the people by requiring the concurrence of two distinct bodies in schemes of usurpation or perfidy, where the ambition or corruption of one would otherwise be sufficient." And, to decrease the likelihood of "sinister combinations," the two houses should be rendered, "by different modes of election and different principles of action, as little connected with each other as the nature of their common functions and their common dependence on the society will admit."[12]

If the principle of separation of powers was universally taken for granted by the delegates when they arrived in Philadelphia, the concept of a bicameral legislature had almost as wide an acceptance. George Mason said the concept was "well settled" in "the mind of

---

11. Although the power of the judicial branch to invalidate laws on grounds of unconstitutionality was not stated explicitly in the Constitution and was not established until the Supreme Court's 1803 decision in *Marbury v. Madison*, it was clearly envisioned by at least some of the framers. When the convention was considering whether the power to veto legislation should be vested in a "council of revision" that would include representation from the judiciary, Elbridge Gerry observed that the judges "will have a sufficient check against encroachments on their own department by their exposition of the laws, which involved a power of deciding on their Constitutionality." Similarly, Rufus King of Massachusetts noted that "the Judges will have the expounding of those Laws when they come before them; and they will no doubt stop the operation of such as shall appear repugnant to the constitution." When the convention returned to the subject, James Wilson, Luther Martin of Maryland, George Mason, and Gouverneur Morris of Pennsylvania all acknowledged that the judiciary would have that power. John Francis Mercer of Maryland and John Dickinson of Delaware protested that the judiciary ought not to possess the authority, but Dickinson "was at the same time at a loss what expedient to substitute." Farrand, *Records*, vol. 1, p. 97, June 4; p. 109, June 4, notes of William Pierce; pp. 73, 76, 78, July 21; pp. 298–99, August 15. That the veto was ultimately placed solely in the president suggests that the majority of the delegates agreed with the Gerry-King view of the judicial role.

12. *Federalist*, no. 62, pp. 378–79; no. 51, p. 322.

the people of America." All the states except Pennsylvania had created two-house legislatures, he pointed out, and the unicameralism of the Continental Congress was one of the factors that made the people averse to conferring greater powers on it. Pierce Butler, acknowledging that he had been among those opposing a stronger Congress, said on seeing that the Virginia plan proposed a two-house legislature he would approach the subject with an open mind. Explaining the Constitution to the North Carolina ratification convention the next year, William R. Davie reported that approval of a strengthened national government by the convention had depended on dividing the legislature into two branches, so that a longer-tenured group of men who were "more experienced, more temperate, and more competent to decide rightly" could check a popular branch "which might be influenced by local views, or the violence of party." George Washington put it more simply in his famed interchange with Thomas Jefferson. When Jefferson asked over the breakfast table why a second legislative chamber had been created, Washington asked, "Why did you pour your coffee into your saucer?" "To cool it," Jefferson answered. "Even so," said Washington, "we pour legislation into the senatorial saucer to cool it." [13]

Delegates were explicit that the new Senate would be designed "to secure the rights of property," as George Mason put it. Gouverneur Morris reasoned that if the Senate was to check the excesses of the House of Representatives, its members should have a "personal interest" in doing so, and they should therefore be persons of "great personal property," as well as an "aristocratic spirit," and they should be unpaid, to assure that only the rich would serve. The House of Lords was the ready model. John Dickinson of Delaware lamented the difficulty of nurturing on American soil the "House of Nobles" that was essential in any perfect government, but he urged the delegates to create a Senate whose members would be distinguished "for their rank in life and their weight of property, and bearing as strong a likeness to the British House of Lords as possible." Elbridge Gerry yearned for a "house of peers." [14]

13. Farrand, *Records*, vol. 1, p. 339, June 20, and p. 34, May 30; vol. 3, p. 340, debate in North Carolina convention, July 24, 1788, and p. 359, anecdote of Washington and Jefferson.

14. Ibid., vol. 1, p. 428, June 26; pp. 512–13, July 2; p. 87, June 2; p. 150, June 7; p. 221, June 12, notes of Robert Yates.

This concept of the role of the Senate determined both the length of senators' terms and the method of selection. Morris held that to protect the independence of the Senate from the more democratic House of Representatives, its members should be chosen for life,[15] but that was too blatant a departure from republican principles to win acceptance. Stability would be guaranteed by giving the senators a longer term than that accorded members of the House; the delegates initially approved a term of seven years, but later shortened it to six to facilitate the staggering of terms.

As for the method of selection, the Virginia plan proposed that senators be chosen by the members of the House from lists of persons nominated by the state legislatures, but this scheme ran at once into the criticism that it violated the principle of bicameralism by making the senators' election dependent on the very House whose excesses the Senate was being created to check. Charles Pinckney of South Carolina suggested at the outset that the Senate be the body in which the states showed their "sovereignty,"[16] and this idea quickly gained wide acceptance. Popular election of senators was discarded, then, on three grounds—first, that one popularly elected branch of the legislature would not be well designed to check another branch similarly chosen; second, that popular election could not be relied on to place men of experience, stature, and wealth in the republican counterpart of the House of Lords; and third, that if the states were to control the Senate, the members of that body had to be appointed by the states themselves rather than elected by the people. So selection of senators by the state legislators was approved by unanimous vote of the state delegations. To George Mason, this mode of election added another to the checks and balances in the Constitution; the states would have the power through the Senate to defend themselves against encroachment by the federal government, just as the presidential veto enabled the executive branch to defend itself against the legislature.[17]

There being no "levelers" in the convention, scarcely any argument for the unicameral alternative was advanced at any time. Franklin reportedly considered two houses unnecessary, but he did not speak

15. Ibid., p. 512, July 2.
16. Ibid., p. 59, May 31, notes of Pierce.
17. Ibid., pp. 155–56, June 7; p. 407, June 25.

out, and bicameralism was initially adopted without discussion or, apparently, dissent. Roger Sherman of Connecticut subsequently remarked that, on principle, he saw no need for a two-house legislature, but concluded by saying that if bicameralism was necessary to solve the quarrel between the large states and the small states over the formula for representation in the legislature, he would agree to the creation of two houses.[18] Bicameralism did turn out to be the magic solvent for that great dispute that had threatened to destroy the convention. The large states would get in one house the representation on the basis of population they had demanded, while the small states would gain in the other the equal representation of states on which they had been adamant. The large states would control the House, the small states would have their disproportionate weight in the Senate. When that great compromise saved the convention, it riveted the principle of bicameralism into the Constitution.

As an element of the compromise, the House was given the exclusive power to originate revenue bills. As originally proposed by the committee that drafted the compromise, the provision denied the Senate the right to amend such bills—a feature copied from the similar restriction on the British House of Lords—but this yielded to the argument that in this as in other matters the more deliberate Senate should serve to check the impulsive House. The original version covered appropriations as well as revenue bills, but the narrower wording that came from a later committee—the famed Committee on Postponed Matters—was not challenged.

Independent Election of the President

The Virginia plan that was the basis for the convention's deliberations provided that the chief executive should be selected by the legislature. This obvious breach of the separation of powers principle was at once recognized as such, and inventive members turned their minds to devising a suitable—and salable—alternative. But it took all summer, and recurrent intense debate, before they could agree on one. "This subject has greatly divided the House," said James Wilson

18. Ibid., p. 48, May 31; vol. 3, p. 297, Franklin letter of April 22, 1788; vol. 1, pp. 341–43, June 20.

in September, as the convention neared adjournment with the issue still unsettled. "It is in truth the most difficult of all on which we have had to decide."[19]

Wilson had been the first to oppose this element of the Virginia plan, and it was he who first suggested the electoral college scheme that finally found its tortuous way into the Constitution. But the initial reaction was that the general electorate would be too poorly informed to make a wise choice of electors, and the "great trouble and expense," as Hugh Williamson put it, made the plan unacceptable. In the first test of Wilson's idea, on June 2, he could not even carry his own state, and election by the legislature was affirmed by a vote of eight states to two. After that, however, the convention formally changed its mind four times. On July 19, it voted for an electoral college, six states to three. Five days later, it reverted to selection by the legislature, seven states to four. On a reconsideration on August 24, the electoral college plan lost by a five-to-six vote and again on a four-to-four tie vote, with two states divided and the eleventh absent. It was this deadlock, more than any other, that occasioned the appointment of the Committee on Postponed Matters, consisting of one member from each of the eleven participating states, and that body after four days of intensive deliberation came down on the side of taking the election of the president out of the hands of Congress. That settled the matter, and the novel idea of the electoral college was decisively approved.

Had this close decision gone the other way, the United States would have had a form of government much more closely akin to those of the parliamentary democracies of the world, where the chief executive—the prime minister—is chosen by, and from, the legislature and remains in office only so long as he or she holds the confidence of the majority of that body.[20] But throughout the summer, the opponents of the original Virginia proposal hammered away at the argument that for the legislature to choose the chief executive would destroy the independence of that office and make its occupant "sub-

19. Ibid., vol. 2, p. 501, September 4.
20. In bicameral legislatures, practices vary, but typically the more popular, or "lower," chamber has the dominant or exclusive role in the selection and removal of prime ministers. In Britain, the model for many parliamentary systems, the House of Commons has the exclusive role, the House of Lords having long since been reduced to a minor and essentially advisory legislative capacity.

servient" to the will of the legislators. The Virginians had recognized this problem and had tried to resolve it by making the executive ineligible for a second term; this provision, argued George Mason, would remove "a temptation on the side of the Executive to intrigue with the Legislature for a re-appointment." To most of those who favored limiting the executive to a single term, it seemed logical that that term should be a long one, and a length of seven years was initially approved, by a one-vote margin, over the objection of those who, like Gunning Bedford, Jr., of Delaware, worried about what would happen to the country "in case the first magistrate should be saddled on it for such period and it should be found on trial that he did not possess the qualifications ascribed to him, or should lose them after his appointment." Impeachment, he pointed out, "would reach misfeasance only, not incapacity."[21]

But the seven-year, single-term solution still fell short of satisfying those who were most concerned about assuring the independence of the executive. Even if he were barred from reappointment, the initial appointment would make him "the mere creature of the Legislature," particularly since he would also be impeachable by that body, argued Gouverneur Morris. "If the Legislature elect, it will be the work of intrigue, of cabal, and of faction . . . real merit will rarely be the title to the appointment." And, in the absence of an independent executive to serve as "the great protector of the Mass of the people," "usurpation and tyranny on the part of the Legislature will be the consequence." James Wilson agreed that the executive would still be "too dependent to stand the mediator between the intrigues and sinister views of the Representatives and the general liberties and interests of the people."[22]

Their position was immensely strengthened when, in mid-July, the convention reversed itself on the question of the single term. Ineligibility for a second term, Morris had contended, would tend "to destroy the great motive to good behavior, the hope of being rewarded by re-appointment." Roger Sherman and Rufus King added the argument that "he who has proved himself to be most fit for an Office, ought not to be excluded by the constitution from holding it."[23] On

21. Farrand, *Records*, vol. 1, pp. 68, 69, June 1.
22. Ibid., vol. 2, pp. 29, 31, July 17; p. 52, July 19; p. 30, July 17.
23. Ibid., p. 33, July 17; p. 55, July 19.

the strength of these arguments, the one-term limit was removed on July 19, six states to four. That permitted a shortening of the executive's term, but it was reduced only from seven to six years. And it precipitated the July 19 swing over to the electoral college method of choosing the executive, even Virginia joining the majority.

The electoral college was still, however, too novel an institution. Delegates wondered whether first-rate men would choose to serve as electors, and whether introducing a new group of officials into the structure would not make the new government too complex. With New Jersey and Delaware changing sides, the convention on July 24 rescinded its decision of five days earlier and restored the power of presidential selection to the legislature. The related decisions on the presidential term were reversed as well, and the delegates were back where they began, with a single seven-year term for their new executive.

But the matter remained far from settled, for the advocates of an independent executive were more adamant than ever. Morris was still insisting that an executive chosen by the legislature would be its "mere creature." He, along with Wilson, King, and others, still contended that the country should be enabled to retain an able president in office for another term, even if the first were as long as seven years. And their ranks attracted an influential recruit: the principal author of the Virginia plan, Madison himself, who had finally thought the matter through and concluded that in this particular feature his plan did indeed violate his own exalted principle of independent branches and separated powers. For the legislature to choose the chief executive encountered now, in his mind, "insuperable objections." He summed up the opposition case. It would "agitate and divide the legislature so much that the public interest would materially suffer by it." The candidate would intrigue with the legislature, and foreign powers would join in the intrigue. Above all, the appointee would be "subservient" to the majority faction that selected him; and that must not be, for legislatures "betrayed a strong propensity to a variety of pernicious measures" and one object of creating an executive with the power of veto was "to control the National Legislature, so far as it might be infected with a similar propensity."[24]

All these arguments were reiterated by Gouverneur Morris when

24. Ibid., p. 103, July 24; pp. 109–10, July 25.

the matter was again considered, on August 24, but in another test vote the electoral college was defeated, six states to five. The proponents had won back New Jersey and Delaware but lost Maryland. A week later, the convention did what such bodies always have to do (and this convention had already done on the great controversy between the large and small states over representation in the legislature); it appointed a committee. Among the eleven members chosen by ballot, one from each state, happened to appear the two most eloquent and insistent enemies of selection of the executive by the legislature, Morris and Madison. Perhaps that ordained the ultimate victory of the electoral college.

Once the committee had agreed that the president would be chosen by electors, two related decisions came easily. The president could be made eligible for reelection, as most delegates had desired all along. And, that being the case, his term could be shortened, and four years was agreed on. As for how the electors would be chosen, that was left to the state legislatures. And their distribution reflected a compromise between the large and small states, with the number of electors assigned to each state equal to its representation in the Senate and House of Representatives combined. The electors would meet in their respective states, and each would cast two votes, only one of which could be for a resident of his own state—an idea advanced earlier in the summer as an answer to the contention that electors would invariably vote for candidates from their own states (at least after George Washington had completed his expected service), making it impossible for anyone to receive a majority. If, despite that precaution, no candidate received a majority, the Senate would choose from among the top five; or, in cases when two candidates received majorities but tied, from the top two. In each of these selection processes, the runner-up would become the vice president.

When the plan was presented, on September 4, defenders of the original Virginia plan for presidential selection by the legislature grumbled but on a test vote could muster the support of only two states. Debate then focused not on the central question of independent electors but on the role of the Senate when the electors failed to produce a clear majority. To many delegates, indeed, this became the overriding issue, for they envisioned the electoral college as little more than a nominating body, consisting of men who would meet in scattered state capitals and, out of touch with one another, disperse their votes among many candidates. Some delegates argued that more and more leaders with national reputations would emerge, but none of the men of Philadelphia—with all their experience and sagacity— were able to look even two decades into the future and foresee the emergence of national political parties with central nominating processes and national campaigns. Nineteen times in twenty, predicted George Mason, the president would be chosen by the Senate.[25] Many were less gloomy than that, but probably no delegate would have dared predict that the electoral college would work as well as it has done, failing only twice in the first fifty-one presidential elections under the Constitution to give one candidate a clear majority.[26]

This, then, raised the specter of too much power in the Senate. Charles Pinckney foresaw the president as a "mere creature" of the Senate, who would ally with that body against the House of Representatives and thus fix himself in office for life. When the president became its "minion," argued Wilson, the Senate would control all appointments, including those to the judiciary, and since it also was being given the power to try impeachments and to make treaties, all three branches of government would be "blended" into the Senate.[27] After a couple of days of floundering, two members of the committee that had designed the proposal, Williamson of North Carolina and Sherman of Connecticut, hit on a scheme that would allay delegates' fears of an overbearing Senate yet preserve for the small states the voting parity with the large states that they enjoyed in that body. The House of Representatives would be given the disputed responsibility, but there the members would vote by states, with each state having a single vote. Thus was resolved the "most difficult" of the convention's problems of governmental architecture.

25. Ibid., p. 500, September 4.
26. Those were the elections of 1800 and 1824, and the first failure was the result of the peculiar provision in the electoral college plan that gave each elector two votes. When the Republican party nominated Thomas Jefferson and Aaron Burr, with the intent that Jefferson serve as president and Burr as vice president, the party's electors cast ballots for both, with the result that both received a majority but tied. This flaw in the Constitution was corrected by the Twelfth Amendment, which was ratified before the next presidential election.
27. Farrand, *Records*, vol. 2, p. 511, September 5; pp. 522–23, September 6.

The Presidential Veto

In a government of separated powers, the legislative branch could not hold an absolute power to make laws. If so, it could encroach on the powers of the other branches and so, in the phrase Madison liked to repeat, "draw all power into its impetuous vortex." The questions before the convention, then, were not whether a veto should exist but who should exercise it, whether the legislature should have the power to override the veto, and, if so, by a majority of what size.

The Virginia plan had called for a "council of revision," consisting of the executive and an unspecified number of judges, with power to veto laws but subject to being overridden by an extraordinary majority of both houses (the size of the majority left blank).

Granting the veto power to both the executive and judicial branches, acting jointly, was proposed on the logical ground that both were in equal need of a mechanism of defense against an ambitious legislature. The weakness of this argument was that the veto power was more than a defense mechanism; it was needed also, said Mason, to "discourage demagogues" in the legislatures from attempting to pass "unjust and pernicious laws," and Morris was explicit as to the types of laws: "emissions of paper money, largesses to the people—a remission of debts and similar measures." If the judges were to participate in vetoing laws on policy grounds, they would be "meddling in politics and parties," as Sherman put it, and they would be biased in interpreting laws they had played a part in writing. "The judges ought never to give their opinion on a law till it comes before them," contended John Rutledge of South Carolina, the presiding judge of his state's supreme court.[28] As for defending the judiciary against legislative encroachment on its powers, some delegates observed that the judges had their power to declare any such laws unconstitutional. These arguments prevailed each time in repeated tests of the issue, leaving the veto power in the executive branch alone.

A few delegates, notably Wilson and Alexander Hamilton of New York, thought the logic of separation of powers required that the executive have an absolute veto. "Without such a Self-defense," said Wilson, "the Legislature can at any moment sink it into nonexis-

28. Ibid., pp. 78, 76, July 21; p. 300, August 15; p. 80, July 21.

tence."[29] But an all-powerful executive was only somewhat less fearsome than an unchecked legislature, and not a single state supported it. Debate then centered on the size of the legislative majority required to override the veto. Two-thirds of each house was the proportion chosen in June. In August, when the plan still called for the executive to be chosen by the legislature and delegates worried about his becoming the legislators' captive, the figure of three-fourths was substituted. But in September, when the executive had been strengthened by the plan for independent election, delegates feared that the three-fourths requirement gave him excessive power. With the support of only a small minority of legislators, protested Sherman, he could prevail over the "general voice" and "mistake or betray" the "sense of the people."[30] In one of its last decisions before adjourning, the convention restored the two-thirds figure.

Checks on the President

As the convention went about creating a strong executive to check what most delegates perceived to be the more dangerous branch of the new government—the legislature—the safeguard advanced originally by Randolph and others who feared monarchy was a plural rather than a unitary executive, to be composed of three men representing different regions. But this proposal was never able to attract the support of more than three states. A plural executive, argued Wilson, would lack "energy, dispatch, and responsibility." Instead, it would produce "nothing but uncontrolled, continued, and violent animosities." All of the states, he observed, had unitary executives.[31]

True, replied his opponents, but they all had a council of some sort to advise and restrain their executives. This became the line of retreat for those who feared an elective king. Gerry, Madison, Mason, Sherman, and Franklin were among influential members who insisted on some form of council—although they disagreed on whether it should be strictly advisory to the executive or should possess a veto power over executive actions—and in August, Oliver Ellsworth of Connecticut suggested one consisting of the president of the Senate,

29. Ibid., vol. 1, p. 98, June 4.
30. Ibid., vol. 2, p. 585, September 12.
31. Ibid., vol. 1, p. 65, June 1; p. 96, June 4.

the chief justice, and the heads of the executive departments, to be limited to advisory functions. The Committee of Detail added the Speaker of the House to this body and named it the privy council, after the group who advised the British king. Mason proposed an alternative, a council elected by the House of Representatives. But the Committee on Postponed Matters resolved the question by giving to the Senate the right to "advise and consent" on the two elements of executive power that most concerned the delegates—the power to make appointments and the power to make treaties—and a separate council then became superfluous.[32] The Senate, Luther Martin of Maryland advised his state's ratifying convention, was to serve as a "privy council" for the president, residing permanently in Washington. Rufus King of Massachusetts, a member of the Committee on Postponed Matters, summarized for his state's convention the reasons the council was abandoned. Since every state would insist on having at least one member, any council would be similar to the Senate. Under the Constitution as drafted, the Senate would advise the president on some matters and he could obtain the opinions of other officers on others. Finally, "secrecy, despatch, and fidelity were more to be expected than where there is a multitudinous executive." None of these arguments satisfied George Mason, who gave among his reasons for not signing the Constitution the absence of the constitutional council that "any safe and regular government" must have. Without a council, the president would rely for advice on "minions and favorites" or become "a tool to the Senate," Mason gloomily predicted.[33]

The principal checks on the executive, then, in addition to the oft-cited power of the purse, were to lie in the Senate's control of appointments and of treaties, the legislature's retention of the power to declare war, and the power of the legislature, in extremity, to remove the president from office through impeachment. In addition, legislators would be protected from executive influence by denying the president the right to offer them positions in the executive branch as long as they remained in the legislature.

32. Alexander Hamilton identified the power to make treaties and the power of appointment as "the only instances in which the abuse of the executive authority was materially to be feared." *Federalist*, no. 77, p. 464.

33. Farrand, *Records*, vol. 3, p. 194, Luther Martin to the Maryland legislature, December 28, 1787; p. 269, Rufus King in the Massachusetts convention, January 28, 1788; and vol. 2, p. 638, September 15.

Senate Confirmation of Appointments

The original Virginia plan assigned the power to appoint judges to the legislature (a practice followed to this day in Virginia), but in its early consideration of the subject the convention restricted the power to the Senate. The "more numerous" House of Representatives, Madison had argued, would be inclined to "intrigue and partiality" and would be too disposed to appoint from its own membership or from lawyers who had served its members. The Senate, as "a less numerous and more select body," would do a better job. But to many delegates, even the Senate would be too numerous, "too little personally responsible," and too much given to "intrigue and cabal," as Nathaniel Gorham of Massachusetts put it.[34] He suggested appointment by the executive with the "advice and consent" of the Senate, a method used in his state for 140 years. But others thought that the executive, too, would be subject to intrigue, and the small states rallied as usual around the Senate, the one institution in which they enjoyed an equal status. The proposal lost on a tie vote, four states to four, and here the matter stood until the final days of the convention.

The argument was finally resolved as part of the grand reconciliation of interbranch relationships worked out by the Committee on Postponed Matters. It adopted the Gorham proposal and applied it not only to the appointment of judges but also to the selection of ambassadors (which the Committee of Detail had earlier assigned to the Senate also) and to the appointment of "all other officers of the United States." Almost as an afterthought, among last-minute amendments, Gouverneur Morris pointed out that "all" was too many, and a clause was added permitting the Congress to vest the appointment of "inferior officers" in the president alone, in the courts of law, or in the heads of departments. Morris, one of the architects of the compromise, summed it up: "As the President was to nominate, there would be responsibility, and as the Senate was to concur, there would be security."[35]

34. Ibid., vol. 1, p. 120, June 5, and pp. 232–33, June 13; vol. 2, pp. 41–42, 44, July 18.
35. Ibid., vol. 2, p. 539, September 7.

Senate Approval of Treaties

The question of who should exercise the treaty-making power had been left to the Committee of Detail, and that body placed the authority in the Senate. When that proposition was considered, in late August, some members protested that the House of Representatives should have a right of approval of the Senate's handiwork, while others contended that the president should be involved. With that much disagreement, the treaty-making power took its place among the other interbranch issues on the agenda of the Committee on Postponed Matters. That body reduced the Senate role to one of "advise and consent" and gave the treaty-making power to the president, but with the proviso—adapted from the Articles of Confederation—that two-thirds of the senators present must concur.[36] A motion to add the House to the approval process won the support of only a single state. A motion to reduce the Senate approval requirement to a simple majority likewise was backed by but one state, but a proposal to reduce the requirement to a majority of the entire Senate membership was defeated by only a single vote, six states to five.

The War Power

From the beginning, it was understood that the executive would be the commander in chief of the army and navy, but that he would be restrained by the ultimate power of the legislative branch to determine when, and against whom, the country would be at war. Thus, in the report of the Committee of Detail, the authority "to make war" was listed among the powers of Congress.

In the only discussion of this issue, Charles Pinckney of South Carolina objected to assigning the responsibility to both houses of Congress, because the House of Representatives would meet only once a year, its proceedings would be "too slow," and it would be "too numerous" for such deliberations. He suggested, accordingly, that the power to make war should be vested in the Senate alone.

36. In *Federalist*, no. 38, p. 238, Madison still held to the original concept, writing that the Constitution "empowers the Senate, with the concurrence of the executive, to make treaties." But Hamilton, in ibid., no. 69, p. 419, places the power "to make treaties" in the president, subject to senatorial concurrence.

But his colleague Pierce Butler observed that the same objections would lie, to a great degree, against the Senate also, and proposed that the power be assigned to the president, "who will have all the requisite qualities, and will not make war but when the Nation will support it." That aroused Elbridge Gerry, who expressed shock at the thought that in a republic the executive would be empowered alone to declare war, and George Mason agreed that the president could not safely be entrusted with such power. Madison and Gerry hit on the compromise that satisfied nearly everyone. The president would be empowered "to repel sudden attacks" but not to thrust the nation into war. To this end, the congressional power was narrowed from "to make war" to "to declare war," and that wording was accepted.[37]

Impeachment

When the convention met, impeachment was a well-established—though infrequently used—process in Britain for the removal of errant officers of the crown, and like other elements of the British constitution the concept had found its way into constitutional doctrine in America as well. Accordingly, when the Virginia delegates put their plan before the convention, they listed among the functions of the judiciary the power to try impeachments that that branch of government exercised under the Virginia constitution. The plan was silent, however, on what body would be empowered to initiate the impeachment and bring it before the judges.

Since the president would be by far the most important of the "national officers" subject to removal, the question entered into the complex calculus of interbranch relationships in three aspects. Who would have the power to impeach the president? What would be the permissible grounds? And who would try the impeachment and render the verdict?

Few were prepared to go as far as Roger Sherman of Connecticut, the convention's leading advocate of legislative supremacy, who considered an independent executive "the very essence of tyranny" and wanted him "absolutely dependent" on the legislature, because it was that branch's will "which was to be executed." To this end, he contended that the legislature should not only appoint the executive—

37. Farrand, *Records*, vol. 2, pp. 318–19, August 17.

as the convention initially agreed to propose—but have the power to remove him "at pleasure."[38] In a test vote when the convention was only a week old, only three states were prepared to transfer the removal power from the judicial to the legislative branch.

Nor were many prepared to go to the other extreme and protect the executive from impeachment altogether. The idea of impeachment was "dangerous," protested Gouverneur Morris; if the executive "is to be a check on the Legislature, let him not be impeachable." But Morris announced after another day's debate that he had been converted by arguments such as those of George Mason: "Shall any man be above justice? Above all shall that man be above it, who can commit the most extensive injustice?" And Franklin: "What was the practice before this in cases where the chief Magistrate rendered himself obnoxious? Why, recourse was had to assassination."[39] Morris then retreated to the position that the grounds for impeachment should be limited and defined. Only two states voted to make the executive unimpeachable.

The Committee of Detail, offering the definition Morris had suggested, limited impeachment of the president to cases of "treason, bribery, or corruption." It also made its choice of the impeaching body: the House of Representatives—which, in a phrase deleted from its final language, the committee had initially held "shall be the grand Inquest of this Nation."[40] These proposals were approved without a roll call vote.

It was Morris, again, who objected to making the Supreme Court the trial body and got the matter referred to the Committee on Postponed Matters. In that committee, Morris must have won a debate with Madison, for the group decided to make the Senate the adjudicator of impeachments brought by the House, but with a two-thirds vote required for conviction and removal. It also limited the grounds to treason and bribery, but on this matter Mason had the last word. This, he objected, "will not reach many great and dangerous offenses. . . . Attempts to subvert the Constitution may not be Treason as above defined." With Gerry seconding him, he proposed to add "maladministration," but when Madison protested that this would

38. Ibid., vol. 1, p. 68, June 1; p. 85, June 2.
39. Ibid., vol. 2, p. 53, July 19; p. 65, July 20.
40. Ibid., p. 154, Committee of Detail records.

amount to the president's serving "during pleasure of the Senate," Mason substituted "other high crimes and misdemeanors," and in this form the language was approved, eight states to three. At this point, Madison renewed his argument in favor of trial by the Supreme Court or by some special tribunal outside the legislative branch, for if the House were empowered to impeach—"and for any act which might be called a misdemeanor"—and the Senate to convict, the president would be "improperly dependent." But Morris responded that the Supreme Court "were too few in number and might be warped or corrupted" and Sherman reminded the delegates that the Court would be made up of presidential appointees.[41] Madison could win the support of only two states, and the Senate was confirmed as the trial body.

Prohibition of Dual Officeholding

As a safeguard against corruption of the legislature, the authors of the Virginia plan proposed that members of that branch be ineligible for appointment to offices in the executive and judicial branches during the terms to which they were elected, and for an unspecified length of time (later set as one year) thereafter. Without such a prohibition, its advocates predicted, legislators would create unnecessary offices that they would then seek to fill. "If not checked," contended Mason, "we shall have ambassadors to every petty state in Europe— the little republic of St. Marino not excepted." Elbridge Gerry saw a legislature mired in "intrigues of ambitious men for displacing proper officers, in order to create vacancies for themselves."[42] Others, led by Madison, argued against an absolute disqualification, on the ground that it would discourage able men from seeking legislative service.

But delegates saw that the issue was not simply one of preventing venality in the legislature but one of power also. For the distribution of appointments would be a prime source of influence for the new national executive that was to be created, and the proponents of a strong executive were loath to exempt the members of the legislature

41. Ibid., pp. 550–51, September 8.
42. Ibid., vol. 1, p. 380, June 22, Yates notes; p. 388, June 23.

from the range of that influence. Thus Alexander Hamilton argued, quoting a British politician, that what "went under the name of corruption" was in fact "an essential part of the weight which maintained the equilibrium of the Constitution." If the executive is deprived of influence by rendering the members of the legislature ineligible for executive offices, agreed John Francis Mercer of Maryland, "he becomes a mere phantom of authority."[43] Those who, like Mason and Sherman, preferred, if not a phantom, at most a weak and controlled executive, supported the prohibition.

Eventually, the convention found what Madison called "a medium between the two extremes."[44] First, the delegates removed the restriction, in the case of House members, on appointments to positions in the executive branch after their terms expired, and the Committee on Postponed Matters removed that prohibition for senators as well. That committee also turned the clause into a two-way restriction; not only could legislators not be appointed to offices in the executive or judicial branches during their terms, but any civil officeholder must resign his post if elected to Congress. The delegates then, by the narrow vote of five states to four, limited the disqualification to only those offices that were created, or whose salaries had been increased, during a legislator's term, thus making him eligible for appointment to any other office provided he resigned his seat.

The Process of Amendment

The Virginia plan proposed that the articles of union the delegates were to draft should include a process for amendment, but it did not define that process except to specify that "the assent of the National Legislature ought not to be required thereto." The proviso, explained George Mason, was necessary because the legislature "may abuse their power, and refuse their consent on that very account."[45] Responding to this concern, the Committee of Detail placed the responsibility for initiating amendments in the state legislatures, pro-

---

43. Ibid., p. 376, June 22, vol. 2, p. 284, August 14.
44. Ibid., vol. 3, p. 316, debate in the Virginia ratifying convention, June 14, 1788.
45. Ibid., vol. 1, p. 22, May 29; p. 203, June 11.

posing that on application of two-thirds of the legislatures the Congress would call a convention for the purpose, and that procedure was approved.

The matter was not reopened until the final days of the convention, when Alexander Hamilton urged that a second means of amendment be added—initiation by the Congress. "The National Legislature," he argued, "will be the first to perceive and will be most sensible to the necessity of amendments" and should therefore be empowered to call a convention on its own motion, by a two-thirds vote of each house. Madison remarked that the language was still vague, asking "how was a Convention to be formed? by what rule decide? what the force of its acts?" His questions were only partly answered as the delegates pondered the procedure. First, they modified Hamilton's idea by providing that when the two houses of Congress by two-thirds votes agreed on the need for amendments, they would submit them directly to the states rather than call a convention. After voting down, by a six-to-five margin, a proposal that amendments take effect on ratification by two-thirds of the states, the delegates agreed to require approval by three-fourths. Madison then succeeded in adding language authorizing the Congress to decide, in the case of each amendment, whether ratification should be by state legislatures or state conventions called for the purpose. Finally, in the last act of the convention before the Constitution was engrossed, the delegates responded to "circulating murmurs of the small States" by agreeing, without debate, that no state without its consent could be deprived of its equal representation in the Senate.[46]

46. Ibid., vol. 2, pp. 558–59, September 10; p. 631, September 15.

CHAPTER THREE

Two Centuries of Constitutional Debate

At no time in the two centuries of national life under the 1787 Constitution have its fundamental principles been subjected to any serious challenge. As noted in chapter 1, only five of the twenty-seven amendments adopted since the Constitution was ratified have affected the governmental structure at all, and none has altered its essential architecture. Even more significant, no amendment that would contravene the separation-of-powers principle has ever been debated on the floor of either house of Congress, and few have even been proposed. One can search the more than one million pages of the *Congressional Record* and its predecessor publications without finding anything more than the rarest of muted and tentative suggestions that the founding fathers might have erred in designing the unique American system of independent executive and legislative branches replete with checks and balances, that the republic might have fared better with a more unified governmental structure like those that have evolved in Europe, Canada, and other nations of the British Commonwealth. Such criticism of the fundamentals of the constitutional system as has been spoken by scholars and observers outside the government has aroused no echo in the public utterances of presidents, senators, and representatives—the men and women who have borne the responsibility for making the system work. The great debate of 1787–88 has never been reopened, despite the expectations of the framers themselves that their decisions made in a single summer—and some by narrow and shifting votes—would be subject to review by every succeeding generation.

When structural amendments have been debated in the halls of Congress, proponents have been at pains to insist—if the question were raised at all—that their proposed changes would certainly not weaken, or would even reinforce, the constitutional structure of checks and balances. In this context, however, important changes in various elements of the constitutional system have been on occasion debated, as experience appeared to cast doubt on some of the details—if not the basic principles—of the framers' design.

Presidential Tenure

The most persistent, recurring topic of debate bearing on the constitutional structure has been the question of presidential tenure. The argument has revolved around two questions. First, did the right of a president to run for reelection for an unlimited number of terms threaten the United States with "an elective monarchy"? Second, if the president were restricted to a single term, should that term be lengthened from four to six years?

George Washington had set the precedent of an eight-year limit on presidential tenure by declining to run for a third term in 1796, and Jefferson and Madison had followed his example. By James Monroe's day, the two-term limit was seen as an element of the country's "unwritten constitution," yet as Monroe was nearing the end of his seventh year in office, supporters of the various candidates to succeed him considered it prudent to fix the principle in writing. Historians have reported no evidence that Monroe ever considered violating the precedent set by his three illustrious predecessors, but the Senate in January 1824, by a 30-to-3 vote, approved a constitutional amendment placing a two-term limit on presidential tenure. The House saw no need for any such precaution, and the effort ended there.[1]

Monroe's successor, however, was chosen in a process that ended in charges of scandal and corruption, and the subject was reopened in a new context. When the electoral college cast its votes following the election of 1824, none of the four candidates—John Quincy Adams, Henry Clay, William H. Crawford, and Andrew Jackson—

---

1. Two years later, the Senate reaffirmed its position by a 25-to-4 vote, but again the House did not act.

had a majority, and the choice was thrown into the House of Representatives for the second—and, as of now, last—time. Andrew Jackson had a plurality of electoral votes, and a plurality of the popular vote in those states that chose their electors by direct election, but Clay threw his support to Adams in what Jackson's supporters condemned as a "corrupt bargain" by which Clay would be named secretary of state. When Adams, thus elected, appeared to confirm the charge by appointing Clay to that office, the Jackson followers had a campaign issue for the whole four years leading up to the election of 1828. Successful in that election, Jackson set out to reform the Constitution to prevent the recurrence of the kind of episode that he felt had denied him his rightful reward four years before.

In his first annual message to Congress, Jackson proposed that the electoral college be abolished and the president be chosen by popular vote, with a runoff election between the two high candidates if none achieved a majority in the initial ballot. Incidental to his principal recommendation, the president included a single sentence suggesting that "it would seem advisable to limit the service of the Chief Magistrate to a single term of either four or six years."[2]

A year later, in his second annual message, Jackson presented the rationale for the one-term limit that was missing from his original recommendation. Such a limit, he said, would "strengthen those checks by which the Constitution designed to secure the independence of each department of the Government." A president ineligible for reelection would "as far as possible be placed beyond the reach of any improper influences." He would be able to approach the "solemn responsibilities" of his office "uncommitted to any course other than the strict line of constitutional duty."[3] Jackson reiterated his proposals in every one of his six succeeding annual messages, but his recommendations were not considered on the floor of either house.[4]

2. Jackson suggested, however, that the popular preference could be registered by states, each state to cast the same number of votes as it would cast in the electoral college. "Message of December 8, 1829," in James D. Richardson, ed., *A Compilation of the Messages and Papers of the Presidents (1789–1897),* vol. 3 (Bureau of National Literature, 1897), p. 1011.

3. "Message of December 6, 1830," in ibid., p. 1082.

4. Jackson did not pause to explain why he had not imposed a one-term limit on himself, beyond a remark in his second inaugural address that his reelection was "unsolicited." Ibid., p. 1222.

After Jackson, no president won reelection until Abraham Lincoln in 1864, so the question remained quiescent. But Lincoln was shot early in his second term and the office passed to the hapless Andrew Johnson, who fell at once into the conflict with the Radical Republicans over Reconstruction policy that led to his impeachment. In the lame-duck session that followed the midterm election of 1866, the Senate Judiciary Committee reported a resolution introduced by Radical Ben Wade of Ohio that would bar from a second term any president, including one succeeding to that office on the death of his predecessor. Although the measure was aimed obviously at Johnson, the brief debate that was accorded it rose to the level of principle. Even the "greatest and best" of presidents, argued Wade, had been tempted to adopt measures "looking quite as much to the continuance of the incumbent in office as to the public good"; the desire for reelection "will sway the judgment of any man, whether he knows it or not."

Those who supported Wade divided on whether the single term should run for four years or six. Advocates of the six-year term contended that every four years was too often to suffer the "great agitation and excitement" of the presidential campaign and, if a president chosen for so long a term proved incompetent or otherwise unsatisfactory, Congress could render him "impotent"—as it had already done in the case of Johnson. But opponents waxed passionate on the danger of so long a tenure for a chief executive who proved unsuitable. Wade denied that a president who disagreed with Congress could be rendered harmless. "His word is law," insisted the Ohioan; "and suppose the people make a mistake, as they are always liable to make a mistake . . . and get a man who is false to all they wanted of him, who thwarts all their ideas, who overthrows all their principles; and there he sits, clothed with a power that you cannot get rid of." Asked Jacob M. Howard, a Michigan Radical: "Was it not a most fortunate thing for this country and the cause of human liberty" that the term of Lincoln's predecessor, Democrat James Buchanan, expired in four years instead of six? "The government would have been destroyed," cried Howard. "It is in the nature of our institutions that the people may from time to time be imposed upon by an incompetent, faithless, or traitorous Chief Magistrate." Against the one-term limit was presented the same argument used in 1787: the people's freedom to choose their chief executive should not be limited. After a single session of inconclusive discussion, the Senate did not return to the measure before adjournment.[5]

The next serious discussion of term limitation came nearly half a century later, in the aftermath of the clash between President William Howard Taft and Theodore Roosevelt for the Republican nomination in 1912 and the subsequent third-party candidacy of Roosevelt that brought about the election of Democrat Woodrow Wilson. Republican Senator John D. Works of California introduced an amendment for a single six-year term with a vivid condemnation of the manner in which both Roosevelt in 1904 and Taft in 1912 had, in his view, misused the resources of the federal government to obtain renomination and, in Roosevelt's case, reelection. Thousands of federal officeholders, he charged, had been mobilized into a "political army," working for the candidate rather than the country. And, after Roosevelt's reelection, pending suits against trusts that had supported him were dismissed. Senator Works continued:

> The effort to elect a President to a second term is a prolific source of political corruption, neglect of official duty, and betrayal of trust on the part of public servants. It is degrading to the President himself, and brings his great office into disrespect, often contempt. . . . A large part of his time that should be devoted to public service is given over to politics and the effort to secure his reelection. . . . He expects every man he appoints to support his political aspirations. . . . The White House is turned into the headquarters of a political party.[6]

Taft himself agreed with at least a part of the indictment. Even if a president does not divert his energies, his appointees do, the president conceded after his defeat. "It is difficult," said Taft, "to prevent the whole administration from losing part of its effectiveness for the public good by this diversion to political effort for at least a year of the four of each administration." If reelection were to be prohibited, Taft preferred a six-year term, because four years was "too short a time in which to work out great governmental policies."[7]

Senator Elihu Root, New York Republican, argued that the government of a president seeking reelection is immobilized not just for a single year but for two, as was demonstrated in the last half of

5. *Congressional Globe*, February 11, 1867, pp. 1140–45.
6. *Congressional Record*, December 9, 1912, pp. 295–97.
7. Speech at Lotos Club, New York City, quoted by Senator Works, ibid., December 10, 1912, p. 361.

President Taft's term. Just when a president "gets to the point of highest efficiency," argued Root, "people in the Senate and in the House begin to figure to try to beat him. You cannot separate the attempt to beat an individual from the attempt to make ineffective the operation of the Government which that individual is carrying on in accordance with his duty."[8]

But, countered Henry Cabot Lodge, Republican of Massachusetts, a president barred from reelection would still use the powers of his office to elect a successor of his own party, one in sympathy with his views, who would carry out the uncompleted policies of the incumbent. And William E. Borah, Republican of Idaho, agreed. Having attended the last two Republican conventions, he "could not discover any perceptible difference between the effect of the influence which was exerted upon the convention in 1908 by the gentleman [Roosevelt] who was nominating his successor [Taft] and that exerted in 1912 by the gentleman [Taft] who was nominating himself." If a president is fit to be in the White House, "he will be a political leader and will direct the political fortunes of his party. . . . He . . . will seek to lead his party, if not for his cause, then to the advantage of his successor." Besides Roosevelt, Borah cited Jefferson and Jackson as presidents who had run "aggressive" campaigns for their chosen successors.[9]

John Sharp Williams, Democrat of Mississippi, drew from the executive-legislative deadlock of 1911–12 a conclusion opposite to that of Senator Root. The 1910 election, which gave the Democrats control of the House of Representatives while Republican Taft remained in the White House, ushered in two years of divided government— what Williams called "lame and impotent and unsatisfactory government." But a six-year presidential term would extend any such period of divided government for two additional years, thus "emphasizing rather than diminishing the defect of our system as it is." Joseph L. Bristow, Republican of Kansas, concurred that the six-year term would result in suspension of governmental action for four years instead of two and make the government "less flexible and more irresponsive to the public will." It would entrench the president in office beyond the reach of the people, "regardless of the character of his administration," said Bristow, suggesting a provision for recall of

8. *Congressional Record*, January 30, 1913, p. 2265.
9. Ibid., pp. 2259, 2269.

the president at any biennial election. And Miles Poindexter, Republican of Washington, put it simply: Six years "is entirely too long for a bad man, and it is too short for a good man." Trust the people to decide at the end of the fourth year was his theme.[10]

An amendment by Senator Bristow to reduce the proposed six-year term to four years was beaten, 25 to 42, and the resolution cleared the Senate, 47 to 23. But it went to a House controlled by the Democratic party, and now that party was looking forward to the inauguration of President Wilson and to complete control of the government for the first time in nearly two decades. In the summer, the Democratic platform had endorsed a single-term constitutional amendment and pledged the party's nominee to "this principle," but Wilson had also promised to "say what I really think on every public question." The president-elect said what he thought in a letter that killed the resolution:

> Four years is too long a term for a President who is not the true spokesman of the people, who is imposed upon and does not lead. It is too short a term for a President who is doing, or attempting, a great work of reform, and who has not had time to finish it. To change the term to six years would be to increase the likelihood of its being too long, without any assurance that it would in happy cases be long enough. . . . As things stand now the people might more likely be cheated than served by further limitations of the President's eligibility. His fighting power in their behalf would be immensely weakened. No one will fear a President except those whom he can make fear the elections.[11]

The next president to win election twice was Franklin Roosevelt, and when he went on to victory for a third and fourth time he steered the reform movement in a different direction. In the 1946 election, the Republicans won control of the Congress for the first time since before the age of FDR, and they came to Washington intent on inflicting posthumously on their long-time adversary the defeat they could never visit on him in four election contests. Barely a month after the Eightieth Congress assembled, the Republicans pushed through a resolution to fix in the Constitution the two-term limit on presidential tenure that Washington, Jefferson, and all their successors, until Franklin Roosevelt, had voluntarily adopted.

10. Ibid., pp. 2265–66, 2271.
11. Letter to Representative Alexander Mitchell Palmer, Democrat of Pennsylvania, February 5, 1913, in Arthur S. Link, ed., *The Papers of Woodrow Wilson* (Princeton University Press, 1978), vol. 27, pp. 98–101.

Quoting George Washington on the dangers of monarchy, Republicans contended that the destruction of Washington's precedent made a constitutional amendment necessary to protect the country against "totalitarianism" and "dictatorship." Representative John M. Robsion of Kentucky, one of the amendment's authors, insisted that the growth of the powers of the executive enabled a president who enjoyed indefinite tenure not only to gain a "very large control of the legislative branch" but also to appoint most members of the judicial branch, posing a "real threat to our republican form of government." "The simple issue," said Representative Edward J. Devitt of Minnesota, "is whether or not we shall add one more check to our present system of checks and balances" as a safeguard "against the possible— even the probable—rise of an executive dictatorship." In the Senate, Alexander Wiley, Wisconsin Republican, likened the "long-time continuance in office by so-called indispensable leaders" to the *"fuehrer prinzip."* And for the anti–New Deal Democrats, Senator John H. Overton of Louisiana warned that a strong president could "make a life termer of himself," from which the country could "drift into an undemocratic form of government . . . a dynasty."[12]

Democratic loyalists countered that the people should not be denied the freedom to reelect their president if they wished. "To have had a constitutional limitation on the Presidential tenure of office in 1940 and again in 1944 would have been disastrous," urged Representative Joseph R. Bryson, Democrat of South Carolina; "in the face of a grave national crisis in 1940 the people . . . believed it inadvisable to change their Chief Executive; and . . . in 1944 . . . the people believed that such a change would have thrown our Nation into chaos and jeopardized our security in the face of the gravest military crisis in our Nation's history." "For the people to have the privilege of choosing whom they please to be their leader is democracy, real democracy," argued Sam Rayburn of Texas, the minority leader. Do not put future generations "in a strait-jacket" that might result "in the destruction of our country," pleaded John W. McCormack of Massachusetts, the minority whip. But to this line of argument, the sponsors had a ready reply: The people were not being shackled; on the contrary, they were being given the right to decide for themselves

12. *Congressional Record*, February 6, 1947, pp. 850, 859–60; March 5, 1947, pp. 1681, 1775.

through the ratification process whether they wanted the two-term limit in their Constitution.[13] The resolution, which became the Twenty-second Amendment, was adopted by the House by 285 votes to 121 and in the Senate by 59 to 23. Not a single Republican in either chamber voted in the negative. A substitute proposal offered in the House for a single six-year presidential term was defeated by a voice vote, without serious discussion.

A "tainted amendment," political scientist Clinton Rossiter called it a few years after its ratification, one "based on the sharp anger of a moment rather than the studied wisdom of a generation." The Constitution, said Rossiter, is "not the place to engage in a display of rancor." He predicted that the amendment would prove to have permanently weakened the presidency. "Everything in our history tells us," he wrote, "that a President who does not or cannot seek reelection loses much of his grip in his last couple of years, and we no longer can afford Presidents who lose their grip."[14] President Eisenhower, asked during his 1956 reelection campaign whether as a lame-duck president his influence would be lessened during his second term, conceded that "in some directions, it may be" but the power of the presidency would still be great. He considered the amendment "not wholly wise."[15] Resolutions to repeal the amendment have been introduced on occasion, but none has made headway in the Congress—even Congresses fully under the control of Democrats fiercely faithful to the memory of Franklin Roosevelt.

The single six-year term has continued to have advocates as well. In 1971, two veteran senators, Democratic Leader Mike Mansfield of Montana and Republican George D. Aiken of Vermont, proposed this reform in order "to allow a President to devote himself entirely to the problems of the Nation and . . . free him from the millstone of partisan politics" and from constant "harassment and embarrassment" by political opponents.[16] Senator Strom Thurmond, Republican of South Carolina, added another argument in introducing a six-year-term amendment four years later: it would "enhance the relationship

13. Ibid., February 6, 1947, pp. 844–48.
14. Letter of March 18, 1957, to Representative Stewart L. Udall of Arizona, ibid., March 25, 1957, p. 4323.
15. "News Conference of October 5, 1956," *Public Papers of the Presidents: Dwight D. Eisenhower, 1956* (Government Printing Office, 1958), p. 860.
16. *Congressional Record,* April 1, 1971, p. 9182.

between the President and Congress" because the legislators, "knowing that the President could not be reelected for a second term, would be more likely to work through consultation rather than confrontation."[17] In 1982 backers of the measure organized the Committee for a Single Six-Year Presidential Term to press for its adoption. The committee cited statements in support of the idea by Presidents Eisenhower, Johnson, Nixon, Ford, and Carter and included representatives of all those administrations, as well as of President Reagan's, in its leadership. Cochairmen of the committee were William E. Simon, President Ford's secretary of the treasury; Griffin B. Bell and Cyrus R. Vance, members of President Carter's cabinet; and Milton S. Eisenhower, President Eisenhower's brother and close advisor. But the movement failed to arouse significant public response, and the committee suspended its efforts.

Presidential Selection

The other element of President Jackson's reform proposal—that the electoral college be abolished and the president chosen by direct popular vote—has also been a recurrent subject of discussion, but some of the suggested constitutional changes would merely have modified the electoral college procedure rather than abolished the institution outright.

The arguments against the presidential selection process as it emerged from the compromises of 1787 and was modified by the Twelfth Amendment in 1804 fall into two categories. First, the electoral college is antidemocratic because it departs from the principle of "one person, one vote," disfranchises the voting minorities in each state by allowing their share of the state's electoral votes to be cast for a candidate they voted against, and favors some states and voting groups over others (although which states and groups are advantaged is a matter of dispute); for all these reasons, it could produce the ultimate antidemocratic result of choosing a president who had been beaten in the popular vote. Second, in the event the electoral college votes were split between three or more candidates, none of whom gained a majority, the subsequent contingency procedure—election

17. Ibid., August 1, 1975, p. 26809.

of the president by the House of Representatives, with each state's delegation casting a single vote—would be subject to manipulation and could, in the end, again lead to rejection of the popular favorite.

Those who worry about the undemocratic aspects of the current process have contended that were a president who had lost the election, as measured by the popular vote, to be placed in the White House, a crisis of legitimacy would result. Fortunately, this hypothesis has not been tested since 1888, although the country has skated perilously close on several recent occasions. In 1888, Benjamin Harrison won an electoral majority although incumbent President Grover Cleveland had a plurality of 98,000—almost 1 percent—in the popular vote. Cleveland and the country accepted the outcome, and the circumstances of his election evidently did not hamper Harrison's presidency. He was, however, defeated in his return match with Cleveland in 1892.

A case can be made that the electoral college also reversed the popular decision in 1960. Encyclopedias and other reference books now give a margin of 119,000 votes to John F. Kennedy over Richard M. Nixon. But the Kennedy total includes all of Alabama's vote for its winning Democratic electors, and only five of those were pledged to support Kennedy. The other six were unpledged, but they had run in the Democratic primary as conservative opponents of the dominant liberal wing of the party and, in the end, voted for Senator Harry F. Byrd of Virginia for president. Although the eleven electors were voted on separately, they all received approximately the same number of ballots, and it cannot be known how many Democratic voters thought they were voting for Kennedy and how many knew they were splitting their support. If it is assumed that the voters knowledgeably intended what became the outcome—five-elevenths of their support for Kennedy and six-elevenths for someone else—Kennedy's total is reduced by 177,000 votes and Richard Nixon becomes the popular vote winner. But having lost in the electoral college in any case, Nixon never advanced any such claim, and the Kennedy popular vote victory stands in the record books.[18]

18. Neal R. Peirce and Lawrence D. Longley, *The People's President: The Electoral College in American History and the Direct Vote Alternative*, rev. ed. (Yale University Press, 1981), pp. 65–67. The authors suggest that Nixon declined to make an issue of the popular vote totals because he would be seen as "a poor loser." The 119,000-vote figure is taken from Richard M. Scammon and Alice V. McGillivray, eds., *America Votes 19:*

One can only conjecture whether rejection by the electoral college of a clear popular vote winner would be accepted as calmly in more modern times as it was in 1888. In this century, two elections besides that of 1960—in which Kennedy's accepted margin was less than 0.2 percent of total ballots cast—have been close enough to have made reversal by the electors a possibility. One was in 1968, when Nixon won handily in the electoral college but gained a popular vote margin of just 510,000 votes, or 0.7 percent. The other was in 1976, when Jimmy Carter defeated Gerald Ford by a respectable 1,681,000-vote margin, or 2.1 percent, but his electoral vote margin was 297 to 140 and several states won by Carter were so close that the switch of a relatively few votes could have given Ford the electoral majority.

The nation has been even more fortunate that the electoral college has produced a clear majority in every election since 1824, so that the House of Representatives has not been thrust into the presidential selection process. The electoral college vote has been split among three or more candidates on half a dozen occasions: in 1860, when Abraham Lincoln defeated three opposing aspirants; in 1892, when the Populist candidate picked up twenty-two electoral college votes; in 1912, when both President William Howard Taft and former President Theodore Roosevelt lost to Woodrow Wilson; in 1924, when Senator Robert M. La Follette, Sr., carried his home state of Wisconsin; in 1948, when the States' Rights (commonly called Dixiecrat) candidate Strom Thurmond won four southern states; and in 1968, when Alabama Governor George C. Wallace won five states. But on all of these occasions, the winning candidate had a clear majority of the electoral vote, and so the issue was decided at that point. The Constitution's fallback procedure for election of the president by the House was avoided.

Yet the escapes were narrow enough to compel attention to the anomalies of the presidential selection process. The electoral college became a live issue in 1912, when a three-way split in its ballots appeared likely, and discussion continued after that emergency passed. House hearings were held in 1923, and in 1933 a House committee reported a plan to divide each state's electoral votes in

---

A Handbook of Contemporary American Election Statistics (Washington: Congressional Quarterly, 1991). The size of the margin also depends on whether the Kennedy figure for Alabama is based on the highest total for any elector (the Scammon-McGillivray number) or the highest of the electors pledged to Kennedy, which was 5,747 fewer.

proportion to the popular vote for each candidate—which would presumably increase the likelihood, although not make certain, that the electoral college decision would reflect the popular vote. In 1934, at a time when Democrats feared some anti–New Deal Democratic electors might not cast their ballots for Franklin Roosevelt, the Senate supported a measure to eliminate the electoral college as a body of persons and record each state's electoral vote automatically for the popular vote winner in that state. The vote for the so-called faithless elector amendment was 42 to 24 in favor, but that fell short of the necessary two-thirds, and the proposal died.[19]

The electoral college issue was vigorously revived when Dixiecrat Thurmond won thirty-nine electoral votes in 1948--the most of any third-place finisher since 1860. Both houses organized for action in the following year, and proposals reached the floor in 1950. The Senate approved by 64 to 27 a proportional plan that Senator Henry Cabot Lodge, Jr., Republican of Massachusetts, and Representative Ed Gossett, Democrat of Texas, had kept alive with committee hearings throughout the 1940s, but in the House the amendment was stalled by the Rules Committee, and when Gossett moved to suspend the rules to pass the measure he was defeated, 134 to 210. The Senate approved a similar measure in 1956 by a 48 to 37 vote, but that was short of the two-thirds requirement.[20]

Twenty years after the Dixiecrat scare, George Wallace and his American Independent party came even closer to throwing the electoral college into deadlock, winning forty-six electoral votes, and reformers again mobilized for action. This time they rallied around the concept of direct election of the president by the people. The public was with them. Opinion polls found decisive popular majorities disapproving the existing contingency procedure for election by the House of Representatives (60 to 24 percent, with the remainder undecided) and approving direct election (66 to 19 percent before the 1968 election and 81 to 12 after). In September 1969, after six days of

19. Wallace S. Sayre and Judith H. Parris, *Voting for President: The Electoral College and the American Political System* (Brookings, 1970), summarize these and earlier efforts for electoral college reform, including adoption of the Twelfth Amendment, on pp. 25–32. Peirce and Longley recount the history of reform debates in greater detail in *The People's President*, pp. 131–206. They point out that the proportional plan would have resulted in more, rather than fewer, instances in which the electoral college would have selected the loser of the popular vote contest (pp. 154–55).

20. Sayre and Parris, *Voting for President*, pp. 33–36.

debate, the House by 339 to 70 approved a plan for direct election. A candidate would be declared the winner with 40 percent or more of the popular vote; if none attained that level, the top two would compete in a runoff election.[21] In the Senate, the proposal was killed by a filibuster by senators from the South and from small states. Majorities of 54 to 36 and 53 to 34 voted to close debate, on two occasions in September 1970, but these fell short of the two-thirds required by Senate rules.[22]

But only six years later came the next close election—the Carter-Ford contest, where a shift of a relatively few votes could have given Ford an electoral vote victory despite Carter's lead of nearly 1.7 million in the popular tally—and proponents of direct election seized the opportunity to make their case again. A legislative logjam prevented consideration of the issue in 1977–78, but when it did reach the Senate floor in 1979, the reform advocates could muster only a 51-to-48 majority, far short of the necessary two-thirds.[23]

Not until 1992 did a third-party movement or independent presidential candidacy again appear with enough strength, or did an election seem close enough, to revive the electoral college issue. But as the polls in the spring of that year began to show that Ross Perot might carry at least several states as an independent candidate, the hazards—and potential antidemocratic outcome—of an electoral college deadlock, with the decision thrown to the House, became once more the subject of intense speculation by politicians and media commentators. Even though Perot withdrew in July, the threat posed by his candidacy could precipitate a restaging of the constitutional debates that followed the earlier three-way contests.

Linking Cabinet and Congress

One of the earliest authoritative suggestions for altering the constitutional relationship between Congress and the executive branch came from Justice Joseph Story of the Supreme Court, in his *Commentaries on the Constitution of the United States*, published in 1833. His clause-by-clause critique of the Constitution is, for the most part, a

21. Ibid., pp. 14–18.
22. *Congressional Quarterly Almanac, 1970*, vol. 26 (1971), p. 840.
23. Peirce and Longley, *The People's President*, pp. 80–84.

long paean to the wisdom of the framers, but one provision troubled him. That was the paragraph barring officials of the executive branch from membership in Congress. Citing the principle of executive accountability, Story argued that the prohibition compelled an administration "to resort to secret and unseen influences, to private interviews, and private arrangements," to "all the blandishments of office, and all the deadening weight of silent patronage" to get its measures introduced and passed, instead of taking "open and public responsibility" and making "a bold and manly appeal to the nation in the face of its representatives." He also contended that if members of the cabinet had to advocate and defend their measures in Congress, presidents would be forced to appoint as heads of departments "statesmen of high public character, talents, experience, and elevated services . . . who . . . could command public confidence," instead of "personal or party favorites" of "gross incapacity" and "ignorance."[24]

A generation later, this issue reached the stage of debate on the House floor, but in the form of a statute rather than a constitutional amendment. A bill offered by Representative George H. Pendleton, Democrat of Ohio, during the Civil War proposed to authorize cabinet officials to participate in debate on matters affecting their departments and require them to be present for questioning twice weekly, at specified times. In approving the bill, in 1864, a select committee chaired by Pendleton repeated Story's argument that if cabinet officers had seats in the House their influence on the legislature would be "open, declared, and authorized, rather than secret, concealed, and unauthorized," but the proponents appeared to be concerned less with the jurist's concept of executive accountability than with their own notion of congressional responsibility. Protesting executive branch secrecy in the conduct of the war, they complained of a "table . . . groaning with the weight of resolutions asking information from the several Departments that have not been answered" and sought face-to-face confrontation with department heads as a means of obtaining information and thus enhancing their own ability to influence and control administrative action.[25] But, by agreement, the debate was

24. Joseph Story, *Commentaries on the Constitution of the United States*, 2d ed. (Charles C. Little and James Brown, 1851), pp. 605–06. The *Commentaries* appeared at a time when congressional followers of President Jackson were attacking the Second Bank of the United States but Jackson was distancing himself from the conflict.

25. Stephen Horn, *The Cabinet and Congress* (Columbia University Press, 1960), pp.

deferred until the final day of the Thirty-eighth Congress, and the
bill died without a vote when the Congress adjourned. A similar bill
by Pendleton—by then a senator—was endorsed in 1881 by a select
Senate committee but was shelved without debate. In both cases,
opponents challenged the constitutionality of the proposed statutes,
but supporters argued that the constitutional prohibition applied only
to full membership with voting rights, leaving the Congress free to
admit anyone it might choose to mere participation in debate.

In the post–Civil War decades, when parties fought their battles
over the spoils of office and offered little in the way of program,
reformers saw still another merit in giving cabinet members seats in
the Congress: they would provide a nationally minded leadership for
a locally oriented and fragmented legislature. In 1873, Gamaliel Bradford, who advocated the reform consistently and constantly for more
than forty years, was deploring the "absence of progress" by the
Congress on a broad range of pressing problems and attributing it to
a lack of clear responsibility in any institution for formulating proposals and initiating action. Presidents in those days left legislating
to the legislative branch—and congressmen insisted that they do so—
but within Congress, responsibility was parceled out to committees
that were more aware of local than of national interests. If cabinet
members sat in the Congress, contended Bradford, when they presented proposals they would arrest the attention of the country and
stir a national response.[26]

The Pendleton idea was kept alive by Bradford, historian Henry
Jones Ford, and others, and in the next century gained the important
support of Henry L. Stimson. As secretary of war in the administration
of President William Howard Taft, Stimson enlisted the president as
a protagonist. If Taft were successful in his effort to establish an
executive budget system, Stimson persuaded him, it would be of little
avail to any president unless department heads could present and

---

53–71; quotation from Representative James A. Garfield, Republican of Ohio, during
floor debate, January 26, 1865. By coincidence, the Confederate States of America were
engaged in the same debate during the same period. The Confederate constitution
specifically authorized the Congress to grant department heads nonvoting seats in the
legislature, but measures to admit the cabinet officers were defeated by the House in
1862 and the Senate the following year. Ibid., pp. 38–45.

26. "Should the Cabinet Have Seats in Congress?" *Nation*, April 3, 1873, p. 234.
This editorial quotes Bradford's argument, presented in a lecture, and goes on to
question whether cabinet members would in fact have that much influence.

defend the president's budget in congressional debate. Just before leaving office, Taft sent a special message to Congress proposing that cabinet officers be granted nonvoting seats in the legislature, but his successor—the same Woodrow Wilson who had advocated even broader reforms as a young scholar—was satisfied that strong presidential leadership, informal collaboration between cabinet members and Democratic congressional leaders, and the use of party caucuses by the latter to develop unity and discipline would make the existing system effective. In Wilson's first two years, that proved to be the case, for Wilson's New Freedom program was written into law by cohesive Democratic majorities.[27] Wilson's own successor, Warren G. Harding, favored the Pendleton scheme, describing it as "one of the most constructive steps that can be taken," and most of his cabinet were advocates as well, but congressional supporters could muster no corresponding enthusiasm on Capitol Hill.[28] The idea was revived in the 1940s by Representative Estes Kefauver, Democrat of Tennessee, in the more limited form of a question period, when cabinet members would be admitted to the floor to answer inquiries, but neither President Franklin Roosevelt nor the House leadership responded favorably, and the effort failed.[29] It was renewed several decades later by Representative Sam Gejdenson, Democrat of Connecticut, who obtained a House committee hearing on a question period proposal in 1992.

Direct Election of Senators

The Seventeenth Amendment, which provided for the direct election of U.S. senators, did little more than confirm the transformation of the Senate that had been proceeding for more than a century.

By 1913, when the amendment was ratified, the Senate had departed in two major respects from the body the framers had designed. First, it had ceased to be—more accurately, it had never become—a kind of privy council for the president. Second, it had

27. Horn, *Cabinet and Congress*, pp. 104, 114–18; and James L. Sundquist, *The Decline and Resurgence of Congress* (Brookings, 1981), pp. 130–32.
28. Horn, *Cabinet and Congress*, pp. 128–30.
29. Ibid., pp. 136–67.

ceased to be the instrument by which the states participated, as states, in federal policymaking.

In its council role, the Senate was to "advise and consent" in two categories of executive decisions—appointment of officials and making of treaties. As soon as President Washington took office and the First Congress convened, questions arose as to how and where the Senate would give its advice to the president and consent to his actions. A Senate committee, appointed to discuss these questions with the president, evidently preferred that the executive come to the Senate chamber with his proposed nominations or treaties, justify them orally and answer questions, and at the conclusion of the discussion receive the Senate's consent or nonconsent. To Washington, such meetings would be liable both to embarrass the president and restrain the senators, and he insisted that the decision in each case whether to submit a proposal orally or in writing should be left to the president. Experience would determine the most satisfactory and effective methods of communicating.[30]

Experience was not long in coming. Having encountered delays in response to two written messages dealing with diplomatic affairs, President Washington took the oral discussion route on a proposed treaty with the southern Indians. Accompanied by the secretary of war, he appeared at the Senate chamber and asked for advice and consent to a series of propositions. But the Senate asked for time and referred the matter to a committee. The president "started up in a violent fret," protesting that his purpose in coming to the Senate chamber was defeated, and after getting a commitment for a report within two days, sullenly withdrew, declaring "that he would be damned if he ever went there again."[31] Washington did return for the second meeting, which concluded amicably, but thereafter no president repeated the experience. Communication of treaties and nominations has been in writing, and no president has entered into oral discussion with the whole Senate. Particularly since rejection of the Versailles treaty by the Senate after World War I, presidents have been careful to seek advice informally from senators before embarking

30. George Henry Haynes, *The Senate of the United States* (Russell and Russell, 1960; orig. copyright 1938), vol. 1, pp. 55–56.

31. The account of the meeting comes from the journal of Senator William Maclay of Pennsylvania, and the departing comment was repeated by William H. Crawford and reported in the memoirs of John Quincy Adams. Ibid., pp. 63–67.

on major diplomatic initiatives and have even admitted senators to the negotiating process—as when President Franklin Roosevelt appointed senators (and House members as well) to the U.S. delegation to the conference that adopted the United Nations Charter—but such consultation and collaboration have been with influential individual leaders and members, not with the entire Senate as a collective council.

Clearly, the Senate never could have developed as a body of presidential councilors. Its growth in size would alone have precluded any such possibility. So would the constitutional independence of the Senate. When the king of England met with his privy council, he was consulting with advisers of his own choice; no presidential council, no matter how small, made up of persons in whose selection the president had no direct voice and perhaps dominated by political opponents eager to discredit him, could possibly fulfill its intended function.

The concept of the Senate as a body representing the states (like the Bundesrat of today's Germany) disappeared more gradually. In discussing the Senate, the framers saw it as an organ of the states; when that body acted, it was the states themselves taking collective action. And that conception carried over into the early decades of government under the Constitution. State legislatures commonly took stands on national issues, and communicated those positions to their senators as instructions, much as governments have always instructed the ambassadors who represent them in faraway capitals. And a senator could ignore or contravene his instructions only at risk of being denied reelection by his state's legislature at the expiration of his term.

In the post–Civil War decades, however, as the states developed a broader range of activities of their own, their lawmakers ceased trying to share in the direction of national affairs as well. And senators, as powerful and influential state politicians in their own right—the majority party's preeminent leader, or "boss," normally held one of his state's two seats and often chose his colleague—were more likely to be able to control the legislators than the other way around. So as ambassadors they became plenipotentiaries, disciplined not by those who sent them but by the powerful party organizations within the Senate that they joined on arrival. And to complete the transformation of senators from state representatives to autonomous federal officials, beginning late in the nineteenth century some states found ways to circumvent the Constitution and arrange for senators to be chosen—though still nominally by the legislatures—in fact by the people through direct election.

With the Senate thus altered, when early in this century agitation grew for adoption of direct election in all the states, no one even called attention to the fact that the states would be giving up what the framers had conceived as the ultimate guarantee of their place in the federal system. Either the states no longer saw the Senate as their guardian against federal intrusion, or they had ceased to feel the need for such protection. And, if the Senate was to represent not the states as such but the people of those states, the contention that the people themselves should make the choice became irrefutable.

Direct election of senators therefore took its place in the long series of election reform measures that were central to the Progressive creed, all aimed at taking governmental institutions out of the hands of corrupt party machines and making them responsive to the people directly—a series that included also the initiative, referendum, and recall; the secret ballot; nonpartisan local elections; and nomination of party candidates, and even presidential electors, through direct primaries. Senators resisted as long as they could; all of them beneficiaries of the existing process, they were bound to see little to gain and much to risk through change. Five times the House passed the proposed amendment, over a span of twenty years, before the Senate finally allowed the proposition to come to a vote. But by 1912, public sentiment could no longer be ignored. Nineteen state legislatures, as of 1911, had petitioned the Congress to call a constitutional convention to relieve them of their onerous responsibility.[32] The proposal had been a staple in Democratic platforms since 1900 and of the Populists and other minor parties since as early as 1876. Muckrakers condemned the Senate as a "millionaires' club" and decried the influence of corporate wealth as state legislators filled the Senate seats; the same year that it finally approved the amendment, the Senate had to expel one of its members, William Lorimer, Republican of Illinois, when it learned

32. Statement of Senator Weldon B. Heyburn, Republican of Idaho, in Senate debate, *Congressional Record*, May 24, 1911, pp. 1539–40. Heyburn was an opponent of the measure; a supporter, Senator Joseph L. Bristow, Republican of Kansas, had a year earlier claimed the backing of thirty-three state legislatures, but some of these presumably had not formally petitioned for a constitutional convention. Heyburn's figure was not disputed in the 1911 debate.

that a corporate "slop fund" had been used to bribe legislators on his behalf. When Secretary of State William Jennings Bryan proclaimed the amendment ratified, in 1913, he exulted that the Senate would no longer be "filled up with the representatives of predatory wealth."[33]

The amendment affected the makeup and character of the Senate only gradually, for if party organizations could control legislatures they could also control nominating conventions. But many factors, including the whole body of Progressive reforms, were contributing to the weakening of party organizations, and the direct election of senators was both the product of the antiparty movement and a contributor to it. As the direct primary spread, the way was opened for insurgent politicians to challenge entrenched party organizations and defeat them, and when the rebels arrived in the Senate they brought their independent attitudes with them. The tightly disciplined party organizations that characterized the Senate in the last decades of the nineteenth century were already beginning to disintegrate when the Seventeenth Amendment was adopted, but that action speeded their dissolution. Steadily the Senate—and the House as well—moved from party cohesion and discipline to individualism, and the direction of change has not been reversed.

The Amendment Process

In that heyday of reform, the Progressive Era, when advocates of social change were pressing for a whole series of constitutional amendments—to bring about, among other things, the direct election of senators, women's suffrage, the income tax, prohibition of alcoholic beverages, banning of child labor—it was natural that they should direct their reforming zeal also to the amendment process that made the achievement of any of their goals exasperatingly difficult. Theodore Roosevelt's Progressive party of 1912, in the same platform that endorsed four of the above proposals, pledged itself "to provide a more easy and expeditious method of amending the Federal Constitution." The platform did not say how, but individual Progressives had been pushing for a federal version of the process that they had succeeded in inserting into various state constitutions, whereby

33. Quoted by Haynes, *The Senate*, vol. 2, p. 1042.

amendments could be adopted through popular initiative and referendum, bypassing the state legislatures altogether. One resolution,
introduced by Senator Robert M. La Follette, Sr., of Wisconsin, would
have amended the Constitution to provide that on application of ten
states or a majority of both houses of Congress, a constitutional
amendment could be submitted to referendum and would be adopted
if a majority of all voters, and a majority in each of a majority of states,
approved it.

For the immediate purposes of the reformers, however, that proved
unnecessary. Even as the Progressives met in 1912, the income tax
and direct election of senators were on their way to ratification by
three-fourths of the states—each achieving that goal in 1913. Prohibition entered the Constitution in 1919 and women's suffrage the
following year. The proposed child labor amendment was submitted
by the Congress to the state legislatures in 1924.[34]

Then it was the turn of the conservatives to be upset with the
amendment process. Spurred by reports that some legislatures had
ratified Prohibition and women's suffrage through irregular and questionable procedures, Republican Senator James J. Wadsworth of New
York, an opponent of both of those constitutional innovations, proposed an amendment to require that each state legislature's action be
subjected to a popular referendum within the state. As reported by
the Senate Judiciary Committee, however, the amendment simply
substituted the popular vote for the legislative vote as the ratifying
action, reducing the legislature to an advisory role if it chose to act
at all. Wadsworth contended that he sought only a "more deliberative" process, but answered affirmatively when asked whether his
"underlying motive" was to "make it more difficult to amend the
Constitution in any way." In the case of the Prohibition amendment,
he pointed out, the voters of five states had rejected the amendment
in advisory referenda but the legislatures had approved it anyway,
and when the women's suffrage amendment was submitted to the
states, the same sequence occurred in four instances.[35] Wadsworth

34. Only twenty-eight states ratified this amendment—four short of the necessary
two-thirds—but the Supreme Court in 1941, reversing an earlier decision, held that
Congress had the power to regulate child labor and so made the amendment unnecessary.

35. *Congressional Record*, March 10, 1924, pp. 4495, 4497, 4489. In the case of the
Eighteenth Amendment, the five states were California, Iowa, Maryland, Massachu-

and his allies charged that these amendments—to which some southern senators added the Fifteenth Amendment (Negro suffrage) as
well—had been "railroaded" or "stampeded" through the legislatures
by "fanatics," "agitators," "organized minorities," and "professional
reformers." "I would rather trust the conservatism of all the people,"
said Frank B. Brandegee, Republican of Connecticut.[36]

The remnants of the Progressive movement took the occasion to
demand that the amendment process be made easier, not harder.
Smith Brookhart, the insurgent Iowa Republican, argued that the right
of amendment should rest squarely on the people in a democracy,
and that Congress should therefore be able to submit amendments
by a simple, rather than a two-thirds, majority. "We have fenced
around the amendment of our Constitution by so many barriers,"
pleaded Brookhart, "that it is only after a generation of campaigning
and of education that we are able to get an amendment at all."[37] But
several test votes made clear that none of the proposed changes in
the amending clause could muster two-thirds of the Senate, and after
several days of debate the effort was abandoned.

Approval of Treaties

As World War II approached its end and statesmen began con-
ceiving of a world organization to prevent any third cataclysmic conflict, some remembered the struggle over an earlier body designed to
preserve the peace—the League of Nations. After World War I, President Woodrow Wilson had been an architect of the League of
Nations, but after an arduous campaign that sapped his energies and
ultimately left him incapacitated, the Senate rejected the Treaty of
Versailles and, with it, U.S. membership in the League. A majority
of senators approved the treaty—49 to 35—but that fell 7 votes short
of the necessary two-thirds. Similarly, American adherence to the
World Court had been blocked—the last time, in 1935, by thirty-six
opponents overriding fifty-two proponents.

---

setts, and Ohio; in the Nineteenth, the four were Massachusetts, Missouri, Texas, and
West Virginia.
  36. Ibid., March 20, 1924, p. 4566.
  37. Ibid., p. 4564.

Even as representatives of the victors of World War II were gathered in San Francisco in 1945 to create the United Nations as successor to the League of Nations, the House Judiciary Committee reported a constitutional amendment that would make it impossible for as few as thirty-three of the ninety-six senators to block U.S. membership in the new world organization. The amendment, sponsored by Hatton W. Sumners, Democrat of Texas and chairman of the committee, would have altered the treaty clause to rest congressional approval on a majority vote of both houses, as in the case of ordinary legislation or even a declaration of war. It was anomalous, suggested Sumners and his committee, that the Constitution rendered it more difficult to make peace than to make war, and the committee report quoted James Wilson's remark during the 1787 convention: "If two-thirds are necessary to make peace, the minority may perpetuate war, against the sense of the majority."[38]

The original reasons for the two-thirds requirement, argued the committee in its report, had disappeared, as the conflicts between the northern and southern states that caused the framers to fear rule by simple majorities—disputes over old issues such as fishery rights and new questions arising from the westward expansion of the nation—had been resolved. The Senate had never become the intimate advisory and consultative body to the president that had warranted its special role in treaty making to the exclusion of participation by the House. Members of the House served as long as senators, and acquired as much expertise. And because treaties normally had to be implemented through legislation and appropriations, in which the House held a parity of power with the Senate, it should play an equal part in treaty making also. In the day when the nation was protected by its ocean barriers, "the emasculation and rejection of our treaties by a minority of the upper House of Congress could be tolerated," said the committee, but now "the very life and death of the Nation depends on smooth-working machinery for regulating our international relations." And the two-thirds requirement "ties the hands of our negotiators."[39]

The opposition based its case on the special nature of treaties under the Constitution. Unlike the legislative power, which is restricted to

38. Ibid., May 1, 1945, p. 4011.
39. Ibid., pp. 4011–12.

the purposes enumerated in the Constitution, the treaty-making power is unlimited. It overrides all state laws and constitutions, and it is not subject to judicial review.[40]

A proposal to require House approval, but by a two-thirds vote as in the Senate, was defeated, 61 to 103. Then a modification to require that the approval in each house be by a majority of the total membership was adopted, and the proposed amendment was approved overwhelmingly, 288 to 88. But the Senate never considered the measure. Each house may be viewed, perhaps, as asserting its self-interest. But in the case of the Senate, ironically, its inaction served not to protect the interest of the majority of its members but rather to preserve the power of a minority.

The United Nations was accepted by the Senate with virtually no objection, and the other treaties that embodied much of the postwar U.S. foreign policy—including the North Atlantic Treaty and the Southeast Asia Treaty—were approved with relatively little struggle. In a spirit of bipartisan and legislative-executive cooperation, the country rejected the isolationism that had marked the previous postwar period and entered wholeheartedly into a role of world leadership, and the question of the extraordinary majority required for treaty ratification lost its urgency.

But a cry of alarm soon came from the opposite direction. Organs of the United Nations were preparing to carry out their duty under the charter of promoting human rights and economic and social reforms; and the United States, in signing the charter, had pledged itself to support such programs. Conservatives suspicious of socialist and communist influence in the United Nations protested that the United States might join in approving, through treaties or executive agreements entered into under those treaties, measures having the force of law in the United States without the direct approval of the Congress. In so doing, moreover, the federal government could act in fields that under the Constitution had been reserved to the states.

A constitutional amendment to limit the executive's treaty-making power, introduced by Senator John W. Bricker, Republican of Ohio, plunged the Senate into acrimonious debate for an entire month in early 1954. As redrafted by an American Bar Association committee

40. Summation by Representative John W. Gwynne, Republican of Iowa, ibid., p. 4019.

and reported by the Senate Judiciary Committee, the measure provided that no treaty or executive agreement could become effective as internal law except through legislation "which would be valid in the absence of treaty." Thus the amendment would both restore a degree of congressional control over executive agreements and restrain the federal government from usurping the powers of the states.

President Eisenhower objected that the amendment as written would put the country back to the days of the Articles of Confederation, when any state had the right to repudiate a treaty, and said he could not accept any amendment that would "change or alter the traditional and constitutional balances among the three departments of Government."[41] Both Republican and Democratic leaders in the Senate then sought the basis for a compromise. One proposed by Senator Walter F. George, Democrat of Georgia, that eliminated most of the objectionable language was accepted by a 61–30 vote, but lost on final passage by 60 to 31, a single vote short of a two-thirds majority. Senator Bricker vowed to continue his fight, but in that year's election the Democrats recaptured their congressional majorities and interest waned.

Congressional Tenure

The two-year term for members of the House of Representatives is "too brief for the public good," President Lyndon B. Johnson said in a special message to Congress in 1966 recommending that the term be extended to four years. In his plan, all 435 members of the House would be elected in the presidential election year.

The longer term, argued the president, would free the representatives from the "inexorable pressures" of biennial campaigning. A representative "is scarcely permitted to take his seat in the historic Hall of the House, when he must begin once more to make his case to his constituency." That reduces his effectiveness as a legislator, deprives his constituents of full representation in Congress, and

41. "News Conference, January 13, 1954," and "News Conference, February 3, 1954," *Public Papers: Eisenhower, 1954*, pp. 51–53, 225.

increases the cost of holding office. All this discourages some of the country's best men from aspiring to serve in the House, concluded the president, himself a former representative.[42]

These arguments repeated those of an earlier debate. The House considered a four-year term for its members in 1906, when the proposal was attached by committee to an amendment providing for direct election of senators. The four-year term was not voted on separately, and the resolution containing both proposals was approved that year by only 89 to 86, substantially short of the two-thirds required for constitutional amendments.[43]

By 1966, the volume of legislation had increased as the scope of government expanded, and a Congress that in 1906 could adjourn in June to permit its members to go home to campaign now stayed in session in even-numbered years until September or October. Burdened by a constantly increasing work load, longer sessions, and higher campaigning costs—for primary as well as general elections—members of the House might have been expected to embrace the proposal for a longer term as heaven-sent relief. Informal polls had suggested that they would. One survey of House opinion on a four-year term, conducted by Representative Abraham J. Multer, Democrat of New York, in 1949, obtained 319 favorable responses to 110 opposed, and a similar inquiry in 1965 by Representative Frank Chelf, Democrat of Kentucky, found 254 members favorable against 41 opposed and 67 doubtful.[44] In eight days of hearings in 1965–66—four before Johnson's message and four after—66 members supported a longer term (65 for four years and 1 for three) against a lone opponent. Yet, after the hearings, the proposal died in the Judiciary Committee without ever being considered on the floor.

One reason was that the committee's chairman, Emanuel Celler, Democrat of New York, was among those hostile to the measure.

42. "Special Message to the Congress Proposing Constitutional Amendments Relating to Terms for House Members and the Electoral College System, January 20, 1966," *Public Papers of the Presidents: Lyndon B. Johnson, 1966* (GPO, 1967), bk. 1, pp. 36–39. Oddly, as late as 1966 a president could still refer to potential congressional candidates as "men."

43. Charles O. Jones, *Every Second Year: Congressional Behavior and the Two-Year Term* (Brookings, 1967), pp. 16–17.

44. *Congressional Tenure of Office*, Hearings before the House Judiciary Committee and Subcommittee No. 5, 89 Cong. 1 and 2 sess. (GPO, 1966), pp. 29, 19.

But, clearly, many of the resolution's less committed supporters simply changed their minds after close examination of the probable consequences of a four-year term.

The central issue was the timing of the congressional election, but that question became significant because of a more profound consideration, the balance of power between the Congress and the president. Whereas Johnson proposed that the congressional election coincide with the presidential, sixty of the sixty-five proponents who testified before Celler's committee had advocated electing half the members each two years. Johnson justified his position on the ground that the voter turnout is higher in presidential years. A system of staggered terms, he contended, would render the House less representative than the Senate and the presidency by "perpetually condemning half its membership to a shrunken electorate."[45] Members were bound to suspect a less altruistic motive in a president renowned for political realism and toughness, and Attorney General Nicholas deB. Katzenbach supplied it. "In presidential years," Katzenbach testified before the committee, "the public in general elects a Congress that is running on the platform of the President. Those elected candidates of the same political complexion as the President are basically in sympathy with the views of their party. In this climate, the President and the Congress are more likely to be able to carry out a program without unreasonable deadlocks. . . . And I would think we had in this country, by and large, better government in times when a majority of the Houses were in basic philosophical sympathy with the President than when they are not. When they are not, it makes it much more difficult to do anything."[46]

The apparent unspoken Johnson objective, then, was to produce a Congress more to the president's liking and enhance his power over it. The Republican minority, of course, was quickest to sense the implication. Democrats, from the first Franklin Roosevelt victory in 1932 through Johnson's, had won seven of the last nine presidential elections. And, whether because of the "coattail" effect, the larger voter turnout in presidential years, or other reasons, Republican representatives had been swept out of office, their party accruing a net loss of 210 seats in the seven elections. But in every midterm election

45. "Special Message of January 20, 1966," p. 39; see also Jones, *Every Second Year*, pp. 30–31.

46. *Congressional Tenure*, Hearings, pp. 183, 204.

after losing the presidency, except 1934, the Republicans had snapped back; in the seven midterm polls from 1938 through 1962 they had recorded a net gain of 148 seats and were headed for another midterm victory (which turned out to be a smashing 47 seats) in 1966.[47] "Small wonder," observed Charles O. Jones, "that the overwhelming majority of minority party members oppose the concurrent-term proposal."[48] Of ninety-two Republicans who expressed a view on the four-year concurrent term in responding to a questionnaire Jones distributed in 1966 to all House members, ninety were opposed, with two neutral. Staggered four-year terms, with half the members elected each two years, were approved by 33 percent of Republicans responding, but the overwhelming majority preferred no change at all.

But neither did Democrats rally behind the Johnson concurrent-term proposal. Only 25 percent of 142 majority party members who expressed a view on the questionnaire approved the plan, with 65 percent opposed and 10 percent neutral. Staggered terms won majority support, 55 to 37 percent with 8 percent neutral. When the returns for Republicans and Democrats were combined, even the most popular form of the four-year-term idea—staggered elections—could not win majority approval. Only 47 percent of the respondents expressed favor, with an equal number disapproving and 6 percent neutral. "No change" was approved by 61 percent.[49] "Certainly . . . as of 1966," Jones concluded, "there was very little enthusiasm for a change. . . . The number opposed to any change is impressive and those who favor some change cannot agree on the form it should take."[50]

As the decade of the 1990s opened, discussions related to congressional tenure centered on quite a different question: whether individual members of Congress should be compelled to retire after serving in office for a specified length of time. This was not a new issue, for resolutions to limit service in Congress had been introduced by more than a few of its members in recent decades, usually specifying

---

47. Jones, *Every Second Year*, p. 43; and Norman J. Ornstein, Thomas E. Mann, and Michael J. Malbin, *Vital Statistics on Congress, 1991–1992* (Washington: Congressional Quarterly, 1992), pp. 53.

48. *Every Second Year*, p. 43.

49. Ibid., pp. 110, 106. Of the 433 House members at the time, 318 returned their questionnaires (73 percent) but some members did not express a view on every alternative. Respondents were not asked to choose among the options, and some approved one or more of the proposed changes and "no change" as well.

50. Ibid., pp. 107, 112.

twelve years as the maximum length of tenure. But the sponsors of these resolutions did not press the issue, in view of the built-in resistance they were bound to encounter among their colleagues, and the reform was never seriously considered.

The issue came to the fore in 1990 when voters in three states—California, Colorado, and Oklahoma—approved term-limitation measures that had been placed on the November ballot by initiative. In California and Oklahoma, the restrictions were applied to state legislators only, but in Colorado the initiative extended to members of Congress as well, limiting them to twelve years of service (though it would not affect any then-incumbent member until after twelve years, or 2002). Among those who endorsed limiting congressional terms was President George Bush, and when the 102d Congress opened in 1991, Representative Bill McCollum of Florida, vice chairman of the House Republican Conference, introduced two versions of term limitation. Both would limit senators and representatives to twelve years of service, but one added a provision to lengthen the House term from two years to four. The latter proposal had fourteen cosponsors, the former fifteen. In the Senate, Senators Dennis DeConcini, Democrat of Arizona, and Steven Symms, Republican of Idaho, introduced a measure to set a twelve-year limit for both houses.[51]

Removing a Failed President

Eight decades after President James A. Garfield lay incapacitated for eighty days before dying from an assassin's bullet, four decades after President Wilson spent sixteen months in seclusion after a stroke, but less than one decade after Eisenhower suffered three serious illnesses, the Congress finally came to grips with the question of how to maintain the country's leadership "in a nuclear age . . . fraught with danger" when the president became disabled. The outcome was the Twenty-fifth Amendment, which established a procedure for removing an incapacitated chief executive (as well as a method of filling a vacancy in the vice presidency). The objective was not con-

51. McCollum, at the time, was in his eleventh year of service. DeConcini was then in his fifteenth year in the Senate, Symms in his eleventh year, following eight years in the House. Several other representatives introduced term-limitation amendments in various forms as the Congress opened.

tested—sixty-nine senators had cosponsored a constitutional amendment offering a solution—and George A. Smathers, Democrat of Florida, presented it to the Senate in 1965 as "not an effort to revise" the Constitution but simply one "to remedy an obvious defect."[52] But the committee had been forced to wrestle with a difficult question. Who should have the authority to declare the president incapacitated? One suggestion was to let the Congress decide, but the committee rejected that as violating the principle of separation of powers. The responsibility was therefore assigned to the executive branch itself. The president could declare himself disabled and devolve his powers upon the vice president or, if he was unable to do so or chose not to, the vice president "and a majority of either the principal officers of the executive departments, or of such other body as Congress may by law provide," could take the initiative. If the president protested the action and the vice president and the cabinet majority insisted on it, the Congress by a two-thirds vote of both houses could overrule the president and continue to repose the presidential powers in the vice president.

The amendment provides a useful safeguard under circumstances in which the president recognizes his inability and has full confidence in his vice president—as was the case when President Reagan delegated his powers to Vice President George Bush during his cancer surgery in 1985. If a seriously impaired president were to insist on retaining his responsibilities, however, the amendment could be invoked only by a kind of palace coup engineered by the vice president and a body of the president's own appointees—or, as an alternative to the cabinet, an "other body" (such as an independent panel of physicians) that the Congress under the amendment is authorized to create. But in either case the vice president is required to join in the decision to ask the Congress to oust the president, and as the prospective inheritor of the presidential duties, he or she would be in a particularly awkward position to initiate or even support such a move. So the original question of whether it is sufficient to locate the power to initiate removal of a disabled president solely in the executive branch did not wholly lose its pertinence when the Twenty-fifth Amendment was adopted.

A few years later, the question of presidential removal arose in a different form: what to do about a president who was disabled not

52. *Congressional Record*, February 18, 1965, pp. 3168–69.

physically but morally, who had lost the capacity to lead the country but was not removable under the new amendment and was not guilty of the "high crimes and misdemeanors" that under the Constitution must be the basis for impeachment. In May 1973, as the Watergate scandals were destroying President Nixon's standing and respect, Representative Jonathan B. Bingham, Democrat of New York, proposed an amendment to authorize Congress to call a new presidential election by law (which would require two-thirds majorities, since the president could be expected to veto any such bill) whenever it found that, in Bingham's words, "the President has lost the confidence of the people to so great an extent he can no longer effectively perform his responsibilities." The president would be eligible to run in the special election. This procedure would circumvent the impeachment process, which Bingham argued was a dangerous expedient because it would bring the government "to a halt" while the president was on trial.[53]

Representative Edith Green, Democrat of Oregon, introduced a few weeks later a slightly different version; her amendment would have empowered the Congress to call an election by a two-thirds vote of both houses without referring the action to the president if it found that the chief executive had exceeded his powers, failed to execute the laws, or executed them illegally. "We presently have no option between the extreme option of impeachment or the other extreme of maintaining in office for as long as three years an administration whose stature and ability to govern has been greatly impaired," she argued. As in the Bingham resolution, the president would have been eligible to run in the special election.[54]

Still a third approach was developed by Representative Henry S. Reuss, Democrat of Wisconsin. His proposal would have permitted the Congress to remove the president by a "no confidence" vote of 60 percent of each house, but as a deterrent to opportunistic, partisan action it provided that all seats in Congress as well as the presidency and vice presidency would be filled in a new election. The question provoked enough academic interest that one law journal devoted an entire issue to a symposium on the Reuss resolution,[55] but when Nixon resigned in August 1974 the issue died. A new president was sworn

53. *Congressional Record*, May 8, 1973, p. 14579.
54. Ibid., July 17, 1973, p. 24232.
55. *George Washington Law Review*, vol. 43 (January 1975).

in, the country enjoyed the fresh start under new leadership that the Bingham, Green, and Reuss proposals were designed to make possible, and the previously anxious public relaxed in the confidence that once again "the system worked."

The War Power

At the height of the national turmoil over the Vietnam War and the extension of that conflict into Cambodia and Laos, the Congress set out to clarify an ambiguity in the Constitution that had once again touched off a quarrel between the branches. Just how far could the president go unilaterally, under his authority as commander in chief, to plunge the country into hostilities without asking for the formal declaration of war that only the Congress could provide?

Senator Jacob K. Javits, Republican of New York, the principal initiator of what became the War Powers Resolution of 1973, announced an ambitious goal: to define precisely, or "codify," the president's authority as commander in chief. He proposed to restrict the president's use of the armed forces, in the absence of a declaration of war, to repelling attack, protecting the lives and property of Americans abroad, and complying with national commitments to which both the executive and legislative branches were a party. His measure passed the Senate by a lopsided margin in 1972, and again in 1973, but the House Foreign Affairs Committee, and particularly its ranking Democratic member, Clement J. Zablocki of Wisconsin, contended that the Congress could not anticipate all contingencies a president might face and therefore should not attempt to codify his power. The committee's bill, therefore, omitted any such restrictive language, and after the House approved it, the House-Senate conference committee constructed an ingenious compromise. It moved the Javits definition of presidential power from the substantive body of the bill to a preamble, which the conferees then in a signed statement interpreted as nonbinding. The operative provisions left it to the president to decide when he should introduce the armed forces "into hostilities or into situations where imminent involvement in hostilities is clearly indicated by the circumstances." But the resolution required him to consult with the Congress whenever possible before doing so, to report within forty-eight hours afterward, and to cease the action if the

Congress did not approve within sixty days. At any time during the sixty-day period, the legislature could terminate the action by concurrent resolution.[56]

But the Congress had chosen as its instrument for clearing up the constitutional ambiguity—insofar as it had succeeded in doing so—not a constitutional amendment but a statute. President Nixon vetoed the statute on the ground that it was not only unwise but unconstitutional. The Congress enacted it over his veto, so it took its place on the statute books. But while Presidents Ford, Carter, Reagan, and Bush each adhered more or less faithfully to its terms, each also either reiterated the Nixon rejection of its constitutionality or expressed doubt. The executive branch therefore, in effect, reserved the right for any future president to flout the resolution at any time he might elect to do so, and the constitutional issue is no nearer to being settled than it was before the Congress acted.

Efficiency, Leadership, and Accountability

While reformers were failing to achieve even the modest link between the executive and legislative branches envisaged in the Pendleton and Kefauver proposals to give cabinet members a congressional role and in Lyndon Johnson's measure for four-year House terms, an occasional scholar, publicist, or retired statesman has risen to challenge the central principle of separation of powers that is embedded in the Constitution. Recognizing the constitutional dilemma confronted by the framers, these critics have urged the opposite solution. In 1787, they have argued, protection of the infant republic against the danger of tyranny may have properly been an overriding concern, and governmental power may have had to be dispersed to assure freedom, whatever the costs in efficiency and decisiveness. But times have changed, and the prospect that the presidency might grow into an elective monarchy or the Congress might ride roughshod over the rights of the people no longer seems so large

56. This provision has presumably been invalidated by the Supreme Court's 1983 decision in *Immigration and Naturalization Service* v. *Chadha*, which outlawed the use of the concurrent resolution to veto executive branch actions. For a fuller account of the origin and evolution of the War Powers Resolution, see Sundquist, *Decline and Resurgence*, chap. 9.

a menace. The danger now, in the reasoning of these critics, lies in the very dispersal of power that was at the heart of the founders' design. They ask questions that were not heard in 1787, that have been brought to the fore by the growth over two centuries in the responsibilities of government, the complexity of the national economy, and the interdependence of the nations of the world. How can institutions set in competition with one another be brought into a sufficient degree of harmony for timely decisions to be made and governmental action organized effectively? How can strong and decisive leadership be assured in a government of divided powers? How can the people fix responsibility when power is scattered and thereby, through the electoral process, hold their elective officers accountable?

The earliest systematic criticism of the constitutional system, and still among the most trenchant and pertinent, came from the pen of Woodrow Wilson, the only political scientist to attain the presidency. While still a senior at Princeton University, in 1879, Wilson picked up the Story-Pendleton-Bradford idea and carried it several steps further, proposing not merely that cabinet members have seats in Congress but that they be chosen from among the legislators and resign when their proposals were rejected, as in Great Britain. That, as Wilson saw it, would clearly fix responsibility and accountability in a government where both were now hopelessly dispersed.[57] In his classic *Congressional Government*, completed in 1884, he developed his critique of the American system as it had evolved, terming it "a government by the chairmen of the Standing Committees of Congress" and condemning it in eloquent language:

> *Power and strict accountability for its use* are the essential constituents of good government. . . . It is, therefore, manifestly a radical defect in our federal system that it parcels out power and confuses responsibility as it does. The main purpose of the Convention of 1787 seems to have been to accomplish this grievous mistake. . . . Were it possible to call together again the members of that wonderful Convention . . . they would be the first to admit that the only fruit of dividing power had been to make it irresponsible.
>
> As at present constituted, the federal government lacks strength because its powers are divided, lacks promptness because its authorities are multiplied, lacks wieldiness because its processes are roundabout, lacks

---

57. Thomas W. Wilson, "Cabinet Government in the United States," *International Review*, vol. 7 (August 1879), pp. 146–63.

efficiency because its responsibility is indistinct and its action without competent direction.[58]

But Wilson did not reiterate his support for a constitutional amendment to provide for a cabinet drawn from and responsible to the legislature or propose other changes in the tripartite governmental structure, although his preference for the British parliamentary system was clear.

Since Wilson, others who have pondered the American system have reached much the same conclusion about the weaknesses of the constitutional structure and put their minds to redesigning it. Some of these efforts produced book-length products.

In 1921, William MacDonald, terming the American system "rigid and irresponsible," thoughtfully set forth the advantages of the British parliamentary system. To convert the U.S. government into a parliamentary form, he proposed that the president select a "premier" from among members of Congress, that the premier head a cabinet made up of legislators, and that the cabinet resign whenever it lost the confidence of both houses. The cabinet would administer the executive branch, and the president would become a ceremonial head of state whose only consequential duty would be the designation of the premier in the event this was not predetermined by the parties in the legislative branch—much as in the parliamentary republics of Germany and Italy today.[59]

William Yandell Elliott's rethinking of the constitutional design, published in 1935, was clearly a product of the times—the crises of the Great Depression and Franklin Roosevelt's New Deal. Seeing the need for national planning and the "control" of industry by government, Professor Elliott found the system of constitutional checks and balances "unworkable" and outlined a scheme for much stronger executive power—ratifying, in effect, the shift in real authority from the legislative to the executive branch that, in the emergency, had already taken place. To strengthen the president, Elliott proposed that members of the House of Representatives be given four-year terms concurrent with the president's, and that the executive be

58. Woodrow Wilson, *Congressional Government: A Study in American Politics*, 15th ed. (Houghton Mifflin, 1913; originally published 1885), pp. 102, 284–85, 318. (Italics in original.)

59. William MacDonald, *A New Constitution for America* (B. W. Huebsch, 1921), p. 37; see chap. 8.

granted the right to dissolve the House and order a new election once during the four years. After the election, the president would lose his veto power for the rest of his term, permitting the Congress to set policy. The right of dissolution might extend to the Senate as well, but to reduce the power of that body, its right to act on money bills would be limited to one of delay, and approval of treaties would be by a simple majority rather than a two-thirds vote. Elliott would also have authorized the president to veto items in appropriation bills and riders (that is, nongermane provisions) in any bills.[60]

Seven years later, journalist Henry Hazlitt saw the exigencies of war as demanding a flexible, parliamentary form of government for the United States. "The grave defects in our Constitution," he contended, "are in large part responsible for our failure to organize efficiently for the conduct of the war. . . . We cannot permit ourselves to lose this war, or even to prolong this war, merely because we have become too hidebound to reexamine and to change that document." His reasoning, and his constitutional design, owed more to Mac-Donald (and to the nineteenth century English critic Walter Bagehot) than to Elliott, but he did concur in the latter's proposal to reduce the powers of the Senate. Having done that, Hazlitt would have centered power in a cabinet drawn only from the House and responsible to it, headed—like MacDonald's cabinet—by a premier designated by the president. Since the president's role would be so largely ceremonial, Hazlitt would have dispensed with direct election and permitted the Congress, with the two houses sitting jointly, to choose the chief of state. If the premier lost a vote of confidence, he would have had the choice of resigning or dissolving the Congress. In the latter case, a new election would fill all the legislative seats and the new Congress would either support the outgoing premier or choose a new one. Hazlitt also argued for a simplified amendment process.[61]

As the war approached its end, Thomas K. Finletter, a wartime assistant to the secretary of state, feared that the postwar need for "creative and affirmative" foreign and domestic policies would outstrip the capacity of a government "designed to achieve political negatives and the *laissez-faire* state." "You cannot," he wrote, "have a

60. William Yandell Elliott, *The Need for Constitutional Reform: A Program for National Security* (Whittlesey House, 1935), pp. 86, 207; see pp. 31–34, 200–02.

61. Henry Hazlitt, *A New Constitution Now* (Whittlesey House, 1942), pp. 15, 8; see pp. 9–14, 102–05, 180.

government capable of handling the most difficult problems that peacetime democracy has ever faced with the two main parts of it at each other's throats." His solution was to have simultaneous election of the president and all members of the Senate and House for six-year terms, which he assumed would result in unified party control of both branches and both houses. A joint executive-legislative cabinet would set policy. If a deadlock arose between the Congress and the joint cabinet, the president could call a new election for the presidency and the entire legislature, which would produce "a unified government, armed with a fresh authority from the people."[62]

Nearly three decades passed before another full-scale study of constitutional reform appeared—probably a testimony to the effective working of the government in the postwar decades, when the United States enjoyed prosperity and economic growth at home and successfully led and organized the free world's resistance to communist advance. But in the 1960s, this record of success gave way to inflation, an unpopular war in Southeast Asia, and riots in the ghettoes and on the campuses. By 1973 Charles M. Hardin could write that "America was gripped by its gravest political crisis since the Civil War," with the presidency "all too often . . . out of control," the incumbent president threatened with impeachment, and bureaucracies "unbridled" and arrogant. Professor Hardin conceded the need for "strong executive leadership," but proposed to bring the presidency under control through "party government." But unlike other political scientists who had been advocating strengthened and disciplined political parties as the key to attaining a workable degree of cohesion between the executive and legislative branches, Hardin contended that "constitutional surgery" was a precondition for successful party government. He proposed to reduce the Senate's legislative power to one of delay, strip it of its right to approve treaties, extend House terms to four years concurrent with the presidential term, give the party winning the presidency one hundred at-large representatives in order to assure that party's control of the House, grant a smaller number of at-large seats to the minority party to provide it with a rostrum for its leader, permit the House to override a presidential veto by a simple majority, and provide that elections would be set

62. Thomas K. Finletter, *Can Representative Government Do the Job?* (Reynal and Hitchcock, 1945), pp. 5, 6, 9, 111; see pp. 106–12.

by law rather than by the calendar, thus shortening the length of campaigns.[63]

In the same year that Hardin's book appeared, Rexford G. Tugwell, an original member of Franklin Roosevelt's "brain trust," published his model of a new constitution, based on discussions at the Center for the Study of Democratic Institutions. Without relating his new language closely to supporting argument, Tugwell rewrote the Constitution in its entirety, renaming some governmental offices and institutions and introducing new ones. He proposed a nine-year term for the president, subject to removal by a 60 percent vote of the electorate after three years; three-year terms for House members, with one hundred elected at large; and a Senate with life membership, made up of former officials and candidates and of presidential appointees, some selected from private groups and associations recognized by the president as "nationally representative."[64]

All of these books were the products of individual scholarship. In 1987, there appeared for the first time the result of a collective study of constitutional issues, the report of the Committee on the Constitutional System, which Hardin had helped to organize six years earlier (see chapter 1). The CCS concluded that "the present system of staggered elections has the effect of pulling the branches apart" because at the midterm election the incumbent representatives and senators who are running find it useful "to distance themselves from the President and from presidential programs that may involve a difficult, short-term adjustment on the way to a worthwhile, longer-term result." It recommended eliminating the midterm election by lengthening the House term to four years and the Senate term to eight, with all House members and half the Senate to be chosen in each presidential election year. It also recommended removing the constitutional prohibition against members of Congress serving in the cabinet or in other executive branch positions; relaxing the present requirement that two-thirds of the Senate must approve treaties by permitting

---

63. Charles M. Hardin, *Presidential Power and Accountability: Toward a New Constitution* (University of Chicago Press, 1974), pp. 1, 2; for his proposals, see especially chaps. 1, 10. Notable among other works proposing measures to strengthen party organizations were American Political Science Association Committee on Political Parties (chaired by E. E. Schattschneider), *Toward a More Responsible Two-Party System* (Rinehart, 1950); and James MacGregor Burns, *Uncommon Sense* (Harper and Row, 1972).

64. Rexford G. Tugwell, *The Emerging Constitution* (Harper's Magazine Press, 1974), p. 14.

approval by a constitutional majority of both houses or, if that were not acceptable, 60 percent of the Senate; and amending the Constitution to allow Congress to set "reasonable limits" on campaign expenditures.

The committee members considered at length some more drastic proposals for constitutional reform but, unable to agree, discussed these measures under the heading of "additional proposals worth considering." These included mandatory straight-ticket voting for national offices, which would require voters to choose between party tickets for president, vice president, senate and House, just as they do now for the first two of those offices; and developing some scheme for the president or Congress, or both, to call special elections to reconstitute a government that "had palpably failed" or was rendered ineffective by deadlock between the branches.[65]

Meanwhile, some of the academic participants in the CCS deliberations were refining and presenting their individual views in separate books. James MacGregor Burns, in *The Power to Lead*, brought up to date his critique of the American political system presented in various writings over the course of more than two decades.[66] He attributed the country's "leadership failure" to the institutional structure rather than simply to the shortcoming and weaknesses of individuals and concluded by endorsing three constitutional changes. These included one of the major measures that the CCS was later to endorse—removal of the prohibition against members of Congress serving in the executive branch—and one of the measures that the CCS would list among additional proposals "worth considering"— the mandatory straight ticket, to which Burns applied the more popular label of "team ticket." He rejected the other major measure that CCS would list as worth considering—special elections to reconstitute a failed or deadlocked government—in favor of a simple expansion of the impeachment power to enable removal of a president who had "dramatically and irremediably lost the confidence of the nation."

65. Committee on the Constitutional System, "A Bicentennial Analysis of the American Political Structure" (Washington, January 1987), pp. 10–13. Recommendations that could be made effective by statute or by changes in political party rules are omitted from this discussion.

66. James MacGregor Burns, *The Power to Lead: The Crisis of the American Presidency* (Simon and Schuster, 1984), summary of recommendations on p. 237.

The effectiveness of these changes, he argued, would depend on a strengthened role for "more organized, disciplined, programmatic, and principled" political parties, but the measures recommended for that purpose could be carried out without altering the Constitution. Six years later, in another book, he added to his list of constitutional reforms two more measures—a four-year term for House members coincidental with the presidential term and repeal of the Twenty-second Amendment, which limits presidential tenure to two terms—and did not repeat his earlier endorsement of the team ticket.[67]

Donald L. Robinson, who has served as director of research for the Committee on the Constitutional System since its organization, presented his own proposals at the conclusion of a treatise on the presidency and the Constitution.[68] Advocating a bold rather than an incremental approach to constitutional change, he placed his major emphasis on introducing a power of dissolution into the American system, whereby either the president or Congress could initiate procedures for calling a special election in which the presidency, the vice presidency, all House seats, and half the Senate seats would be at stake. He also joined Burns in endorsing the proposal to allow members of Congress to serve in the executive branch, the repeal of the two-term limit on presidential tenure, and the extension of House terms to four years, to which Robinson would add an eight-year term for senators (half to be elected in each presidential year) in order to eliminate the midterm election altogether. He also advocated creation of a national council made up of a hundred "notables" chosen for life, which would elect from its ranks a "chief of state" who would issue the call for special elections, superintend their conduct, and "provide continuity" until the new government was installed. Reminiscent of the British House of Lords in its makeup, it would also have power, like the Lords, to delay and propose amendments to

67. James MacGregor Burns, *Cobblestone Leadership: Majority Rule, Minority Power* (University of Oklahoma Press, 1990), pp. 132–36.

68. Donald L. Robinson, *To the Best of My Ability: The Presidency and the Constitution* (Norton, 1987), pp. 270–81. Robinson also prepared for the CCS what the organization called its "debate book," a volume setting forth arguments for and against various proposed amendments to the Constitution, including most of those discussed in this book. Robinson, *Government for the Third American Century* (Westview Press, 1989).

legislation but not the power to veto. And to this body of recent reformist literature should be added the first edition of this book.[69]

These voices raised outside the halls of Congress have at no time aroused response within. In their unconcern, the legislators have reflected faithfully the voters whom they represent, for the critics have inspired no mass movement in support of any fundamental change in the governmental structure. Proposals for structural amendments to the Constitution, in the absence of a governmental breakdown that is indisputably traceable to institutional rather than individual failure, are inherently technical and abstract, not likely to arouse emotion. Moreover, the very fact that government has not broken down attests, in the popular mind, to the wisdom of the constitutional design. The absence of criticism surely reflects a faith that the structure that has survived so long without formal alteration must have served the country well since the beginning and can be counted on to serve it no less well in times to come.

This does not mean that the balance of power between the branches, and the relationships between them, have remained constant for two centuries. As Don K. Price has emphasized, the written Constitution was flexible enough to permit "the evolution of a richly varied unwritten constitution that can be adapted by political bargaining to new needs and circumstances."[70] It has permitted the Congress to delegate extraordinary power to the president, as in wartime and during the economic catastrophe of the Great Depression, but to curtail that power when circumstances change. The Congress may submit to presidential leadership, but it does so voluntarily and for only as long as it may choose. The president may act unilaterally, particularly in foreign relations, but he does so at the peril of having his policy undermined, or repudiated, by the Congress later. Throughout this century, until the 1970s, Congress accepted—and to some extent initiated—the strengthening of the presidency as the essential point of national leadership. But when the "imperial presidency" overreached itself in the 1960s and 1970s, Congress was aroused to rein it in, through such measures as the War Powers Resolution of 1973, the Congressional Budget and Impoundment Con-

69. James L. Sundquist, *Constitutional Reform and Effective Government* (Brookings, 1986).

70. Don K. Price, *America's Unwritten Constitution: Science, Religion, and Political Responsibility* (Louisiana State University Press, 1983), pp. 149–50.

trol Act of 1974, and the intensification of congressional oversight of administrative actions.[71]

In a very real sense, the public acts as an invisible referee as the bargaining among the branches takes place. The American people have never wavered in their support of the essential concept underlying the tripartite structure of the government, that power shall not be concentrated, that none of the branches shall be unduly aggrandized at the expense of the others. And, although the appropriate balance of power is neither stable nor precisely definable, the people— aroused by vocal public officials, elder statesmen, and other opinion leaders—sense when it is upset and support those who seek to restore the balance. Through democratic processes, the judgment of the people prevails.

Most of the reform proposals that are considered in the next five chapters have been advanced, however, on the assumption that the effectiveness of government can be impaired when the bargaining and rivalry between the executive and legislative branches degenerate, as they often do, into conflict and stalemate. The object must be to bring the branches to collaborate in greater harmony without subordinating either. Specific measures are thus analyzed from the point of view of whether, and how, they will contribute to the unity of the government—while preserving the balance of its elements—and hence to its efficiency, the strength of its collective leadership, and its accountability to the people.

71. The phrase is from Arthur Schlesinger, Jr., *The Imperial Presidency* (Houghton Mifflin, 1973). Sundquist, *Decline and Resurgence*, reviews the evolution of the legislative-executive balance through the 1970s.

CHAPTER FOUR

Forestalling Divided Government

Since the beginning, those who have feared that the separation of powers might render the government weak and indecisive have looked for salvation to an institution that the Constitution did not contemplate—the political party. That the framers did not prepare the way for parties was quite deliberate. One can search the entire proceedings of the 1787 Convention in vain for a favorable reference to the concept of parties, but the record is replete with condemnation of what were usually called "factions" or "cabals." No more forceful diatribe against political parties has ever been written than *The Federalist*, in which Madison denounced "the mischiefs of faction" and described the whole constitutional structure as designed to prevent any "interested and overbearing majority" from assembling all the powers of the government, thus enabling it to oppress the minority. "The accumulation of all powers, legislative, executive, and judiciary, in the same hands, whether of one, a few, or many . . . may justly be pronounced the very definition of tyranny," wrote Madison.[1]

In his celebrated farewell address, President George Washington echoed these sentiments, warning his countrymen "in the most solemn manner against the baneful effects of the spirit of party generally," which he called "the worst enemy" of democratic governments

---

1. See particularly *The Federalist*, nos. 10, 47, 48, 62 (New American Library, 1961). Quotations from no. 10, pp. 78, 77, and no. 47, p. 301.

everywhere.[2] And Washington's successor, John Adams, reiterated that "the spirit of party" is one of the "natural enemies" of the Constitution.[3] They had good reason to be concerned, for the party spirit had begun to appear even during Washington's first term, and in the election of 1800 that ended Adams's tenure two political parties contested on a national scale. Once they assumed responsibility for actually running the government, the framers' own generation— including many of the convention delegates themselves—thus repudiated the theory of nonpartisanship embodied in the Constitution. Madison himself was elected president in 1808 and 1812 as a party nominee and in his retirement years acknowledged that parties are "a natural offspring of Freedom."[4]

By the 1830s, in Andrew Jackson's time, the familiar American two-party system had settled firmly into place. The party processes were quickly formalized. Every four years, each party held a national convention, adopted a platform embodying its program, and nominated candidates for president and vice president. Each party also ran candidates for the Senate and the House on the same party ticket and, in doing so, asked the people to grant it control of the entire government—exactly what the constitutional design was intended to forestall. But the politicians' concept of *party* government, with full responsibility and accountability in a single group of like-thinking leaders, was also accepted by the people. For the next century and a quarter—until 1956—the voters regularly assigned all of the powers of the two elective branches to the same party, apparently without dread that tyranny and oppression would be the consequence. (And the preponderance of new appointees to the judiciary would of course also be of that party.) With only four exceptions—in 1848, 1876, 1880, and 1884—an incoming president enjoyed the support of majorities of his own party in both houses of Congress. Sometimes the president's party lost control of one or both houses at the midterm election, but unified party government was normally restored in the next pres-

2. James D. Richardson, ed., *A Compilation of the Messages and Papers of the Presidents (1789–1897)*, vol. I (Bureau of National Literature, 1897), pp. 210–11.

3. Ibid., p. 221.

4. Note apparently written about 1821, when Madison was preparing his record of the convention proceedings for publication. Max Farrand, ed. *The Records of the Federal Convention of 1787*, rev. ed., vol. 3 (Yale University Press, 1966), p. 452.

idential balloting. In the first half of this century, even the midterm voting normally supported the president's party; the only exceptions occurred in 1910, 1918, 1930, and 1946. Between those four two-year hiatuses, either the Republicans or the Democrats were granted full responsibility for the entire government for long periods, the former in the 1900s and the 1920s, the latter in the 1910s, the 1930s, and the 1940s.

The Accepted Theory of Party Government

As soon as political science was born as a scholarly discipline, its spokesmen developed a theoretical rationale for the system of unified party government that political leaders and the electorate at large had put firmly in place. They reasoned, just as had the founding generation shortly after it began to run the government, that the institutions that the framers had so deliberately separated had to be brought together in some degree of unity for the government to function— and the instrument for that purpose was the political party.

In 1954, Austin Ranney traced the thinking of what he called the "party government school" from pre-presidential Woodrow Wilson through A. Lawrence Lowell, Henry Jones Ford, and Frank J. Goodnow.[5] By that time, the doctrine had attained virtually universal acceptance in the scholarly literature—an agreement that continued into the 1980s. Thus to V. O. Key, Jr., writing in 1942, parties were the means to overcome "the obstructions of the governmental structure"; to James MacGregor Burns (1949), they fulfilled the "vital function" of integrating "the separated organs of government"; to Howard Penniman (1952), they made "the dispersed and disconnected organs of government . . . respond to a common impulse and work in harmony"; to Clinton Rossiter (1960), they provided the needed "bridges across the gaps" that "separate the executive from the legislature"; to Frank J. Sorauf (1968), they "bring a unifying force . . . which helps to hold the disparate fragments together"; to David B. Truman (1971), they were the "sole efficient means" of producing "union between the executive and legislative branches"; to Gerald Pomper (1980), the parties bridged the "gaps" in the constitutional structure; and to Mil-

5. Austin Ranney, *The Doctrine of Responsible Party Government* (University of Illinois Press, 1954).

ton C. Cummings, Jr., and David Wise (1985), "they serve to link different parts of the government," a "vital" function.[6]

The consensus was so complete that when the Committee on Political Parties of the American Political Science Association produced its landmark report in 1950 it did not even feel the need to argue the case for political parties, but simply asserted that they are "indispensable instruments of government" necessary for, among other things, "integration of all of the far-flung activities of modern government."[7]

Corollary to the theory of party government was the doctrine of presidential leadership. To perform its function of unifying the government, the party had to have a leader, and that role fell logically to the man who had been nominated by the party's national convention, who had victoriously carried its banner in the last election, and who had all the resources of the executive branch to assist him. Just as treatises on political parties had hailed the political party as the government's unifying instrument, so did scholars of policymaking processes and executive-legislative relationships extol the president's place as prime mover of the entire governmental system. Textbooks included sections on his proper extraconstitutional function as "chief legislator" along with those describing his constitutional duties as chief executive. He set the legislative agenda for the Congress, submitted the bills that were the basis of its deliberations, and met reg-

6. V. O. Key, Jr., *Politics, Parties and Pressure Groups* (Crowell), p. 495; James MacGregor Burns, *Congress on Trial* (Harper and Brothers, repub. by Gordian Press, 1966), p. 45; Howard Penniman, *American Parties and Elections*, 5th ed. (Appleton-Century-Crofts), pp. 164–65; Clinton Rossiter, *Parties and Politics in America* (Cornell University Press), pp. 62–63; Frank J. Sorauf, *Party Politics in America* (Little, Brown), p. 18; David B. Truman, *The Governmental Process* (Alfred A. Knopf), pp. 531–32; Gerald Pomper, in Pomper, ed., *Party Renewal in America: Theory and Practice* (Praeger), p. 7; and Milton C. Cummings, Jr., and David Wise, *Democracy under Pressure: An Introduction to the American Political System*, 5th ed. (Harcourt Brace Jovanovich), p. 248. Fuller quotations from these writers, as well as a more detailed historical account and a fuller exposition of the theory of party government and the issues raised by divided government, are contained in Sundquist, "Needed: A Political Theory for the New Era of Coalition Government in the United States," *Political Science Quarterly*, vol. 103 (Winter 1988–89), pp. 613–35.

7. Committee on Political Parties, *Toward a More Responsible Two-Party System*, supplement to the *American Political Science Review*, vol. 44 (September 1950), also published by Rinehart, 1950. Quotation from Rinehart ed., pp. 15–16. The report was widely criticized, but for its specific proposals to make parties more responsible rather than for its acceptance of the concept of party government. None of the critics reasserted the framers' theory that unified government was to be feared and discouraged.

ularly with the leaders of the congressional majorities who collaborated in planning the enactment of the party program. Indeed, the legislative leaders were seen, at times, as little more than agents of the presidential will. On one historic occasion, in 1945, Senator Alben W. Barkley, Democrat of Kentucky, felt obliged to resign as majority leader because he could not support a tax proposal submitted by Democratic President Franklin Roosevelt. (He was promptly reelected by his Democratic colleagues.) In order that the government may be able to "take swift, coherent, and purposeful action," which Congress by itself cannot initiate, "the basic problem of American government is finding and perfecting institutions that will enable the president to lead Congress with maximum effectiveness," wrote Austin Ranney.[8]

But when the legislative branch followed the president's lead, it was not because of his constitutional position as head of the executive branch—in that role he was the legislators' rival, not their leader—but because their majorities were tied to him by the bond of party. That had long been the normal order of things, and the models of presidential leadership took for granted that it would continue. Phrases such as "the party in power" and "the president's majority in Congress," contrasted with "the opposition party" or "the minority party," recur throughout the literature. After the 1947–48 period of divided government, writers had to acknowledge the possibility that sometimes there might be no single "party in power," but they tended to see that circumstance as only the occasional outcome of a midterm election that would be righted in the next presidential year. And they deplored it. Sorauf, for instance, writing primarily about state governments, called division of government between the parties "by far the most important institutional barrier to the coordination of legislative and executive decisionmaking under the aegis of a unifying political party."[9] During the long era of unified government, no one—either practitioner or scholar—was heard to suggest that what was needed was to do away with unity and divide the government between the parties.

8. Austin Ranney, "The President and His Party," in Anthony King, ed., *Both Ends of the Avenue: The Presidency, the Executive Branch, and Congress in the 1980s* (Washington: American Enterprise Institute for Public Policy Research, 1983), pp. 131–32. For quotations from other political scientists on the necessity for presidential leadership, see Sundquist, "Needed: A Political Theory," pp. 621–24.

9. Sorauf, *Party Politics*, p. 361.

The New Era of Divided Government

Yet even as these theories of party government and presidential leadership were being developed and expounded, the political world was changing. When President Dwight Eisenhower was sworn in for his second term in 1957, he became the first president since Grover Cleveland seventy-two years earlier to confront on inauguration day a Congress in which either house was controlled by the opposition party. In Eisenhower's case, both houses had Democratic majorities. The divided government produced by the 1954 midterm election had continued into a new presidential term, a happening without precedent for more than seven decades. Unified government was restored during the 1961–69 period, under Democratic Presidents Kennedy and Johnson, but thereafter divided government was to be the norm, unity the exception. As in 1956, so in 1968, 1972, 1980, 1984, and 1988, Republican presidents were chosen to govern in an unintended and unsought coalition with Democratic majorities in Congress, always in the House and usually also in the Senate. From 1955 through 1992, the government was divided for twenty-six of thirty-eight years—six of Eisenhower's eight years, all of Nixon's and Ford's eight, all of Reagan's eight, and all of Bush's four—or 68 percent of the time. Measured from 1969 through 1992, divided government prevailed in twenty of twenty-four years, or a staggering 83 percent of the time. And the forecast has been for more of the same; political observers have written routinely of a Republican "lock" on the presidency and an insuperable Democratic "incumbency advantage" in the House and, most of the time, in the Senate as well.

A century and a half of practice and theory are thus now invalidated. The political party cannot "bridge the gaps" between the executive and legislative branches, become the "unifying force" and bring "union," "harmony," and "integration" to the government as a whole—to use political scientists' terms—if it links the executive only to the congressional *minority*. The majority party in Congress cannot accept the president as its leader, as the long-prevailing theory requires. After all, they strove to defeat him in the last election, and either he or his party's successor nominee will be their opponent in the next. If they accept his program, they will be adding to his stature as the nation's leader and strengthening his party for the electoral battles ahead. By the same token, the president cannot follow the lead of the congressional majorities, for that would enhance the credibility of their party and bolster its standing for the next election. All of the obstacles to governmental harmony and cohesion that pertain in times of unified government are therefore heightened when the government is divided. Then the partisan debate that is normal, healthy, and essential in a democracy is no longer confined to the majorities and minorities in Congress but spills over into confrontation between the two branches of the government that, for everything that is accomplished, have somehow to be brought into agreement. At worst, the executive and legislative branches become intent on discrediting and defeating each other's initiatives, and the government is immobilized. And neither party can be held responsible for governmental failure, for neither has in fact had responsibility.

Those who have felt that the separation-of-powers structure did not work well even in what had been normal circumstances—that is, in times of single-party control—have found what they consider substantial evidence that the now-normal partisan division of the government has made matters worse. In the Eisenhower years, the president's foreign policy received bipartisan support, but on the domestic side the period was unproductive. The president and his Democratic opponents quarreled over what to do about such important issues as education, health insurance, housing, unemployment, and water pollution. Each side had the capacity to block initiatives by the other; neither a Republican nor a Democratic program could be enacted, and action on pressing domestic issues had to await the establishment of unified Democratic control after the election of 1960. The Nixon years, likewise, saw the emasculation or outright defeat of such presidential initiatives as Nixon's family assistance plan, his health insurance proposal, and his New Federalism, and by the end of Nixon's first term relations between the branches had degenerated into open warfare. In his second term, Nixon later boasted, "I had thrown down a gauntlet to Congress, the bureaucracy, the media, and the Washington establishment and challenged them to epic battle."[10] The Congress took up the challenge and, even after forcing Nixon out of office, continued the battle with his successor, and he with it. As the result,

---

10. Richard Nixon, *RN: The Memoirs of Richard Nixon* (Grosset and Dunlap, 1978), p. 850.

President Ford set what is surely the modern-day record for vetoes of important measures—no fewer than sixty-six vetoes in his brief twenty-nine-month tenure, sparing hardly any bill of significance, as recriminations flowed back and forth between the White House and the Capitol. Among the measures vetoed were foreign affairs bills, in which Ford protested that Congress was seeking to reverse his decisions made under "authority previously conferred" and to "forge impermissible shackles on the President's ability to carry out the laws and conduct the foreign relations of the United States." America, he complained, "can have only one foreign policy," and "foreign governments must know that they can treat with the President on foreign policy matters, and that when he speaks within his authority, they can rely upon his words."[11]

In the next period of divided government, President Reagan did succeed in driving his radical economic program through a Democratic House, but his victories were confined, for the most part, to his first year in office. After that, relations steadily deteriorated, and by the third year the government was once again reduced to ineffectiveness. The House—and to some extent the Republican-controlled Senate as well—was resisting further domestic budget cuts, and it was frustrating the president's foreign policy, particularly in Central America. But the government's impotence was reflected most dramatically in its incapacity to cope with gigantic and unprecedented budget deficits. As the annual revenue shortfall pushed past $200 billion by 1983, the

---

11. "Veto of the Foreign Assistance Bill," *Public Papers of the Presidents: Ford, 1976–77*, vol. 2 (Government Printing Office, 1979), pp. 1481–85. The president was reproaching Congress for a long series of interventions that often amounted to the legislators' taking command of foreign policy, relating to the war in Vietnam, relations with the Soviet Union, intervention in Angola, response to the Greek-Turkish dispute over Cyprus, allocation of foreign assistance, trade policy, arms sales to Arab nations, and relations with international organizations. This broad and sustained conflict, which began during the Nixon administration, is detailed in my *The Decline and Resurgence of Congress* (Brookings, 1981), pp. 247–52, 274–93. When unified party government was restored with the inauguration of Democratic President Jimmy Carter, perfect harmony between the branches was never achieved, but both sides sought conciliation, and relations were "marked not, as in the Ford years, by a series of drastic reversals but by a mixture of successes, narrow escapes, minor setbacks, and issues deferred to forestall confrontation." Ibid., p. 297. Lloyd N. Cutler, who served as counsel to President Carter, notes that "Congress never challenged the president's deployment or use of our forces abroad" and "although Congress insisted on various minor modifications, Congress never acted to block his arms transfers." Cutler, "Beware Ticket-Splitting," *Washington Post*, November 1, 1988, p. A19.

president and spokesmen for both parties in both houses of Congress separately warned the nation of impending disaster, but together they could not—then or for most of the next decade—muster the will to act.

Nor, in a divided government, could anyone be held accountable. In the 1984 and 1988 elections, the Democrats could—and did— charge the president with responsibility for the record deficits, but he in turn could—and did—blame the Democrats in Congress who, after all, approved all the appropriations. Yet both parties were entirely right in denying responsibility, because neither was responsible. And the voters, having declined to vest an undivided authority in either party, could not register a clear-cut approval or disapproval of what had happened and so could not set the future course of government, either by returning a responsible party to office or by turning it out of office. Not until 1987 was a bipartisan agreement reached to check the expansion of the deficit, but the action was years late and billions short. "The general fund deficit sailed past the $300 billion mark in 1990," as Comptroller General Charles A. Bowsher put it, and by 1992 the president's budget for the 1993 fiscal year proposed a deficit of $399.4 billion.[12] Observed one of the budget negotiators, Senator Warren B. Rudman, Republican of New Hampshire, during the 1990 discussions: "What we are seeing is a very good illustration that divided government doesn't work any more. Our system of checks and balances that worked in a simpler time is now an obstruction to governing. The people don't know who to blame because no one is accountable."[13]

Evaluations of Divided Government

The Committee on the Constitutional System (CCS), in its 1987 report, found that the "confrontation, indecision and deadlock" and the diffused accountability that are always present in the separation-

12. Bowsher, "Major Issues Facing the 102nd Congress," *GAO Journal*, no. 12 (Spring 1991), p. 24; and *Budget of the United States Government, Fiscal Year 1993*, pt. 1, table 2–3, p. 25.
13. Susan F. Rafsky, "The Budget Battle Reflects the Strains in the System," *New York Times*, October 28, 1990, p. E1.

of-powers structure are exacerbated by divided government. The division "has led to inconsistency, incoherence and even stagnation in national policy," to "*non*decisions resulting from frequent deadlocks." "If divided government is recognized as the preeminent cause of interbranch conflict and policy stalemate and deadlocks," CCS concluded, measures to reduce its likelihood should be considered.[14] Under divided government, wrote Lloyd N. Cutler, cochair of CCS since its founding, "responsibility is very muddled" and "most of the time, on essential issues, really remains either in a deadlock or in a state where no real decision can be made."[15]

J. William Fulbright, former chairman of the Senate Foreign Relations Committee, wrote that the "inevitable result" of divided government is "acute bickering, polemical stalemate, and governmental paralysis. Each side blames the other for our national failures." Inability to cope with the deficit "is to a great extent due to the rivalry between executive and legislature," he continued, and in foreign affairs no one can "speak for the country. . . . Presidential agreements are inevitably tentative and provisional. Nixon's agreements with the Russians were effectively undercut in Congress. Foreign leaders, for their part, hesitate to make agreements with a leader who cannot deliver."[16] As a current illustration of that point, members of the executive board of the International Monetary Fund are quoted as describing the failure of the Congress to approve President Bush's request for a $12 billion appropriation to the Fund "as the potential casualty of an American coalition government that isn't really working."[17]

Before the 1988 election, journalist William Rusher pleaded with voters not to divide the government and hence "compel" the two branches "to fight like two scorpions in a bottle"; after the election, he admonished his readers to "stop asking a Republican president and a Democratic Congress to defy human nature by 'working together

14. Committee on the Constitutional System, "A Bicentennial Analysis of the American Political Structure" (Washington, January 1987), pp. 3, 5, 15.

15. Lloyd N. Cutler, "Some Reflections about Divided Government," *Presidential Studies Quarterly*, vol. 18 (Summer 1988), pp. 489–90.

16. J. William Fulbright with Seth P. Tillman, *The Price of Empire* (Pantheon Books, 1989), pp. 55–58.

17. Hobart Rowen, "America Owes the IMF," *Washington Post*, January 9, 1992, p. A21.

for the good of the country,' when they have sincere and profound differences as to precisely what that might be."[18]

By 1992, public opinion polls revealed an appalling level of frustration and disgust with the political system in the electorate at large. Journalists who roamed the country interviewing voters and attending "focus group" sessions reported with virtual unanimity that the country was in a sour and angry mood. Voting participation in the early primary elections fell markedly below the levels of four years earlier, particularly on the Democratic side; in New York, for example, only 7 percent of eligible voters went to the polls, and the Democratic turnout fell by 39 percent from the 1988 level. "There are unhappy and angry voters, and they don't feel they have any outlet," said Curtis B. Gans, director of the Committee for the Study of the American Electorate.[19] Most dramatically of all, a political neophyte whose views on most major issues were unknown and who was not even an announced candidate—H. Ross Perot, Texas billionaire—was leading both major party candidates, Republican President George Bush and Democrat Bill Clinton, in a series of public opinion polls.[20]

The Perot phenomenon was the direct result of divided government, contended House Minority Leader Robert H. Michel, Republican of Illinois. "Perot," he said, "is exploiting a real, disturbing, genuine disaster that our political system has been undergoing for some time now, and I'm talking about divided government in Washington. . . . We've come to a point in American history where a president of one party simply cannot lead if the Congress is dominated by the other party."[21] Earlier, Senator Rudman, in announcing his retirement from the Senate because of "frustration"—primarily because

18. William Rusher, "What Bush Should Say," *Washington Times*, October 25, 1988, p. F3; and Rusher, "Voting District Dilemma," ibid., May 17, 1989.

19. Dan Balz, "Turnout in Primaries Down Almost 12%, Study Finds," *Washington Post*, April 14, 1992, p. A7. Public opinion poll data showing voter disillusionment with the government are summarized in chapter 5.

20. A *Newsweek* poll conducted June 4–5, 1992, found Perot preferred by 35 percent of registered voters, Bush by 33 percent, Clinton by 25 percent. The poll, conducted by the Gallup organization, interviewed 753 persons by telephone. "President Perot?" *Newsweek*, June 15, 1992, pp. 18, 24. A *Washington Post*/ABC News poll conducted by telephone June 3–7, covering 1,512 adults, reported that 36 percent of registered voters preferred Perot; 30 percent, Bush; and 26 percent, Clinton. E. J. Dionne, Jr., "Perot Leads Field in Poll; Bush Rating at New Low," *Washington Post*, June 9, 1992, pp. A1, A7.

21. Robert H. Michel, "Perot: A Siren Song but a Wake-Up Call Too," *Washington Post*, May 22, 1992, p. A25.

of the inability of the government to cope with the deficit—had placed a large part of the blame on divided government. "You have no sense of who is accountable to whom," he complained.[22]

From Scholars, a Mixed Appraisal

All of these expressions about divided government, from mild concern to deep disquiet to outright alarm, have inspired an outpouring of study and comment from the political science community—four volumes on the subject in 1991 alone. Interest has become so keen that the author of a 1992 book, preemptively titled *Divided Government*, speculates that the subject "has the potential to become the new organizing principle of American politics research in the 1990s."[23]

As would be expected, the scholarly judgments thus far are mixed. Some writers confirm the traditional doctrine in emphatic terms. Divided government "cannot but contribute to systemic paralysis," contends James MacGregor Burns, long an advocate of unified party government and founding chair of the Committee for Party Renewal.[24] Barbara Sinclair concludes that united party government "does not guarantee good decision making" but "it does allow voters to affix blame and take retribution. . . . When control is divided, it is difficult for the public to hold anyone accountable. Voters are left angry, disgusted, and wondering why the people they elect always seem to be incompetent, inept, and ineffectual."[25] I.M. Destler, reviewing recent executive-legislative conflict in foreign policy, found that interbranch discord brought occasional benefits but led to "tactical inflexibility" and "policy unpredictability," which "undermines . . . U.S. diplomatic credibility;" on balance, he concluded, "by the mid-seventies the policy costs of conflict and decentralization [within the Congress] were substantially exceeding the gains."[26] Benjamin Ginsberg and

22. Helen Dewar, "Rudman to Leave Senate," *Washington Post*, March 25, 1992, pp. A1, A4.

23. Morris P. Fiorina, *Divided Government* (Macmillan, 1992), p. 3.

24. James MacGregor Burns, *Cobblestone Leadership: Majority Rule, Minority Power* (University of Oklahoma Press, 1990), p. 110.

25. Barbara Sinclair, "Governing Unheroically (and Sometimes Unappetizingly): Bush and the 101st Congress," in Colin Campbell and Bert A. Rockman, eds., *The Bush Presidency: First Appraisals* (Chatham House, 1991), pp. 183.

26. I. M. Destler, "Executive-Congressional Conflict in Foreign Policy: Explaining It, Coping with It," in Lawrence C. Dodd and Bruce I. Oppenheimer, eds., *Congress Reconsidered*, 3d ed. (Washington: Congressional Quarterly, 1985), p. 352.

Martin Shefter condemned the "institutional combat" produced by divided government, with the Democrats seeking to strengthen the Congress and to "weaken the presidency" and the Republicans attempting "to undermine Congress and increase the autonomy of the White House," all of which "undermines the governing capacity of the nation's institutions."[27]

Other analysts who expressed a preference appeared to give the edge to unified party government. Unity makes it easier for presidents to gain support, forge effective coalitions, and achieve their legislative goals, several writers noted. Divided government, in contrast, was described as an "impediment to legislative-executive cooperation," as conducive to "gridlock," and as making "initial agreement less likely and implementation more difficult." One writer found "abundant" evidence of "legislative-executive policy stalemate" but attributed these failures to the constitutional structure in general without passing judgment on whether divided government had made matters worse. Another merely found the partisan division a cause of "added concern" but not enough concern to provide "strong grounds for an indictment" of it.[28]

Fiorina, at the end of his short book, comes close to neutrality. While he finds "compelling" in some circumstances the argument that "divided control exacerbates the already serious problems of responsibility . . . in American politics," he also sees merit in the ability of the Congress to block executive branch military adventures, as in Vietnam and Nicaragua, when the government is divided. He concludes that "divided governments and unified governments as yet have not differed significantly in their capacity to meet challenges."[29] But the judgments among all the many political scientists now writing on the subject range only from outright condemnation of divided government, at the one end, to approximate neutrality, on the other.

27. Benjamin Ginsberg and Martin Shefter, *Politics by Other Means: The Declining Importance of Elections in America* (Basic Books, 1990), pp. 161, 163.

28. James A. Thurber, "Introduction: The Roots of Divided Democracy," in James A. Thurber, ed., *Divided Democracy: Cooperation and Conflict Between the President and Congress* (Congressional Quarterly Press, 1991), p. 5; Walter J. Oleszek, "The Context of Congressional Policy Making," in ibid., p. 95; Sinclair, "Governing Unheroically," p. 182; Michael L. Mezey, "Congress within the U.S. Presidential System," in ibid., p. 20; and Paul J. Quirk, "Domestic Policy: Divided Government and Cooperative Presidential Leadership," in Campbell and Rockman, eds., *The Bush Presidency*, p. 87.

29. Fiorina, *Divided Government*, p. 111.

None has found divided government so superior that it should be advocated as the preferable model for the future.

Many of the writers who, on balance, prefer unified government offer the caveats that unity does not guarantee success and that, in Walter Oleszek's words, "divided government, despite its drawbacks, can be made to work."[30] But to say that divided government *can* be made to work leaves unanswered the critical questions of how, under what circumstances, and how reliably; whether the goals that motivate the behavior of politicians are conducive to providing the leadership and accommodation necessary to make a divided system succeed or, if not, whether motivation can or will be altered; what institutional devices may need to be developed, or invented, for divided government to succeed; and, of course, how accountability is established when it fails.

In a book certain to be highly influential, also published in 1991, David R. Mayhew attempts to provide what has been lacking in all the discussion of divided government: a solid empirical base for analyzing its merits and disadvantages. Based on contemporary and historical judgments, Mayhew identifies the most important enactments across the whole range of national policy during the period 1947–90—listing 267 in all. Dividing these between times of unified party government (eighteen of the forty-four years) and times of divided government (twenty-six years), he finds no significant difference; important measures were as likely to have been enacted under one pattern of control as the other. Unified and divided government each averaged about a dozen enactments per two-year Congress.[31]

Mayhew found wide variations between times of intense activity— notably the early New Deal era and the period that began with Pres-

30. Oleszek, "Context of Congressional Policy Making." in Thurber, ed., *Divided Democracy*, p. 96.

31. David R. Mayhew, *Divided We Govern: Party Control, Lawmaking, and Investigations, 1946–1990* (Yale University Press, 1991), The book reviews not only legislative enactments but also major congressional investigations of executive branch behavior. From the latter, it reaches the same conclusion that whether the government is under unified or divided party control makes no significant difference. As a measure of the book's influence, Frank J. Sorauf, in a jacket endorsement, asserts that "Mayhew has accomplished the demolition of a major belief about American politics." Sorauf had himself been a leading exponent of that belief. See his comments quoted on pp. 90 and 92, above.

ident Kennedy's election, crested with President Johnson's Great Society, and continued to run strongly through the entire eight years of the Nixon and Ford administrations—and periods of doldrums, which included some of the Truman and Eisenhower years and most of the Reagan-Bush decade. But the fluctuations did not coincide with shifts from divided to unified government and back again. Rather, surges of productivity appeared when the public mood turned activist and ended when the reformist impulse burned out, and the influence of the dominant mood cut across shifts in the partisan configuration of the government. Thus the burst of lawmaking that began in the Kennedy-Johnson period of unified government continued at a scarcely reduced pace through the Nixon-Ford years of divided control despite the extreme degree of conflict between the branches over the Vietnam War, the Watergate scandal, Nixon's impoundment of appropriated funds, Ford's sixty-six vetoes, and other issues—and came to its end about the time the inauguration of Jimmy Carter restored governmental unity under Democratic auspices. Although in some circumstances divided government may have obstructed the passage of important legislation, in other circumstances it may have facilitated it, because when the public was plainly in favor of action on a given issue the opposing parties and their leaders (conspicuously including legislators ambitious to run for president) competed in their response and collaborated across the branches in order to avoid the onus of having blocked a popular measure.

Mayhew's findings will surely be the starting point for future debates on the issue of divided government, but they are not so conclusive as to end discussion, and the author is careful to enter his own caveats at many points. First of all, the study is limited to an examination of instances when the government succeeded—when it enacted something—whereas the criticism of divided government has centered on instances of failure, of *non*performance. It can be speculated that if divided government serves as well as unified government in enacting measures, then it will be no more likely to fail when action is called for, but in any case the study did not deal with governmental nonperformance. Nor did it attempt to judge whether the ultimate enactment was timely enough and good enough or might have been better with a different executive-legislative relationship. For instance, Mayhew identifies the deficit reduction package that grew out of the 1990 bipartisan "summit" conference as not only an important measure but one of "historic" importance, and hence a major success of divided government.[32] But that this response to fiscal imperatives came, in the judgment of most observers, both too little and much too late does not count as one of divided government's failures.

Mayhew terms it an "act of faith" to believe that the deficit would have been dealt with more decisively had the government been unified throughout the 1980s, but Allen Schick, who has made careful empirical analysis of the budget process his specialty, is one who has reached that judgment. With unified government, he writes, "stronger measures would surely have been taken on the spending or revenue side, depending on the party in power."[33] A unified Republican government would have reduced the deficit further by cutting spending, a Democratic one by raising taxes, but a divided government, "while conspiring to diffuse responsibility," could adopt no bold policy of either kind. Mathew D. McCubbins has stated, and documented, an even more forceful conclusion "that divided partisan control of Congress in the 1980s was the *principal* cause of the rapid growth in budget deficits seen during that decade." During the six years (1981–86) when the Senate was controlled by Republicans and the House by Democrats, the two houses had different spending priorities, and the "stalemate" was compromised, he found, by each house's accepting the other's increases, which led to "increased spending on nearly every function of government." When the Democrats recaptured the Senate in the 1986 election, the stalemate was broken, the Senate accepted House policies for lower expenditures for national defense, and the rate of increase in total spending was slowed. McCubbins found the same pattern in other periods of divided government since 1929.[34] Similarly, Mayhew lists the Clean Air Act of 1990 as an achievement of divided government, but David Vogel, in a case study of environmental policy, condemns the "thir-

32. Mayhew, *Divided We Govern*, pp. 73, 74.
33. Ibid., p. 190; Schick, "Governments versus Budget Deficits," in R. Kent Weaver and Bert A. Rockman, eds., *Do Institutions Matter? Government Capabilities in the United States and Abroad* (Brookings, forthcoming).
34. Matthew D. McCubbins, "Government on Lay-Away: Federal Spending and Deficits under Divided Party Control," in Gary W. Cox and Samuel Kernell, eds., *The Politics of Divided Government* (Westview, 1991), pp. 114, 141–42. (Italics added.)

teen-year impasse" that preceded its passage as a governmental failure, which he attributed in part to the partisan division that prevailed
during the last nine of those years.[35]

One reason that the legislative process appears about equally productive in times of governmental unity and times of division, Mayhew
argues, is that by the time a law is ready for passage it usually commands enough broad bipartisan support to assure its enactment in
any circumstance. Sometimes events compel the parties to overcome
their differences and get together.[36] Sometimes, as Vogel noted in the
environmental case, public support for action is so evident that the
parties vie for credit in responding. But Mayhew's methodology does
not measure whether the parties, when they are forced to get together,
compromise so much as to unduly "water down" the legislation,
which may have already been diluted before presentation in adherence to the law of anticipated reactions. Mayhew points out that
"awkwardly stitched-together" compromises that fail to reach the
goals sought occur when the government is unified—the Natural Gas
Policy Act of 1978 is cited—and contends that during the "frenzied

35. David Vogel, "Representing Diffuse Interests: Environmental Policymaking,"
in Weaver and Rockman, eds., *Do Institutions Matter?* Lloyd Cutler had previously
observed that years of excessive budget deficits have coincided with periods of divided
government ever since the end of World War II. The only years when the deficit
exceeded 3 percent of the gross national product (excluding years of war and recession)
were 1948, when Democratic President Truman faced a Republican Congress, and 1975
and 1976, when Republican President Ford dealt with a Democratic Congress. Beginning in 1982, the deficit again rose above 3 percent, where it has since remained. It is
projected to exceed that level at least until 1993. Cutler, "Some Reflections on Divided
Government," p. 489. The data are in *Budget of the United States Government, Fiscal Year
1992*, table 1.2.

36. Charles O. Jones goes even further in suggesting that divided government—
or, as he terms it, "diffused responsibility"—may actually be necessary in order to
make possible major reforms in such areas as taxing, welfare, social security, health
care, trade, and budgeting. "It is unlikely," he writes, "that such reforms can be enacted
if one side has to bear the full responsibility for the changes. . . . Diffusion of responsibility may be essential at certain points in a policy's history if large-scale change is
to occur. . . . If . . . politics allows crossing over a partisan threshold to place both
parties on the same side, then agreements can be reached which will permit blame
avoidance, credit taking and significant policy change." Jones, "The Diffusion of
Responsibility: An Alternative Perspective for National Party Politics in the US," in
Governance, vol. 4 (April 1991), pp. 171–72. Catherine E. Rudder reaches a similar
conclusion in discussing the passage of the Tax Reform Act of 1986 but emphasizes
the importance of presidential leadership in such circumstances. "Non-Incremental
Policy-Making under Divided Party Control," *American Politics Quarterly*, vol. 19 (October 1991), pp. 426–37.

drive" for new laws in the Great Society period many of the enactments were hastily drafted and recklessly overcommitted the government.[37]

But while most legislative enactments ultimately win bipartisan support, Mayhew still presents a not insignificant list of important bills approved by Democratic presidents and Democratic Congresses that were opposed by most Republicans in both houses and would presumably therefore have been blocked had the government been divided. They include President Truman's Point Four program of aid to developing countries, seven major elements of the Kennedy and Johnson domestic program, and President Carter's energy package, his minimum wage increase, the bailout of Chrysler, and the Panama Canal treaties. On these matters, a unified Democratic government was able to enact program measures as postulated by the party government theorists while a divided government would probably have failed.[38] And the Democrats were clearly accountable, too; the perceived excesses of the Great Society legislation may well have contributed to the voters' rejection of the Democrats in 1968, and the Panama Canal became an issue to be used against their party in 1980.

This leads to what appears as the most important omission in Mayhew's work—any discussion at all of what the critics of divided government have considered as perhaps its greatest weakness: its lack of accountability.

When a single party has responsibility for both branches, the people in their one sovereign act—the act of voting—can render a verdict and thus set the general direction of governmental policy. If in their collective judgment a party has failed, the voters can turn it out of

---

37. Mayhew, *Divided We Govern*, p. 181. One may attribute the "frenzy" in large measure, perhaps, to President Lyndon Johnson's conviction that the "window of opportunity"—the period when bold departures would be possible, before the government would once again be deadlocked—would be short and therefore had to be seized upon. The window-of-opportunity phenomenon is discussed in chapter 5.

38. Ibid., pp. 180–83, 124–25. Although Republican opposition to the listed measures suggests that had that party controlled any element of a divided government the bills would not have been enacted, Mayhew notes seven occasions when Republican presidents signed bills passed by Democratic majorities but opposed by most Republican legislators, including the deficit-reduction package of 1990. The seven Kennedy-Johnson bills were the Area Redevelopment Act, two housing acts, the establishment of the Department of Housing and Urban Development, the Economic Opportunity (war on poverty) Act, the Appalachian Regional Development Act, and the model cities program.

office, as they did the Democrats in 1920 and 1952 and the Republicans in 1932; if the party has succeeded, it can be sustained in office, as the Republicans were throughout the 1920s and the Democrats in the 1930s. Divided government permits—even encourages and rewards— finger pointing and blame avoiding. As in the decade-long issue of the deficit, a Republican president and a Democratic Congress can blame each other and the people cannot hold either clearly responsible. Elections lose some of their meaning, the voters lose some of their power, and the constant buck passing and evasion of responsibility may contribute to the rise of disgust with politics and politicians as a class and the decline in electoral participation that are universally deplored. Terming accountability "the ultimate test of any republican form of government," David S. Broder offers a succinct illustration: "When the financial system collapsed in 1929, the Republicans were voted out of office, losing the White House and Congress. But when the savings and loan system collapsed in 1988, no one was punished politically, because there was no way to apportion blame between a Republican executive and a Democratic Congress." The long experiment of "government without parties" has failed, he contends, and "people have every right to be disillusioned." [39]

Effects on Administration

Most scholarly, as well as popular, discussion of divided government has dwelt upon its effect on legislative productivity (although Mayhew, as noted, extends his analysis to congressional investigations). But the partisan clash between the branches has highly significant effects upon administration too, many of them adverse. A panel of the National Academy of Public Administration (NAPA), after a two-year study of congressional-executive relations bearing upon the implementation of federal programs, concluded that heightened distrust between the branches has impaired program execution. Since the 1970s, the panel wrote, divided control of the government has become "dominated by high partisanship" and, in these circumstances, "distrust, ideological differences, and profound policy differences frustrate the consummation of even routine policy changes."

---

39. David S. Broder, "Politics without Parties," *Washington Post*, January 5, 1992, p. C7.

Some White House partisans repeatedly expressed the view "that *no* legislation would be better than any legislation enacted by congressional Democrats," reported the panel, and "such a stance, joined by its partisan congressional counterpart, frustrates useful interbranch dialogue to the point of crisis and breakdown."[40]

When Congress distrusts the executive branch, it is more likely to withhold discretion from administrators, write detailed prescriptions into law, impose constraints that may prove to be unworkable or result in the inequitable distribution of benefits, and intervene in day-to-day administration to the point of "meddling." It is also more likely to create quasi-administrative or supervisory bodies outside the executive branch (or even within the legislative branch itself) and informal relationships that make the legislature (or individual legislators) to some degree coadministrators of particular programs, thus departing from the accepted notion—accepted, notably, by the Supreme Court and enforced by it when pertinent cases arise—that administrative responsibility should be fixed clearly and exclusively in the executive. The NAPA panel concluded that congressional intervention had salutary as well as deleterious effects and, on the whole, probably did more good than harm. It found less meddling than the complaints of administrators had led it to expect, and it recognized as necessary some degree of coadministration and some blurring of the channels of administrative responsibility. Yet its plea was for coadministration to take place in an atmosphere of collaboration rather than antagonism, an atmosphere more likely to prevail when the government is united.

John Chubb and Paul Peterson, editors of a volume looking back upon the Reagan era, observed that the "inherent tensions between the legislative and executive branches had been reinforced and heightened by conflict between the parties," making interbranch disputes "the central issue of governance in the modern era." The Reagan administration "intensified the partisan conflict . . . in a systematic way," and negotiations between the branches were "often marked by mutual recriminations, allegations of malfeasance, and accusations

40. National Academy of Public Administration, *Beyond Distrust: Building Bridges between Congress and the Executive* (Washington: NAPA, 1992), p. 74. (Italics in original.) The panel, with eighteen members experienced in both branches, was chaired by James R. Jones, former White House chief of staff, Democratic member of Congress from Oklahoma, and chair of the House Budget Committee.

of power usurpation." Legislation emerging from the continuing conflicts embodied compromises not only in policy but also in administrative structures, and "an agency whose structural integrity is compromised or perhaps even sacrificed in the battle for political control cannot carry out the assigned policy effectively." Terry Moe found that each of three agencies he studied was "a grotesque combination of organizational features that clearly are not conducive to effective performance." Similarly, Ginsberg and Shefter contend that as administrative agencies become the "battleground" in the partisan executive-legislative struggle for policy control, they "can become incapable of carrying out their governmental tasks."[41]

A longer historical view illuminates the relation between divided government and the breakdown of trust between the branches. During the era of normally unified party government that spanned the first half of the twentieth century, the Congress joined in developing the doctrine of presidential leadership referred to early in this chapter and acquiesced in—indeed, often initiated—the aggrandizement of presidential power. Beginning with the congressionally initiated Budget and Accounting Act of 1921, Congress willingly made the president the general manager of the government, modeled on the position of chief executive officer that every corporation found necessary. With the Employment Act of 1946, it assigned him responsibility for planning and recommending measures for full employment and economic stability. During and after World War II, it accepted his primacy in foreign policy and even, in a series of resolutions, yielded the power to take the country into war. And it accepted his role as chief legislator, setting the congressional agenda and providing the drafts of major bills.

But once the years of unified party government gave way to an era of a government usually divided, the Congress set out quite consciously to recapture the powers it had ceded to the president. For the majority Democrats, it was one thing to delegate authority to the leader of their own party but quite another to enhance the power of the leader of the opposition. So, beginning with extricating the country from the Vietnam War, the Congress took major foreign policy

41. John E. Chubb and Paul E. Peterson, "American Political Institutions and the Problem of Governance," in Chubb and Peterson, eds., *Can the Government Govern?* (Brookings, 1989), pp. 30, 35, 36, 37; Terry M. Moe, "The Politics of Bureaucratic Structure," in ibid., p. 324; and Ginsberg and Shefter, *Politics by Other Means*, p. 34.

decisions into its own hands. With the War Powers Resolution of 1973, it sought to recapture the power to make war. In the Congressional Budget and Impoundment Control Act of 1974, it curtailed the president's power to control spending. The executive budget to which the Congress had formerly made not much more than marginal adjustments now became "dead on arrival," and the legislators, with a complex new budget apparatus, assumed primary responsibility for the nation's fiscal plan. In many ways, it extended the intervention in administrative matters that gave rise to the NAPA study discussed above. And for all these purposes, it vastly expanded its staff—in the offices of individual members, on committees and subcommittees, and in ancillary research and advisory agencies in the executive branch.[42] In short, it equipped itself to, in Fred W. Riggs's words, "second guess every basic policy issue," and in doing so it generated for itself "a vast and intractable agenda."[43] There is little sign that it has been able to master that agenda, or ever can. Certainly, the opinion polls reflect a profound public impression that Congress is failing to discharge satisfactorily the role it has claimed for itself.

Unified Government in the Future

Finally, comparisons between unified and divided government should not be allowed to rest entirely on how the two systems have functioned in the past, because what matters is the outlook for the future. And the prospect, when and if unified government is restored, is that the potential benefits of unity will be realized in greater measure than they have been in the past half century.

Since 1933, whenever the government has been unified, the responsibility for its effectiveness has lain with the Democratic party (except for the two-year period 1953–54). But the Democratic party, from Franklin Roosevelt's time at least through the 1960s, often failed to unify the government because it could not unify itself. Reformist zeal in the 1930s, 1940s, and 1960s was directed not at attaining unified partisan control—that was the normal state of affairs—but at reorganizing parties, particularly the party structures in the House and

42. The history of the aggrandizement of presidential power in the first half of this century and the efforts of Congress in the 1970s to recapture its former status are recounted in my *Decline and Resurgence of Congress.*
43. Fred W. Riggs, "Problems of Presidentialism," draft manuscript.

Senate, so that the governing majority could fulfill the responsibilities that the theory of party government and presidential leadership imposed upon it. That was the goal of the APSA Committee on Political Parties in its famed 1950 report.

When Mayhew and others compare the effectiveness of the competing forms, then, they are matching the performance of divided government in the current period with that of unified government in a period when, in the judgment of many respected scholars, it was not working well. Much of the time, in fact, it had the characteristics of divided government more than those of unified government. The Democratic majorities in Congress assigned important committee chairmanships to party members who voted with the Republicans on crucial issues, and effective control often lay with the conservative coalition of Republicans and their Democratic ideological soulmates who opposed the domestic policies of Democratic presidents. The government was nearly as divided in the administrations of Truman and Kennedy (and even Roosevelt after 1937) as in those of Reagan and Bush.

But the ancient rift in the Democratic party between its liberal and conservative, or northern and southern, wings has been gradually closing for several decades, the result of the party realignment that has been progressing steadily. Democrats sent to the Congress from the South rarely align themselves with the Republican opposition nowadays; rather, they take their place close to the ideological mainstream of their party. And thanks to the elimination of the automatic seniority system and other democratizing reforms in the Congress, the relatively few remaining Republican-minded Democrats can be denied committee chairmanships, or removed from them, if they set out to obstruct the party's programs. On the Republican side, the corresponding liberal-conservative chasm that once existed has likewise largely disappeared. During most of the Reagan-Bush era the party has attained a phenomenal degree of unity.

Under the new circumstances, unified party government will come far closer in the future to the theoretical ideal. Divided government should not be compared with unified government as the country has known it—which has often been a travesty of the concept—but with unified government as in theory it ought to be, as it is in other countries, and as it is likely to be whenever it is installed by the voters in coming years.

The Origins of Divided Government

The remainder of this chapter is devoted to explaining, first, why divided control has come to be the prevailing form of government and, second, how the likelihood of partisan division may be reduced. Those who may be convinced, by scholarly studies or their own observation and experience, that divided government is not a serious problem—or may even be a boon—may skip the remaining sections and proceed to the next chapter. Those who think there is still merit to the argument that unified party government is to be preferred, all things considered, may read on.

The Increase in Ticket Splitting

The transition from the long era of party government to the new age when divided government has become the norm may be dated with the elections of 1954 and 1956—or, if one prefers, that of 1968—but powerful forces that had been at work for several earlier decades had eroded the foundations on which the unity of the government had rested. The straight-ticket voters who had characterized the nineteenth century gradually gave way to new generations of ticket splitters who, when there were enough of them and they split their tickets preponderantly in the same direction, were bound to divide the responsibility for government.

Thus the proportion of congressional districts carried by the presidential candidate of one party and the House candidate of another averaged only 3.9 percent in the three elections of 1900–08, but rose to 13.5 percent in the four Franklin Roosevelt victories of 1932–44 and reached 29.9 percent in the 1956 Eisenhower election, 38.0 percent in the two Nixon elections of 1968–72, 38.2 percent in Reagan's 1980–84 victories, and 34.8 percent in Bush's 1988 race. For the six elections that produced divided government, then, an average of 36.3 percent of the districts recorded split results—a phenomenal tenfold increase in half a century. Even in the three intervening elections that produced unified Democratic governments—those of 1960, 1964, and 1976—an average of 29.3 percent of the districts still divided their support between the parties.[44] To resolve the problem of divided government,

44. Norman J. Ornstein, Thomas E. Mann, and Michael J. Malbin, *Vital Statistics*

then, will require checking and reversing one of the central trends of modern political history.

Ticket splitting is the electoral expression of the antiparty, or at least nonparty, ideology that has attracted a growing proportion of the voting public since the beginning of this century. Revolting against the corruption of patronage-oriented political machines, the reformers of the Progressive Era struck at the parties as institutions, seeking to supplant venal and self-seeking party bosses with new leadership free of party taint. In the newer states of the West, nonpartisan municipal elections were introduced for the purpose of eliminating altogether the influence of political parties in city politics. In the older states, reformers often organized independent reform parties or backed independent candidates in municipal races. At the state level, direct primaries were instituted to enable reformers to challenge the machines and their bosses for party nominations.

For the reformers to succeed, aroused citizens had to be willing to shed their established allegiances and cross the party line, if necessary, to vote for antimachine progressives. Nonpartisan attitudes, political independence and ticket splitting became civic virtues. Independent voters could weed out the "party hacks" and so compel the organizations to nominate honest and competent individuals. The new independent newspapers that arose to replace the party-affiliated journals of the nineteenth century had to demonstrate their independence by endorsing a split ticket in each election, as a matter of principle. Interest groups and civic organizations that laid claim to political independence had to do likewise.

A precondition to independent political action, of course, was fundamental reform of the ballot itself. In the nineteenth century ballot procedures made it difficult, if not impossible, for voters to split their tickets. Ballots were customarily printed by party organizations rather than by governmental agencies, and individual voters on arriving at the polling place simply obtained their party's ballot, marked it, and dropped it in the box. The single publicly printed ballot, marked in secret, that nowadays seems so central to the democratic process that one assumes it must always have existed, was in fact one of the many electoral innovations of the Progressive Era—imported from Australia.

Even after the universal adoption of the Australian ballot early in this century, however, both tradition and the form of the ballot encouraged straight-ticket voting. In most states, the election officials listed each party's nominees in separate columns, with a square or circle at the head of the column that could be checked by those who wished to vote for a party's entire slate. A straight ticket could be voted quickly; to split one's vote required time and care, and party workers could identify the ticket splitters simply by observing the length of time the individual voters spent in the polling place. To protect voters against pressure from party organizations, reformers in many states—backed up, of course, by the minority party in each state—gradually brought about alterations in the form of the ballot to eliminate the straight-ticket square or circle at the head of the party column. By 1972, the first year for which the Council of State Governments published data on the subject, barely half the states, or twenty-six, made it possible to vote for a party's entire slate in a presidential election by marking one box on the ballot or pulling a master lever on the voting machine. Eight years later, the number had declined to nineteen.[45] At least one state, Virginia, even went so far as to eliminate party identification from the ballot altogether, leaving it to party workers outside the polling place to remind voters of the identity of a party's candidates.

The hold of political parties on their traditional supporters was also weakened through the loss of patronage. Civil service merit systems, introduced in the 1880s, spread to encompass more and more jobs at all levels of government, denying those posts to party loyalists and so weakening one of the incentives for loyalty itself. Meanwhile, the boom in the private sector relative to public employment was reducing the value and appeal of those jobs that remained at the disposal of party organizations. And the informal welfare functions of parties— the traditional ton of coal and Christmas basket for the needy—gave way, after the 1930s, to public welfare.

As ticket splitting became both mechanically possible and morally acceptable—even virtuous—it would appear whenever voters found themselves out of sympathy with their party's candidate for president

45. Council of State Governments, *The Book of the States, 1974–75* (Lexington, Ky., 1974), p. 35; *1982–83* (1982), p. 104. One of the nineteen, Oklahoma, had separate straight-ticket boxes or levers for each level of government. *The Book of the States* has not reported these data in editions since 1982–83.

or the program he espoused. Thus Theodore Roosevelt as a third-party candidate for president in 1912 could attract millions of voters who remained loyal Republicans in state and local contests. Alfred E. Smith as the Democratic candidate in 1928 could impel millions of southern Democrats to scratch the top of their ticket while steadfastly supporting the rest of the party slate. With the realignment of the 1930s came massive ticket splitting among northern Republicans backing Franklin Roosevelt's New Deal and both northern and southern Democrats opposing it.

The bonds of party were clearly attenuating, but their weakness was concealed as long as the Democrats, the country's new majority party, were able to elect their president. So Roosevelt and Harry Truman succeeded in doing what every twentieth century president before them had accomplished; they carried into office with them majorities of their own party in both the Senate and the House. Journalists and political scientists who for years had accepted the "president's coattails" as one of the immutable phenomena of political life saw no reason to reverse their judgment. Nor did they after the 1952 election, when a Republican president brought a Republican Congress to Washington with him.

But in 1956, the frayed and tattered state of the presidential coattails was dramatically exposed. In that year, President Eisenhower won forty-one of the forty-eight states and 58 percent of the two-party vote, but his party still lost both houses of Congress. The GOP lost eleven of the senatorial elections in the states that Eisenhower won—or 42 percent—and nearly the same proportion of House seats in the districts Eisenhower carried. The voters who gave the president 58 percent support gave the Republican House candidates only 49 percent. Yet even this extraordinary degree of ticket splitting was exceeded in Richard Nixon's landslide reelection in 1972. The president carried every state but Massachusetts, with a popular vote margin 4 points higher than Eisenhower's—62 percent of the two-party vote—but lost the Senate and House by even greater margins. Democratic candidates won exactly half the Senate races in the states that Nixon carried, sixteen of thirty-two, and about half the House seats in districts Nixon won. The president's 62 percent fell off to 47 percent for his party's House nominees.

In 1980 the presidential coattails proved somewhat stronger: Republican candidates won only twenty of the thirty-one senatorial contests in states carried by Ronald Reagan—or 64 percent—but since most of the seats in those states had been held by Democrats, the GOP was able to capture control of the Senate for the first time since the first Eisenhower landslide. But the results of House elections made clear that the political system had by no means returned to the pre-1956 years. Republican House candidates still polled only 49 percent of the two-party vote, lagging 6 percentage points behind Reagan, and the Democrats emerged with a fifty-one-seat margin—enough to enable them to organize that body and chair all of its committees, even though they lacked the unity and discipline, and perhaps the will, to defeat the Reagan economic program during the honeymoon year of 1981. In 1984 the number of states with split results between the presidency and the Senate rose almost to the halfway mark, as Democrats won in fifteen of the thirty-two races in states carried by Reagan and a Republican won in Minnesota, the only state supporting the Democratic candidate, Walter Mondale. Of the 370 congressional districts carried by President Reagan, Democrats were elected to the House in 189, or 51 percent.[46] The 1988 election showed a drop in the number of House districts with split results, from 190 to 149, but the crossing of party lines was still almost solidly in one direction; of the total, 136 districts voted for President Bush and the Democratic candidate for Congress, while 13 split in the opposite direction, for the Democratic candidate for president, Michael Dukakis, and the Republican nominee for Congress.[47] In senatorial races, the number of contests with split results exceeded 50 percent for the first time in history; of the thirty-three states with Senate elections, fourteen voted for Bush but elected a Democratic senator while three supported Dukakis and sent a Republican to the Senate.

The pattern of ticket splitting has been so preponderantly in one direction throughout the whole era of divided government since 1956 that the partisan division has taken only one of its two possible forms—Republican presidents have confronted Democratic Con-

---

46. Richard E. Cohen, "Despite His Landslide Win, Reagan Trailed House Winners in Most Districts," *National Journal*, April 20, 1985, pp. 854–57. One district carried by Mondale, in New York City, reelected a Republican representative, making a total of 190 districts with split results. Cohen's preliminary total of 192 is reduced to 190 in Ornstein and others, *Vital Statistics, 1991–1992*, p. 64.

47. Richard E. Cohen, "Lonely Runner," *National Journal*, April 29, 1989, pp. 1050–54.

gresses. To find a government divided in the opposite manner, one would have to go back all the way to 1947–48, when Democratic President Truman faced the Republican Eightieth Congress (the "do nothing, good for nothing" Congress, as he termed it, that he made the target of his victorious 1948 campaign). Why, in more recent times, have the people consistently preferred Republican presidents and Democratic legislators—to the point where commentators routinely refer to the two parties' "locks" on their respective branches?

Reasons for Ticket Splitting

Some have suggested that the voters consciously seek to divide their government out of distrust for politicians of both parties, and some evidence from current public opinion polls supports this view. Thus an NBC/*Wall Street Journal* survey in July 1991 found that 61 percent of the respondents thought it "better to have different political parties controlling the Congress and the presidency, to prevent either one from going too far," while only 28 percent endorsed the view that the same party should control both branches "so they can work together more closely." Earlier NBC/*Wall Street Journal* polls using the same wording in 1986 and 1990 showed comparable results. During the 1984 campaign, two Harris polls showed 55 percent and 60 percent believing the country would be "worse off" if the voters gave President Reagan "a Republican-controlled Congress that would pass nearly everything he wants." Yet, in November 1976, after the election had restored unified party government under President Carter, Harris found a 45-39 percent margin in favor of single-party control. And in April 1987, a *Washington Post*/ABC poll produced a 51-35 percent majority in favor of unified party government under Democratic control. Clearly, the results vary with the degree of confidence the people may accord their government, particularly their president, at any particular time. Moreover, the polling results should be interpreted with caution, because it is difficult to achieve perfect neutrality in the wording of the question.[48]

48. The NBC/*Wall Street Journal* surveys were conducted by the polling organizations of Peter D. Hart and Robert M. Teeter and reported in their summary of "Study #4019," dated July 1991 (question 4d). The 1984 surveys by Louis Harris and Associates were conducted September 21–25 and October 26–31 and reported in Harris Survey news release no. 98, November 2, 1984. The 1976 figures are taken from Austin Ranney,

But although a popular majority at a given time may favor divided government as an abstract principle, there is no evidence that many voters think in abstract terms when they make their actual decisions in the voting booth. The majority that sometimes tells pollsters it distrusts unified government is converted on election day to a three-quarters majority that by its votes supports the principle of unity.

To begin with, divided government is determined, in the case of the House, by a minority of the nation's 435 congressional districts. In the recent elections with the most ticket splitting, those of 1972 and 1984, only 192 and 190, respectively, of the 435 districts turned in split results; the majority of districts supported presidential and House candidates of the same party. And within most of the split districts, a minority of voters—possibly a very small minority—determined the results. In 1972, when Nixon ran 15 percentage points ahead of Republican House candidates, on the average, that proves only that as many as 15 percent of the voters split their tickets between the presidential and House candidates (disregarding the impact of those who may have voted for only one of the two offices). Assuming that 5 percent of the voters split their tickets in favor of George McGovern—a generous assumption—while 20 percent split in Nixon's direction, for a net of 15 percentage points, the ticket splitters would still total only 25 percent. The results for 1984, when Reagan's percentage of the presidential vote was 12 points higher than the Republican share of the aggregate House vote, indicate that the proportion of ticket splitters may have been less, but the election-year poll of the Survey Research Center of the University of Michigan found it to be about the same—25 percent (19.6 percent who voted for Reagan and the Democratic candidate for Congress and 5.6 percent who supported Walter Mondale for president and the Republican nominee for the House). Exit polls in the 1988 election indicated that

---

"What Constitutional Changes Do Americans Want?" *This Constitution: A Bicentennial Chronicle* (Winter 1984), reprinted in Donald L. Robinson, ed., *Reforming American Government: The Bicentennial Papers of the Committee on the Constitutional System* (Westview Press, 1985), p. 286. The *Washington Post*/ABC poll results were published in the *Post*, April 22, 1987, pp. A1, A14. As an example of a possible misleading question, one may cite the *Post*/ABC poll, which asked, "Do you think it is better for the country to have a Democratic president or a Republican president when the Democrats control the U.S. Congress?" The response of 51-35 percent in favor of a Democratic president may have reflected current presidential preferences rather than an endorsement of unified party government as a principle.

ticket splitting declined to less than 20 percent. In that year, Bush ran just eight points ahead of his party's candidates for Congress.[49] Partisan division between the presidency and the House therefore results from the behavior of a minority of voters in a minority of districts.

In the case of the Senate, divided government after a presidential election may result from the carryover of an opposition majority from earlier elections. Insofar as the division is produced by ticket splitting in the most recent election, that is similarly the result of the voters' actions in a minority of states. On no occasion have as many as half the states with both presidential and senatorial elections split in favor of the winning presidential candidate and the senatorial nominee of the opposing party, although, as noted earlier, 1984 and 1988 came close to producing that result.

It would be equally fallacious, of course, to assert that the majority of voters has any steadfast interest in, or desire for, united government as such. Confronted with an abstract question as to the merits of united government, the reply of the typical Democrat or Republican would no doubt be: "By which party? If you mean by my party, I'm in favor of united government. If you mean by the other party, I'm against it." This attitude seems clearly enough demonstrated, in the case of the Democrats at least, by the results of midterm elections. In 1954, 1958, 1970, 1974, 1982, 1986, and 1990, a majority of the voters preferred Democratic control of the House of Representatives—or at least did not consider it undesirable—at times when they knew a Republican president would be in office two more years. In five of those seven elections, the electorate also increased the number of Democratic senators—in 1954 and 1986, by enough seats to restore the Democratic majorities that had been swept away in the earlier Eisenhower and Reagan landslides. But it can be doubted that the voters deliberately sought divided government as such, in those years or in the six presidential election years with divided outcomes. Those results can be better understood as the unplanned consequence of voting choices made for other reasons.

What, then, are the reasons? Why does the minority of split-ticket voters whose behavior produces divided government prefer a Repub-

---

49. Data for 1984 and 1988 from Donald L. Robinson, *Government for the Third American Century* (Westview Press, 1989), pp. 69–70.

lican for president most of the time yet prefer Democrats to represent them in the Congress?

The preference for Democrats in Congress may be explained in large part by the simple fact that the Democratic party has been, throughout the era of divided government, the country's majority party, and for that to be reflected in representative legislative bodies is to be expected. More citizens have identified themselves as Democrats than as Republicans, and the Democrats have been successful in translating this popular support into a majority of governorships most of the time (56 percent in 1991), a majority of state legislative seats (60 percent in 1991), and control of more city halls and county courthouses in populous areas.

Even if the Democrats were to lose their advantage in voter identification (as some recent polls indicate they are on the verge of doing or have already done), they would be much slower to lose their majorities in public offices at the state and local levels, for a reason that has been advanced most convincingly by Alan Ehrenhalt. The Democrats, as the party of positive government, have greater natural appeal to able and ambitious young people who are willing to undertake arduous political campaigns for the right and power to use government for constructive purposes. Young people who believe that, in Ronald Reagan's words, "government is the problem, not the solution" find their home in the Republican party, but the negative objective of dismantling government is a less powerful motivator for seeking office. Consequently, the Democratic party has been better able to recruit competent, aggressive, and vigorous campaigners for local offices and state legislative seats and hence wins more elections at those levels. And it is from the ranks of successful state and local officeholders that congressional candidates are drawn. With a richer resource of such officials, the Democratic party has, on the whole, been able to offer more appealing candidates for Congress.[50] Congres-

50. Alan Ehrenhalt, *The United States of Ambition: Politicians, Power, and the Pursuit of Office* (New York: Times Books, 1991). For data on the advantage of the Democrats in nominating congressional challengers with experience in state and local office, see Gary C. Jacobson, "The Persistence of Democratic House Majorities," in Cox and Kernell, eds., *Politics of Divided Government*, pp. 66–68. Fiorina suggests another reason for the Democratic recruitment advantage may be the professionalization of state legislatures: as holding, and campaigning for, legislative seats has become a full-time job, the salaries and perquisites of those jobs are more likely to attract Democrats, whose

sional elections, as Gary Jacobson and others have argued, are won or lost not on election day but many months earlier when potentially attractive candidates make their decisions about whether to run.

Republican party spokesmen have emphasized two other explanations: the power of incumbency and gerrymandering of congressional districts. Members of the Democratic majority in Congress are able to entrench themselves in office by the superior ability of incumbents to attract campaign funds, by the use of the postal franking privilege to gain name recognition, and by the service they are able to render to constituents. True, more than 90 percent of incumbents running for the House and Senate have been regularly returned to office—in 1990 the percentages were above 95 percent for both houses—but the argument loses weight when it is noted that the Democrats have been winning a majority of *open* seats (those in which no incumbent is running). During the decade of Republican ascendancy in presidential elections, beginning in 1980, well over half the seats in the House of Representatives have been open at least once; of the members of the House in 1991, 266, or 61 percent, began their present service in 1981 or later, and of those, 154 were Democrats. Thus, even in the Republican decade, 58 percent of House newcomers were Democrats. A corresponding analysis of the Senate shows that of the 100 members, exactly half have taken their seats since the first Reagan election in 1980, and 28 of those 50, or 56 percent, were Democrats.[51] Clearly, the Democratic "lock" on Congress cannot be attributed to the power of incumbency.

That leaves, for the House, the possibility that gerrymandering of congressional districts accounts for the Republicans' failure to capture control in years when their presidential candidates were winning overwhelming victories. Republican spokesmen cite one statistic: the aggregate vote for Republican congressional candidates in all 435 districts has in some elections come close to equaling the total Democratic vote. If district boundaries were fairly drawn, they argue, their nearly equal share of the aggregate congressional vote would be translated into the same proportion of House seats. Gerrymandering has, of course, been a constant feature of American political life ever since

membership is drawn more heavily from lower-income groups, than Republicans, who have greater opportunity for "more lucrative careers in the private sector." Fiorina, *Divided Government*, pp. 45–52.

51. *Congressional Directory 1991–92* (GPO, 1991), pp. 376–77, 383–89.

Governor Elbridge Gerry of Massachusetts gave his name to the process almost two centuries ago, and each party has seized the opportunity in some instances when it was in full control of a state government in the year following a decennial census. California Democrats redrew boundaries in a blatantly partisan fashion after the 1980 tally, but so did Indiana Republicans—a process that backfired in the latter case, as Democrats increased their proportion of Indiana representatives when the gerrymander took effect. Aggregate congressional vote is an unreliable measure of actual party strength, however, because the totals are skewed by the figures from districts where one or the other party does not attempt a serious challenge. The most careful scholarly studies of reapportionment after the 1980 census indicate that gerrymandering accounts for very little, if any, of the Democratic margin in the House.

Indeed, Gary Jacobson's equations suggest that the Democrats did "slightly *worse*" after redistricting. When other factors—incumbency, national tides, and the Democratic vote in the previous election—are taken into account, they explain fully the twenty-five-seat Democratic House gain in 1982, and the same is true of earlier reapportionment periods. These equations, "do not prove the absence of partisan gerrymandering, of course," writes Jacobson, "they merely indicate that partisan effects, if any, have balanced out."[52] A more significant sta-

---

52. Jacobson, "Persistence of Democratic House Majorities," p. 63. (Italics in original.) In the same volume, John R. Petrocik finds Jacobson's calculations—and those of other scholars who have reached the same conclusion—unpersuasive but does not offer alternative methodology or estimates. "Divided Government: Is It All in the Campaigns?" note 2, pp. 36–37.

One form of malapportionment was outlawed when the Supreme Court in 1962 (*Baker* v. *Carr*, 369 U.S. 186) required that all districts in a state have approximately equal population. But beyond that, no system for drawing boundaries can be devised that will not advantage one or the other major party, depending on which among conflicting criteria are chosen to guide the process. If, for instance, blacks are concentrated in black-majority districts (which is the criterion being applied, pursuant to federal law, in the 1991–92 redistricting in the South), the Republicans gain the advantage. If, on the other hand, districts are drawn to conform as nearly as possible to political subdivision boundaries, the black vote may be spread to provide a Democratic edge in several districts. A logical case can be made for either approach, and any nonpartisan redistricting commission would have to choose among competing values at the outset. Even if the latter course is followed and the effort made to avoid dividing cities and counties, those natural political communities can be grouped in various patterns that possess equal logic but any of which will give an advantage to one party or the other. The fact that no ideally nonpartisan system can be designed has left legislators free to do whatever they can to maximize partisan advantage.

tistic is the number of congressional districts carried by the Republican presidential candidate in each election; in the six presidential elections that produced divided government, that number has reached as high as 377 in 1972 and 372 in 1984—or 87 and 86 percent—and in every case far exceeded the number won by the Democratic presidential nominee.[53] But Republican congressional candidates have run as many as 15 percentage points behind their presidential ticketmates. If that margin could have been reduced significantly, the Republicans would readily have won control of the House. The target of GOP wrath should therefore be ticket splitting, not gerrymandering. The party's aim should be to restore the ancient power of presidential coattails.

Jacobson and other scholars have developed what may be the most cogent explanation of why that goal will be difficult to attain. The ticket splitters who give the country divided government use different criteria, they suggest, in determining their presidential and congressional preferences. That in turn reflects the ambivalence of voters: they want the benefits of active government, particularly for their districts—which they associate with the Democratic members they send to Congress—but they also want the low taxes, as well as the strong national defense, that they are promised by Republican presidential candidates. "Democratic majorities in Congress," writes Jacobson, "make a Republican presidential candidate's promise (however ephemeral) of 'no new taxes' more appealing; at the same time, people may feel more comfortable voting for a Republican president knowing that the Democrats in Congress will keep him from gutting their favorite programs. . . . Conversely, it becomes more difficult to persuade voters to boot Democrats out of Congress when there is a Republican in the White House to control their collective excesses."[54] Ronald Reagan and George Bush have succeeded in cutting taxes, while congressional Democrats have succeeded in preserving, or even expanding, popular programs. "The resulting budget deficits have so

---

53. Ornstein and others, *Vital Statistics, 1991–1992*, table 2-15, for 1964 and 1972–88. For 1968, tabulated from data in Michael Barone, Grant Ujifusa, and Douglas Matthews, *The Almanac of American Politics 1972* (Gambit, 1972).

54. Gary C. Jacobson, *The Electoral Origins of Divided Government: Competition in U.S. House Elections, 1946–1988* (Westview, 1990), p. 134. See also the concluding pages of his "Persistence of Democratic House Majorities."

far brought little palpable pain," and perhaps never will, so the voters have little reason to be unhappy about divided government.[55]

Herman Belz makes the point from a historical perspective: "The people appear to elect presidents who will satisfy the anti-government tendency that has been a conspicuous feature of American political thought, while choosing as their representatives politicians who will maintain the welfare state programs that have become virtually a part of the constitutional order since the 1930s."[56] John R. Petrocik puts it somewhat differently: The Republicans have not been able to make the issues that they "own"—such as maintaining military security, handling foreign policy matters, reducing the deficit, controlling inflation, and holding down taxes—"take hold" in congressional races, while the Democrats have been unable to make the issues on which they win congressional races—such as social security, education, farm policy, and "fairness"—the "centerpieces" of presidential contests."[57]

These explanations are reinforced by still another, which rests on the greater ideological homogeneity of the Republican party compared with the Democratic. The Republicans have encountered relatively little difficulty in finding candidates for president who can appeal successfully to the whole range of the Republican spectrum, while the Democratic party still suffers from its ancient schism—between its northern big-city, ethnic, liberal, pro-labor wing and its southern rural, native-stock, conservative, anti-union wing, and more recently, to complicate matters, between its massive block of black adherents and many of its traditional white supporters who are resisting black demands. These divisions are not a bar to success in congressional elections, because individual state and district Democratic candidates do not have to embody any national party line; they can and do win

55. Gary C. Jacobson, "The Roots of Divided Government Are Political, Not Structural," *Public Affairs Report* (Institute of Governmental Studies, University of California at Berkeley), vol. 32 (July 1991), p. 7.

56. Herman Belz, "The Constitution and the 21st Century," in *Mr. Madison's Constitution and the Twenty-First Century* (Washington: American Historical Association and American Political Science Association, 1988), p. 9.

57. Petrocik, "Divided Government," pp. 16–17, 21. Petrocik determines the "ownership" of particular issues according to survey responses as to which party can better handle each issue. He finds the responses, and hence the party images, relatively stable from one campaign year to another.

by reflecting the nature and attitudes of their respective diverse constituencies. But bridging the gap in presidential contests is quite another matter; to put it simply, a candidate who will excite northern Democratic voters is likely to alienate the South, while one conservative enough to appeal to that region will fail to mobilize the party's potential northern strength.[58]

Designing a Solution

For those who, like the CCS, see divided government as the "preeminent cause" of interbranch conflict, four approaches to a remedy are discussed below. One would proceed directly to the point, by simply making ticket splitting impossible. The second and third would employ less drastic methods, relying on a change in the ballot format and in the electoral schedule to encourage straight-ticket voting. The fourth would assure the president a congressional majority by arbitrarily assigning his party enough additional Senate and House seats to outnumber the opposition.

One point bears on the feasibility of any of these solutions. Any measure that held real promise of bringing about a reduction in split-ticket voting would be anathema to the incumbent members of the Senate and the House. The reason is simple; members of Congress are the direct and personal beneficiaries of ticket splitting.

Of the one hundred members of the Senate in early 1992, ninety-three had had personal experience running for the Senate or the House, or both, during a presidential election year. Of those ninety-three, fifty-eight—or well over half—had saved their political careers by separating themselves from their party's candidate for president; they had managed to survive through ticket splitting—usually reflecting the power of incumbency—in a year when their party's presidential candidate failed to carry the legislator's state or district. And almost two-thirds of the others, or twenty-two, had run ahead of their presidential candidate in one or more elections, by margins ranging

58. Martin P. Wattenberg notes that since 1964 competition for the Democratic presidential nomination has usually been more divisive than the corresponding Republican contest, which leaves the Democrats less united as they enter the autumn campaign. "The Republican Presidential Advantage in the Age of Party Disunity," in Cox and Kernell, eds., Politics of Divided Government, pp. 39–55.

as high as 28 percentage points. Thus, exactly four-fifths of the Senate's membership—eighty of the one hundred—had been in a race where they found their party's presidential candidate to be at least a drag on the ticket, if not a sure loser from the start.

Similarly, of the 435 members who organized the House in 1991, at least 45 percent (196) had won in a year when their party's presidential candidate had gone down to defeat in the member's district. This included 65 percent of the House Democrats, or 174, some of whom had survived three or even four or more Republican presidential victories in their districts. On the other hand, only 22 House Republicans, or 13 percent, had won when a Democratic presidential candidate carried their districts—a few of these results go back as far as 1964—but many of the others had had the experience of running more strongly than their party's nominee for president.[59]

Under these circumstances, a Democratic member of Congress would have to believe very deeply in the abstract principle of straight-ticket voting to see merit in any reform that linked his fate more closely to that of Michael Dukakis in 1988, Walter Mondale in 1984, or Jimmy Carter or George McGovern in earlier years. And a Republican senator or representative could anticipate the danger of someday being found on a ticket with a presidential candidate as weak as Goldwater proved to be in the North in 1964 or Gerald Ford in the South in 1976.

The Presidential-Congressional Team Ticket

The most direct and effective, but most arbitrary, way to end ticket splitting between candidates for president and Congress would be simply to prohibit it. Each party's candidates for president, vice pres-

---

59. Barone and others, *Almanac of American Politics, 1972, 1980* (Dutton); and Michael Barone and Grant Ujifusa, *Almanac of American Politics, 1984, 1990* (Washington: National Journal) contain presidential election returns for most congressional districts from 1968 to 1988. Cohen, "Despite His Landslide Win," pp. 855–57, presents 1984 results for all districts, if one accepts Cohen's estimates for nine districts for which calculations were not complete. For the missing districts in the earlier elections, I relied on presidential election returns by counties (or big-city wards). In the very few cases where there were no detailed data, I tried to err on the side of minimum ticket splitting in dividing a county's or ward's presidential vote between congressional districts. Hence the "at least" phrase in the tally of House elections.

ident, senator, and representative could be bound together as a slate—
or team ticket, as it has been called—with each voter casting a single
vote for one of the competing teams.

The team ticket would be less than a foolproof protection against
divided government, to be sure. Since only one-third of the Senate
seats are filled in each presidential election, a lopsided Senate majority—such as the Democratic majorities of the 1960s—would not be
overturned in a narrow presidential election won by the opposition
candidate (assuming that the system of staggered six-year terms is
not altered, a possibility discussed in chapter 5). And even in the case
of the House, where all the seats are at stake in each election, a slim
mathematical possibility would exist that in a close election the presidential candidate winning the most electoral votes might not carry
a majority of House districts. Nevertheless, the prospects for unified
party control of the government would be tremendously enhanced.
Divided government following a presidential election would become
the kind of rarity it was during the first century of Republican-Dem-
ocratic competition.

Beyond that, the team ticket would have a profound effect on the
conduct of politicians of the majority party in office. Throughout a
president's first term, the chief executive and legislators of the winning party would recognize that when reelection time came they
would stand or fall together. Members of Congress of the president's
party would be at pains to enhance the president's success, since they
as well as he would be dependent on the public's acceptance of his
record in office. Would this produce a Congress too docile, too subservient to exercise its responsibility to oversee, and where necessary
investigate, the executive branch? Certainly—at least until a president
was reelected and entered his lame-duck second term—the members
would lose a measure of their independence, as is the case in parliamentary countries where legislators are forced to run on the party
record. Members would no longer be free to score political points in
their home states or districts by opposing, and embarrassing, a president of their own party. They could no longer denounce their leader
and reject party discipline altogether, as leading senators and representatives have done so often in the past, reducing their party's
program to a shambles. They would have to accept the president's
leadership, like it or not, as long as he remained the party's likely
nominee for reelection.

Nevertheless, in their own interests, individual legislators would be forced to oppose the president where his policies and programs appeared likely to undercut support for the party in a particular state or district. Their incentive to make the president's record look good would extend to the prevention of mistakes, and their oversight and investigative powers would still be important for that end. If the president persisted in a locally unpopular course, dissenting legislators would have the recourse always available in any democracy when the positions of a party's leadership become unacceptable—to bolt the party and either join another party or form a new one. The likelihood of splinter parties, such as Strom Thurmond's States' Rights Democratic (Dixiecrat) party of 1948 or George Wallace's American Independent party of 1968, might be increased somewhat.

While the pressures for accommodation and harmony within the governing party would weigh most heavily on the legislators, it would be felt to some degree by the president as well. The threat of third-party challenges would be one source of pressure. But short of that extremity, a president would be aware that in each presidential election the party team would be dependent not only on the president's record in office but on that of the legislators, too. A president would have to attend to building their reputations and records as well as his own. To that end, patronage and local projects would be of prime importance; the "pork barrel" would lose none of its current significance. But the president would have reason to accommodate the legislators' viewpoints on legislative matters, too. At both ends of Pennsylvania Avenue, the culture of individualism, of "every politician for himself or herself," would give way, to some considerable extent, to an ethos of teamwork.[60]

Crucially affected, also, would be the presidential nominating process. As a precondition to accepting the team-ticket idea, the legislators would surely insist they have an effective veto over the selection of the presidential and vice presidential nominees to whom they would be bound. Some device to enhance their influence, such as those discussed in chapter 7, would be in prospect.

---

60. James MacGregor Burns concludes that the team ticket would have a less profound effect on congressional and presidential behavior than is suggested here. *The Power to Lead: The Crisis of the American Presidency* (Simon and Schuster, 1984), p. 199.

The Challenge to Tradition

The idea of a team ticket has one notable precedent. Since the formation of parties in the United States, candidates for president and vice president have been bound together; the voter casts a single ballot for a slate of electors committed to one or another party's presidential–vice presidential team. No one has been heard to advocate a right for voters to split their ticket for those two offices.

Nevertheless, to further restrict the voter's right of choice would do violence to a tradition that has been cherished by the American polity ever since Progressive reformers introduced the secret ballot. One may anticipate the response of typical southern ticket splitters in 1988 had it been suggested that, in order to support the candidacy of George Bush, they be required to vote to oust their friendly and effective Democratic representative. Or if they wanted to retain their representative in office, that they be forced to accept Michael Dukakis. And these southern voters have their counterparts in every region, who split tickets in both directions and would defend vehemently their right to do so. If those voters had thought about divided government at all, they would be apt to see its adverse consequences as remote and speculative—and of a kind that could be averted if only the responsible officials would put aside partisanship and do their duty in the national interest—while the restriction on their freedom to vote as they please would be immediate, clear, and personally felt.

If the individual voter would be difficult to persuade, the average member of Congress, as noted earlier, would be even more so. For every winner in general elections, of course, there is a loser. For every incumbent senator or representative who survived only because of ticket splitting, there is a candidate of the other party who would have been elected if the practice had been forbidden. Southern Republicans, for example, should find great merit in the team-ticket idea. Indeed, if the scheme had been in place over the past thirty years, the entire Republican party would have benefited, for it would have been the majority party in Congress during many of the years when it was consigned to what appeared to be perpetual minority status. That assumes, as seems likely, that the support given the team ticket would have come closer to that accorded the GOP presidential candidates in 1956, 1968, 1972, 1980, 1984, and 1988 than to the much lower level of support given its nominees for Congress. And with Republican control of both branches, the GOP would have had the opportunity to enact its program unobstructed by the opposition.

But Republican House and Senate members have not stepped forward to advocate the team ticket, in spite of their apparent self-interest, and the Democrats surely will not do so, for their self-interest runs, of course, in the opposite direction. Had the team-ticket scheme been in effect, they would have lost their House majorities long ago— if not in 1956, surely by 1972—and probably the Senate in those years also. Those whose own political careers, or whose colleagues' careers, were saved by ticket splitting are not likely to step forward quickly to outlaw the practice. Adoption of the team ticket would therefore depend, in all likelihood, on bypassing Congress in the constitutional amendment process. That has never been done, but it can be. On petition of two-thirds of the state legislatures, Congress must call a constitutional convention, which would submit its proposed amendments directly to the states for ratification—and that method would have to be used to accomplish any of the changes discussed in this book that might be perceived by sitting members of Congress to be against their interest (a possibility considered in chapter 9). However, the state legislators who would have to initiate such a convention have much in common with members of Congress. Many of them, too, have survived through ticket splitting in state elections, and their outlook might not differ greatly from that of their counterparts in Washington.

An electoral system should never be judged, of course, according to the degree of comfort and convenience it accords political candidates and officeholders. It should be measured by its effects on the performance of the political system as a whole. And for those who accept the model of unified, responsible party government, the very features that discommend the team-ticket idea to members of Congress are its merit. By requiring a party's presidential and legislative candidates to share a common success or failure at the polls, it would compel them to work together once elected. Inevitably, some members of Congress would be dragged to defeat by a presidential candidate unpopular in their states or districts. Occasionally, a presidential candidate might be dragged down, too. But one candidate's loss would be another's gain. And, if reducing conflict and averting deadlock would benefit the political system as a whole, the public at large would gain from the incentives to party cohesion and cooperation that the team ticket would provide.

The Effect on Third-Party Prospects

In all of U.S. history few third-party candidates have been elected, and no third party has ever waged more than one strong presidential campaign since the Republicans as a party only six years old elected Abraham Lincoln in 1860. But a free and open political system must at least allow the opportunity for a Theodore Roosevelt or a George Wallace to organize a party and make a try.

Under a team-ticket system, as observed above, party splintering and third-party attempts might very well become more common, because there would be less room for dissidents within the major parties. Conceivably, the tendency toward splintering could become so pronounced that the familiar American two-party system would at times give way to multiparty competition. If the minor parties were to gain enough strength to hold a balance of power, some of the advantages of the team-ticket scheme would be lost; coalitions would have to be formed, and responsibility and accountability would be diffused. It may be assumed, however, that third parties in this country would tend to have short lives under the new electoral system just as under the present one. Stable multiparty systems are associated, the world over, with proportional representation in parliamentary elections. Wherever representatives are chosen from single-member districts, no matter how tightly disciplined the parties may be, two strong parties usually dominate the scene. That is the case in Great Britain and in the nations formed from the British Commonwealth, including Canada up to the present. Even France, with its long tradition of multiparty competition, appears to be evolving into a two-party nation.

If team tickets were required, a candidate for president who was running essentially as an individual rather than as the head of a genuine party, such as John Anderson in 1980, would be at a marked disadvantage. Without capable running mates for the Senate and House, he could hardly hope to compete on equal terms against team tickets with strong candidates for the legislative seats. He would be forced to organize a full-fledged party, one capable of governing—and that would be all to the good, for an independent in the presidency could hardly succeed against the combined opposition of both the majority and minority parties in both houses of the Congress. Any presidential candidacy would have to reflect, as it should, more than the individual ambition of a maverick politician. It would have to grow out of broad political forces—like, for example, the Populists in the 1890s or the Dixiecrats and the American Independent party (AIP) in the postwar South. And such solidly based parties would have probably as favorable a prospect in a team-ticket electoral system as they do now, for they should encounter no difficulty in recruiting capable and appealing candidates for Congress. That would be particularly the case if a legislative candidate were permitted under the plan to run on more than one team ticket, with his or her votes aggregated. The success and acceptance of the present New York method of totaling the votes of candidates running on more than one party slate suggests its adaptability to the national level. But even without such a device, the experience of the Populists suggests that any party with a depth of popular support can field a winning team. In carrying five states for its presidential candidate in 1892, the People's party elected three senators and eleven representatives. The Dixiecrats and the AIP did not attempt to field full slates, but there is no reason to think they would have found it difficult to do so.

Independent candidacies for the Senate or the House, on the other hand, would be virtually barred if the team-ticket idea were adopted. The number of independents in Congress has been so negligible— there is only one, a Socialist from Vermont, in the 1991–92 Congress— that this problem can probably be disregarded. In any case, independents in the Congress can contribute only to the disintegration, not integration, of the government.

Two Simpler Approaches

Recognizing the radical character of the team-ticket solution, and the enormous practical obstacles to its adoption, those who decry the consequences of divided government have sought simpler, less drastic approaches that would stop short of compelling straight-ticket voting. The CCS endorsed one of these—a statute to require states to give voters the option of casting a single straight-ticket vote (as contrasted with the mandatory requirement of the team-ticket proposal). And it recommended another as worth considering: scheduling congressional elections to follow shortly after the presidential election each four years rather than be held concurrently.

Any reform that still permitted ticket splitting would, by definition, be less effective than the team ticket as a safeguard against divided government. But any substantial reduction in the number of split ballots would help. The question is how much help could be expected—whether any measure lacking the element of compulsion would have sufficient effect to make its adoption worth the effort. To the extent it did hold promise of results, it would, of course, arouse the opposition of incumbent members of Congress for all the same reasons that apply to the more drastic team-ticket proposal discussed above.

Change in the Ballot Format

If the elimination of the straight-ticket voting box on the ballot, or the master lever on the voting machine, in most of the fifty states has contributed to the rise in ticket splitting, restoring that box or lever would presumably induce a decline. A return to the nineteenth century practice of open voting, with party-printed ballots, could not be seriously proposed, but within the context of secret ballot procedures voters in every state could be enabled to support all or a portion of a party's list of candidates by checking a single box or pulling a single lever.

For the purpose of encouraging unity in the national government, the opportunity for straight-ticket voting would need only to extend to a party's candidates for federal offices. A reform so limited would be a simple, minimal change in existing practices that could be accomplished by legislation in the thirty or so states not now providing the straight-ticket opportunity. Yet the slowness and uncertainty of a state-by-state approach suggests the desirability of national action, through an act of Congress, to make the reform universal.

Any suggestion that the Congress take responsibility for any aspect of the design of ballots on a nationwide scale would encounter a states' rights objection that so intimate a feature of the local election process is none of Washington's business. Yet the national government has regulated elections in many respects. It has set rules governing the financing of national campaigns. It has intervened by constitutional amendment to overrule state decisions as to who may vote—by prescribing Negro suffrage and women's suffrage, setting the minimum voting age at eighteen years, and abolishing the poll tax as a prerequisite for voting. In the Voting Rights Act of 1965, it outlawed discrimination at local polling places and authorized federal enforcement. Federal officials have been assigned as local voting registrars, and changes in the election laws of some states, including drawing of congressional and state legislative district boundaries, are subject to review and approval by the U.S. Department of Justice, which has on occasion invalidated a state statute. For the Congress to act on a related matter of clear national concern and interest should not appear as an unreasonable extension of federal power, assuming the regulation applied only to candidates for national office.

But if the states that now do not provide the option to vote a straight ticket for president, vice president, senator, and representative with a single ballot mark were to do so, how many voters would exercise the option? Not many, if one may judge from a comparison of voter behavior in 1980 between the states that did offer the straight-ticket opportunity and those that did not. Of the thirty-three states that chose senators in the 1980 presidential election, fourteen offered the straight-ticket option, while nineteen did not.[61] In the fourteen, the average percentage-point spread between the proportion of the two-party vote given a party's presidential candidate and its senatorial candidate was 8.2 points, the median 6.0 points. In the nineteen states not offering the straight-ticket option, the spread was only slightly greater, an average of 10.9 and a median of 8.6 points. The proportion of split outcomes was about the same. Seven of the nineteen states, or 37 percent, gave their electoral votes to a president of one party while choosing a senator of the other, while five of the fourteen straight-ticket option states, or 36 percent, did likewise. Democratic Senators Dodd of Connecticut, Dixon of Illinois, Ford of Kentucky,

61. The nineteen states with the straight-ticket option as of 1980 were Alabama, Connecticut, Illinois, Indiana, Iowa, Kentucky, Michigan, Missouri, New Hampshire, New Mexico, Oklahoma, Pennsylvania, Rhode Island, South Carolina, South Dakota, Texas, Utah, West Virginia, and Wisconsin. Louisiana holds its senatorial and presidential elections separately, with the former choice made in its unique nonpartisan primary in September. Council of State Governments, *The Book of the States, 1982–83*, p. 104. The calculation for 1984 assumes that the same nineteen states had retained the option. Subsequent editions of *The Book of the States* have not reported data on the subject.

Eagleton of Missouri, and Hollings of South Carolina all survived the
Reagan tide in their states, despite the straight-ticket option, by running from 6 percentage points (Eagleton) to 21 percentage points
(Hollings) ahead of President Carter as a candidate on the same ballot.
This may be evidence enough that a change in the form of the ballot,
standing alone, is unlikely to reduce significantly the likelihood of
divided government in Washington. In 1984 the states with the
straight-ticket option actually showed a higher proportion of split
results in senatorial elections—seven of thirteen, or 54 percent, compared with nine of nineteen, or 47 percent, in states without it.

Separate Congressional Elections

A second relatively simple proposal would be to separate the presidential and congressional elections by a short interval—two weeks,
say—so that when the voters came to choose their senators and representatives they would already know whom they had sent to occupy
the White House. Then they would, it is suggested, be disposed to
elect members of Congress of the president's party, to help make
successful the administration of the person they had just entrusted
with the nation's leadership. This is what happened in France in 1981.
Having just placed the Socialist François Mitterrand in the Elysée
Palace, the French electorate in a separate poll five weeks later
returned a substantial Socialist majority to the Chamber of Deputies.

The question, of course, is whether the American electors would
behave as the French did on that occasion. Perhaps in some years
they would be in the mood expressed in the NBC/*Wall Street Journal*
poll of 1991, when a 61-to-28 percent majority favored divided government to prevent either the president or the Congress from "going
too far." In that event, separating the elections would have the opposite effect from that intended. Perhaps at other times the voters would
be in the mood of November 1976, when they felt that the president
they had just elected deserved a Congress controlled by his partisan
allies.

In guessing what the public response to such an appeal might be
in any future circumstances, the history of midterm elections may be
relevant. Every four years under the present Constitution, the people
in a separate congressional election have the opportunity to send to
Washington a Congress that will support the president or one that

will oppose him. Invariably, the president campaigns on behalf of his party's nominees and pleads with the people to elect them. The nominees in turn ask for election on the ground the president deserves support. But with monotonous regularity the president and his party are rebuffed. Only once in this century, in 1934, has the president's party increased its proportion of members of the House in the midterm election, and in only seven midterm contests has it picked up Senate seats.[62] (The Senate, because the seats at stake in a given year may be preponderantly of one party or the other, is a less revealing measure of a president's persuasive power than is the House.) Woodrow Wilson's nationwide campaign for a Democratic Congress in 1918 was perhaps the most energetic such appeal to the electorate—and the most spectacular failure. To all these demonstrations of the absence of presidential coattails in the midterm elections must be added President Franklin Roosevelt's equally historic failure in 1938 to persuade members of his own Democratic party to "purge" senators and representatives unsympathetic to the Roosevelt New Deal in favor of candidates pledged to cooperate with the party's leader.

Granted, if the presidential and congressional elections were separated by a brief interval, the question of divided government might become the focus of the separate congressional election, and the president-elect might make it so by actively campaigning for congressional majorities of his party. One may then speculate as to whether that issue would create a bandwagon effect in favor of the president-elect's party or have the opposite result—more ticket splitting—because the voters resented the interference of even a popular president-elect and rejected his advice, just as they have spurned the advice of sitting presidents. Or it might make little difference at all, as the electorate continued to make its congressional choices as it does now, on the basis of many other considerations beyond a preference for, or an aversion to, divided government. In any case, the CCS argues, the president should be granted "an opportunity to persuade voters to elect a majority of the same party to Congress and thus give the party a better opportunity to carry out its program."[63]

Perhaps the best prediction is that the voters would behave just about as they do now. Those who believe the president should have

62. Ornstein and others, *Vital Statistics, 1991–1992*, p. 53.
63. CCS, "A Bicentennial Analysis," p. 15.

a cooperative Congress controlled by his own partisans have every opportunity now to vote a straight ticket—and do. Those who positively favor divided government, or for other reasons favor the opposing party's candidate for senator or representative, split their tickets. Only one factor would be altered by separating the elections: the voter would know the outcome of the presidential election. Yet why would this knowledge change behavior? Surely, the voters who supported President Eisenhower in 1956 expected him to be elected— almost everyone else did, too—yet enough of them voted Democratic for congressional candidates to deny the GOP control of either body. Similarly, the supporters of Richard Nixon in 1972, Ronald Reagan in 1984, and George Bush in 1988 must have been nearly as certain of the election outcome when they cast their ballots as they were the morning after. All these candidates in the course of their campaigns—as well as all the other party spokesmen—had regularly asked the voters to vote the straight party ticket for national offices. Nevertheless, enough tickets were split to produce divided government.

The inevitable congressional resistance to any proposal that might possibly lessen the electoral independence of the legislators would be compounded, in this instance, by an added circumstance—the falloff in voting turnout that could be expected between the first and second elections. All members of Congress would ponder whether their chances would be helped or hurt by the lower turnout—which party's supporters would be more likely to stay home in the second balloting?—and would be influenced accordingly. If in doubt, members would shy away from change—after all, under the existing schedule of elections, they have been successful. And opponents of the dual-election plan would be given a persuasive argument: any scheme that would result in reducing the electorate for congressional balloting would be demonstrably antidemocratic. Whether correct or not, the idea that a large voter turnout is a sign of high civic morale, and a low turnout bad for a democratic polity, is a national article of faith. If the Congress could be persuaded to experiment with separate elections, the experience would be illuminating. But whether the election outcome would be different—or different enough, at least, to warrant the cost and the nuisance of two elections instead of one—is doubtful. And any differences that appeared would be stigmatized as the result of an antidemocratic reduction in the size of the electorate.

Bonus Seats in Congress

A direct and effective way of eliminating the possibility of divided government following a presidential election—although one with no precedent in American experience—would be to create additional seats in Congress for the president-elect's party in a number sufficient to give it control of the Senate and the House.

If control were to be guaranteed, the number of additional seats awarded in some years would have to be substantial. To have provided President Nixon with Republican majorities after the 1968 election would have required the addition of 17 GOP senators, enlarging that body from 100 to 117, and 52 representatives, increasing the size of the House from 435 to 487. After 1984 President Reagan would have needed 72 added Republicans in the House, and after 1988, President Bush would have required 11 additional senators and 78 representatives of his party. And even these numbers would provide only bare majorities that could be overturned with a single death or resignation; to give the president a margin reasonably safe against such contingencies would require somewhat more bonus seats.

The addition of bonus members, it has been argued, not only would assure the president's party of a majority (if only a one-seat margin) and so permit it to organize the Congress but also could bring to the legislative bodies a group of leaders elected from the country at large who would approach their legislative duties with a national rather than a parochial perspective and could, if properly selected, bring a wealth of experience and wisdom to congressional deliberations. It is this very prospect, of course, that would be sure to arouse the most intense opposition to the proposal from incumbent members, who would see some of their power and influence flow to a group of newcomers who might outclass them in stature and prestige.

This objection would be mitigated if the number of bonus seats were fixed at a small figure, but the effectiveness of the approach would be reduced to the extent that the number of seats was limited. If the additional House seats had been fixed at a number even as high as fifty, for example, it would have been insufficient to assure Republican House majorities in the 1956, 1972, 1980, and 1984 elections, all won by Republican presidents. To make the idea acceptable to incumbent members as an experiment would probably require reducing the number to the point where the prospect of preventing divided government at any given time would be so small as to make the effort hardly worthwhile.

In the case of the Senate, the proposal encounters a constitutional obstacle, for it could be interpreted to contravene the one unamendable clause of the Constitution—the provision in Article V that "no State, without its Consent, shall be deprived of its equal Suffrage in the Senate." While proponents could argue that the bonus senators would represent the nation, and hence all states equally—and this could be specified in the language of the amendment—opponents would advance the plausible contention that whatever state was the home of a national senator would in fact have extra suffrage.

Leaving aside these practical and constitutional difficulties, one may speculate as to how a scheme for adding members to the Senate and the House could best be designed to serve the purposes sought. Much depends, of course, on the method of selection, and on this point a range of possibilities is open.

At-large candidates could be nominated by the party at its national convention, along with its choices for president and vice president. If the numbers were large enough to cover any need that could be reasonably anticipated—twenty candidates for the Senate and seventy-five for the House would be the minimum suggested by recent elections—each quadrennial party convention would be faced with an enormously complex task. Presumably, it would simplify its job by delegating the selection in fact to the presidential nominee, as it does now in the case of selecting its candidate for vice president. But that in turn would thrust an onerous and distracting burden on presidential candidates, who while engrossed in the contest for the nomination would have to find time to make judicious choices among the persons seeking places on the party list. In a hotly contested race, a candidate would have to delegate the selection process to advisers and assistants and would, to some extent, lose control. Whether the public would have confidence in a selection process that was in the hands of anonymous, behind-the-scenes negotiators is conjectural. Moreover, such a process would surely defeat the aims of those who see in at-large members the opportunity to place in the Senate and House a corps of the ablest, most nationally minded party leaders. The list makers would be confronted with overwhelming pressures from all of the organized and unorganized groups and factions within the party—state and local party organizations, women, blacks, Hispanics, Asian-Americans, other ethnic and religious groups, liberals and conservatives, business and labor, and all the rest—for representation. Any group that could claim the allegiance of a few hundred thousand voters would make its demands and would have to be heard. Group representatives, when elected, would hardly be nationally minded. They would be seen, and would probably behave, as the representatives of the interests responsible for getting them included on the slate in the first place.

If the number to be elected were uncertain, to be determined after the election by the need of the president's party for additional seats to attain its majority, all of the candidates would have to be ranked in order—as is done in some proportional representation systems of election in parliamentary democracies—which would compound the pressures for inclusion on the party list with jockeying for high positions on the slate. This suggests the desirability of fixing the number of at-large seats in advance. But any fixed number would necessarily turn out, in any given election, to be either too small to give the president's party the control sought or larger—perhaps much larger—than necessary for that purpose, and hence unnecessarily disruptive.

The rank-ordering could be done, of course, by the voters themselves. At the time of the presidential election, voters could be permitted to cast a ballot for a specified number of persons listed on the slate of the party of their choice, and the candidates could be ranked according to the results. Whether an individual voter could obtain the information necessary to make an intelligent choice among eighty competing candidates may surely be questioned. That problem could be ameliorated if the choice were made by regions, from smaller lists, but it would remain. And a regional system would defeat the purpose of electing nationally minded members to the Congress. Finally, for the voter to make the choice, on either a national or regional basis, would lead to a general election season in which candidates for the at-large seats would be campaigning against one another within their party, thus extending the primary season through the whole general election period, with all of the divisive consequences that hard-fought primaries can have. The Italian proportional representation system has been widely criticized within Italy for having that result.

These weaknesses and difficulties suggest still another alternative—that the at-large seats be filled *after* the election, by appointment.

The responsibility could be vested in the president alone,[64] or in the president subject to confirmation by his party's members in the house affected, or even exclusively in the legislative body. The first of those methods would probably strike all concerned as giving the president excessive authority over the legislature, upsetting the balance between the branches. If the legislators chose their added colleagues, one may surmise that former legislators, including some retired by their constituents, would be chosen for many of the at-large seats, and that eminent, nationally minded statesmen likely to outshine the members who selected them would be scrupulously avoided. In fact, it might come to be understood, as a condition of appointment, that the at-large members would take no active role in the legislative process. The middle course—appointment by the president subject to confirmation—might well lead to an assertion by the legislative parties of the right not merely to confirm but to nominate some or all of the at-large members, just as senators now in fact nominate many of the presidential appointees who are subject to Senate confirmation, including judges, federal district attorneys, and many other officials who head regional and state offices of federal agencies.

If the at-large members were so selected, then, they might be mediocre party hacks, sure to vote as the party leaders dictated but otherwise committed to stay in the background, appearing in committee or on the floor only for the purpose of voting. But that at least would make for harmony within the Senate and the House. Any method of selection that in fact placed in the Congress experienced and eminent leaders would inevitably create tension within the legislative houses that would make those bodies even less manageable than they are now. The Senate and the House would be made up of two classes of members—those elected in the usual way, who shared a common outlook because they had survived the obstacle course of state or district electoral politics, and those who had achieved their status by one or another form of appointment. How committee and subcommittee chairmanships would be assigned, how seniority would be measured and recognized, how patronage and office space would be distributed (indeed, costly new Senate and House office buildings would have to be constructed and the legislative payrolls substantially

64. The possibility of a president's appointing officials of the executive branch to the at-large seats, which would require repealing the constitutional prohibition against dual officeholding, is discussed in chapter 7.

expanded)—all these would be subjects of incessant antagonism pitting the two classes of legislators against each other.

There remains the question of what would happen after the first two years. Would the at-large members of the House be appointed for only the two-year terms that their regularly elected colleagues enjoy? Assuming they were elected in the first instance, would they run for reelection nationwide (or regionwide if originally chosen regionally)? Since they could not have competition from the opposing party (which would have no right to fill the at-large seats), would challenges by members of the same party be admitted? Would an election serve any real purpose in the absence of interparty rivalry? But if the seats were filled by appointment at midterm, the at-large members would lose any semblance of independence during the first two years. These complications suggest that whatever method of selection were used in the first instance, the at-large members be given four-year terms.

In the case of senators, six-year terms corresponding to those of the regularly elected members would appear inappropriate, for that would extend the term of a member appointed to give one president a Senate majority into the term of a president who might be of the opposing party. Four-year terms for at-large senators would pose no difficulty, except for setting them apart from their colleagues in one more way.

In no event, however, would appointments of any length made at the outset of a presidential term provide a safeguard against divided government after the midterm election, when the president's party normally suffers a setback. To provide that assurance would require the possibility of additional appointments at midterm. But such a provision would authorize the appointing authorities, in effect, to reverse the electorate's midterm decision—an idea so patently antidemocratic as to be surely unacceptable. In the absence of such a provision, would the at-large members remain in office the full four years even if the midterm election put them in the minority and so rendered them unable to serve the purpose for which they were elected or appointed? The midterm problem would be eliminated, of course, if the terms of House members were extended to four years, as discussed in chapter 5.

In the case of the House, a variant of the team-ticket scheme would avert the complications of at-large selection. The 435 House districts could be divided by the House into 87 groups of 5 districts each, with each party to nominate a candidate in the superdistrict who would run as a member of a curtailed team ticket with the presidential and vice presidential nominees. Where the superdistricts crossed state lines, the nominating process would have to be worked out through interstate agreements, which could be negotiated by the state party organizations within the terms of flexible authorizing legislation. Several objections to this proposition are apparent. Since the bonus seats would not all go to the party of the winning presidential election, in a close election the added seats might merely enlarge the House without giving the president's party control. The grouping of the House districts would create internal stresses within that body, with the opportunity of—and certainly the charges and countercharges related to—gerrymandering on a national scale. The organization of multistate nominating processes would encounter technical difficulties that, while not insoluble, would produce conflict and dissatisfaction.

A corresponding process could be conceived for the Senate, with twenty-five bonus senators representing pairs of states or ten chosen by five-state regions. If the votes of individuals were weighted to give the states equal influence on the result, the requirement of equal state suffrage in the Senate would presumably be met. The bonus senators could be given four-year terms coincident with the president's. But the same objections that apply in the case of the House apply also to the Senate, plus the additional obstacle of devising a weighted voting scheme that would not strike too many as illogical and undemocratic.

Effectiveness versus Feasibility

The problem of divided government, it is clear from this analysis, will not yield to ready resolution. Neither of the two schemes that would prove truly effective—the team ticket and the congressional bonus seats—could hope to garner significant support among incumbent members of Congress. And both would arouse strong public opposition as antidemocratic—the former by destroying the voter's freedom of choice and the latter by "packing" the Congress. The two more modest proposals—the requirement of a straight-ticket box on the ballot and the separation of presidential and congressional elections—would draw less hostility only because they would give less promise of making any real difference. To the extent that they appeared likely to succeed in their purpose—that is, to tie the fate of senators and representatives seeking reelection to that of their parties' presidential candidates—they would be fought by the same incumbent members, less vociferously perhaps but no less firmly, and would be likewise attacked as antidemocratic. The pervasive question of the feasibility of these and other approaches to constitutional reform is reexamined in chapter 9.

CHAPTER FIVE

Altering Terms and Electoral Processes

Reviewing the outlook for the federal budget deficit in the spring of 1984, Budget Director David A. Stockman observed that "we only have one more chance: that is in the first six months of 1985." The reason? "In the cycle of the American political system, there is about a six or seven month window every four years when concentrated efforts need to be made to grapple with problems."[1]

The same prediction was offered four months later by Representative Trent Lott of Mississippi, the House Republican whip. Even assuming substantial Republican gains in the 1984 election and reestablishment of the conservative coalition of 1981, said Lott, "We'll have six months, and that's all."[2] Barber Conable of New York, about to retire as the ranking Republican member of the House Ways and Means Committee, was more generous. He thought "the window of opportunity" might last for the entire congressional session of 1985—but not beyond.[3] After his election as Senate majority leader in late 1984, Robert J. Dole, Kansas Republican, made the same estimate.

1. Speech to the United States Chamber of Commerce, Washington, D.C., *New York Times*, May 24, 1984.

2. Steven V. Roberts, "Republicans Cultivating Swing Votes," *New York Times*, September 17, 1984.

3. Steven Presman, "President's Leadership Style and Split in GOP Ranks Are Key to Second-Term Success," *Congressional Quarterly Weekly Report*, October 27, 1984, p. 2786; and Martha M. Hamilton, "Conable: Tax Hike Necessary," *Washington Post*, October 28, 1984, pp. G1–G9.

Windows and Honeymoons

This view that little can be accomplished except in the first year—or half year—of any presidential term had been something approaching accepted doctrine in the Washington political community for a long time. Journalists and politicians alike had long noted the phenomenon of the "honeymoon" that the Congress was supposed to accord each new president. But the honeymoon, by definition, was expected to be brief. President Lyndon Johnson, an old Washington hand, justified his frenetic attempt to pass a controversial measure in 1965—the first year after his election—on the ground that "this was the only chance I would have." In 1966, he said, members of Congress would "all be thinking about their reelections. I'll have made mistakes, my polls will be down, and they'll be trying to put some distance between themselves and me." Johnson went on: "You've got to give it all you can, that first year. . . . You've got just one year when they treat you right, and before they start worrying about themselves. The third year, you lose votes. . . . The fourth year's all politics. . . . So you've got one year."[4]

Reviewing presidential policy leadership over two decades, Paul C. Light concluded that "speed is a key to presidential success in Congress" and "the first year provides the prime opportunity for legislative influence."[5] In the second year, as Johnson graphically observed, members of Congress are engrossed in staking out positions for the midterm election scheduled for November, and serious issues tend to be deferred. And in that election the incumbent president's party is almost invariably dealt a setback. The president's ability to lead is impaired, and he—especially if he is running for reelection—and the members of Congress as well begin to feel the pressures of the coming presidential election. Difficult issues tend again to be postponed, political risks are sidestepped, and politicians await the new mandate from the people that the presidential election is expected to confer. So goes the one-year-in-four "window-of-opportunity"

---

4. Harry McPherson, Jr., *A Political Education* (Little, Brown, 1972), p. 268. The measure that prompted Johnson's comments was one granting home rule to the District of Columbia.

5. Paul C. Light, *The President's Agenda: Domestic Policy Choice from Kennedy to Carter* (Johns Hopkins University Press, 1983), p. viii.

theory. If it is valid, it suggests the desirability of opening the window wider by lengthening the present two-year interval between elections, which is the shortest in any of the world's advanced democracies.

The 1980s: Testing the Theory

The first term of Ronald Reagan—just coming to its close when Stockman, Lott, and the others were speaking—had been a classic illustration of the one-year-in-four cycle. The president's achievements in reversing the unbroken trend of half a century toward the welfare state were massive and historic. But the breakthroughs came almost exclusively in 1981. After the initial year, the dismantling of governmental agencies and programs came to a halt. The president could lead the Congress no further in the direction he had set for it; indeed, the most significant movement in 1982 was a slight retreat, as the Congress forced the president to accept a tax increase he had not sought and initially resisted. In the midterm election, the Democrats added twenty-six seats to their House majority, and the government reverted to its familiar stalemate. The president lacked votes to impose further sizable cuts in governmental spending and in taxes, but he had the power to block any significant initiatives by the Congress in the opposite direction. Meanwhile, the deficit, acknowledged on all sides to be dangerously high, remained out of control. The president and the Congress did manage to get together on a "down payment" reduction, but that was all; decisive action was deferred. And that measure and a bill to rescue the social security system (which had to be fashioned outside the regular legislative process by a special bipartisan commission and then ratified without alteration by the Congress) were the only major legislative achievements of Reagan's third and fourth years.[6] Not only was a concerted effort to cope with

---

6. The National Commission on Social Security Reform, chaired by Alan Greenspan, was appointed by the president and the congressional leadership in December 1981 and reported its recommendations in January 1983. This method of overcoming policy deadlocks between the branches, used successfully on occasion in the past, was tried twice more during the Reagan first term. A commission on the MX missile, chaired by General Brent Scowcroft, made recommendations that were the basis of a bipartisan agreement that kept the missile program alive until after the 1984 election. But a commission on U.S. policy toward Central America and the Caribbean basin, headed by former Secretary of State Henry A. Kissinger, failed to establish its credibility and win support for its recommendations.

the deficit left for 1985; so too, for example, was action—likewise seen as a necessity by legislators and executive alike—to stem the flood of illegal immigrants across the Mexican border.[7]

As it happened, despite the predictions of so many seasoned observers of the Washington scene, the events of Reagan's second term did not repeat the pattern of his first. Contrary to the window theory, the initial year of the second term—1985—was not the most productive of the term, but the least. True, that was the year in which the Congress acted on the budget deficit through the Gramm-Rudman-Hollings Act, but the "window-of-opportunity" phrase refers to a time when politicians are assumed to have their chance to enact bold, decisive measures that may be unpopular and involve political risk, and Gramm-Rudman-Hollings was not that kind of enactment. More evasion than decision, it established deficit-reduction targets for the next five years but set the immediate targets high enough to avert the need for raising taxes or making draconian budget cuts and left to future Congresses the determination of what to do if the later targets were not met. If the later Congresses did not act otherwise, the goals would be achieved through automatic, uniform cuts spread across most agencies of the government. Were that to happen, it would likewise amount to evasion—avoidance of the responsibility of Congress to distribute expenditure cuts on a considered, rather than arbitrary, basis. Even one of the sponsors of the measure, Senator Warren B. Rudman, Republican of New Hampshire, called it "a bad idea whose time has come."[8]

7. David Mayhew's listing of important measures enacted during the period 1947–90, discussed in the previous chapter, includes only five others from the 1983–84 Congress, for a total of seven—barely half the average output of twelve per Congress over the forty-four-year span. Mayhew, *Divided We Govern: Party Control, Lawmaking, and Investigations, 1947–1990* (Yale University Press, 1991), pp. 70–71. By any measure, 1983 and 1984 were among the least productive years, in terms of significant legislation, of the entire period.

8. *Congressional Quarterly Almanac, 1985*, vol. 41 (1986) p. 459. Officially entitled the Balanced Budget and Emergency Deficit Control Act of 1985, the measure was universally referred to by the names of its sponsors, Senator Phil Gramm, Republican of Texas; Rudman; and Ernest F. Hollings, Democrat of South Carolina. Whenever the automatic cuts in appropriated funds took effect, they were to be divided equally between defense and nondefense programs. Certain nondefense programs were exempted from the cuts, including social security, interest on the public debt, veterans' pensions, medicaid, aid to families with dependent children, food stamps, child nutrition, and other welfare programs; and the reductions in five health programs, including medicare, were limited. The first automatic cuts—termed "sequestrations"—were

Only one other measure passed in 1985 makes David Mayhew's list of important enactments—a $52 million farm bill—but the next three years saw the passage of no fewer than eighteen of his listed measures, a productivity equal to the six-per-year average of the entire forty-four-year period covered by his study. These included the historic tax reform act, an immigration bill that dealt at last with the problem of illegal entry, and measures concerning environmental protection, drug abuse, welfare reform, civil rights, catastrophic health insurance for the aged (later repealed), reorganization of the Department of Defense, housing, foreign trade, and water and transportation projects.[9] Perhaps most significant, Congress and the administration were forced in late 1986 and early 1987 to face again the deficit issue they had evaded in 1985. They succeeded in agreeing on a two-year deficit-reduction package estimated as yielding $75 billion over the two years, of which $28 billion would be in increased revenues. Once more, however, the issue was substantially evaded, for the cuts were based on rosy economic projections (such as a fall in interest rates that would lower the cost of servicing the national debt), one-time windfalls from asset sales, and improved tax collections. After the agreement, the deficit continued to rise, and the issue would harass the next administration.[10]

---

applied early in 1986, amounting to 4.3 percent for nondefense programs and 4.9 percent for affected defense programs (the Defense Department was authorized to exempt some expenditure categories and concentrate the reductions in the remainder.) Congress solved the problem for the 1987 fiscal year mainly by one-time actions—estimating a $11 billion windfall from the immediate effects of the Tax Reform Act of 1986, anticipating increased tax collections from stepped-up enforcement, projecting net sales of government assets, delaying one military payday so as to push the expenditure into the following fiscal year, and so on. Sequestration was thus temporarily averted.

9. Mayhew, *Divided We Govern*, pp. 71–73.

10. The agreement on the budget deficit was precipitated by the largest one-day drop in the history of the stock market's Dow-Jones average, on October 19, 1986. When Wall Street analysts with near unanimity blamed the federal deficit as one of the contributing causes, President Reagan agreed to the "summit meeting" on the budget that Democratic congressional leaders had long been pleading for. The summiteers were confronted with estimates from the Congressional Budget Office that to meet the original Gramm-Rudman-Hollings target for the coming fiscal year would require sequestration of 17 percent of funds appropriated for nondefense programs and 26 percent for defense. The negotiators responded not only by calling for higher revenues, some budget cuts, and bookkeeping legerdemain but also by raising the targets, and the agreed changes were enacted. The new targets were, of course, also exceeded.

On most of the other measures, the initiative for this burst of achievement came less from the Reagan administration than from Democratic leaders on Capitol Hill, particularly House Speaker Jim Wright of Texas, and four of the eighteen measures—sanctions against South Africa, authorization of sewage treatment projects, authorization of highway and mass transit projects, and a civil rights bill that overturned a 1984 Supreme Court decision—were enacted over Reagan's veto.

As George Bush prepared to enter the White House in 1989, the "window-of-opportunity" discussion of four years earlier did not recur, for the reason that the Bush campaign had been singularly lacking in program proposals. Quite the opposite; Bush "had fought a campaign based on a premise of no precipitous shifts in policy," as two British observers wrote in a collection of essays by political scientists appraising the first two years of the Bush administration. Other contributors to the symposium concurred that the absence of an agenda was a distinctive feature of the first Bush years, offering the sharpest of contrasts with the opening of Reagan's presidency eight years before. The "Bush presidency is more inclined to react to events than to anticipate them" was the editors' summation. The 1988 campaign was "devoid of policy ideas" and "fed on symbols and innuendoes" instead, specifically of "hyperrhetoric on no new taxes, more flags, and no furloughs for (black) criminals," wrote one analyst. Others referred to "a no-mandate, limited-action president," "a lack of clear direction," "a consensus that the election carried no policy mandate," and an agenda that was "modest and, by and large, nonconfrontational."[11]

The absence of a presidential program was matched by a corresponding lack of congressional initiative. The House was distracted by the public outcry against a pay raise that Speaker Wright put through early in the year, and then Wright himself became embroiled in a scandal that eventually led to his resignation in mid-1989, at about the same time as the resignation of the majority whip, Tony

11. Colin Campbell and Bert A. Rockman, eds., *The Bush Presidency: First Appraisals* (Chatham House, 1991), quotations from Anthony King and Giles Alston, "Good Government and the Politics of High Exposure," p. 275; Campbell and Rockman, "Preface," p. viii; Rockman, "The Leadership Style of George Bush," p. 9; Charles O. Jones, "Meeting Low Expectations: Strategy and Prospects of the Bush Presidency," pp. 38, 58; and Barbara Sinclair, "Governing Unheroically (and Sometimes Unappetizingly): Bush and the 101st Congress," pp. 157, 163.

Coelho of California, for involvement in questionable outside activities. Meanwhile, the Senate was breaking in a new majority leader, George J. Mitchell of Maine.

The experience of Reagan's second term and of Bush's administration offer no confirmation of the window-of-opportunity theory, then, but they do nothing to invalidate it either. In effect, they did not test it, for if neither the president nor the Congress has much of a program to enact, little will be pushed through an open window nor thwarted by a closed one. In 1985, Reagan was a spent leader, whose legislative revolution had been accomplished four years earlier and who had been locked in stalemate since; the 1984 election, which confirmed the Democratic control of the House, did nothing to break that stalemate nor give his administration a new mandate or new burst of energy. In 1989, the president was new, but mandate and program were missing. Thus the theory is tested not in every quadrennial cycle but only in some: those in which a president takes office fresh from a campaign centered on policy issues, with what he conceives to be a mandate from the voters to put his policies into effect, and with the vigor and skill to make himself the leader not only of the executive branch but of the Congress as well.

Confirmation from History

Four times in this century all of these circumstances came together to produce bursts of legislative achievement that set the country in a new direction. The first of those occasions covered the opening years of Woodrow Wilson's first term, when the Federal Reserve Act, the Underwood Tariff Act, and other elements of Wilson's New Freedom were enacted. The second was the era of Franklin Roosevelt's New Deal, which began with his fabled "hundred days" and lasted throughout his first term and into his second. The third spanned 1964, the first year of Lyndon Johnson's presidency, and 1965, the year following his landslide election, when the Great Society was enacted. The fourth was Ronald Reagan's first year, with its historic reversal of the half-century trend toward expansive government and the welfare state.

Of these four bursts of creative activity, only the New Deal survived the midterm election. Wilson's New Freedom came to an end when war in Europe and the issue of preparedness split his Democratic party, leading to a loss of fifty-nine House seats in 1914. Johnson's Great Society ran out of energy when inflation, riots in the black ghettoes and on the campuses, and the Vietnam War all discredited his leadership. And Reagan's revolution stalled when the Democratic Congress concluded that its honeymoon with the opposition had gone on long enough and assumed its normal posture of resistance. In those three cases, the window-of-opportunity theory appears to have been validated, and the fourth case adds confirmation as well, for while the desperate circumstances during the Great Depression solidified the Democratic majorities in Congress behind Roosevelt's leadership for a longer than normal honeymoon, it too—despite FDR's overwhelming electoral majority in his 1936 reelection—came to an end by the time of the next midterm balloting.

The experience of almost every other president in this century likewise confirms the window-of-opportunity theory: honeymoons are brief, and the midterm election normally deals a setback to presidential leadership. The election of 1906 cost the Republicans twenty-eight seats in the House and plunged Theodore Roosevelt's final two years into fruitless conflict with Congress. William Howard Taft fared even worse; the Republicans lost ten Senate and fifty-seven House seats—and control of the House—in 1910. Herbert Hoover likewise lost the House to the Democrats in the middle of his only term, in 1930. Harry Truman's first midterm election, in 1946, gave the opposition Republicans control of both houses; in domestic matters, the two notable initiatives were those of Congress, the Taft-Hartley Labor Relations Act and an income tax cut, both passed over President Truman's veto. Dwight Eisenhower's Republican party likewise lost control of Congress in the midterm election of 1954, resulting in a stalemate on domestic legislation that lasted six full years—broken ultimately by the restoration of unified governmental control by the elections of 1960-64. Gerald Ford, Jimmy Carter, and George Bush all saw their parties' numbers in Congress reduced at midterm.

Eliminating the Midterm Election

Yet if the "window of opportunity" is open for only six months to a year at most, will a new president necessarily be ready with a program to thrust through that opening? Reagan was better prepared than most; he had a clear vision of the massive retrenchment of governmental operations that he desired to accomplish and he had a budget director in David Stockman who was extraordinarily well equipped—in background, in a zeal that matched the president's, and in ability to master budgetary detail—to translate the president's philosophy into specific fiscal decisions. The accomplishments of 1981 were legendary, yet before that year was over Stockman had drawn a vivid picture of the costs of haste:

> The thing was put together so fast that it probably should have been put together differently. . . . The defense numbers got out of control and we were doing that whole budget-cutting exercise so frenetically. . . . We didn't know where we were ending up for sure. . . . In other words, we should have designed those pieces to be more compatible. But the pieces were moving on independent tracks. . . . And it didn't quite mesh. . . . and we didn't think it all the way through. We didn't add up all the numbers. We didn't make all the thorough, comprehensive calculations about where we really needed to come out. . . .[12]

For a president who is less well prepared, more time is required to assemble a staff, analyze the issues, and define a program, and by the time the organizing and learning period is over, much of the first year may have passed. Even Richard Nixon, long experienced in Washington, failed to seize the opportunity. "The more we seemed to learn about the domestic system," a Nixon aide told Paul Light, "the less we could do. We had our best shot at the start of the term but didn't have the organization to cash in. By the time we had the organization, the opportunity was closed." Jimmy Carter had even more need for time to learn and organize; he was new to Washington and so were most of the members of his staff. So the first year was lost, and with it the chance for any notable achievement in the entire term. Light observes that in each presidency a "cycle of increasing effectiveness" coincides with a "cycle of decreasing influence." "Regardless of the President's initial expertise and information," he writes, "the first year of the first term is characterized by a surprising level of confusion. As the President and the staff settle the chaos, the opportunities disappear. By the third and fourth years, the President and the staff are fully trained for domestic choice, but the agenda must be restricted."[13]

---

12. Quoted by William Greider, "The Education of David Stockman," *Atlantic Monthly* (December 1981), pp. 40, 43, 45, 54.

13. Light, *The President's Agenda*, pp. 36–38.

If the midterm election could be delayed, or even eliminated altogether, the "window of opportunity" would presumably be opened wider. A four-year term for House members, as proposed by President Johnson in 1966, would allow the representatives two full years before the next election loomed as close as it does now on the day each member is sworn in. If the window has been, and is, six to twelve months, it would become thirty to thirty-six months. A midterm election would still choose one-third of the Senate, however, unless senatorial terms were either shortened to four years or extended to eight so that all senators could be chosen in presidential years. Since the latter would clearly be more acceptable to senators, whether or not more desirable on its merits, what has been called the four-eight-four plan (four years for president, eight for senators, four for representatives) represents one approach for those who believe a too-soon midterm election schedule contributes to the debilitation of the government.

For those who pause at the prospect of waiting four full years before rendering an electoral verdict on the course of government, a three-year term for House members represents an intermediate solution. This would appear to depend, however, on extending the president's term to six years, so that congressional elections would occur in each presidential election year. The six-year term for presidents has recently been advocated on its own merits, quite independent of any accompanying adjustment in House terms, usually with a proviso that the president would be ineligible for reelection. If the presidential term were so changed and the House term set at three years, a six-six-three pattern would result. This, it will be noted, would not eliminate the midterm election, only delay it. And after the midterm setback, the normal period of stalemate would last three years instead of two.

The Four-Eight-Four Plan

The case for short terms, for any elective office, rests on the contention that frequent elections keep officeholders "close to the people" and hence more responsive, more representative, more accountable. In a word, short terms are more democratic. Those who advocate longer tenure reply that too-frequent elections are a burden and a distraction, that an elected officer in fact needs some distance from the people in order to concentrate on the responsibilities of office and have the freedom to act courageously without fear of immediate retribution at the polls. This issue of responsiveness and accountability versus freedom to act is as old as representative government itself. Granted, elected officials must submit themselves periodically to the voters. But, in the case of the House of Representatives, how frequently is too frequently? How often is often enough?

If one looks to other governments, the judgment there is that every two years is unquestionably too frequent for legislators. A British Parliament sits for five years, or until whatever earlier date the government of the day may designate. Nations of the British Commonwealth have continued this tradition of long tenure. Some European countries elect for shorter terms, but three years appears to be the least; no other advanced country gives its legislature only a two-year life. These models must be considered with a caveat: constitutions are designed by politicians, usually by the legislators themselves, who can be expected to prefer long terms, and what is most convenient for the legislators themselves is not necessarily best for a nation. If it were, all terms should be for life.

Responsiveness versus Freedom to Act

A four-year term for the House of Representatives was not considered at the 1787 convention—a time when annual elections were the vogue—but in its first decision on the matter the framers did approve a three-year term. Too-frequent elections, contended Daniel of St. Thomas Jenifer of Maryland, rendered the people indifferent "and made the best men unwilling to engage in so precarious a service." James Madison seconded Jenifer's motion for a three-year term. One year, he observed, would be consumed in preparing for, and traveling, to the capital, and three years "will be necessary . . . for members to form any knowledge of the various interests of the States to which they do not belong." Elbridge Gerry of Massachusetts made the case for annual elections "as the only defence of the people against tyranny"; to him, a triennial House was as undemocratic as a hereditary executive.[14] After their initial defeat, Gerry and his allies contin-

14. Max Farrand, ed., *The Records of the Federal Convention of 1787*, 1937 rev. ed., 4

ued to protest the three-year term as too great a departure from the current practice (only South Carolina elected legislators for more than a single year) and from the presumed expectations of the people who would have to approve the document that came out of Philadelphia. The obvious compromise was a two-year term. That was adopted on reconsideration, and the matter remained settled.[15]

Some of the arguments of 1787 in favor of the three-year term are now outdated. Madison's argument about time-consuming travel disappeared in the last century. And his contention that three years were necessary for a representative to gain sufficient knowledge for his job lost its pertinence when the early practice of rotating House seats among the counties making up a district, and thus assuring a House comprised largely of freshmen, was abandoned. When the 102d Congress met in 1991, only 33 of the 435 House members—or 7.6 percent—were freshmen learning their jobs. More than 80 percent of the members had more than four years of experience in the House when the session opened.

The Jenifer argument that short terms discourage "the best men" from seeking legislative seats seems also to have scant validity today—even though Lyndon Johnson in 1966 reiterated Jenifer's position and repeated his very words. Frequent elections may be a nuisance, and an expensive one, but prospective candidates know that if they ever reach the House of Representatives their tenure is, in fact, likely to be long. In any event, while this judgment is necessarily subjective, the electorate in almost any district does not nowadays lack highly qualified and highly motivated candidates from whom to choose. Most of the House members and staff who discussed the issue at a 1966 meeting "either did not consider the two-year term harmful to recruitment or thought it played only a small role."[16] And the two-year term does not deter members from seeking to continue in the House, for few voluntarily retire after brief service. The eleven members—or 2.5 percent—who retired from the House, and from politics, at the end of 1990 (excluding those who were retiring to seek another elective office) averaged sixty-five years of age and fifteen years of

---

vols. (Yale University Press, 1966), vol. 1, pp. 214–15, June 15, from notes of James Madison.

15. Ibid., pp. 360–62, June 21, notes of Madison.

16. Charles O. Jones, *Every Second Year: Congressional Behavior and the Two-Year Term* (Brookings, 1967), p. 47.

House service. A similar list for 1984 comprised nine members, averaging fifty-eight years in age and fifteen in service.[17] The average age for the combined groups—sixty-two years—does not differ greatly from the typical retirement age of persons in other occupations who have early retirement options with generous pensions. In short, most members end their House careers not voluntarily because of the strain and the cost of biennial elections but because of death, defeat (or the fear of it), or ambition for higher office. House members have—up to the present, at least—found their careers satisfying and attractive despite the two-year term.[18]

The language used by Elbridge Gerry in advocating the one-year term likewise does not ring true today, but if "defense . . . against tyranny" is translated into modern phraseology—defense against "lack of responsiveness," against "lack of sensitivity," against "arbitrariness"—his position still defines the central issue. Reviewing hearings and discussions that followed President Johnson's four-year-term proposal of 1966, Charles O. Jones summarized the position of the opponents this way: "The House of Representatives . . . was intended to be close to the people. It is the job of representatives to stay in touch with their constituents so as to reflect their needs, wants, and changes in attitude. It is highly unlikely that members will do this job if they are elected for longer terms. The only way to assure that they will stay close to the people is to force them to come home frequently so as to be reelected."[19]

But, to repeat, how frequent is frequent enough? Senators, blessed with six-year terms, commonly describe their attention to their constituents as cyclical. In the first two years, they stick to their business in Washington and go home only occasionally (the frequency influenced by the distance of their states from the capital); in the next two, they appear in their states more frequently, looking for occasions to make speeches and greet constituents; in the last two, they go home at every opportunity and campaign as assiduously as members of the

---

17. *National Journal*, November 10, 1990, p. 2719, and November 10, 1984, p. 2147.

18. The average age of the twelve senators who retired from the Senate and from politics (at least temporarily) in the six-year period ending in 1990 was also sixty-two, suggesting that job satisfaction has been as great in the House as in the Senate, despite the longer terms and higher prestige of senators. In 1992 the proportion of House members retiring voluntarily was markedly higher than in any other postwar year, a development discussed later in this chapter.

19. Jones, *Every Second Year*, p. 35.

House. The latter, if given a four-year term, would surely behave similarly. In their final two years, they would visit their districts as often, and follow the same campaign schedules, as they do now. It is the first two years that would be different; the representatives would stay in the capital more, spend less time in their districts.

But the argument that representatives should stay "close to the people" applies least forcefully to those first two years. During the election campaign, they have been constantly and intensely in touch with their constituents. They have listened to thousands of them. They have presented their platforms, explained and defended policy positions, and received approval. Their mandate to fulfill their campaign promises, whatever those may have been, is clear. Why should they have to worry during the next few months about whether their constituents have changed their minds? If they have, of course, their representatives are not likely to remain unaware of it. But beyond keeping informed, which representatives can scarcely avoid doing, there would seem to be every reason, from the standpoint of responsiveness, for legislators to be kept free of campaign pressures—including the pressures of early and constant fund-raising—during their first two years so that they can devote themselves to responding through legislative activity to the promises they made to their constituents in their campaigns.

It is in the last two years that the real question arises. If the constituents by then have changed their "needs, wants, and attitude," the mandate of the last election will be obsolete and the member may be no longer representative. By that time, of course, the representative will be well aware of the next election and alert to every indication of opinion in the district. Will that suffice to assure responsiveness, or must the constituents have a chance to make their views clear by approving or relieving their representative and, in so doing, delivering a new mandate? That they may wish to do so is clearly shown by the midterm elections of 1946, 1954, 1958, 1966, 1974, 1982 and 1986, each of which revealed that a wide swing in public opinion had occurred since the preceding presidential election.

The difficulty is that the president elected two years earlier remained in office. Unless the president's term is shortened to two years—which no one has proposed—the midterm election cannot result in a clearly defined change in governmental direction anyway. All it can do is deadlock the government, or tighten an existing deadlock, as it did in each one of those cases. If a new direction cannot be decisively charted, would it not be wiser to permit the country to proceed along the old path a little longer, giving the governing administration and Congress another couple of years to prove the merit of their policies? Sometimes a policy that may look like a failure after only two years may appear much more successful after four. Especially when a new government introduces drastic changes, for the electorate to be obliged to render a verdict after only two years may be unfairly, and unwisely, premature. Stability and continuity of a government's policies are sacrificed, along with the opportunity for a sound test of the wisdom of those policies.

And, given the speed with which the midterm election bears down on governments, policies requiring political courage may not even be adopted. "I think that the four years would help you to be a braver congressman, and I think what you need is bravery," observed a representative during the 1966 discussion of President Johnson's proposal. Fair housing and situs picketing bills were cited as measures that were "too hot" for House members to be willing to consider that year with an election imminent. "If we had a four-year term," said another member, "I am as confident as I can be the situs picketing bill would have come to the floor and passed."[20] And those were not intricate bills. Complex measures that require an extended period for drafting or that require negotiation of differences among multiple conflicting interests are even harder to accommodate within the election cycle. The failure of Congress to enact President Carter's energy legislation, for example, is often attributed to the haste with which the program was put together and sent to Capitol Hill without sufficient advance consultation with leading members of Congress or with interest groups. Carter hoped that an early start would enable Congress to act equally quickly, well before the midterm election. But on so complex and hotly controverted a matter, extensive negotiations were unavoidable; they dragged on into the election season, and the program was for the most part lost.

In a debate on the budget in March 1992, Senator John C. Danforth, Missouri Republican, deplored the effect of the two-year election cycle on efforts to control entitlement spending:

20. Ibid., pp. 28–29. The situs picketing bill, which would have legalized "common site" picketing by labor unions at construction sites, was a key legislative objective of organized labor at the time, strongly opposed by the construction industry.

But no sooner is that suggestion put forward than people are saying, "Wait a second. Not now. No. Wait until next year. Let us not talk about controlling the entitlement programs, because this is an election year and we do not want to offend anybody by talking about the entitlements. That is too risky politically. We want to get through the election. Wait until next year."

So I am sure we will wait until next year. . . . to deal with the entitlements, to deal with the problems of the tax system, to deal with health care cost control. . . . And next year people will say, "Well, wait a second. Let us not do it because an election is coming." An election is never more than two years away in Congress. . . .

Deep down in our hearts we know that we have bankrupted America and that we have given our children a legacy of bankruptcy. We have been so intent on getting ourselves elected that year after year we have put off the hard issues.[21]

While all the consequences of any change in a governmental system can never be predicted with assurance, one can be certain that the changes in attitude and behavior at both ends of Pennsylvania Avenue that would flow from a longer time horizon would be profound and would affect the outcome of many legislative issues. The wider "window of opportunity" would enable the administration and the legislature alike not only to deal with Senator Danforth's "hard issues" but also to proceed in a more orderly fashion. Action that must now be compressed into a single year could be extended over two or even three. Bills that now expire at the end of two years would survive for four. In some cases, the result might be simple procrastination. If there is no hurry, why exert oneself? Yet congressional committees would be under pressure from the president, colleagues, and constituents to get on with the work. The legislative traffic jam in both houses would be alleviated, making easier the orderly scheduling of members' time among the multiple committees and subcommittees on which they serve. And the number of required hearings would themselves be reduced. Now, any subject of legislative concern not disposed of by one Congress must be reopened by the next from the beginning, with wholly new hearings (although they are sometimes abbreviated).

The four-eight-four plan was the solution chosen by the Committee on the Constitutional System to the problem it identified as too-brief "honeymoons" between newly elected presidents and their Con-

21. *Congressional Record*, daily ed., March 26, 1992, p. S4306.

gresses. The present system, argued the committee, encourages legislators "to distance themselves from the President and from presidential programs that may involve a difficult, short-term adjustment on the way to a worthwhile, longer-term result." The proposed change would "lengthen and coordinate the political horizons of all incumbents," provide a greater opportunity for "decisive action on domestic problems," and eliminate the "setback to the President's party" that "usually results" from the midterm election, weakening his leadership, increasing the possibility of stalemate and deadlock, and sometimes bringing the government "close to immobility."[22]

This recommendation has been criticized on the grounds that, first, it would fail to have the desired effect because the differing motivations and constituencies of presidents and legislators would still collide, leading to lack of cohesion and deadlock between the branches, and, second, that it would impair the legislators' autonomy and make them subservient to the president. These diametrically opposing arguments have even been embraced in the same critique, without explanation of how a constitutional change could be at the same time both harmless and dangerous.[23]

The former of these two arguments has the greater merit. Elimination of the midterm election would not in itself assure harmonious cooperation between the branches. If the House and half the Senate were chosen on the same date as the president, they could be as hostile to the executive as, say, the Democratic-controlled Congress chosen in 1972 was to Richard Nixon; their feud began well before the election and continued afterward, with a bitterness that only intensified until the day of the president's resignation nearly two years later. All that can be said is that the Congress elected in the presidential year is usually somewhat more compatible with the president

22. Committee on the Constitutional System, "A Bicentennial Analysis of the American Political Structure" (Washington, January 1987), pp. 5, 10–11.

23. Mark P. Petracca, Lonce Bailey, and Pamela Smith, "Proposals for Constitutional Reform: An Evaluation of the Committee on the Constitutional System," *Presidential Studies Quarterly*, vol. 20 (Summer 1990), pp. 516–19. These authors first contend that the four-year term "will not alter the compelling effects of constituent differences which motivate House members" and therefore "efforts to foster executive-legislative cohesion will be frustrated." Then they argue, without acknowledging the contradiction, that cohesion would be so great that the reform "eliminates the independence of the House from the fate of the executive" and would result in legislative "subservience" to the executive.

than the one elected at the midterm. Eliminating the midterm ballot would simply prevent relations from getting worse, as they are now bound to do whenever the opposition party scores its normal gains. To assure that they are harmonious at the outset of a presidential term would require attention to the problem of divided government, discussed in chapter 4, and other measures directed toward encouraging cohesion within a united party government, considered in chapter 7.

As for the contention that eliminating the midterm election would lead to "subservience" of the Congress to the president, this ignores the fact that every four years, since the beginning of the republic, a Congress has been elected with each president, and—in recent decades at least—those Congresses could scarcely be described as acquiescing in presidential wishes. While not significantly affecting the first two years, in terms of cohesion, the four-eight-four plan reform would designedly bring the level of cohesion during the last two years up to the level of the first two—which should trouble only those, if there are any, who consider the degree of unity between the president and Congress during those first two years to be usually so excessive that it needs to be regularly shattered by the holding of a midterm contest.[24]

In the discussion of the four-year term after the Johnson initiative of 1966, representatives who favored the longer tenure generally opposed election in the presidential year. Instead, they advocated staggered terms, with half the House elected each two years, or the election of the entire House at the presidential midterm. But neither of these schemes would eliminate the midterm election, lengthen the life of Congresses, or draw the executive and legislative branches closer together.[25] If those are the objectives to be sought in introducing

24. See my "Response to the Petracca-Bailey-Smith Evaluation of the Committee on the Constitutional System," ibid., pp. 538–40. The CCS recommendation finds academic support as well. Concluding his study of relations between the president and Congress over more than three decades, Mark A. Peterson—who describes himself as skeptical of most constitutional reform measures—argues strongly for the four-year term. Peterson, *Legislating Together: The White House and Capitol Hill from Eisenhower to Reagan* (Harvard University Press, 1990), pp. 287–93.

25. The same applies to the variant, sponsored by Representative Richard J. Durbin, Democrat of Illinois, based on that state's constitutional provisions governing state legislators' terms; members of the House would serve two four-year terms and one two-year term during the ten-year period following each reapportionment, with members divided into three classes for the purpose.

the four-year term, only a term coincident with that of the president will serve the purpose; any variant would probably widen, not narrow, the distance between the branches.

The Eight-Year Senate Term

In the four-eight-four plan, senators would be divided into two classes rather than the present three, one member from each state chosen in each presidential election. With half rather than one-third of the Senate at stake in that election, a trend toward either party would have greater impact on the partisan makeup of the Senate, giving the president's party somewhat more seats and reducing to some degree the likelihood of divided government. Fifty rather than thirty-three or thirty-four senators would share the mandate of each election, and to that extent the Senate would be more rather than less responsive to the popular will at the outset of each presidential term.

The House term could be lengthened without altering the present six-year term for senators, resulting in a four-six-four plan. This would not satisfy those who would like to see the midterm election eliminated altogether, but retaining that election for only one-third of one house would reduce its disruptive impact. The electorate of the thirty-odd states holding senatorial elections would be able to register a limited verdict on the course of government and by that means might bring about a modification of its policies without necessarily rendering it immobile. And if freedom from an immediate election can turn congressional cowards into heroes, two-thirds of the senators as well as all House members would be free to become statesmen—as they are now—although those two-thirds would be under pressure, as at present, from the one-third up for reelection.[26]

On the other hand, a four-six-four plan would surrender the advantages to be gained from extending the life of each Congress from two

26. A vote on May 1, 1985, vividly illustrates the effect of an imminent reelection contest on senatorial behavior. The issue was whether to support the agreement reached between President Reagan and the Republican Senate leadership to freeze cost-of-living increases for social security recipients as part of the deficit-reduction effort. Republican senators not up for reelection in 1986 (including one whose term would expire and had announced his retirement) voted 24 to 8 to sustain the leadership. But Republicans facing reelection voted 11 to 9 against the party position. With only one Democratic senator supporting the freeze, the full cost-of-living increase was restored, 65 to 34.

years to four. Theoretically, a four-year Congress could be introduced even without altering the terms of senators, by simply allowing one-third of the senators to take their seats at the midpoint. For a whole new class of freshman senators (usually from four to a dozen, but sometimes more) to enter at midpoint in each Congress would doubt-less strike the Senate as awkward and incongruous—even though a few new senators and representatives selected to fill vacancies during each Congress now enter after the sessions have convened. To assure the benefits of a four-year Congress, the four-eight-four scheme appears more promising than four-six-four. Senators would undoubt-edly be reluctant to initiate any move to lengthen their own terms, for fear of voter retribution, but the adverse reaction could be miti-gated by making the change effective at a date far enough in the future to be at or beyond the expiration date of the term of any current senator. And if the proposal were being pushed vigorously by House members and groups outside the government, the senators' self-inter-est would clearly lie in acquiescing.[27]

Those who object that eight years is a term of excessive length for any elective office, even that of senator, have an arguable case. If the electorate makes a mistake in its initial choice, even six years is a long time to wait for the opportunity to rectify it. Yet an eight-year term would not alter the makeup of the Senate significantly. Few senators fail now to extend their service beyond six years. Of the sixty-six senators who left office during the twelve-year period from 1979 to 1990, twenty-two had served one term or less—and of these, only seventeen were retired by action of the voters, or fewer than three per biennial election.[28] Sixteen had served all or part of two terms; fourteen, three terms; eight, four terms; two, five terms; two, six terms; and two, seven terms, for an average tenure of almost exactly

27. One obstacle to the idea of a four-year House term has been the fear of senators, and governors as well, of challenges from representatives who could run against them in midterm without giving up their seats in the House. This objection has, however, been met in recent versions of four-year-term amendments—including the one pro-posed by President Johnson—by the inclusion of a simple proviso requiring House members to resign if they choose to run for any other office.

28. Of the others, one (John P. East of North Carolina) died during his first term; three (Paul E. Tsongas of Massachusetts, Paul S. Trible, Jr., of Virginia, and Daniel J. Evans of Washington) retired voluntarily after completing full terms; and one (Nicholas F. Brady of New Jersey) was an interim appointee who chose not to run for a full term. Two of the seventeen defeated (James T. Broyhill of North Carolina and David K. Karnes of Nebraska) were also interim appointees.

fourteen years. Clearly, the electorate is not appalled at the idea of long service for its senators; the number screened out after a single term, for whatever reason, is small, and extending the terms of those few senators by two years each would have a negligible effect on the makeup of that body. To be precise, during 1979–90 eighteen senators would have served two years longer each than they did under the present system, for an average of exactly three of the one hundred senators.[29]

A four-four-four plan would, of course, remove this objection. While there has never been any significant adverse criticism of the present six-year term for senators, the voting public might well respond favorably to the notion of a shorter tenure. And if the entire Senate were chosen in each presidential year, the prospect for united party government would be enhanced. Yet the implacable opposition of a hundred senators to any suggestion that terms be shortened is not to be lightly counted by advocates of reform—even if it were contemplated that the constitutional amendment would be initiated by a convention rather than by the Congress. Staggered Senate terms, moreover, are now embedded in tradition. Since extending the present six-year term would have so little effect on the actual makeup of the Senate, the four-eight-four plan appears to be the more promising of the alternatives.

The Six-Six-Three Plan

Those who agree that two years is too short a time between national elections but worry that four years may be too long have an obvious compromise to consider—a three-year term for House members, as initially approved by the Constitutional Convention. But unless presidential and Senate terms were also changed, House three-year

29. The eighteen include the twenty-two who served one term or less except for East, Brady, Broyhill, and Karnes. None of the interim appointees' terms would have been extended under an eight-year plan, because each would have had to face the voters at the next regular election in order to complete the remainder of the term. Tsongas, Trible, and Evans would all have been heavily favored for reelection had they chosen to run, so the number of senators who would have served an extra two years against the will of their constituents can be put at fifteen (the seventeen whom the voters defeated at their first opportunity, excluding Broyhill and Karnes), amounting to an average of 2.5 of the one hundred senators.

terms would be incongruent with both. Half the time, the House election would occur in odd-numbered years. Only one House election in four would coincide with the presidential balloting. A national election would be held in three of every four years. Accordingly, the three-year term is not usually advocated except in conjunction with extending the president's term from four to six years and rescheduling senatorial elections so that half the Senate is chosen each three years. And since altering the president's term would be by far the most consequential of all these changes, the question of the three-year House term becomes subsidiary to the issue of making the presidency a six-year office.

The proposal for a six-year presidential term, in turn, usually incorporates a condition that the president be ineligible for reelection. And that provision is, indeed, the principal motivation for advocating any change at all—as it has been whenever the subject has arisen since Andrew Jackson's day. Much as in the Senate debate of 1913 (reviewed in chapter 3), six-year-term advocates consider that campaigning for reelection is a burdensome distraction for a president, and one that tends to reduce him from the level of statesman to that of politician and hence to corrupt the processes of government. But if reelection is to be forbidden, they argue, four years is too short a time for a president to accomplish the goals to which he committed himself in his original campaign.

The White House as Campaign Headquarters

Running for reelection does assuredly consume a president's time and energies, diverting him from attending to what may be pressing policy and administrative matters. "The public would be outraged if they knew, really knew, how much of the president's time is engaged in devising reelection strategy, which begins about 20 minutes after his election," writes Jack Valenti, who served as special assistant to President Lyndon Johnson. "Unhinge the president from the reelection process," Valenti urged, and thereby "increase his productive time in studying, learning, probing the economic riddles."[30] Johnson himself made the same point in his memoirs: "The old belief that a

30. Jack Valenti, " '6 Years in the White House?' You Bet," *Washington Post*, January 1, 1983, p. A15.

President can carry out the responsibilities of his office and at the same time undergo the rigors of campaigning is, in my opinion, no longer valid."[31]

And those rigors have been magnified in the three decades since Johnson campaigned. The proliferation of presidential primaries in the 1970s opened the opportunity for serious challenge to an incumbent's renomination at his own party convention, as Gerald Ford learned in 1976 and Jimmy Carter in 1980. Campaigning for reelection now may have first call on a president's time not just for a few months but for more than a year. Ford, to fend off a challenge by Ronald Reagan, was a half-time campaigner during the entire period between the New Hampshire primary in early February and the close of the delegate-selection season in early June. In that eighteen-week period, he made nineteen trips to twenty-one states, spending a total of forty-two days on the campaign trail. Jimmy Carter made clear that, had it not been for the Iranian hostage crisis, he would have done likewise in his contest with Senator Edward Kennedy, but under the circumstances he chose a "Rose Garden strategy," confining himself to a single one-day campaign trip before the Democratic nominating convention. In both cases, of course, the incumbent presidents campaigned extensively during the traditional two-month electoral period that begins on Labor Day. Even in 1992, when President Bush faced in Patrick J. Buchanan a far less dangerous primary opponent than those Ford and Carter had confronted, Bush spent twenty-nine days campaigning in nineteen states during the primary season, not counting a dozen trips outside Washington to address politically influential groups, though not ostensibly campaigning.

Even more important than the drain on presidential time and energy, in the view of those who would prohibit reelection, is the temptation for presidents and their subordinates to misuse the powers of their offices to win a second term. The Watergate burglary may be the ultimate illustration of governmental corruption to advance a president's ambition to remain in office, but surely every administration loses part of "its effectiveness for the public good" during the reelection campaign, as President Taft conceded after his own unsuccessful effort to win a second term. Edward Tufte has shown that some

31. Quoted by Foundation for the Study of Presidential and Congressional Terms, *Presidential and Congressional Term Limitation: The Issue That Stays Alive* (Washington, 1980), p. 19.

presidents have sought to manipulate the economy to achieve a peak of prosperity in their reelection year, at the expense of more stable and desirable long-run policies.[32] And presidents try to manipulate public opinion as well. "During my administration," Richard Nixon wrote in his memoirs, "excessive euphoria built up around the 1972 Peking and Moscow summit meetings. I must assume a substantial part of the responsibility for this. It was an election year, and I wanted the political credit for what I believed were genuinely major advances toward a stable peace. . . . Euphoria is dangerous in dealing with the Soviets, or with any adversary."[33]

Finally, it is argued that presidents, like members of Congress, would be more courageous if they did not have to worry about the effect of every action on their reelection prospects; they would rise above politics and make the "hard, tough, abrasive decisions" that they now tend to put off.[34] Cyrus Vance, secretary of state in the Carter administration, attested that in its last eighteen months the administration had lost "a great deal of the boldness and drive that we earlier had. . . . I am convinced that our handling of affairs in the Middle East, with regard to Salt II in 1979, and the situations that arose in the Caribbean would have been different had we not been in an electoral period."[35]

And when a president did act, his motives would be less likely to be questioned. As Jimmy Carter noted in endorsing the six-year term midway in his administration, "No matter what I do as President now, where I am really trying to ignore politics and stay away from any sort of campaign plans and so forth, a lot of the things I do are colored through the news media and in the minds of the American people by 'Is this a campaign ploy or is it genuinely done by an incumbent President in the best interest of the country without any sort of personal advantage involved?' " And because a president made ineligible for reelection would be given credit for acting in the national rather than his personal interest, his standing would be higher in the country and his influence in Congress would be greater.

32. Edward R. Tufte, *Political Control of the Economy* (Princeton University Press, 1978).
33. Richard M. Nixon, *The Real War* (Warner Books, 1980), pp. 266–67.
34. Valenti, " '6 Years in the White House?' "
35. Statement at meeting at the University Club, New York City, April 21, 1982, reported in "In Pursuit of Stronger Leadership from Presidents of the United States" (undated), distributed by the Committee for a Single Six-Year Term, p. 3.

"I think it would strengthen my hand with the Congress," Carter suggested.[36]

Lame Ducks, Influence, and Partisanship

The last point is the crucial one, for most hard, tough, and abrasive decisions require some form of acquiescence by the Congress, and a courageous president will still be ineffective if the legislators are not willing to accept his leadership. And the traditional view has been the opposite of Carter's; it holds that once a president becomes a lame duck, ineligible for reelection—which a one-term president would be from the moment of his inauguration—he loses influence with the members of his own party in the Congress. "One of the strengths of the presidency is that the fellow will be around tomorrow," Lyn Nofziger, long a Reagan associate, told an interviewer. "And remember the threat of running again and being reelected is about the only party discipline we have in this country."[37] The same argument has been, and is, the core of the case against the Twenty-second Amendment, which makes every president a lame duck in his second term. "You have taken a man," said President Truman with reference to that amendment, "and put him in the hardest job in the world, and sent him out to fight our battles in a life and death struggle . . . with one hand tied behind his back."[38]

The question becomes, then, how much would presidential behavior really change? One test can be found in the record of two-term presidents who, in their second terms, were in fact lame ducks, either because (in the cases of Eisenhower, Nixon, and Reagan) the Twenty-second Amendment was in effect or, before its adoption, they had renounced any ambition to extend their service.

No two-term president, in this century at least, passes the test of rising above partisan political activity in his second term. Senator Borah, in the 1913 debate, contended that Theodore Roosevelt had

36. "Interview with United Press International Advisory Board," *Public Papers of the Presidents: Jimmy Carter, 1979* (Government Printing Office, 1980), vol. 1, pp. 738, 739.

37. Ken Bode, "Reagan Runs Ahead," *New Republic*, February 18, 1978, p. 14; quoted in Foundation for the Study of Presidential and Congressional Terms, *Presidential and Congressional Term Limitation*, p. 17.

38. Paul B. Davis, "The Results and Implications of the Enactment of the 22nd Amendment," *Presidential Studies Quarterly*, vol. 9 (Summer 1979), p. 290.

exerted as much effort to win the nomination for Taft in 1908 as Taft had shown in seeking his own renomination four years later. Woodrow Wilson in the midterm election of his second term campaigned vigorously for a Democratic Congress. In 1952, President Truman spent twenty-six days of "whistle stop" campaigning in twenty-seven states to win election of Adlai E. Stevenson as his Democratic successor—and in doing so to vindicate his own record. This comes close to the thirty-five days spent in campaigning for his own return to the White House in September and October of 1948 (although Truman had spent another fifteen campaign days in sixteen states in June of that year). Dwight Eisenhower, the first president to be made ineligible for reelection by the Twenty-second Amendment, spent nine campaign days on behalf of Richard Nixon as his successor in 1960, which again comes close to the twelve days he spent on political tour to win his second term four years before. In Nixon's case, reelection did nothing to dampen his intense partisan ardor. He entered his second term determined to confront and master the Democratic Congress; he "threw down the gauntlet" to them, as he said in his memoirs. Freed of concern about ever having to campaign again, he appeared to consider himself relieved of the need to be conciliatory—which hardly makes for harmonious institutional relationships. And Ronald Reagan spent fifteen days on the campaign trail following the 1988 Republican convention, making thirty-one appearances at party gatherings in thirteen states and the District of Columbia, to support the election of George Bush and Republican candidates for Congress.

Among the second-term presidents, Nixon, Truman, and Reagan were unusually intense partisans. But surely Eisenhower would not be so characterized. Yet even a president with nonpartisan inclinations cannot attain his office without fighting the partisan battle as nominee of one political party and opponent of the other. And in that fight he depends on his party for support, develops loyalty and emotional attachment to it, and acquires obligations to it that he cannot lightly cast aside. Moreover, if his party is repudiated at the polls when his term ends, he will see it as a personal repudiation; by the same token, its victory becomes his. Any president elected for a single six-year term, therefore, would be far from indifferent to the interests of his party and of its candidate for election as his successor. Assuming that he retained his public popularity, he would speak at party rallies, as he does now, and would be photographed with his party's candidates for Congress. He would insist that the national chairman of his party be his personal choice, or at least acceptable to him. And he would probably take steps to make sure that the party's candidate for the next six-year term would be someone who would carry on the policies he had initiated. In short, he would not become a political neuter. That being the case, he would still face the temptation to use the powers of government for partisan advantage. And he would still be under public suspicion that his actions were politically motivated— perhaps not to the same degree that Carter said his motives were suspected, but certainly to some degree.[39] And what is true of presidents is true of their political appointees; those who are not yet ready to retire from public life will use their influence on behalf of their party's nominee, as President Taft acknowledged his own appointees did. Before the nominating convention, some will back various candidates. Their zeal may be somewhat less than if their president were himself running, but it will still exist. The difference in impact on the government will be of degree, not of kind.

Whether or not President Eisenhower behaved differently in his second term, there is little in his experience to support the Carter view that a president ineligible for reelection has a stronger hand with the Congress. Eisenhower, it is true, had to contend in his last six years with a Congress controlled by the opposition Democratic party, but divided government, as noted earlier, has become virtually the normal state of affairs in Washington. In any case, Eisenhower and the Congress were deadlocked on domestic policy issues throughout that six-year period. Relations were, if anything, worse in the second term. The Congress rejected virtually every presidential initiative as too timid and ineffective on domestic matters, and he in turn vetoed a long series of Democratic bills as too far-reaching and too expensive. In 1959 he disapproved two housing bills, two public works appropriations bills, and a farm bill, and in 1960 measures to assist economically depressed areas, to raise federal pay, and to expand con-

---

39. Carter suggested that "there could be some appropriate constitutional prohibitions against trying to be a kingmaker and being involved in choosing one's own successor." Such a prohibition applies, he said, in Venezuela. "Interview, April 27, 1979," p. 739. But one may question both the theoretical wisdom of trying to remove a political party's chosen leader from participation in the party's affairs and the practical enforceability of any such provision.

struction of sewage treatment plants, all on the spending issue.[40] In foreign and military affairs, the Democrats generally supported the president in his second term, but they had also done so in his first term. The tabulation by *Congressional Quarterly* of Democratic congressional votes cast for or against Eisenhower's position on individual measures shows no significant change between the two terms. In the four Congresses, Eisenhower was supported by 45, 50, 51, and 41 percent of the Democratic votes, with 40, 37, 35, and 44 percent in opposition.[41]

As for the effect of President Eisenhower's second-term lame-duck status on his own party, the *Congressional Quarterly* figures show some deterioration of support among congressional Republicans. Republicans in the two houses voted with the president four times as often as they opposed him in his first Congress, 72 percent to 18 percent. In the following Congress, the ratio fell to 67 to 22 percent, or about three-to-one. But in Eisenhower's second term, the ratios for both Congresses were only a little better than two-to-one, at 61 to 27 percent and 66 to 30 percent, respectively.[42] Similarly, President Reagan's support scores from members of his party fell sharply, from an average of 72 percent in his first term to 56 percent in 1985–86 and 45.5 in his final two years, after the Democrats regained control of the Senate.[43] These presidential-support "box scores" are far from a definitive measure of presidential influence; they do not attempt to distinguish between crucial votes on issues where presidential interest was intense and votes on questions where the president had announced a position but exerted no pressure. But whatever they are worth, the figures lend more support to the Truman-Nofziger contention that a president ineligible for reelection loses influence in the Congress than to the opposing view that he gains.

40. James L. Sundquist, *Politics and Policy: The Eisenhower, Kennedy, and Johnson Years* (Brookings, 1968), p. 428.

41. *Congressional Quarterly Almanac, 1955*, vol. 11 (1955), p. 66; *1956*, vol. 12 (1956), p. 107; *1958*, vol. 14 (1958), p. 101; *1960*, vol. 16 (1960), p. 107. The sharp decline in Democratic support in the final Congress, that of 1959–60, is probably less a reflection of a stiffening of partisan attitudes than the change in composition of the Democratic party in Congress with the increase in its ranks of fifteen senators and forty-nine representatives following the election of 1958.

42. Ibid.

43. *Congressional Quarterly Weekly Report*, December 22, 1990, p. 4208.

It remains dubious, then, that a single six-year term would significantly alter presidential behavior and, in so doing, enhance presidential prestige and influence. But to gain those speculative benefits, the people would have to give up three rights they now have—first, to retain a successful president for eight years instead of six; second, to retire a failed president after four; and third, to force a president seeking reelection to respond to the mood and policy views of the electorate.

Fifteen of the twenty-nine presidents who sought a second term after serving a complete or near-complete first term were adjudged successful and returned to office—Washington, Jefferson, Madison, Monroe, Jackson, Lincoln, Grant, McKinley, Theodore Roosevelt, Wilson, Franklin Roosevelt (for third and fourth terms also), Truman, Eisenhower, Nixon, and Reagan. Except for Lincoln, McKinley, and Nixon, all served for more than six years. In some of those cases, what the president had to offer was given fully in his first six years, and two more added little luster to his name, while in others, the president's leadership was undiminished in the final years of the second term. Not more than one or two of the eleven full second terms, however, could be fairly called a failure, and some of the presidents were so successful—as was eventually demonstrated with Franklin Roosevelt—that they could have had a third term for the asking.

On the other hand, of the fourteen presidents who sought reelection and were rejected, whether by their own party or by the country at large—John Adams, John Quincy Adams, Van Buren, Tyler, Fillmore, Pierce, Andrew Johnson, Arthur, Cleveland (after his first term), Benjamin Harrison, Taft, Hoover, Ford, and Carter—how many would have been effective leaders if their terms had continued for two more years? Some, such as Andrew Johnson and Hoover, had been discredited and reduced to futility long before their single terms had ended, and had even aroused such hatred that two more years of inept leadership might have brought violence, with its threat to every institution. In many cases, the country could hardly wait to admit its mistake and send packing the president it had chosen at the last election. In the absence of any mechanism for removing presidents who have failed but remain innocent of any "high crimes and misdemeanors" that justify impeachment (a subject discussed in chapter 6), a four-year term presents more than sufficient risk. Six years for an incompetent, erratic, or listless president would have been disastrous on at least several past occasions—and could be again.

Moreover, a president facing a reelection contest is forced to remain in touch with, and be responsive to, the people. That, of course, is precisely what advocates of the single six-year term are seeking to avoid. They seek to insulate the president from popular pressure so that he may act with courage. Certainly the Supreme Court, heading the branch of government that is wholly insulated, has been able to enunciate policies—school integration, for example—that the executive and legislative branches could not muster the courage to adopt. Cyrus Vance, Jack Valenti, and others are surely right in contending that a president protected from popular reprisal would be able to act more courageously in the face of either adverse public opinion or the hostility of politically influential pressure groups.

But a president protected from public opinion is also a president unrestrained by it. If he is free to act in the national interest, as six-year-term proponents insist, that national interest will be as he defines it. And will his definition be superior to the one that is hammered out, under the current system, in the heat of a reelection contest? It is significant that Richard Nixon did not throw down the gauntlet to the Washington establishment until his second term, when he assumed he could disregard the hostility that he might—and, as it turned out, did—arouse. In his case, lack of restraint led to disgrace and resignation, but another president might pursue policies equally unwise and, with greater luck, survive a full term of office unrestrained in those areas of national policy where the Congress lacked the means to take control.

President Reagan's 1984 campaign for reelection illustrates the power of the voters both to moderate and to stiffen an incumbent's policy positions during the season when he pleads for their support. In response to public opinion polls showing that many, or even most, voters considered him too belligerent toward the Soviet Union, he dropped the harsh and condemnatory language from his vocabulary and adopted a tone of conciliation. Goaded by the charge that he was the first president since World War II not to meet with the Soviet leadership, he met with the Soviet foreign minister and reopened communication on disarmament and arms control. Under pressure from the nation's elderly, he was pushed into a categorical commitment not to propose reducing social security benefits. Seeking to exploit the antipathy of most voters to increased taxes, he pledged never to raise taxes except as a last resort, which would prevent any such action for at least a substantial period after his second inauguration. Perhaps with an eye to Hispanic voters, he participated in killing the bill to control illegal immigration. Entering his second term, the president held to his reelection campaign positions and cited his pledges in opposing tax increases and social security benefit cuts.

In these five cases, each person will have his own judgment as to whether the shift in President Reagan's position reflected the national interest. Democratic theory holds that, ultimately, the people must control and direct the government; as Gouverneur Morris said in 1787, the hope of reelection is "the great motive to good behavior." But democratic theory also finds room for institutions, such as the Supreme Court, that are removed wholly from the electoral process. A judgment on whether popular restraint on presidents through the requirement that they face the electorate after four years is good or bad depends on one's view as to where lie the greater promise and the greater risk—in submitting the president to public pressure through the reelection process, in the interest of presidential responsiveness to the mood of the electorate as a whole and to organized interests within the polity, or in insulating the president from such pressure, in the interest of presidential courage and decisiveness.

However the six-year presidential term might improve presidential behavior, it would not improve to a corresponding degree the workings of the *whole* government because it would alter only one element of that whole. It would set back the date of only one election—the presidential—without recognizing that for all elements of the government the midterm election is the one that comes too soon. Unless House terms were also lengthened, the legislative branch would still be in a state of perpetual distraction, would still suffer the loss of courage attributable to the constant imminence of the next election, and would still adjourn every two years in a crush of hastily drawn and ill-considered legislation and unfinished business. Although the six-six-three plan would delay the midterm test by one year—which would be an improvement—it would compensate for that gain by extending to three years the period of deadlock that commonly follows each midterm election.

In contrast, either the four-four-four or the four-eight-four plan confronts the problem of the midterm election and extends the time horizon of all three elements of the governmental structure. Both provide more time for deliberation and courage, not just for the president but for representatives and senators as well. In choosing between those two plans, the difference in the practical effect is so slight that the question can be decided on the basis of feasibility. By that criterion, four-eight-four would appear to hold the greater promise.

Neither, of course, would resolve the problem of divided government discussed in chapter 4, but either would help. Despite the rise of ticket splitting, presidential coattails still have some effect. The party of the winning presidential candidate normally gains strength in Congress, as the 1980 Republican capture of the Senate so dramatically demonstrated. The probability of united government would be enhanced to some degree with a four-year House term. And the incentive to intraparty cohesion would last for the full four years, because members of Congress would know that in the next election, as in the one just past, they would be running not on their own but as a part of their party's presidential ticket. The force of this incentive would be even stronger during a president's second term if the Twenty-second Amendment were repealed.

Repeal of the Twenty-second Amendment

The Twenty-second Amendment has probably made no difference, so far, in determining who actually occupies the White House. The only presidents so far denied a possible third term by the amendment have been Dwight Eisenhower and Ronald Reagan. Surely Eisenhower, with his history of serious illnesses and his belief that no man over seventy should serve as president (he reached that age just before his second term expired), would never have considered another race. Reagan turned seventy a few days after taking office and would have reached eighty midway through a third term. If he would have considered seeking such a term in 1988 (in the absence of a constitutional barrier), it is likely that objections from within and outside the Republican party—magnifying the incidents during his second term that suggested age was already an impairment—would have been sufficiently fierce to dissuade him. Most future presidents would also voluntarily retire after eight years in the absence of the amendment, if the past can be taken as a guide. Only Franklin Roosevelt, of the ten presidents who completed a second term before the amendment took effect, even considered seeking a third consecutive term.

The importance of the amendment, then, is not its bearing on who occupies the White House, but its effect on the behavior of politicians when they know for certain that any president's second term must be his last. Harry Truman expressed with characteristic simplicity the view quoted earlier: with a two-term limit, the president would enter battle in his second term with one hand tied behind his back. The evidence from the Eisenhower and Reagan years suggests that the president is not as critically handicapped as Truman's language portended, but that he does lose influence over the Congress to some degree. The president's party in both the executive and legislative branches becomes less cohesive as candidates for president emerge and contest for power. If that is the case, repeal of the Twenty-second Amendment would tend to strengthen the president as party leader and hence improve cooperation between the executive and the members of his party in Congress.

Even a lame-duck president, as Eisenhower himself pointed out, still possesses great power, and strong and active presidents have managed to maintain their influence as party leader to the end—as Theodore Roosevelt, for one, demonstrated in mobilizing the GOP in support of William Howard Taft as his successor. So while logic might suggest that the Twenty-second Amendment was unwise, both in denying the people a free choice of leaders, particularly in a time of crisis, and in depriving the presidency of one element of its power, its adoption does not appear to have had major consequences, nor is it likely to. Meanwhile, the existence of the amendment does provide reassurance to those who still worry now, as many did in the 1940s when the amendment was adopted, that the presidency has grown so strong that an unscrupulous leader could sustain himself in office indefinitely through the abuse of power. Now that one president has been forced to resign his office as the consequence of abuse, that concern is less credible today than forty years ago, but the presence of the amendment may contribute in some small measure to public confidence in the presidential office and hence in the constitutional system as a whole.

Limiting Congressional Terms

As the decade of the 1990s opened, the public attitude toward government at all levels was sour. Journalists and pollsters alike reported that the people were in a mood to "throw the rascals out," both in state capitals and in Washington. They saw the national capital as full of bumblers and, to some extent, of crooks (the Wright, Coelho, and "Keating five" scandals were in the news) who could act decisively to raise their own pay but could not otherwise come to grips with such problems as the budget deficit, drugs and crime, or the loss of American preeminence in the world economy.[44]

People blamed the Congress more than President Bush, whose standing in the polls was then exceptionally high. At the beginning of 1990, one poll found that only 15 percent of the public had "a great deal of confidence" in the Congress while 59 percent had "only some" confidence and 23 percent had "hardly any"—proportions that had been relatively constant ever since the Watergate scandal had rocked the country nearly twenty years earlier. Another survey in early 1990 reported that only 20 percent of respondents rated the "honesty and ethical standards" of representatives as "high" or "very high." Senators came out a bit better, at 24 percent, but local and state office-holders were given high ratings by only 21 and 17 percent, respectively. In August, 24 percent of those interviewed expressed "a great deal" or "quite a lot" of confidence in Congress, a percentage lower than such institutions as organized labor (27 percent), big business (25 percent), and the Supreme Court (47 percent). And on election day, voters interviewed as they left their polling places disapproved

---

44. House Speaker Jim Wright, Democrat of Texas, and House Democratic Whip Tony Coelho of California both resigned their seats in 1989 following investigations of their financial affairs. The Keating five were senators who intervened to varying degrees on behalf of Charles H. Keating, a savings and loan executive whose institution had incurred heavy losses and who had contributed generously to the senators' campaign funds. After a long investigation, the Senate committee on ethics expressed disapproval of the conduct of all five, but "strongly and severely" reprimanded only one—Alan Cranston, Democrat of California, who had already announced his retirement at the end of his term. The committee termed his activities on behalf of Keating "improper and repugnant." Phil Kuntz, "Cranston Case Ends on Floor with a Murky Plea Bargain," *Congressional Quarterly Weekly Report*, November 23, 1991, pp. 3432–35.

of Congress's record by 73 to 20 percent.[45] Questions in other surveys produced comparable results. When asked "Do you think most members of Congress have done a good enough job to deserve reelection, or do you think it's time to give new people a chance?" 20 percent opted for reelection, 67 percent for new people. Similarly, 52 percent said the American people "should fire Congress for the difficulty it has had in passing a deficit reduction plan."[46] And all this negativism was expressed before revelation of the scandal that implicated by far the most members and suggested that corruption and self-seeking were pervasive: check kiting at the House bank.[47]

The Voters' Frustration

When the voters are in a throw-the-rascals-out mood, they can act directly on their chief executives—mayors, governors, and presidents—who are elected at large (except for some mayors, usually in small cities) and can be turned out by a majority of voters when and if they stand for reelection. But this is not true of legislators. All members of Congress, as well as all state and many city and county legislators, are elected by districts. And therein lies the frustration of the voters. The Congress *as a whole* is not accountable to the people *as a whole*. Each voter can act to throw out one rascal, but the others are beyond reach. And it is the others who have aroused the citizens; the single one on whom the individual voter is permitted to pass judgment is, in all likelihood, one with whom he or she usually agrees

45. The four polls were by National Opinion Research Center, February–April, 1990; the Gallup Organization, February 8–11, 1990; Gallup, August 16–19, 1990; and exit interviews by Voter Research and Surveys, November 6, 1990, covering 9,001 voters, all reported in *The American Enterprise*, vol. 2 (January–February 1991), pp. 82–83, 92.

46. CBS News/*New York Times* survey, October 10, 1990; and Yankelovich Clancy Shuman for *Times*/Cable News Network, October 10, 1990. *The American Enterprise*, vol. 2 (January–February 1991), pp. 85, 92.

47. The House Ethics Committee, which opened an investigation of operations of the House bank late in 1991, revealed in April 1992 that 269 present and 56 former House members had overdrawn their accounts. Some had done so only once or a few times, however, and blamed the bank for not crediting their deposits promptly. The committee considered 22 of the 325 to have "abused" their banking privileges. Speaker Foley emphasized that no government funds were involved (except that bank employees were on the government payroll), but he ordered the bank closed. Opponents seeking to oust incumbents were making the most of the issue; several of the most flagrant abusers were defeated in the 1992 primaries, and others were in trouble as the general election approached.

and who is often, too, a friend, neighbor, or at least a casual acquaintance to whom the citizen has access when it may be needed, and one who may have brought tangible benefits to the state or district— and, with reelection and greater seniority, will be able to bring more. Thus the Congress is in a very real sense an irresponsible body, beyond control by the voters, whatever their mood. And the same is true of state legislators.

The voters' dilemma and frustration were vividly evident in 1990. Despite disapproving of Congress's record as a whole by 73-20 percent, the electorate sent back to Washington 391 of the 407 incumbents running for reelection (or 96 percent), and only one of twenty-eight senators seeking new terms was defeated (Rudy Boschwitz, Republican of Minnesota).[48] Survey data confirmed that the voters were absolving their own familiar and popular representative from the blame that they affixed to the Congress as a whole. Thus the same polls that found a more than three-to-one majority believing that members of Congress in general *did not* deserve reelection in 1990 reported that a 44-40 percent majority thought their own representative *did* deserve to be returned to Washington. The 53-46 percent majority of poll respondents who rated the level of ethics and honesty of all members as "not so good" or "poor" became a 69-29 percent majority rating of "excellent" or "good" for their own representative. And while 41 percent thought at least half the members to be corrupt, only 15 percent so characterized their own representative. As the popular disapproval of the Congress as a whole reached an all-time low in 1992, falling below 20 percent, approval of "your own representative" still stood at 49 percent, but that was well under the 71 percent rating of May 1989 and scores above 60 percent throughout 1990 and 1991.[49]

That explains the popularity in the electorate at large of the movement to limit the number of terms for members of Congress. Term limitation is the only means by which the individual voter could get at all those *other* members—that largely nameless and faceless body of unethical, corrupt, and unrepresentative legislators who are sent

48. "Lame Ducks: Who's Leaving Congress and Why," *National Journal*, November 10, 1990, p. 2719. Of the defeated House members, one lost in his party's primary, the others in the general election.

49. Richard Morin and Helen Dewar, "Approval of Congress Hits All-Time Low, Poll Finds," *Washington Post*/ABC News Poll, March 20, 1992, p. A16. Other surveys produced similar results. *The Public Perspective*, vol. 3 (May–June 1992), p. 102.

to Washington by all those *other* voters. The disgruntled individual citizen is not satisfied to hear that what exists is the result of the democratic process, that the other voters are entitled to be represented by whomever they select, and that they can, and will, sort out the honest from the dishonest, the responsive from the unresponsive, and the energetic from the wornout and superannuated. Those other voters have not done so in the past; why should they be expected to do so now or later? The power of incumbents to win reelection whether they are dishonest or honest, bad or good, is simply too great; they are entrenched by years or even decades of shaking hands, distributing newsletters, speaking at luncheons and banquets, writing letters, doing favors, and taking credit for federal benefits awarded to their districts. The power of incumbency is so great that even when the country is in a conservative, pro-Republican mood, liberal Democrats will be returned to Congress to thwart the leadership of Republican presidents. What other solution is there than to impose some arbitrary restriction on the freedom of the voters in all districts to choose whom they please? The answer would appear to be in limitation of tenure, applying the same logic by which the electorate was deprived, through the Twenty-second Amendment, of its right to decide whether to give a third term to Dwight Eisenhower in 1960 or Ronald Reagan in 1988.

There is no question as to the popularity of the idea, in the abstract. The 1990 election-day pool of 9,001 voters leaving their polling places answered affirmatively by 70-28 percent the question, "Should there be limits on the number of years a member of Congress can serve?" Another survey a month later produced a 74 percent response in favor of term limits. When the Gallup organization combined the issue of term limits for House members with that of lengthening their terms, it obtained a 59-31 percent majority in 1977 in favor of a limit of three four-year terms and an almost identical 59-32 percent majority for the same proposition in 1981.[50]

50. Voter Research and Surveys, November 6, 1990; NBC/*Wall Street Journal* survey conducted December 8–11, 1990; both, as well as the Gallup results, are reported in *The American Enterprise*, vol. 2 (January–February 1991), p. 87. On the question of limiting House members to three four-year terms, the Gallup poll obtained less favorable responses earlier, with a positive majority of 49-37 percent in 1964 and a negative majority of 45-43 percent in 1969. The latter came after the public debate on President Johnson's proposal for four-year terms (with no limit on the number of terms), and the negative vote was probably more an expression against the longer term than against

In three states, voters had the chance in 1990 referenda to impose term limits on state legislators, and in all three they did so. Oklahoma, by a two-thirds vote, limited state legislators to twelve years. California approved its measure by only 52 percent, but that was a far stricter proposition, limiting state House members to six years of service and state senators to eight. Colorado, by 71 percent, placed caps of eight years on its legislators and—alone among the three— also set a twelve-year limit on U.S. senators and representatives. The action was prospective, however; it merely started the clock running, and the twelve years will not actually expire for any member of Congress until the year 2002—at which time the action will undoubtedly have to survive a court test to determine whether a state has the power to set term limits for members of the national legislature.

In the meantime, the term-limitation movement in 1991 suffered its first setback, when the voters of Washington state rejected a referendum measure to restrict the tenure of U.S. senators to twelve years and House members to six. There, consistent with national attitudes, the state's voters heavily favored the proposal at the outset, but in an intensive campaign, led by Speaker Thomas S. Foley, opponents were able to persuade a 54-46 percent majority that, however they might feel about term limitation in theory, in practice it would mean that senior and influential lawmakers from their state, particularly Foley, would be replaced at the end of 1994 by inexperienced newcomers who would have to begin their climb to influence from the bottom of the seniority ladder—and, once they had attained it, would have to retire. Washington would thus be placing itself at a disadvantage in competition with other states in protecting and advancing its own interests.

Advocates of term limitation elsewhere proved to be undeterred by the Washington defeat, and were going ahead with plans to place referenda measures before the electorate in 1992.[51] However, the logic of the Washington state experience would appear to be inescapable: any state acting alone would be deliberately reducing its relative clout

---

the idea of limits. When presented as a separate question, term limitation has consistently won large majorities in public opinion surveys.

51. Preparations for referenda were reportedly going forward in fifteen states, and all but one of the propositions would affect federal as well as state offices. David S. Broder, "Term Limits: The Movement Gathers Momentum," *Washington Post*, July 29, 1992, p. A23.

on issues coming before Congress. Moreover, even if all the states whose constitutions permit adoption of amendments or legislation by popular initiative imposed term limits, those states still would collectively suffer in the competition with all the other states whose constitutions contain no such provision. If all states are to be on an equal footing, the U.S. Constitution would have to be amended to impose uniform restrictions. And it hardly needs to be remarked that Congress is unlikely ever to initiate any such amendment; senior members are enjoying their lifetime careers in Congress, and most junior members are looking forward to doing likewise. Proposals for term limits (usually twelve years) have been introduced in every recent Congress, but have not even been granted a hearing. In the improbable event that public pressure for term limits becomes overwhelming, however, Congress would have the opportunity to couple the limiting of terms with the lengthening of them—which, a decade ago, the Gallup poll tells us the voters would have found acceptable.

Freshness versus Experience

Proponents of term limits contend that the forced retirement of senior senators and representatives would, by increasing the turnover rate, assure a younger and fresher Congress, one closer to the people, more representative of them, more open to new ideas, and more sensitive and responsive to developments in the country and the world. There is a partisan aspect to this, of course. More Democrats than Republicans are among the senior members in both houses who would be forced from office, and a more representative Congress that reflected prevailing political attitudes would presumably be, these days, more Republican. Indeed, some Republicans see term limits as the relatively quick and easy road to capturing control of the House of Representatives after four decades of Democratic hegemony.[52]

If the experience of the past decade can be taken as a guide, however, the GOP would be in for a disappointment. As seats have become open through unforced retirements during the Reagan-Bush era, the Republicans have not made significant gains. They held only

52. The arguments for and against term limitations are well summarized by former Representative Bill Frenzel, Republican of Minnesota (for), and Thomas E. Mann (against) in *Brookings Review*, vol. 10 (Spring 1992), pp. 18–25.

three more seats in the Senate and nine in the House after the 1990 election then they held in 1979, before President Reagan's first election victory. For all the reasons discussed in the preceding chapter, the Democrats have maintained a consistent advantage in recruiting attractive candidates for Congress and in electing them, and limiting congressional terms would not appear to affect directly any of those reasons. If the allowed period of service were so short as to discourage able people altogether, the effect would be felt by both parties, and presumably about equally. If the limit were set at twelve years, as usually proposed, congressional service would still be as attractive to Democratic as to Republican potential aspirants. So, were term limits in effect, the political and ideological makeup of the two houses would in all probability be much the same as now.

If partisanship can therefore be disregarded, it is left to balance the merits of a younger and fresher Congress against the advantages of a legislature with a higher proportion of experienced leaders. Were this being written thirty years ago, one could easily come down on the side of youth, for the critical repositories of legislative power in the two houses—specifically, committee chairmanships—were then bestowed automatically on the basis of seniority, and members who were ideologically rigid, unrepresentive of their bodies' membership, worn out, or even senile could gain and retain immense power. But since then the Congress has reformed itself. First, committee chairs have been stripped of much of their arbitrary authority and subjected to democratic control, both by the committee members acting collectively and by the majority party caucuses and the leaders and leadership bodies elected by them. Second, the automatic seniority system has been jettisoned; although seniority is still the principal criterion in choosing committee chairs, enough senior chairmen have been rejected by their party caucuses to make clear that competence, energy, and a reasonable degree of representativeness are requisites for leadership positions. The requirement of competence was reaffirmed in 1992, when Jamie Whitten, Democrat of Mississippi, was persuaded by the leadership to relinquish voluntarily—under threat of involuntary removal—his duties as chair of the House Appropriations Committee after suffering a stroke.[53] So the question becomes

53. Eric Pianin, "Rep. Whitten Gives Up Duties as Appropriations Chairman," *Washington Post*, June 10, 1992, p. A2. In his fifty-first year of service, Whitten was the longest-serving member in the history of the House.

one of whether senators and representatives who are competent, energetic, and representative should be cast out of Congress along with their colleagues who may lack those qualities, simply on the ground of length of service.

Here it is difficult for even the most dispassionate analyst to be objective, for one inevitably thinks in terms of personalities. Would the present Congress perform better if such figures as Senators Sam Nunn, Robert Dole, Edward Kennedy, and Jesse Helms and Representatives Thomas Foley, Robert Michel, Lee Hamilton, and Henry Hyde—all of whom are beyond the twelve-year limit—had been forced out some years ago? If the people of Kansas want Senator Dole to represent them, and if the Republicans in the Senate want him as their leader, why should they not be allowed to work their democratic will? And the same can be said of the people of the Fifth Congressional district of Washington and the House Democrats in regard to Speaker Foley. And would the United States have been better served in recent times if such conservative stalwarts as Robert Taft and Everett Dirksen and such liberal pillars as Hubert Humphrey and Paul Douglas had been limited to twelve years of service? A strong ideologue from either extreme might be willing to make the trade and eliminate them all, but observers from anywhere near the middle of the ideological spectrum would probably agree that the Senate was graced by the continued presence of all four. Moreover, despite the high reelection rates of incumbents, every two years the voters do retire at least a few unworthy or superannuated members.

Opponents of term limits point out that a legislative branch stripped of its most experienced members would be disadvantaged in competing with, and overseeing and controlling, long-tenured military officers and civil servants—not to mention their own highly experienced congressional staffs. People succeeding to leadership positions in the Congress would not necessarily be any different politically or ideologically from their predecessors, or more able or even more energetic. They might have more fresh ideas, but not the skill to make their thoughts effective. All that can be said for sure is that they would be younger, on average, but whether youth in and of itself is to be preferred to experience and accumulated wisdom in the workings of a complex government and society is certainly a questionable proposition.[54]

54. It has been suggested that the objective of rejuvenating the legislative bodies would be at least partially served if the tenure of members on committees—as distinct

Finally, the power of incumbency may well be overstated. True, recent elections have shown an extraordinarily high rate of reelection. But in the past when the electorate has been deeply disgruntled, it has often lowered that rate sufficiently to remold its legislative bodies. This happened in 1946, 1948, 1952, and 1954, when partisan control of both bodies was shifted from one party to the other; in 1980 and 1986, when control of the Senate was switched from the Democrats to the Republicans and back again; in 1958, 1974, and 1982, when recession and the Watergate scandal resulted in large Democratic gains in one or both houses; and in 1966, in addition to 1980, when the tide flowed strongly in the Republican direction.[55] In 1990, while the anti-incumbent mood did not drastically lower the incumbent reelection rate, it did reduce the reelection margins of incumbents of both parties.[56] Indeed, some supposedly "safe" members, such as Democratic Senator Bill Bradley of New Jersey and Republican Representative Newt Gingrich of Georgia, barely survived. If many months earlier, when potentially strong opponents were making their decisions not to challenge the incumbents, they had anticipated the prevailing mood in November and decided otherwise, the results might have been startlingly different. And the ability of the voters to oust entrenched incumbents was dramatically demonstrated in the 1991 off-year state elections; both houses of the New Jersey legislature were converted from Democratic majorities to "veto-proof" Republican majorities of more than two-thirds, and the Republicans

---

from tenure in Congress—were limited. See Albert R. Hunt, "Reform Congress by Limiting Committee Stints," *Wall Street Journal*, October 30, 1991, p. A16. The objection that experience and expertise would be sacrificed applies also, of course, to this form of service restriction.

55. Although the reelection rate of House members has been rising steadily for more than a century, the average age of new members has declined sharply since the 1930s—from nearly fifty to the low and middle forties—with the result that the average age of House members had declined to about fifty in recent years. The average length of service has also declined since 1970 and stands at about the level of the 1950s. Nelson C. Ometrius and Lee Sigelman, "Costs, Benefits, and Careers in the U.S. House of Representatives: A Developmental Approach," *Congress and the Presidency*, vol. 18 (Spring 1991), pp. 61, 67, 68. Proponents of term limitation who see the House as a body whose members are too old and have served too long may take at least a small measure of comfort from recent trends.

56. This was the first election since World War II in which the average reelection margin of House incumbents of both parties declined from the previous election, according to calculations by Alan Baron. Quoted by Hunt, "Reform Congress."

increased their representation in the Virginia Senate from ten to eighteen, or nearly half the membership.

The year 1992 was to give further evidence that incumbency was no longer king and that the voters are still sovereign and capable of registering their will. By August, voluntary retirements from the House had reached sixty-five—a postwar record—and another sixteen members had been defeated in primaries. Thirteen of the retirees were leaving to run for the Senate or for state office. Of the remaining fifty-two, who were ending their political careers, the reasons varied. Some members whose district boundaries were redrawn following the 1990 census stepped aside rather than campaign in unfamiliar territory, which in some cases would also have meant competing against an incumbent of the same party. Some of the House bank check kiters preferred retirement to spending an entire summer and autumn trying to defend their financial behavior. Some expressed frustration at the ineffectiveness of the government and the low repute of the Congress; Matthew F. McHugh, the New York Democrat who chaired the House bank scandal investigation, complained of being "frequently put in the position of defending my character for simply being a member of Congress."[57] Some of the primary losers were also the victims of redistricting and the bank scandal.

The Senate was likewise experiencing a high retirement rate, with seven voluntary departures and one primary defeat (Alan J. Dixon, Democrat of Illinois). The two youngest retirees—Kent Conrad, 44, Democrat of North Dakota, and Timothy E. Wirth, 52, Democrat of Colorado, each leaving after only a single term—both cited the government's incapacity to cope with the deficit as among their reasons for frustration. "The Federal budget is out of control," said Wirth. "Our debt is crippling. . . . The Congress is stymied by relentless and pointless maneuvering for short-term political advantage." He also described the "continuous money chase" required in campaigns as "not just time-consuming and energy-wasting, but ultimately demeaning."[58]

As the people were tiring of their political incumbents, so were those incumbents tiring of their jobs—and for much the same reasons. The anti-Washington mood was taking its toll even before the voters

57. Kenneth J. Cooper, "House Bank Probe Leader to Leave," *Washington Post*, May 5, 1992, p. A1.
58. Statement by Senator Timothy E. Wirth, April 8, 1992, Denver, Colorado.

made their final choices in November. The prospect was for the heaviest turnover in half a century in the House, and a relatively high proportion of newcomers in the Senate as well. Perhaps the Congress will appear sufficiently fresh to persuade the voters that tenure is already being limited effectively enough, and the movement for arbitrary ceilings on legislative service will lose its powerful momentum.

Electing the President

No feature of the governmental structure has departed further from the intent of the Constitutional Convention of 1787 than the method of selecting the president. In designing the electoral college, the framers thought they had created a body made up, as Hamilton put it, of "a small number of persons" who would "possess the information and discernment requisite" to deciding who of the nation's citizens could best serve as chief magistrate.[59] And those persons would not necessarily even be chosen by the voters; they would be appointed in a manner prescribed in each state by its legislature, and initially the legislators simply made the appointments themselves. The process was thus twice removed from popular decision: the voters would choose the legislators, who would choose electors, who would choose the president.

But within a few decades, the decision had been placed squarely in the people's hands. National parties had formed early, the country's familiar two-party system was fully operative by Andrew Jackson's time, the parties nominated candidates for president and vice president, they chose electors in each state who would support the party nominees, and the voters made the decision between the party elector slates. The electoral college, far from being a search committee composed of the country's most eminent, informed, and discerning citizens with the heavy responsibility of selection, became a body of relatively obscure party functionaries whose duty was simply the mechanical registration of the decision the voters had made.

But that still left three questions that have brought the electoral system under challenge repeatedly from the Jacksonian era to the present day:

59. *The Federalist*, no. 68 (New American Library, 1961), p. 412.

First, what happens if and when individual electors decide not to rubber-stamp their party's choices but to exercise the independent judgment the framers expected them to use?

Second, what happens if and when the electoral college, in its discretion, rejects the popular vote of the national electorate?

Third, what happens if and when the electoral college voting produces no majority and the contingency procedure of election by the House of Representatives is invoked?

The Faithless Elector Issue

Faithless electors have been a rarity. Historians count, at most, sixteen electors who have cast their votes for persons other than the party nominees they were expected to support, and not since 1824 has there been more than one such instance in any single year. In 1988, a West Virginia Democratic elector reversed the positions of his party's candidates, voting for vice presidential nominee Lloyd Bentsen for president and Michael Dukakis, the presidential nominee, as his running mate. Before that, the most recent aberrant ballot was cast in 1976, when a Washington state Republican elector voted for Ronald Reagan instead of Gerald Ford. Five others bolted their party tickets between 1948 and 1972, but of those who tried to organize a concerted effort, none could get even a single ally. These maverick electors appear as zealots, eccentrics, or publicity seekers who gained their positions through the negligence of the party organizations that appointed them, and none has affected the outcome of an election.[60]

It is possible, of course, that an election could be so close that even a single stray elector could determine the outcome. Larry Longley has noted that in the narrow election of 1976, if 5,560 voters in Ohio had cast their ballots for Ford instead of Carter, the latter's electoral college tally would have been reduced to 272, only two more than a majority; in that case, if only three Democratic electors could have been persuaded, by whatever means, to switch to Ford, the electoral vote would have been a tie, and a switch of four would have given Ford

60. A history of faithless electors from 1796 through 1976 is in Neal R. Peirce and Lawrence D. Longley, *The People's President: The Electoral College in American History and the Direct Vote Alternative*, rev. ed. (Yale University Press, 1981), pp. 97–99. The six defecting Democratic electors from Alabama in 1960, mentioned in chapter 3, are not counted as faithless, because they ran explicitly as unpledged to their party nominees.

the victory. The faithless elector issue, he concluded, is "neither theoretical nor unimportant."[61] And the Senate considered the problem real and important enough in 1934 that it approved by a substantial majority a constitutional amendment to eliminate the electoral college as a body of individuals and record a state's votes automatically for the winning candidates.

On the other hand, the faithless elector issue is one that can be—and perhaps is being—resolved by means short of a constitutional amendment. State political parties (or independent presidential candidates) can easily make certain that persons designated as electors pledge to support the party nominees, even requiring written promises to that effect. Moreover, fifteen states had by 1966 passed legislation forbidding electors to betray their party's nominees.[62] The constitutionality of such legislation has been questioned, but in any case the problem vanishes if state parties exercise vigilance, and most appear in recent years to have been doing so.

Nevertheless, the electoral college is an archaic and unnecessary institution that poses some degree of risk, however minimal. Should consideration be given to amending the Constitution to deal with the more serious questions discussed in the next two sections, the substitution of faithful computers for not always reliable human electors could and should be included in any reform package.

Electing a Defeated Candidate

Those who criticize the electoral college as undemocratic begin with two philosophical propositions: every citizen's vote should be equal to every other citizen's, and the candidate with the most votes should be the winner. If these propositions are accepted, the electoral college fails on several counts. First, the small states carry added weight because the number of electoral votes granted each state is equal to its representation in the Senate and House combined; thus Wyoming with three votes will have 0.56 percent of the electoral vote in 1992

61. Lawrence D. Longley, "Electoral College System," in L. Sandy Maisel, ed., *Political Parties and Elections in the United States: An Encyclopedia* (Garland, 1991), vol. 1, p. 329.

62. Robert L. Tienken, *Proposals to Reform Our Electoral System*, Library of Congress, Legislative Reference Service, 1966, pp. 9–11, cited by Peirce and Longley, *The People's President*, p. 100. They indicate that the number had not increased by 1981.

although it contains only 0.18 percent of the nation's people, while California will cast fifty-four votes, or 10.04 percent, representing 11.97 percent of the population. Second, because every state but two (Maine and Nebraska) casts its votes under a winner-take-all rule, the minority of voters in each state is not represented in the electoral college at all. If, for instance, California's presidential vote of 10 million in 1992 is split 51 to 49 percent, some 5.1 million voters would be represented by its fifty-four electors but the other 4.9 million would be "disfranchised." In a three-way presidential race, the proportion unrepresented could be a majority, as high as 66 percent. Third, the distribution of electoral voters is as out of date as the last census. In 1988, the allocation was based on a census eight years old, which severely underrepresented rapidly growing states such as California, Florida, and Texas while overrepresenting other states that had been losing population.

Each of these points has its counterargument. Not every U.S. institution embodies the principle that every citizen's vote should carry equal weight. While the Supreme Court has enforced the "one-person, one-vote" rule in the construction of state and local representative bodies since 1954, it cannot touch that bulwark of unequal representation, the U.S. Senate, and it is that disparity that was carried over into the electoral college. As for the winner-take-all rule, it prevails throughout the American electoral system, where the continental European concept of proportional representation has never found support. After every election, a minority—sometimes the majority—of voters remains unrepresented. Finally, if a census eight or ten years old is satisfactory for apportioning the House of Representatives, it should be good enough for the electoral college as well, and reapportionment on the basis of either more frequent censuses or estimates of population shifts would not be practicable.

The critical test, however, is whether any or all of those inequities might result in the election of a candidate defeated in the popular vote and thus brand the whole process as antidemocratic and—in the eyes of the losing party and of democratic purists generally—illegitimate. The president's claim to a popular mandate would be undercut and executive leadership weakened. Fortunately, the electoral college has passed that test in every election since 1888 (if only because Kennedy's disputable popular majority in 1960, mentioned in chapter 3, was not challenged). True, the electoral vote has distorted the popular vote margin, often severely, but obligingly has always skewed it in the direction that strengthened the president's position. It has magnified narrow popular vote victories into much more substantial electoral triumphs, adding from three to sixteen percentage points in the close elections of the past century. In 1976, for example, Jimmy Carter's 50.1 percent of the popular vote—a 2.1 point margin over Gerald Ford—was transformed into an electoral college majority of 55.2 percent, with a decisive 10.4 point edge over the incumbent president. In landslide elections, the magnification has been far greater. Thus in 1980 Ronald Reagan received 50.7 percent of the popular vote but 90.7 percent of the electoral vote, for a disparity of 40 points. This gain was almost matched four years later, when his popular vote of 58.8 percent was translated into an electoral majority of 97.6 percent. In 1988 Bush's 53.4 percent of the popular vote became 79.2 percent of the electoral vote.[63]

The historical record can be read two ways. One scholarly study attributes upsets like that of 1888 to the influence of one-party states and concludes that with the nationalization of the two-party system the chance for a divergent outcome between the two votes has become "remote" and "extremely unlikely." Its authors therefore find no reason to jettison the electoral college system on that ground.[64] Others look at the narrow escapes in this century as well as the previous one and contend that because some chance will always exist that the popular vote loser might be chosen by the electoral college, "the authority of the presidency and the quality of American democracy" stand always in danger of being "undermined." Thus the authors of a second treatise point out that in twenty-two "hairbreadth" elections between 1828 and 1976, or 55 percent of those for which popular vote totals are available, a shift of less than 1 percent of the national vote in key states would have changed the outcome. They acknowledge that any trend that produced a shift in key states would also affect voting patterns in other states and hence a greater national swing

63. Differences between the popular and electoral vote percentages in elections from 1800 through 1972 are tabulated in Judith A. Best, *The Case against Direct Election of the President* (Cornell University Press, 1975), pp. 56, 59. Differences for later elections are calculated from data in Richard M. Scammon and Alice M. McGillivray, eds., *America Votes 19: A Handbook of Contemporary American Election Statistics* (Congressional Quarterly, 1991).

64. Wallace S. Sayre and Judith H. Parris, *Voting for President: The Electoral College and the American Political System* (Brookings, 1970), p. 156.

than 1 percent would be required, but contend that the figures demonstrate that "mighty results can come from relatively small voting shifts" and that many past elections have held "real potential for electoral college crisis." In 1976, for instance, a shift of only 11,950 votes in Delaware and Ohio (0.0147 percent of the national total) would have deadlocked the electoral college, leaving the decision either to any one defecting elector among the 538 or to the House of Representatives.[65]

Since the defenders of the electoral college have to concede its clear inequities, they have to base their support on grounds other than principles of fairness. As in other issues of constitutional reform, politicians choose sides not on the basis of abstract principle but according to their judgment as to who would be the winners and losers in the redistribution of political power. In the Senate and House debates of 1969–70 and 1979 on the direct election alternative, some representatives of small states found clear and easy grounds for opposition in their states' prospective loss of the extra relative voting power the electoral college gives them. But, more important, many representatives of the largest states saw their states as losers also, and here the reasoning was more complex.

Because all the large states give their entire blocs of votes to whoever wins the popular plurality, and most of these states are relatively evenly divided between the parties, their vote bonanzas become the grand prizes of the national contest. And within these closely contested states are "swing" groups that, in a close election, may be in a position to decide which presidential candidate gets a state's entire bloc of votes. In the metropolitan areas of these large states, ethnic and religious groups—blacks, Jews, Catholics—gain inordinate importance. They are courted assiduously by every serious candidate, and their demands are heard, while the residents of smaller states—as well as middle-sized states where one party is dominant and the outcome is foreordained—can be taken for granted. Many of those states get only a token visit from a presidential candidate, if they are not ignored altogether.

Spokesmen for minority groups have been candid in defending the strategic advantage the present system gives them. Vernon E. Jordan, president of the National Urban League, testified in 1979 on behalf

65. Peirce and Longley, *The People's President*, pp. 206, 258–63. The three elections of the 1980s had popular vote margins large enough to keep them out of the hairbreadth category.

of a coalition of black organizations: "We like it [the electoral college]. We see our vested interest in it. We choose to retain it." The direct election alternative, he said, would have a "disastrous impact" on black people. Similarly, Howard M. Squadron, president of the American Jewish Congress, saw "unpredictable and possibly baneful results" in direct election and praised the electoral college because it "gives greater weight to Jews in the heavily populated states."[66] Other progressive groups, whose strength also tends to be centered in metropolitan areas, likewise predicted that direct election would dilute their influence. If liberals were to gain from retention of the electoral college, conservatives would lose, and when a vote on the issue came in 1979, some legislators aligned themselves in accordance with the ideological divide. But more followed party lines, with most Democrats—backed by President Carter—for direct election and most Republicans against. The ultimate voting pattern in 1979, wrote Peirce and Longley, was "somewhat muddled by complex cross pressures." The change was approved by a majority of senators, 51 to 48, but that was 15 votes short of two-thirds. Significantly, senators from the twenty-seven smallest states, the beneficiaries of the vote allocation inequities of the electoral college, split almost evenly for and against retaining their supposed advantage.[67]

If the electoral college gives disproportionate influence to the large metropolitan areas and their potent minority groups, that is defended by some scholars on the ground that, in effect, they deserve to be. Thus Wallace Sayre and Judith Parris argued that metropolitan areas "encompass many of the nation's urgent domestic problems—notably hard-core, long-term poverty . . . and environmental pollution" to a disproportionate degree, which are beyond the capacity of local jurisdictions and "have long been ignored by state and national legislatures." Moreover, the major metropolitan areas are "seriously underrepresented elsewhere in the political system," they contended—presumably referring particularly to the Senate—so that extra influence in the electoral college "produces a rough kind of justice . . . that seems to work."[68]

66. *Direct Popular Election of the President and Vice President of the United States,* Hearings before the Subcommittee on the Constitution of the Senate Judiciary Committee, March–April 1979, pp. 172, 183, 220, 196, quoted by Peirce and Longley, *The People's President,* p. 203.
67. Peirce and Longley, *The People's President,* pp. 205–06.
68. Sayre and Parris, *Voting for President,* pp. 136, 140.

Judith Best develops the argument that the electoral college also reinforces the two-party system. If the alternative debated in 1979 were adopted—that is, election by a 40 percent plurality of the popular vote or, if no candidate reached that level, by a runoff between the two with the most votes—it would encourage independent and third- or fourth-party candidates to enter the race, she contends. At present, such aspirants have no chance to influence the outcome unless, like Strom Thurmond in 1948 and George Wallace in 1968, they have a strong enough regional base to enable them to carry one or more states. But under the direct vote alternative, an independent or third-party nominee would not need to carry a single state but would only have to garner somewhat more than 20 percent of the popular vote to force a runoff in which the major candidates could be pushed into a bidding contest for the independent or third-party support. Beyond that, the entrance of a third candidate would invite additional entries, with the cumulative power to impel a runoff. Best speculates that in 1968, in addition to George Wallace, Eugene McCarthy, Nelson Rockefeller, and Ronald Reagan might have entered the presidential race, leading to perhaps as many as ten candidates in all and turning "the general election into a national primary" in which the moderate vote might have been split and extremists would have won the runoff slots. In such a situation, voters would have an incentive to cast a protest vote in the first round, knowing that they would have a second chance in the runoff.[69]

Proponents of direct election point to history to dismiss such speculation. Every president since Lincoln has received more than 40 percent of the popular vote—and even Lincoln, with 39.8 percent, would have passed the threshold if his name had been on the ballot in every state.[70] And this has occurred despite the rise of strong third-party movements from time to time. If a runoff election were to occur occasionally, it would be between the two major party nominees. The winner would be the majority choice of the nation, thus serving the ultimate purpose of direct election—that the popular victor not be denied office and the loser inaugurated amid cries of public outrage. The legitimacy of the presidency, on which its strength must rest, would be secured.

69. Best, *Case against Direct Election*, pp. 136, 140.
70. Peirce and Longley, *The People's President*, pp. 220, 242–45.

An ingenious compromise that would virtually assure the election of the popular choice while still discouraging a proliferation of candidates was proposed in 1978 by a task force created by the Twentieth Century Fund. This group, cochaired by Stephen Hess and Jeane Kirkpatrick, recommended that electoral votes be cast as they are now (although automatically, to eliminate the faithless elector), but that a national bonus of 102 votes be awarded the candidate with the most popular ballots. Under this scheme, independent and third-party candidates would probably find even less incentive than they now have to enter the race, because their chances of deadlocking the electoral college and throwing the decision to the House of Representatives—with all the opportunity for manipulation that would provide—would be reduced to the barest mathematical possibility and for practical purposes eliminated. Members of the task force who were on opposite sides of the direct election issue in the 1970s found common ground in the national bonus plan and were able to recommend it unanimously.[71]

Election by the House of Representatives

When Ross Perot withdrew his not-yet-announced candidacy for president in July 1992, the announcement dissipated consternation that had been aroused earlier, when he led both the Republican and Democratic expected nominees, President Bush and Governor Bill Clinton, in some polls. But the problem highlighted by his potentially powerful campaign remains. That is the anomalous method by which, in case the electoral college produces no majority, the president is elected by members of the House of Representatives.

For that purpose, as described in earlier chapters, the delegation from each state casts a single vote. This is by far the most glaringly undemocratic element of the whole U.S. electoral system; Wyoming's one representative in the House would have weight equal to California's fifty-two, although California's population is sixty-five times that of Wyoming. If a state delegation cannot reach a decision, it can cast no vote. In 1992, eight states had equal numbers of Democratic and Republican representatives; if all representatives from such states

71. *Winner Take All: Report of the Twentieth Century Fund Task Force on Reform of the Presidential Election Process* (Holmes and Meier, 1978).

supported their party nominees, those states would be voiceless. And if a state's delegation split three ways, so that no candidate won a majority, the Constitution is silent as to whether a simple plurality of the delegation could cast the state's vote. Moreover, the winning candidate must receive the support of a majority of the states. Assuming that some states were unable to reach a decision because they were evenly divided or for any other reason, no candidate might be able to obtain the support of the necessary twenty-six. If no decision were reached by March 4, the vice president–elect would be sworn as acting president.

All of this voting would take place under the most intense public pressure, beginning as soon as it was clear on election night that the electoral college had no majority and the election was headed for the House.

First of all, the problem of the faithless elector would arise with a fresh intensity. The independent or third-party candidate who was responsible for the deadlock—and who, given the two-party makeup of the House, would have no chance of election—would be in the position of kingmaker. He could strike a bargain with whichever of the leading candidates would meet his terms—reminiscent of the "corrupt bargain" of 1824—and then try to lead, or instruct, his electors to vote accordingly. But would they? Some would be bound by state laws to vote for their candidate despite his evidenced desires. Others would feel free to make up their own minds, as the framers intended that they should. Some might feel obliged to support whoever won the plurality of the national popular vote, or whoever finished second in the elector's home state. In any event, until the electoral votes were actually cast in December, the pressure on the losing candidate's electors would be intense. The losing candidate and individual electors would no doubt be proffered great rewards, material or otherwise, for their crucial support—and even if that were not in fact the case, rumor would have it so. Ever since George Wallace failed to deadlock the electoral college in 1968, many observers have contended that such a logjam, with its opportunity for deal making on national policy, must have been his real objective, since neither he nor anyone else expected he would win the electoral majority.

But assuming that no deals were struck and the election did proceed to the venue of the House, all of the pressure that had begun mounting on election night would come to bear upon the members of the House.

They would face the same set of questions the electors had already faced. It was commonly assumed in 1992 that if the election went to the House its members would put party loyalty first. Thus, with its virtually guaranteed Democratic majority, the House would automatically elect Governor Clinton even if he had been outpolled by President Bush in the popular tally. But would enough House Democrats take the risk of provoking the voters' wrath by overturning their decision? Most representatives were still uncommitted on their course of action when Perot withdrew, but those who had commented expressed divergent points of view. Some said they would respect the national electorate's judgment and support the favorite. Others demurred that their decision might depend on the closeness of the vote. Some said they would reflect the majority opinion of their own constituents. Others declared a solemn personal responsibility to cast their own votes for whichever candidate they felt would make the better president—once again invoking the intention of the framers. Although couched in terms of responsibility and principle, such a stance could serve primarily as a cover for party loyalty, for the principled representatives would be bound to conclude that the candidate they supported in the election campaign—meaning the candidate of their party—would be the better leader.

As the time of voting approached, the pressure would be concentrated on the fewer and fewer representatives who remained uncommitted. Assuming that the Democrats were close to controlling a majority of states, the decisive votes would be those of potential Democratic defectors. Once again, the opportunity for bargaining would be unsurpassed, as would the prospect of reward. Both sides would cry accusations of corruption, and some of the allegations might even rest on fact. In the spring of 1992, commentators were writing lurid scenarios of the House election prospect. At the extreme, observers noted, it might fall to the one House member who was neither a Democrat nor a Republican—Socialist Bernard Sanders of Vermont, who would have power equal to that of all fifty-two California members combined—to make single-handedly the final decision that chose the president. Perot himself cited the "disruptive" nature of a prospective House election in his withdrawal statement.[72]

72. "Perot: Our Objective Is to Improve Our Country," *Washington Post*, July 17, 1992, p. A19.

By that time, a national consensus appeared to be forming that the contingency procedure had so many flaws that, whatever the outcome of the 1992 campaign, at least that aspect of the electoral college system had to be changed. It was flagrantly unfair in equating Wyoming or Vermont with California. It could readily result in rejection of the popular vote winner in favor of the runner-up. It created alarming opportunities for manipulation and corruption. It conferred enormous power, as well as a tremendous burden, on the few members of the House who would hold the decision in their hands. And, because the decision lay in the legislature, the basic concept of the separation of powers would be violated. It was to shield the president from dependency on the Congress, after all, that led the framers to finally reject the Virginia plan and design the electoral college as the alternative to selection of the president by the legislators.

Various corrective proposals were being discussed before Perot's withdrawal. At the very least, the disparity among the states had to be rectified, perhaps by entrusting the election to a majority of the House or to a larger body combining the membership of both houses. Advocates of the direct popular vote for president saw the discontent with the contingency procedure as another argument on their side: the surest and simplest way was to abolish the electoral college and leave the decision to the national electorate. The "national bonus" plan proposed by the Twentieth Century Fund task force would make an electoral college deadlock the rarest of eventualities, but the task force suggested that if it should occur, there could be a runoff election between the top two candidates. But the two ideas are not interdependent. Without a bonus system, a deadlock could be resolved by a runoff between the two leading candidates, to be decided either by a new electoral college or by the popular vote.

Once a president is securely installed in office in 1993, the American people will in all likelihood put out of mind the perils of the present election process that many saw so clearly half a year before. But if the major national parties continue to disintegrate and each quadrennium brings improved prospects for independent and third-party candidates—especially some as appealing as Perot but more determined and more skilled in politics—the fragile presidential election system needs to be placed at the top of the agenda for constitutional reformers.

CHAPTER SIX

Reconstituting a Failed Government

All governments descend into periods of ineffectiveness, when for any of a wide range of causes leadership fails, public confidence is lost, and conflicts within the government deepen and remain unresolved. When this occurs, parliamentary systems possess a safeguard; their governments can be dissolved at any time and new elections can then install new leaders with a fresh mandate from the people. Or weak leaders can be replaced with stronger ones even in the absence of elections, without provoking a constitutional crisis—as Neville Chamberlain was forced to give way to Winston Churchill following British defeats early in World War II.

The United States, in contrast, is in bondage to the calendar. The nation's leader is elected for four years, and no matter what his failures the office is his as a kind of property right until his term's scheduled expiration—with two exceptions. He may be removed under the impeachment clause of the Constitution if he is convicted of "treason, bribery, or other high crimes and misdemeanors." He may also be relieved of his duties under the Twenty-fifth Amendment, adopted in 1967, if the vice president and a majority of the cabinet declare him to be unable to perform the functions of his office and, in the event the president disputes that finding, two-thirds of both houses of Congress confirm his incapacity.

Eight of the nation's thirty-nine presidents have died in office, but only one has failed for any other reason to complete his term—Richard Nixon. But Nixon's case, perhaps more than any other, illustrates the hazards of the American system. When he resigned after serving nineteen months of his second term, the universal reaction was one of relief that "the system worked," rescuing the country from the final twenty-nine months of a presidency that had hopelessly collapsed. Yet a review of the events of 1973-74 suggests that the outcome was fortuitous.

For more than a year, from the time that the Watergate scandal began to unfold in 1973 until Nixon's resignation in August 1974, the country was in the throes of a constitutional crisis. Most Americans agreed that the president had flagrantly abused his powers, had presided over and tolerated, if not connived in, outrageous and widespread crime. Yet there was a grave question as to whether anything could be done about it under the Constitution. Nixon and his supporters contended that for a president to be "hounded" out of office would establish a precedent that would damage the presidency and destabilize the constitutional system. His opponents had only one recourse under the Constitution—impeachment—and removal would require that the president be convicted of criminal activity. Some argued that the "high crimes and misdemeanors" clause was intended to have a broader meaning, but because conviction and removal would require the assent of two-thirds of the Senate, the interpretation of the clause in any impeachment trial could not ultimately be any broader than any minority of thirty-four of the one hundred senators would permit—and Nixon had more than that number of solid backers. Luckily, on August 5, one more tape was discovered, which contained incontrovertible evidence of the personal, indictable crime—obstruction of justice. Nixon's support melted away, and four days later he resigned.

But the episode laid bare the weaknesses in the impeachment process and the need to consider alternative means for removing unfit presidents. What would have happened if the final tape had never been discovered, or if the crime had not been recorded on tape at all, or if the tape had been destroyed? Surely, no future president will preserve the evidence of his own malfeasance. In any of those events, the House Judiciary Committee would have gone ahead with its impeachment and the country would have been embroiled in the bitterest of debates about whether a president should be convicted and deposed on circumstantial evidence alone. Because crimes were committed by the president's closest associates, he must have "approved, condoned, and acquiesced in" them, the committee charged, but would sixty-seven senators ever agree to that?[1] If they did not, a discredited president would have every right to remain in office unable to lead and govern the country. And in any case, the whole world would witness the U.S. government immobilized while its president sat figuratively in the dock being tried as a common criminal in the glare of television cameras. No one would know whether the trial would last three months, or six, or even longer. And what of other crises that might well up for attention in the meantime?

Criminal activity is only one circumstance that can render a president unable to lead and govern. Andrew Johnson enraged the country not by flirting with common crime but by pursuing unpopular policies and then defying an act of Congress designed to restrain him by what he contended were unconstitutional means. A House majority impeached him, and the Senate failed to convict by only a single vote. While the trial was in progress the government was incapacitated, and long before it was over, Johnson's presidency was destroyed. But a century ago the country could survive without a government better than it could today. Moreover, the trial occurred only a few months before the 1868 election, when a new executive reflecting the views of the Congress and the country would be chosen.

Other longer periods of governmental ineffectiveness can be identified, if one uses as the criterion the public judgment at the time. The clearest recent case is the more than three years that elapsed between the stock market crash of 1929 that precipitated the Great Depression and the inauguration of Franklin Roosevelt in 1933. Herbert Hoover clearly failed to give the country the leadership it was demanding, as evidenced by the Democratic gains in the midterm election of 1930 and even more emphatically by Hoover's personal repudiation in 1932. To cite a case is to invite argument as to whether the public judgment was correct. After all, the people delivered Harry Truman a similar rebuke in the midterm election of 1946 but changed their mind and gave him a new term two years later. And the Democratic tide in the 1982 election suggests that the voters at midterm had adjudged Ronald Reagan's policies a failure—a judgment which, if made, was clearly reversed in 1984. But however one may feel about

---

1. Article I, Obstruction of Justice, adopted by House Judiciary Committee, July 27, 1974, reprinted in *Congressional Quarterly Almanac, 1974*, vol. 30 (1975), p. 884.

a particular case, whether that of Hoover or someone else, it can hardly be disputed that a president *can* fail, that he can early in his term be shown up as inadequate to lead the country and fulfill the heavy responsibilities of his office. That is a hazard of human nature that applies to the occupant of any job, exacerbated in the case of the presidency by the almost superhuman demands of the office and the anything-can-happen process by which those who hold it are originally selected.

In other large organizations, no matter how carefully their chief executives are chosen, it is taken for granted that the power of removal in case of failure must exist. A corporate board of directors may remove its chief executive officer, a school board its superintendent, a university board of trustees its president, a city council its city manager, and so on, and in the case of private organizations there is no necessity even to show cause. A parliament may similarly remove its prime minister, at any time and for any reason. The U.S. government, and the state and city governments modeled after it, are virtually unique among all the world's organizations in possessing no true safeguard against executive failure.

One can identify five categories of circumstances in which a president would lose his capacity to lead the country yet could not be removed from office under the Constitution.

First, a pattern of criminal conduct that clearly stems from the president's office yet cannot be traced to the president personally. In other words, the president covers his tracks—which Nixon so conspicuously failed to do.

Second, a pattern of abuse of power for personal or partisan ends that is corruptive yet not specifically in violation of any criminal statute. A president could be exposed and even impeached, but if one-third plus one of the Senate insisted that the impeachment clause required criminal culpability, he would be sustained in office.

Third, the mental or emotional breakdown of a president that is not clear and provable enough to be grounds for declaring him disabled under the Twenty-fifth Amendment. Under its terms, for a president to be relieved of his duties against his will requires a kind of palace coup; the initiative must be taken by the vice president, invariably a presidential loyalist nowadays, and a majority of the cabinet, all presidential appointees.[2] The presidency is the country's very symbol of

2. The Twenty-fifth Amendment provides that the Congress may create or designate some "other body" to substitute for the cabinet in taking the initiative jointly with

solidity and certitude, so one shrinks from even admitting the possibility that a president might gradually, or suddenly, break under
the strains of office and become erratic or impulsive in his judgments,
or lethargic and indecisive, or suffer delusions of grandeur or per-
secution or the early stages of senility. But it could happen. It has
happened to prime ministers of other countries, to governors, to
members of Congress, to cabinet officers, under far less severe stress
than that to which a president is subjected almost every day.

Fourth, a general and irremediable loss of public confidence in the
president, for reasons other than any of the above, as was the case
with Herbert Hoover.

Fifth, a systemic deadlock between the executive and legislative
branches so severe as to cripple the capacity of the government to
cope with crisis. This could happen to a healthy, competent, and
assertive president, but one unable to lead a Congress controlled by
an opposition that was solidly organized and equally determined.
The Andrew Johnson case is the clearest illustration of executive-
legislative deadlock, but the later years of Richard Nixon's administration and all of Gerald Ford's demonstrated that the president and
the Congress can be so hopelessly at odds on both foreign and domestic policy that the country can have no coherent policy at all. In any
period of a government divided between the parties, the government
can come perilously close to that condition.

Whatever the desirability of an easier method of removing failed
presidents elected for four-year terms, the issue becomes considerably
sharper if extending the president's term to six years is contemplated.
The country can survive short periods of ineffective government, but
with a six-year presidency a failed leader could remain in office for
as long as four to five years after his failure was established. That
would be more than inconvenient. It could well be intolerable.

---

the vice president. When the amendment was being drafted, suggestions were made
that the "other body" might include members of the legislative and judicial branches
or might be made up of physicians. The Congress has not seriously considered any
alternative to the cabinet. A commission created by the White Burkett Miller Center
of Public Affairs at the University of Virginia recommended against any such action,
finding it "unlikely that any other body could be designed that would be free of other
difficulties or receive as much political acceptance." Miller Center, *Report of the Miller
Center Commission on Presidential Disability and the Twenty-fifth Amendment* (University
Press of America, 1988), p. 18.

Similarly, if congressional terms are lengthened in such a way that the present midterm election is eliminated, the question of an additional safeguard against prolonged deadlock gains pertinence. The present midterm election has not in fact proved to be a serviceable mechanism for resolving deadlocks; it tends instead to intensify conflict and reinforce any executive-legislative impasses, by increasing the strength in Congress of the party in opposition to the president. But it at least gives the electorate an opportunity to express a judgment about the course of government and, if it chooses, deliver a forceful mandate. A four-eight-four plan, as discussed in chapter 5, would protect the Congress as well as the president from public retaliation for a full four years. To free elected officials from the pressure of a certain new election after only two years of a new presidential term has the potential benefits outlined in the earlier discussion, but it increases the danger that a failed government could remain in place too long.

Special Elections as the Remedy

Were governmental failure always the consequence of presidential sins of commission or omission—the first four of the five sets of circumstances listed above—the remedy could be sought in some additional method of removing the chief executive from office.

The simplest approach would be to broaden the impeachment clause of the Constitution by adding to "treason, bribery, or other high crimes and misdemeanors" some broad term such as *maladministration*, the word suggested by Mason and Gerry at the convention, or by making presidents impeachable "when they have dramatically and irremediably lost the confidence of the nation," as recently suggested by James MacGregor Burns.[3] At first glance, such a change might appear to place the president too much at the mercy of the Congress, subjecting him to removal for petty, partisan, even whimsical reasons. But the barriers to improper use of a broadened impeachment power would remain formidable. Since two-thirds of the Senate would have to concur in the removal action, it normally could not be

3. James MacGregor Burns, *The Power to Lead: The Crisis of the American Presidency* (Simon and Schuster, 1984), p. 237.

taken without some degree of bipartisan support. The opposition party would almost always lack the votes to act alone; it has rarely held as many as two-thirds of Senate seats in the modern era of two-party competition, and even when it has had that much voting strength it has had neither the ideological unity nor the organizational discipline that would be required to produce anything approaching a solid party vote.

Even in the face of certain defeat in the Senate, a House controlled by the opposition would have the power to impeach a president as a partisan maneuver to embarrass him, because only a majority vote is required there (a requirement that could, of course, be raised). But the very gravity of the action would hold the legislators back; one recalls the agitated faces and agonized words of the House Judiciary Committee members in 1974 as they were making their fateful decision to impeach Richard Nixon, fearful that they might be toppling not just an individual president but the presidency itself. In a parliamentary country, a vote of "no confidence" only changes the government-of-the-day while the chief of state—a monarch or a figurehead president—remains as the symbol of stability. In this country, removing the president deposes the chief of state himself, even though the vice president succeeds immediately to that office.

Legislators would also be deterred by the risk of the voters' retribution if they were perceived to be acting precipitately or from petty or partisan motives. In a parliamentary government, again, the prime minister is selected by the legislators rather than directly by the people, so if they remove that officer they are only changing their own minds. But for an American Congress to remove the president would be to reverse the decision of the people themselves, as expressed in the last election. Presumably, the voters would not look kindly on legislators who acted hastily, without compelling reasons, or out of crass partisanship, to upset the judgment of the electorate. One may guess that they would do so only under overwhelming and sustained public pressure. In this century, probably only Nixon, and perhaps Hoover, aroused mass hostility on the scale necessary to provoke a reluctant Congress, had it possessed an unrestrained removal power.

Whether or not a broadened impeachment power might be overused, however, it would be an undesirable mechanism for other reasons. It would remain a judicial process, with the chief justice of the Supreme Court presiding, members of the House as prosecutors, and the president on public trial. Whether that process is any longer appropriate even when the grounds for removal are limited to crime may be questioned. One may ponder what would happen to the position of the United States in world affairs if the president were subjected to a long proceeding, reported breathlessly each day to the global audience through its television news, even if (like Andrew Johnson) he were ultimately acquitted. One may worry, too, about the consequences of immobilizing the government for the duration of the ordeal. A reevaluation of the suitability of the existing impeachment process in the modern age is needed in any case. But if the grounds for removal were extended to cover maladministration or any other of the many possible forms that presidential failure may take, the impeachment process is clearly inappropriate, for the decision becomes a matter for prudent judgment—for responsible political judgment in the best sense of that word—rather than judicial proof.

As Charles Hardin has written:

> Emphasis on the *legal* criminality of *individuals* hides and even denies the *political* responsibility that must be *collective*. . . . Political adequacy is judged not by weighing individual guilt or innocence according to the rules of evidence but rather by political procedures for testing the prudence and judgment of government. . . . The political process should be capable of registering the collective judgment of responsible politicians—who, in turn, are informed by their sense of public opinion—on the prudence and wisdom of governments. The legality of a president's acts may figure in such judgments, but more important are decisions on presidential prudence, grasp of events, will, wisdom, and self-control.[4]

Finally, were a president to be removed through trial and conviction under an impeachment procedure, for whatever reason, the vice president would succeed to the presidential office, and that person might not be a suitable successor. The vice president might be associated with the acts and policies that destroyed congressional and public confidence in the president and so be equally discredited.

For all these reasons, a simple system for calling a new presidential election would appear to be preferable to modification of the impeachment process. The verdict on removal of the president could then be left to the people, assuming that the president sought vindication and

---

4. Charles M. Hardin, *Presidential Power and Accountability: Toward a New Constitution* (University of Chicago Press, 1974), p. 7. (Italics in original.)

could win the nomination of his party, and whether he or his opponent won, the new president would have a fresh mandate from the country.

The Bingham, Green, and Reuss resolutions introduced during the Watergate crisis (and discussed in chapter 3) all provided for new elections. All placed the initiative for calling the elections in the Congress, and all predicated the action on a vote of "no confidence." Action under the Bingham plan, which would have simply authorized a special election to be called by statute, would have required a two-thirds vote of both houses—a barrier greater than that embodied in the impeachment process itself—assuming that the president would use his veto to reject the derogation of his record. The Green resolution similarly called for a two-thirds vote of both houses. In contrast, Representative Reuss lowered the necessary congressional majorities to 60 percent, but he introduced another inhibition to hasty congressional action; his resolution required that every seat in both houses, as well as the presidency and vice presidency, be filled in the special election. Those elected under any of these resolutions would serve the unexpired terms of the officers whose seats were vacated.

It is understandable that in the Watergate period concern focused on the presidency. It was not difficult then to locate the source of governmental failure—in the character flaws of Richard Nixon. But in the five sets of circumstances listed earlier that can destroy a government's capacity to govern, only the first four represent presidential failure. The fifth circumstance is deadlock between the branches on fundamental policy, which can render even a strong and wholly competent president unable to lead the nation. That was the problem that worried the reformers of an earlier generation, in the 1930s and 1940s. They saw the legislative branch as the source, or potential source, of governmental incapacity. Admirers of Franklin Roosevelt and Harry Truman, they feared that wise and progressive presidents would be prevented by reactionary and parochial legislators from doing necessary things. Some of them, therefore, proposed a power in the executive—the president or a presidentially designated premier—to dissolve the Congress, or one house of it, and order new elections.

The problem appears, therefore, in a context broader than that of simple presidential failure. Governments can fail for other reasons, too, and any amendment to the Constitution establishing a mechanism for special elections as the means for reconstituting a government incapable of governing should be broad enough to deal with the whole range of circumstances that can result in failure.

Designing the Special Election Mechanism

In countries with a pure parliamentary form of government, every national election has the character of a special election. It is called by the government in power, on short notice, at any time of the year. Campaigns are short, and the parties select their candidates and formulate their programs in advance to be ready to run whenever the starting gun goes off. But in this country, the opposite tradition has developed. National elections occur rhythmically and automatically on specified calendar dates—with the sole exception of the occasional by-elections called to fill vacancies in the House of Representatives. And the same is true of state and local elections, with the additional rare exception of recall elections that some state constitutions provide for. From the principle of calendar elections has evolved the whole system of candidate selection. Having unlimited time to prepare and conduct their campaigns, the parties have established extraordinarily complex and elaborate processes for choosing nominees. In recent years, serious candidates for the presidency (except incumbents) have felt compelled to begin full-time campaigning about two years before the date on which they hoped to be inaugurated. Delegates to the national nominating conventions are selected in primaries and caucuses that extend over a four-month period beginning nearly a year before the inauguration day. Campaigns for Congress may be as long as those for president, and the formal nominating process in some states begins as early.

If a provision for calling special elections on short notice were to be introduced into the American political system, the parties would have to be prepared to conduct brief campaigns and to devise anticipatory or simplified processes for nominating the presidential and vice presidential candidates who would compete in the special balloting.

Designing a special election provision also requires selection from a range of alternatives on each feature of the system. Who would have the power to call the special election, and what offices would be filled? Would those elected serve fresh terms or only the unexpired portions of the original terms? Could the special election be called at any time or only at specified times?

The answers to these questions depend on the range of circumstances for which the special election mechanism is intended to be available. An assumption that the governmental failure arises from a divided, deadlocked government may lead to one design, while an assumption that the problem is presidential failure at a time of unified government—for any of the reasons listed at the outset of this discussion—may lead to quite another. Ideally, the mechanism should be flexible enough to serve all the circumstances in which a government may fail. But the more flexible the system the more often, presumably, it would be utilized. That leads, then, to still other questions. How often would special elections need to be held and in what circumstances? And if the process were designed for only the gravest of emergencies—once or twice a century, say—how can it be limited to just those situations? Whether special elections are to be encouraged or discouraged affects the design of the mechanism at every stage.

Calling the Election

Some of the proposals advanced in the past have placed the initiative for calling special elections in only one branch of the government. They were conceived as measures to permit the president to dissolve the Congress, or for Congress to bring about the removal of a failed president, but not both. However, if the cause of the governmental failure were systemic deadlock between the branches (as distinct from an impasse on a specific policy issue, for which a referendum device, discussed in chapter 8, might be appropriate), either the president or the Congress should have authority to initiate the election that would be intended to resolve the crisis.

If the power were so lodged, either branch in a period of government futility could challenge the other to a showdown, with the people to decide. Both the Congress and the presidency would therefore have to be at stake in the special election. To fully ensure that control of the Congress could be reversed by the election, not just some of the House and Senate seats but all of them would have to be submitted to the people's verdict, as in the Reuss resolution. If the president were vindicated, presumably the voters would give him a Congress of his own party that would follow his leadership. Conversely, if the opposition were upheld, the voters would presumably replace the president with the candidate of the other party and solidify its control of the legislature.[5]

In a provision empowering the Congress to call a new election, should an extraordinary majority be required? There is solid precedent for such a standard. For the Congress to declare a president unable to discharge his duties under the Twenty-fifth Amendment, over his objection, a two-thirds vote by both houses is required. For a president to be removed under the impeachment clause, a simple majority of the House can vote to bring the executive to trial before the Senate, but a two-thirds vote by that body is required for conviction. In the Bingham resolution providing for special elections, a two-thirds vote of both houses would have been required unless the president concurred, because the election would have been called by statute.

The essential consequence of a two-thirds rule, as noted earlier, is that the decision becomes bipartisan. Such a rigorous requirement might be appropriate if the special election were always to be conceived as a punitive action against the president as an individual; a broad bipartisan consensus should underlie any action that drives a president from office in disgrace. But if the purpose is to enable the electorate simply to choose between opposing parties when their conflict is so deep as to vitiate the powers of government, a requirement for a bipartisan consensus would be self-defeating. To serve that purpose, either party should be in a position to initiate the showdown, whether or not the other concurred. Indeed, even the 60 percent standard in the Reuss amendment would not enable the congressional majority to act in most circumstances of divided government. Of the eleven Congresses since World War II in which both houses were controlled by the party in opposition to the president, only two—the Eighty-sixth, following the election of 1958, and the Ninety-fourth,

5. The word *presumably* is key, however, for it is entirely conceivable that the president and the congressional majorities, given the power of incumbency, would all be returned, with no mandate other than to resume their quarrel. Such a result might discredit the new procedure, but it might also focus attention on the need for revision of the election system along the lines discussed in chapter 4, to forestall the partisan division of the government.

following 1974—were held by majorities of 60 percent or more.[6] If the provision is to be usable whenever it is needed, the Congress must be able to act by, at most, a vote of a constitutional majority—that is, a majority of the total membership. In instances where the minority gave the action no support, the majority party would have to achieve near unanimity, for a few dissidents could block the election simply by absenting themselves or by abstaining. But if it were fully unified and prepared to take the risk, it would be able to put before the people its case against the president.

A proposal to entrust the power to so small a majority would inevitably arouse fear that the special election mechanism might be overused, that it might be employed by either the president or the Congress in instances where the disagreement was in no sense fundamental but where either party might see the opportunity to capitalize on a transient public mood to improve its partisan position. A special election called in such circumstances might not in fact be undesirable, from the standpoint of effective government, because it could be the means to avert a deadlock—if not to resolve one. Yet even if the Congress were free to act by no more than a constitutional majority, a powerful deterrent would exist in the provision that all seats in Congress as well as the presidency would be subjected to the decision of the voters. The members of Congress who called the new election would be foreshortening their own tenure and putting in jeopardy their own careers as well as that of the chief executive.

That would cause no great risk, and perhaps not even any inconvenience, in the case of members of the House, assuming that the two-year term is continued. The special election could well be scheduled to coincide with the regular midterm election when House members would be running anyway. But it would involve both risk and inconvenience for most senators, one-third of whom at any given time have assured service of four to six years ahead of them, and another third from two to four more years. Only the final third are scheduled to face the voters at the next election. Two-thirds of the Senate, then, would have strong reason to resist acting to dissolve the Congress under any but the gravest circumstances. For this and

6. In the 102d Congress, elected in 1990, the Democratic opposition held more than 60 percent in the House but not in the Senate.

other reasons that were discussed earlier, a special election would not
be called by the Congress except when the incapacity of the government became so palpable that public clamor made a new election
inescapable. If the Senate terms were extended to eight years, with
two classes, the disincentives would be even greater, for half the
Senate at any time would be assured of tenure for more than four
additional years.

The president, however, would not be subjected to quite the same
restraint. Each four years, the presidency is at stake in a national
election, along with the entire House and one-third of the Senate. As
that election approached, a president would have reason to reflect on
the makeup of the Senate and, if a majority of the holdover senators
were of the opposition party, consider the prospect of gaining additional seats for his party by dissolving the Congress and requiring
the entire Senate to be chosen. It is difficult to see a president's taking
such action, however; the cries of outrage from holdover senators of
his own party would be deafening. Again, the initiative for a new
election would be likely only in response to an irresistible demand
from the people—in which case, the Congress might act first or the
two would proceed in unison.

If it be deemed necessary or prudent to devise additional restraints
on the president, however, several may be considered. William Yandell Elliott's suggestions for resolving deadlocks, discussed in chapter
3, would have limited the president to exercising his dissolution
power once in a term, and for the remainder of his term he would
have lost his veto power, leaving the Congress free to establish policy.
The former restriction would be of little import, since it is hardly
conceivable that any president would want to dissolve the Congress
more than once in four years, and it may be questioned whether
outright suspension of the veto—although that would have some
deterrent effect on presidents—would be desirable under any circumstances. The principal purpose of the veto, as the founders saw it,
was to enable the president to defend his powers against congressional encroachment, and at a time of intense conflict between the
branches—which would always be the case during a dissolution
crisis—the veto power would be more than ever important for that
purpose.

A second suggestion is that the president be empowered to call
the election only with the concurrence of either the House or the

Senate. This plan presents a certain symmetry. The government's three policymaking centers—presidency, Senate, and House—can deadlock in any of three ways, with any two combined against the third. Any two, therefore, should be able to initiate the new election. Such a plan would appear singularly appropriate for the circumstance of the first six Reagan years, when a Republican administration and a Republican Senate confronted a Democratic House. But it can be doubted that a requirement for Senate concurrence would add any real restraint to what would exist if the president possessed the power to act alone. In the latter case, he would surely not act without the wholehearted support of his party members in the Senate anyway. And requiring the concurrence of one house would strip the president of the power to deal with the kind of situation that developed during the second term of Franklin Roosevelt, when the president's program was blocked by a conservative coalition that controlled both houses, or in the administrations of Presidents Eisenhower, Nixon, and Ford, when Republican presidents and Democratic Congresses continually thwarted and frustrated each other. If, under those circumstances, neither house were willing to submit its membership to new elections—which they might anticipate would result in popular endorsement of the president—the constitutional amendment that was designed to provide a means for breaking deadlocks would prove inadequate.

A corresponding case can be made for placing authority in just one house of Congress to call the special election. If the deadlock occurred at a time when the opposition party controlled only one chamber, as in the early Reagan period, the president and his party in the other house might anticipate defeat in the new election and hence be reluctant to act. Ideally, it was suggested earlier, either party during a continuing impasse should be able to challenge the other to a showdown by asking the voters to make a choice between the two parties and their respective programs. Logically, then, the opposition-controlled house should be able to initiate the election on its own.[7]

---

7. Donald L. Robinson proposes that special elections be called either (1) by a proclamation of the president, with the consent of either one-third of the House or the Senate or (2) by a joint resolution of Congress (which requires presidential concurrence) or, if the president does not concur, the resolution subsequently passed by majorities of the two houses. *"To the Best of My Ability": The Presidency and the Constitution* (W. W. Norton, 1987), pp. 271, 278–79. This scheme would be more restrictive than

Even so liberal a mechanism would not suffice, however, in the case of a governmental failure at a time when one party controlled both branches and neither the president nor his majority in either house—all fearing repudiation at the polls—was willing to risk a special election. This is a common complaint about parliamentary government in countries such as Britain; since a government holds office for its full term (five years in Britain), unless the ruling party chooses to call an election at an earlier date, the country has no means of dislodging a failed government barring a split within the governing party itself. A parallel situation can, of course, develop in the United States. Perhaps the Hoover administration in 1930 can be accepted as an example, but for those who reject that illustration any number of hypothetical cases can readily be constructed. What would have happened, for instance, if President Franklin Roosevelt, like Neville Chamberlain, had proved totally inadequate as a leader in wartime and was leading his country to defeat at a time when his party had full control of both houses of Congress? He would have been entitled to his office while the war was lost. The midterm election, it must be repeated, provides no safeguard against presidential failure, for the presidency is not at stake. If the special election mechanism were to be available for the entire range of circumstances, authority to call the election would have to be placed somehow in the minority party— perhaps by vesting that power in 40 or 45 percent of the members of both houses. And even a number that small would not enable the minority, in a time of lopsided congressional majorities, to act without the aid of at least a few members of the majority.

---

the one proposed here, by not enabling one house to initiate the special election unless it had the concurrence of either the president or the other house. Robinson would also, "for purposes of continuity," subject only one class of senators to the special election (one-third of the body if terms remain six years, or one-half if eight-year terms, which Robinson advocates, were adopted). This would have the effect of severely reducing the disincentives to calling a special election, thus making the use of the device more likely. It might also enable the carryover senators opposed to the verdict of the special election (assuming the verdict is a clear one) to block the program of the new administration and the House majority and so perpetuate the deadlock. As Robinson argues, they too would probably respond to the election returns—at least during the new president's honeymoon period—just as congressional Democrats largely went along with President Reagan's program in 1981. But they might not, and to that extent the utility of the special election mechanism would be reduced. The argument of a need for continuity does not appear to be a strong one, for far more than half the incumbent senators would surely be reelected (see chapter 5).

Carrying the logic to this extreme leads to the fundamental question posed earlier. If a mechanism is to be available for the gravest of emergencies, should its use be limited to those occasions? And, if so, how can it be?

Some of those who have considered these issues answer the first question in the negative. They find the advantages of special elections, rather than elections fixed by the calendar, to be so great that they would maximize their use by empowering a minority of the two houses, or even of one house, to initiate the action. The reduction in the duration, strain, and costs of campaigning, they argue, would be a boon, and if elections were frequently called on short notice, the parties would be compelled to have their leaders designated and their programs defined in order to be ready. The indirect consequence, then, would be greater party cohesion, which would make whichever party was the victor better prepared to govern.

But making the special election so readily available would open the way to political gamesmanship. If the minority party in Congress were empowered to call the election, it would have an incentive to do so whenever the public opinion polls showed that a majority of voters disapproved of the president's performance. Six postwar presidents, according to the Gallup poll, have experienced that high a rate of disapproval at some point before the expiration of their terms— Truman in 1946 and again in 1951–52, Johnson in 1967–68, Nixon in 1973–74, Carter in 1979–80, Reagan in 1983, and Bush in 1992. But these were sometimes temporary; Truman was rebuffed in the 1946 election but recouped in 1948, and Reagan was set back in 1982–83 but recovered by 1984. One of the arguments for longer terms, discussed in chapter 5, was that a longer time horizon gives officeholders a chance to be statesmen and take actions that are unpopular in the short run but to the country's—and their—longer-run advantage. Enabling the minority party to initiate an election whenever a president's popularity suffered a drastic drop would work in the opposite direction. It would make presidents more cautious than they are now. They would be even more preoccupied with politics, running hard for reelection not just in the last two years of their first terms but throughout those terms and during much of their second terms as well.

To prevent the minority party from being able to call an election capriciously, with a what-do-we-have-to-lose attitude, some have suggested that some form of referendum be interposed, giving the people rather than the minority party the opportunity to decide, by a vote or by petition of a specific proportion of the electorate, whether a special election were in order. But if the contention in chapter 5 that midterm elections now come too soon has merit, adding a midterm referendum on a special presidential election would compound the present problem. The object should be to relieve Congress from the burden of an always-imminent election, not to subject the president to that same strain.

If one concedes this point, then a governmental failure at a time of united government could be solved only by the majority itself. If the present midterm election is retained, that provides a safeguard, for the electorate could give the opposition control of at least one house, which could then invoke its power (if the amendment permitted one house alone to initiate action). If the midterm election were eliminated, however, the American people would be in the same position as the British; they would have no recourse if their leaders were not disposed to move. Yet the power of public opinion should not be discounted. Chamberlain did, after all, relinquish his office, and so at later dates, under pressure from their own party, did Anthony Eden and Margaret Thatcher. Richard Nixon's resignation set a useful precedent in this country. If the public outcry against a failed president and a leaderless governing party were loud enough, revolt would surely stir in the party's congressional rank and file. The fact that either house of Congress possessed the power to call a special election would have a profound effect. By threatening to join with the opposition to provoke such an election, a minority of the majority party in either house could in some cases bring about a presidential resignation. If it failed, and if the situation in the country were bad enough, it could carry out its threat.

On balance, placing the authority to call the new election in either the president or a constitutional majority of either house of Congress would provide a mechanism that would be available in cases of deadlock and—through the pressure of public opinion—in most other cases of failed government as well. To make the mechanism available for every conceivable case, by empowering the minority to act, would have a destabilizing effect so great as to outweigh the advantages of going to that extreme. The remainder of this discussion assumes that the authority to call the special election would be limited to the president or a Senate or House constitutional majority.

Full or Unexpired Terms?

On the face of it, if the nation is to be put through the trauma and turmoil of a special election for the president and the entire Congress, more should be at stake than just the unexpired terms of the current officeholders. The new election would presumably reconstitute a failed government and give the nation a fresh team of leaders. They would enter office eager to carry out their mandate, and the electorate would expect them to do so. It would appear both unnecessary and undesirable to give them less than normal full terms; to do so would thrust them at once into preparing for the next election and would force the country to go through its electoral ordeal twice within a single four-year span.[8]

But the question again arises as to whether, if full terms were to be awarded, politicians would be encouraged to maneuver for personal and partisan advantage. Might the process be invoked unnecessarily or even frivolously, in circumstances for which it was not intended, at times when governments were successful? If a united government were riding high in the public opinion polls, might it choose to go to the electorate for bigger majorities and a reinforced mandate rather than wait for the next regular election when its standing might be lower—much as governments in parliamentary countries strive to schedule their elections on the most advantageous dates?

The Twenty-second Amendment adds a complication here. Under its terms, a person may be elected president only twice, so a hostile Congress could be certain of curtailing a president's tenure by calling

---

8. If the Senate terms continue to be staggered—either as at present, with one-third of the Senate elected each two years, or as discussed in chapter 5, with one-half chosen each four years—any constitutional amendment providing for election of the entire Senate to new terms would have to provide for dividing the Senate into classes with varying terms. That could be done simply, by providing that the class with the shortest time remaining at the time of the special election would have the shortest term, and the class with the longest time remaining, the longest. As used in this section, the full-term option means new terms of two, four, and six years for the Senate classes (or four and eight years for the two classes in the four-eight-four plan) but full terms for the president, vice president, and representatives.

a special election. If it were scheduled during the president's first term, he would serve less than eight years even if he were reelected, and if the Congress scheduled such a vote during his second term, he would be ineligible to run. On the other hand, if the amendment were modified to exempt special elections from its provisions, a president could circumvent the present limitations on his tenure (eight years plus up to two years of the unexpired term of his predecessor) by calling a special election at whatever time seemed most propitious for his purpose. With artful language, the new amendment could set limits corresponding to those now in effect. Thus, if a special election were held during the last half of a president's first term or the first half of his second, the president if reelected could be made ineligible to run again when the new term expired; and if the election were held after the midpoint of his second term, he could be barred from competing in that race. That would give a hostile house of Congress the means to shorten the term of the president it opposed, and it would present an ambitious president with a way to extend his term. But neither the curtailment nor the extension could be for more than two years, and neither the legislators nor the president would be likely to gamble on the electorate's approval for a stake so small.

But even if political gamesmanship appeared to offer some potential gain for a president or his party, the self-interest of senators (and House members too, if their terms were lengthened) would impose the severe inhibition discussed earlier. If the opposition party held a majority in one or both houses, it might find some incentive in the opportunity a special election would offer it to capture the White House (and the other chamber, if controlled by the president's party). Similarly, a majority of the president's party in one house might see a chance for their partisans to capture the other house as well. But the individual legislators, as well as the president, would have to weigh a conjectural gain for the party as a whole against the certain, premature risk to their own careers. They would vacate their offices and undergo the expense and strain of an early election, with no recompense except a renewed tenure in the seats they already occupied. House members could, of course, escape an extra contest (assuming congressional terms remain unchanged) if the special poll were scheduled to coincide with the present midterm election, but two-thirds of the senators would find everything to lose and little to gain. And if House terms were extended to four years, the representatives would find themselves in the same position.

True, the slight extension of a senator's hold on his office if he survived the special election would provide a correspondingly slight incentive. A senator with five years remaining in his term would enter on a new six-year term, one with three years a four-year term, and so on, assuming the present structure of six-year staggered terms. With an eight-year term, the incentive would be somewhat greater, for a senator with five, six, or seven years remaining could win an eight-year term, and one with one, two, or three years left to serve could get a new four-year stay.[9] But even this mild incentive would be removed if the election were for only the unexpired terms of the offices being vacated. The question in that case would be whether the special election mechanism would be utilized in the circumstances for which it was designed—to reconstitute failed government—or whether it would never be used at all.

Only the most intense public pressure, surely, could induce legislators to give up their seats and call a special election with no reward at all beyond being allowed to finish the term to which they were already entitled. The electorate would have to be so aroused that a majority of one house (or the president, but he would surely be sensitive to the attitudes of the legislators in this matter) would reappraise where their self-interest lay and conclude that to resist a special election would imperil them more than would yielding to it. One can identify perhaps a couple of times in this century when public hostility toward governmental leaders might have reached that degree of intensity. If the special election process is to be designed, and reserved, for only such occasions, then the unexpired-term option would be suitable. But it would be unavailable as a method of reconstituting governments whose failure has produced deep public frustration, alienation, and disgust but not yet driven the voters to the edge of revolution.

The full-term alternative would raise the incentive for politicians to act in these kinds of circumstances. Would it, then, lift the stakes

9. This assumes that senators with short tenure remaining would not challenge their colleagues for the longer term. Traditions of comity would discourage such behavior, as would the greater risk involved in challenging an incumbent. But the possibility might well act as another factor discouraging the calling of special elections.

too high and lead to overuse of the new mechanism? Public opinion would again be the key. If it could compel a special election in the most extreme situations under the unexpired-term alternative—and even that is less than certain—it could assuredly restrain any initiative at other times, even if full terms were the winners' reward. At every stage, the fear of an adverse public reaction would be a forceful inhibition on those who held the power to initiate the new election. Since they would be required to submit themselves to the verdict of the special election, they would not be likely to risk the voters' judgment that they had acted precipitously or for narrow, partisan purposes. The governmental failure would have to be patent and compelling, not only in the eyes of the politicians but in the judgment of the electorate at large. In other words, the public itself would have to be the true initiator, with the politicians in the posture of reluctantly responding. And the public could surely be counted on not to clamor for an extra, unnecessary election. Only a plain collapse of governmental leadership and competence would put the country in the kind of mood that would command the response of the Congress, or the president, or both. That would be true under either the full-term or the unexpired-term option, so the advantages of the former may as well be incorporated in any special election scheme.

Timing the Election

Any special election process would be designed for emergencies, and, by definition, emergencies cannot wait. Governments may fail abruptly, and once the public has concluded that the failure is both manifest and irreparable, the sooner a new, invigorated government is put in place the better. The parliamentary model suggests itself— elections to be called at any time, held promptly, and the fresh leadership installed in office immediately after the votes are tabulated. In Britain, an interregnum lasts not much longer than a month.

If the newly elected officials in this country are to serve full terms, however, complete flexibility in scheduling the special election would encounter some difficulties. The first is psychological. If a special election were called for March, say, and the new government installed in May (which is probably as quickly as American tradition would allow), the new terms would also expire in May and the next regular election therefore would be held in March. And so would subsequent national elections, until another special election initiated another series on another date. True, irregular elections do not upset the electorates of other countries, and a few American states and cities elect their leaders in the spring. Until a few decades ago, Maine held its national election in September. Nevertheless, it is argued, November as the proper month for choosing presidents is implanted in the national psyche by two centuries of ritualization; the fixed rhythms of politics are as reassuring as the unvarying, predictable movements of the sun, the moon, and the planets, and to remove the certainty of calendar elections would unsettle and alienate the electorate.[10]

The psychological problem would be compounded by a series of practical ones. If the national election were held in March, every stage of the nominating process would have to be rescheduled accordingly. Assuming that the present nominating processes were left essentially unchanged, the national party conventions would have to be held in midwinter rather than midsummer, and the presidential and congressional primaries now held in the spring would have to be rescheduled in the autumn. A large body of legislation, and an even vaster congeries of political habits, would have to be recast.

These objections could be met very simply, for the most part, by adjusting the full terms by a few months. The amendment could provide that the new full terms would expire in the January that came closest to the date when they would otherwise expire. At the next regular election, then, the familiar November date would be reinstated, although not necessarily in a year divisible by four.

Alternatively, the amendment could provide that special elections would be permitted only on the usual November date. As a further concession to tradition, the opportunity could be limited to the midterm even-numbered year. This could be defended on the ground that the first year after a presidential election would be too soon to ask the electorate to reconsider its decision of the previous autumn and by the third year the country could bear to struggle along until the regularly scheduled presidential balloting. And it could be pre-

10. The extent to which the public is attached to November elections as such may have been overestimated. The Gallup poll reports that a majority of its sample responded favorably to the suggestion that the presidential elections be moved forward to September, in order to give the president more time to prepare for the opening of Congress in January. George Gallup, Jr., "Americans Favor Major Overhaul of Electoral Process," *Dallas Morning News*, December 6, 1984.

sented—somewhat deceptively, to be sure—as a minimal, incremental change. All the reformers would be proposing would be to expand the scope of the familiar midterm election a bit, to include the presidency and vice presidency as well as legislative seats.

But while such a plan would meet the practical tests better, it would serve the theoretical ends less well. A president who became discredited early in his term would remain in office for a full two years, unless, following the Nixon precedent, he could be persuaded to resign. In the country's interest, two years might be too long. But, what is more likely, the governmental incapacity would not become clearly enough established to create a public demand for action until the deadline for calling the midterm election had passed. If that deadline were fixed as September 1—and practical considerations would probably lead to choosing an even earlier date—a new government would have only nineteen months to demonstrate its incapacity.

Once it survived that short period, it would be assured of continuance for its full four years. The crucial year for the people to decide whether a government should be turned out of office before its time is either the later part of the second year or the third. If the decision must be made no later than eighteen or nineteen months after a president's inauguration, the procedure would be unavailable when it would be likely to be needed most. The purpose of the amendment would be vitiated. Whenever governmental deadlock or failed leadership becomes intolerable and a special election imperative, the remedy should be available immediately without waiting for what might be an entire tense and wasted year until the next November.

If the special election process is worth adopting at all, then, the principle of flexible timing needs to be accepted and the psychological objections to elections in unaccustomed months and odd years confronted and somehow overcome (although, as suggested above, the familiar November date could be maintained for all but the special elections). And the political parties would have to face the necessity of designing special nominating processes for use if and when a special election were called.

Adjustment of Nominating Procedures

Whoever called the special election would need to be granted some degree of discretion as to how soon the voting would take place. But, given the premise that emergencies by their nature require a quick response, the normal nine-month span for the entire nominating and electing process would have to be compressed to some degree. The parties would have to be ready at any time to nominate their candidates and present their cases to the voters in a period of weeks rather than, as is now the case, months.

In the case of congressional candidates, existing nominating processes could be preserved in their essentials, by simply expediting each step of the procedure. The one casualty might be the runoff primaries, which would probably have to be suspended by the few states that still conduct them. But a single primary would be feasible. If the special election were called on March 15, say, and set for sixty days later, on May 14, states would have time to organize primary balloting on April 23, with three weeks left for the general election. Candidates could be required to file for nomination within a week, by March 22, which would allow more than a month for arranging the mechanics of the election. So brisk a schedule would be a radical departure from the leisurely pace to which American politicians and election officials have become accustomed, but precedents do exist. Special elections to fill vacancies in the House are usually held within a few weeks after the vacancies occur, and in states that hold runoff primaries the interval between the first and second primaries is usually three weeks but in South Carolina has been only two.

The presidential nominating process is, however, another matter. The present elaborate series of events, beginning with the first primaries and caucuses in midwinter and ending with the national convention extravaganzas in midsummer, followed by a general election campaign of almost three months, obviously could not be compressed into a 60-day period—or even a 160-day period—without fundamental alteration.

One approach would be for the Congress by law, or the parties by their own rules, to prescribe a national presidential primary to be held concurrently with those for House and Senate. The massive party convention would be regretfully abandoned on this occasion, and its functions beyond nominating the president otherwise assigned. The most important of those duties would be the nomination of a candidate for vice president, but that would be scant loss; vice presidential selection has not always been performed satisfactorily by conventions anyway. In most instances, the convention simply ratifies the hasty choice of the presidential candidate, and that ministerial act can be as well left to the party's national committee as to a convention. On the other hand, if the choice is to be made in a more considered fashion, the procedure of the Twenty-fifth Amendment could be invoked, with the new president appointing his vice president, subject to confirmation by Congress, after taking office. A second function of the convention is to write a platform; this duty could be entrusted to the national committee, or the party policy could be left to be enunciated by its presidential candidate, whose pronouncements always carry considerably more weight than party platform declarations. Finally, the convention is the party's plenary rule-making body, but the national committee acts for the convention between its sessions. The calling of a special election would not generate a need for new rules that could not be met by the national committee.

The national primary has other features, though, that affect its suitability as the mode for nominating party candidates in a special election. Most versions of the primary that have been advanced have suggested a runoff feature in the event no candidate gets more than a specified proportion of the vote—usually 40 percent—in order to assure that the winner in a multicandidate contest is the choice of more than a small minority. Allowing eighty rather than sixty days for the entire election process would be sufficient to accommodate a runoff primary—if those designing the process were willing to risk the reaction from an electorate asked to vote three times at intervals of two or three weeks (or four times altogether, if the whole process had to be set in motion by a referendum).

Two alternatives to the runoff primary are available, however. One would be to delegate a preliminary screening responsibility to the national committee, or to that body augmented by some or all of the party's membership in Congress and its governors; it would select two candidates to be presented to the voters. A second alternative would be a theoretically appealing but virtually untried procedure called "approval voting" in which primary voters could vote for as many of the candidates in a multicandidate primary as they considered suitable to lead the party in the general election. The candidate acceptable to the largest number of primary voters would be the nominee, with probably a reasonable chance that he or she would have the approval of a majority.

But while a national primary would appear to be feasible, its desirability is a separate question. It has always been a ready alternative to the present convention process but has never achieved enough support to bring it into serious consideration, despite the widespread and vociferous criticism of the existing system. One objection is that it would give too decisive an advantage to the candidate or candidates with the greatest name recognition or access to the most copious financial resources, or both. It would probably eliminate the possibility that now exists for a relatively unknown candidate with limited resources—such as Eugene McCarthy in 1968, Gary Hart in 1984, or Paul Tsongas in 1992—to burst upon the political scene by making an impressive showing in the earliest caucuses and primaries.

A second objection is that even now too many states hold primaries and the aim should be to reduce rather than increase the number. The proliferation of primaries in the last two decades (see chapter 7) has placed the choice of each party's nominee in the hands of 10 million to 20 million or more rank-and-file voters in each party, but those voters must base their judgment of a candidate's leadership capacity on what is essentially a casual impression, gained mostly over television. What is needed, it is argued, is a return to the balanced nominating process that prevailed as late as the 1960s, when the various candidates could test their public appeal in a few primaries, but the party's leaders—those who had worked with the candidates most closely and knew them most intimately—could make sure that the nomination did not go to one who was unsuitable for the presidential office, however popular he proved to be in the primaries. That hazard would be avoided if, as suggested earlier, two candidates were nominated by the national committee (preferably augmented for the purpose) to run in the national primary.

If, even with that adjustment, a national primary seems undesirable, another alternative suggests itself. That is for the party to establish a much smaller nominating convention, consisting of only a few hundred people who could be assembled on a few days' notice in a prearranged location. The delegates to that convention could be selected during the first year of a new president's term, though that would appear to be an unnecessarily elaborate arrangement since special elections would surely prove to be rare events. Once again, a convention made up of the party's national committee plus its members in Congress and its governors would be both representative and knowledgeable as a nominating body.

To suspend the present nominating process in a time of crisis would inflict no permanent injury on the political system. If the result would be restoration of citizens' faith in their government, that would well justify the temporary disturbance of normal party practice. Moreover, on the positive side, one experience with a quick and relatively inexpensive process of choosing new leaders might show the way to improvements in the interminable, exhausting, and excessively expensive political ordeal that the country now suffers each four years.

The Need for a Safety Valve

How to provide a "safety valve" when governments fail is a conundrum for constitutional designers in any democratic system. The objective is clear enough. When a government proves incapable of leading the country and loses the people's confidence, for whatever reason, the people should have the opportunity through a new election to replace it. But no country has a constitution that guarantees that opportunity.

In theory, parliamentary systems offer the people a recourse, because those who administer the government must maintain the confidence of a parliament made up of the elected representatives of the people, and if they fail to do so they can be removed at any time. When a prime minister fails, he can, like Chamberlain, be replaced. But that is not the same as giving the people a fresh choice. The members of Parliament remain in office, the same majority party or coalition of parties in that body still governs, and the new prime minister comes from that same governing group. If the party or coalition as a whole has lost the public confidence, it remains in power for its full term—or until it decides voluntarily to call an election—just as surely as a president remains in office for his full four years in the United States.

The difficulty in Britain and other parliamentary countries is that the party or parties that control the legislature must make their own decision as to whether and when their government should relinquish its authority. In a two-party parliamentary country, the governing party usually clings most tenaciously to power when it has the least public support, for it can always hope to restore itself if the election is delayed. In a multiparty system, where government is by coalition, a new election is more likely to be called, because in case of governmental failure the coalition may come unglued and there will be no way to restore it short of fresh elections. But coalition governments are so often weak and unstable that they are hardly to be taken as a model.

The framers of the U.S. Constitution sought their safety valve, for the legislative branch, in the biennial election of the House and one-third of the Senate. As for the executive, he would be chosen very carefully, by an electoral college composed of prudent and knowledgeable citizens or by the House of Representatives, and if by chance he proved traitorous or criminal, he could be impeached. Broader grounds for impeachment were rejected to ensure the independence of the chief executive from too tight congressional control.

But with the democratization of the presidential selection process and the growth of executive power, the fixity of a president in office for four full years, no matter how incompetent he may prove to be, is a weakness in the American system that can, in a time of grave emergency, be perilous. For a president to be merely nontreasonous and noncriminal is no longer enough, if it ever were. The president today must be the country's leader in every respect, its chief legislator as well as chief executive, its moral preceptor and its commander in chief, and nowadays the leader of the whole free world and chief strategist and tactician in the global effort to implant and nurture the institutions of freedom and democracy in formerly despot-ridden lands. And in none of these roles will the president be effective if he has become discredited beyond recovery and so lost the confidence of the people in this country and abroad. In an electoral system that permits divided government, moreover, even a competent president can be rendered ineffective if forced to contend with a hostile Congress. And in such situations the biennial election, as was emphasized in chapter 5, turns out not to be a safety valve at all; history tells of no instance when a midterm election resolved a deadlock between the branches, but of many instances where it intensified conflict and immobilized the government.

An attempt to design a provision for special elections as the means to reconstitute a failed government in the United States encounters at once the dilemma that has faced constitution-makers in other countries. If those who control the government must themselves decide when a new election is needed, they may refuse to act no matter how patent the governmental failure and how loud the public outcry demanding action. On the other hand, if the power of decision is located somewhere outside the control of the elected officials who exercise responsibility—in the congressional minorities, perhaps subject to approval by the people themselves through some form of referendum—the stability of government will be undermined and responsible elected officials will suffer the continuous distraction of imminent elections. Yet the American separation-of-powers structure lends itself to an arrangement not available to parliamentary governments, where power is centralized: authority to call the election can be reposed in a *part* of the government, without requiring the concurrence of the other parts.

Because so much of governmental failure in the United States is due to partisan squabbling and deadlock between the branches, any one of the three elements in a deadlock—the president, the Senate, or the House (the latter bodies by constitutional majorities)—should be able to initiate the election. In order that the deadlock can in fact be broken, all elective offices in both branches should be declared vacant and filled in the election. The election should be callable at any time and the newly elected officers should serve new, full terms—except that, in order to preserve the most essential element of the country's traditional political calendar, those terms could be adjusted up or down to expire in the nearest January and thus permit a return to normal November elections.

For all the reasons discussed earlier, the inhibitions to calling a special election—in any of the forms the new mechanism might take—would be so great that the procedure, if added to the Constitution, might never be used. But the very existence of the authority would operate subtly to prevent the kinds of deadlocks that the provision would be intended to resolve. In times of conflict between the president and a Congress controlled in whole or in part by the opposition, the hand of a strong and popular president would be greatly strengthened. If he felt confident that public opinion was behind him, he could challenge recalcitrant legislators to yield to his wishes—or else. The result would be greater cohesion among the elements of the government, even when they were controlled by opposing parties. Theoretically, members of Congress could threaten the president as well, if he were unpopular among the citizenry, but they would be less credible. The Congress is so pluralistic, its power so diffused, the authority of its leaders to impose discipline so limited that it can rarely stand united and steadfast in any battle with even a weak president. Yet its sensitivity to public opinion can never be doubted, and in a circumstance where the problem was one of presidential incapacity and failure, as the electorate's views solidified so would those of the legislators, and they would possess the ultimate sanction to force the president from office. To maintain the confidence of the Congress and forestall any such eventuality, a president could not afford to ignore or defy the legislators and deliberately provoke or intensify conflict, as presidents have sometimes done, but would be forced to seek a close relationship. Yet if in the end he failed and sensed that he would lose in a showdown—probably anticipating that his own party might well deny him renomination—the chief executive would be likely to follow the useful precedent of resignation established by President Nixon.

A constitutional provision for special elections could, in sum, be written in a form that would make it safe from abuse, because the disincentives to use the provision would be compelling and the electorate could readily penalize the politician or party who abused it. It would be a spur toward cooperation between the branches—with a shift in influence from the Congress to any strong and popular president but to the legislature from a weak and unpopular one. And it would provide a safety valve for the country in any of the many varied circumstances that can lead to an inept, failed, and debilitated government.

CHAPTER SEVEN

Fostering Interbranch Collaboration

No one would ever expect to find perfect harmony, for long, between the executive and legislative branches of the American government, even when they are controlled by members of the same party chosen at the same election. Nor is an absence of conflict necessary for the government to function. Indeed, some degree of conflict is not only inevitable but desirable. Legislators must respond to presidential initiatives with a degree of skepticism and assert their independent views; otherwise, the legislative branch could be dispensed with altogether. And the president must review congressional initiatives with a corresponding independent outlook. But the problem arises when skepticism deepens into distrust and outright hostility. Then the power of each branch to check the other can lead to deadlock and immobility, and the government cannot muster the degree of unity necessary to enable it to act.

The problem of deadlock is reviewed in chapter 4 in the context of a government divided between the major parties. But while the most severe and debilitating impasses between the branches in recent decades have come during periods when Republican presidents have confronted Democratic Congresses, stalemate is by no means confined to such periods. Every Democratic president from Woodrow Wilson to Jimmy Carter had his clashes, too, with Congresses at least nominally controlled by his own party. The quarrel over Franklin Roosevelt's "court-packing" plan, and its ultimate defeat, which brought an abrupt end to the whole New Deal reform era, was probably the most divisive of the Democratic disputes. But Democratic governments were devitalized by disputes over preparedness in Woodrow Wilson's time, civil rights and civil liberties in Harry Truman's, Vietnam and inflation in Lyndon Johnson's, and energy policy in Jimmy Carter's. Real power in the Congress was often wielded not by the formal Democratic party structure in alliance with the president but by an informal coalition of conservative southern Democrats and Republicans.

In the pre-FDR era, when the Republicans normally held congressional majorities, GOP presidents and Congresses had their differences, too. Theodore Roosevelt was hardly on speaking terms with the conservative GOP congressional leaders by the time his second term ended, William Howard Taft fell out with those same leaders over the tariff, Warren Harding and the GOP legislators took opposite views on the World Court, and Coolidge twice vetoed Republican-written farm bills with blistering denunciations. In Ronald Reagan's first term, leaders of the Senate Republican majority upset the president's fiscal policy as early as 1982, when they forced him to accept a tax increase he did not want, and they scrapped his military spending buildup in 1985—but in these instances the president graciously accepted his defeats and went along.

Even with united government, then, presidential honeymoons with Congress are often short. Writing in 1940, at a time when Democrats had controlled both branches for nearly a decade, Harold J. Laski could observe that the Congress "is always looking for occasions to differ from" the president, "and it never feels so really comfortable as when it has found such an occasion for difference. In doing so, it has the sense that it is affirming its own essence."[1]

Accordingly, those who have sought a greater degree of unity and cohesion within the government have sometimes attempted to design institutional changes that would somehow force the president and his party majorities in Congress to collaborate, whether they were so inclined or not, or that would at least encourage harmony by creating countervailing pressures against the tendencies toward divergence that arise from the separation of the branches. These schemes can be divided into two categories—those that would formally modify the separation of powers by structurally interrelating the branches, and those that would seek their goal through strengthening the informal

---

1. Harold J. Laski, *The American Presidency: An Interpretation* (Harper, 1940), p. 123.

institution that binds the president and the congressional majorities together in times of united government. That institution is, of course, the political party.

Modifying the Separation of Powers

Proposals to modify the separation of powers necessarily take the form, as Stephen Horn has pointed out, of either putting legislators in the executive branch or putting officials of that branch—usually cabinet members—in the legislature.[2] If the members of Congress or cabinet officers who move across branch lines are to serve in only an advisory capacity, the constitutional separation of powers is not breached and the arrangement can be made through statute or simply by voluntary agreement. But if any official of either branch is to share authoritatively in the exercise of *power* in the other branch, the "incompatibility clause" of the Constitution stands in the way. That is the clause in Article I that declares that "no person holding any office under the United States shall be a member of either House during his continuance in office."

The clause originated, as noted in chapter 2, not out of a concern for dual officeholding as such but out of worry about preserving the independence of the Congress from presidential power. If the president could dangle the prospect of attractive patronage appointments, he could bend the legislators to his will, it was argued. Underpaid, part-time legislators in those days could presumably be easily seduced by the award of full-time offices that would enable them to settle their families in the capital. But much of the antipatronage purpose of the clause was vitiated, even for eighteenth century government, when the original language was modified in the Convention to permit legislators to accept an appointment (other than to new offices or those whose emoluments had been increased during their term) simply by resigning their seats. For modern government, the clause is even less significant, since membership in the Congress has become a full-time job with pay and prestige superior to all but the highest posts in the executive branch—cabinet secretaries, top White House staff posi-

2. Stephen Horn, *The Cabinet and Congress* (Columbia University Press, 1960), p. 211.

tions, or major ambassadorships—and with, normally, a much longer tenure. If the compatibility clause is no longer needed as a safeguard against mass corruption of the Congress through patronage, then, its desirability should be judged on other grounds—that is, whether the dual officeholding that it prohibits might, in some form, contribute to more harmonious relationships between the president and the Congress, without creating problems more serious than those it helps to solve.

The Committee on the Constitutional System (CCS) concluded that dual officeholding would be "an experiment that has considerable promise and little risk." The principal effect of the compatibility clause, its report stated, has been "to deprive the nation of administrators who would have the confidence of both the executive and legislative branches." Repeal of the clause would "broaden both the range of talent available to a President in forming his administration and the base of political leadership in the executive branch," and appointment of leading legislators to cabinet positions "might encourage closer collaboration" between the branches and "help to prevent stalemates."[3]

Members of Congress in the Cabinet

A constitutional amendment that simply deleted the compatibility clause, as recommended by the CCS, would leave it for each president to decide whether to appoint members of Congress to administrative posts, and for each legislator offered a post to decide whether to accept it. In the committee's words, it would permit experimentation; if either the executive or the legislative branch felt that the experiment tilted the balance of power in favor of the other branch, or if the idea proved unworkable for any reason, it could be abandoned at the initiative of either branch. The president could scrap the experiment simply by not offering executive positions to legislators. It would not be so easy for the legislative branch to end the experiment, if the president offered appointments and individual legislators desired to accept them. But if it were clear to the Congress as a whole that the experiment tended to aggrandize the presidency at the expense of the

3. Committee on the Constitutional System, "A Bicentennial Analysis of the American Political Structure" (Washington, January 1987), pp. 11–12.

legislative branch, the latter would have ample means of self-defense. Individual legislators would be pressed by their colleagues not to serve, the Senate would use the confirmation process to extract promises regarding their behavior, and, if they abused the relationship, they would lose the very influence that led the president to appoint them. Either both branches would find the experiment beneficial, or it would be abandoned. One may surmise that mutual suspicion would limit the application of the experiment, and elimination of the compatibility clause would therefore have little consequence, at least until it had been tested over a considerable period.

Those who see dual officeholding as the key to more effective government have therefore proposed, on occasion, to make the practice mandatory. Thus a constitutional amendment introduced in 1979 by Representative Henry S. Reuss, Democrat of Wisconsin, contemplated that fifty legislators would serve in the executive branch. The Congress would designate by statute offices eligible to be filled by its members, and the president each two years would submit his list of nominees for those posts, whether members or nonmembers. They would be voted on by each house en bloc. If either house rejected the slate, it would be revised by the president until he obtained concurrence. The appointments would then be made, subject to individual Senate confirmation in the usual manner, with the legislator to receive a single salary—that of the executive branch position. In addition to the arguments made later by the CCS, Reuss said in offering his amendment that it would "bring a 'hometown touch' to federal agencies now too often isolated in Washington," and "make service in Congress more attractive."[4]

The following discussion will focus on the Reuss proposal and will suggest some of the difficulties that persuaded the CCS to advocate experimenting rather than plunging into a complete unification of the branches through dual officeholding. Some of the objections to appointing fifty members of Congress to executive office would apply also, of course, to the appointment of an experimental one or two.

The first question relates to how the slate of up to fifty candidates would in fact be put together. With either house having the power to reject the slate, the Congress could, if it chose, enforce a demand

4. Memorandum, Office of Representative Henry S. Reuss, July 29, 1979.

that *its* slate be nominated by the president. In Britain, the queen appoints the ministers of the crown but she does not in fact choose them; that power was seized by the House of Commons long ago when it informed the monarch that it would not give a vote of confidence to any cabinet except that of its own selection. The same practice has been applied in this country to offices that are governed by the rule of "senatorial courtesy"; because the Senate as a whole defers to senators representing the state in which the office is filled, those senators are in effect empowered to reject any presidential appointee except the one they insist the president appoint. Such de facto senatorial selection does not apply now to cabinet posts and other positions of high rank, although powerful legislators have on occasion come close to dictating lesser appointments as the price of cooperation with the executive branch. Yet, under the Reuss proposal, when the Congress wrote its statute containing its list of offices, powerful elements within the legislature would surely be developing their own ideas as to which legislators should fill which of the designated posts. Fierce competition would surely ensue; would the legislators prefer to bargain their way to their own solutions or leave the executive free to pick and choose among them? The former, in all likelihood. It would be an extraordinary example of self-restraint if a Congress that—like the House of Commons—had the clear power to impose its will on the executive did not find formal or informal ways of doing so.

This would seem the probable outcome not merely because of the ambition of members of Congress but because of the difficulty—even unworkability—of the alternative. If the president were left truly free to make his own selections, he would have to decide in the first instance how many legislators to put on his list and then whether to appoint the most senior and powerful members of Congress or more junior members who might be more compatible with him. The objective of enhancing cooperation between the branches would appear to oblige the president to go in the former direction and seek as appointees the senior members who would have the greatest influence with their legislative colleagues. This is the theory of dual office-holding in parliamentary governments. The foreign secretary also manages foreign policy legislation and leads debate on foreign policy issues in the British House of Commons, the chancellor of the exchequer on budget and financial measures, and so on. The cabinet is at the apex of both branches, leading both and in so doing keeping them fully coordinated.

Representative Reuss, in presenting his proposal, did not envision that pattern. "It would not be wise," he said, for the president to appoint committee chairmen to the cabinet, "because that would present a real conflict of interest, which would carry us, in my judgment, too far away from the Presidential system, which I certainly don't want to displace."[5] For that reason, he said, a wise president would not, for instance, appoint as secretary of the treasury the chairman of the House Ways and Means Committee. But, to pursue this example, if the chairman wanted the job, for the president to pass over that powerful personage and appoint some other member of Congress or someone from outside the legislative branch would hardly be conducive to improving cooperation between the branches. The chairman would have to possess an unusually benign and forgiving temperament not to make life difficult for the secretary now and then, just to prove the president made the wrong judgment. Staff assistants of the passed-over member would fan the jealousies. Moreover, even in cases where selection of a junior member affronted none of the seniors, the appointee would be apt to lack the stature and influence required to become *their* leader in the legislative process. The junior member would have to win the elders' assent to administration measures by persuasion, with no notable advantage over cabinet members selected under the current practice from outside the Congress, and the potential advantage of dual officeholding would not be realized.[6]

On the other hand, if the president were determined to select senior and influential members, it would still be awkward to exercise free choice among that limited group. The bicameral structure of the Congress, in particular, would put the president at peril. Could the president find a person who would be influential in one house who would not become a liability, because of institutional rivalry, in the other? As ambitious members of the House and Senate competed for the president's favor, it would become increasingly clear that for every

5. *Political Economy and Constitutional Reform,* Hearings before the Joint Economic Committee, 97 Cong. 1 sess. (Government Printing Office, 1983), p. 336.

6. The prospect would be even less promising in a time of divided government. There is little reason to think that cabinet members appointed by a Republican president from Senate and House Republican minorities would be more effective in dealing with the Democratic majority than would officials selected from outside Congress. The discussion in this section therefore assumes unified party control of the branches.

member of one house nominated, the executive would make at least one enemy in the other house who would be in a position to do daily damage to the administration program. If many senior members were offended, the whole slate of nominees might be in danger of rejection. Presidents might eventually conclude that the only way to achieve harmony would be to allow the Congress itself to select its own members for the jobs.

But this presents its own range of problems. The majority party that organizes each house of Congress has found that assigning posts of power within the limited confines of the house itself is a divisive process, which is the reason that both houses, whether the majority is Democratic or Republican, have fallen back on seniority as the simple, harmonious way of filling their committee and subcommittee chairmanships.[7] For the few posts that have been necessarily exempted from seniority, such as party leadership positions, the competition to fill vacancies is distracting and always a threat to party harmony. For the two houses of Congress to attempt to divide between themselves and then respectively allocate up to fifty eagerly coveted executive branch positions would multiply manifold the strains and stresses that arise each two years from merely organizing the Congress. The legislators would undoubtedly fall back on some automatic and nondivisive process based on standing and seniority, assigning those entrusted with leadership in the Senate or the House in particular functional areas to the corresponding executive branch positions, perhaps settling conflicts between the houses by lot.

That might satisfy the Congress, but it would hardly satisfy the president. It would give him a slate of appointees of whom a large proportion might be unsuited for executive responsibility—by virtue of temperament, lack of administrative ability or energy, or ideological incompatibility with the president. One recalls the feud during the Vietnam War between President Johnson and the chairman of the

7. In the 1970s, House Democrats stripped the seniority principle of its previously absolute and automatic character, and the Democratic caucus has since violated the tradition on several occasions. Democrats on some committees have likewise departed from seniority on occasion in selecting subcommittee chairmen. But such departures are still rare, and seniority remains the normal and dominant mode of selection among House Democrats. Republicans in the House and both parties in the Senate still adhere to seniority as rigorously as ever. However, as noted in chapter 5, the reduction in the arbitrary power of committee chairs has made less important the question of who occupies a committee's chair.

Senate Foreign Relations Committee, J. William Fulbright, Democrat of Arkansas, but other examples can be brought to mind from any period. No president could weld an effective and cohesive administration from a slate of officials not of his own choosing.

There remains, finally, the problem of work load. Ambitious members of Congress have managed to make being an American legislator a demanding, exhausting, full-time job. And few cabinet members would contend that their executive branch duties alone do not consume their total energies. The two jobs as now constituted would impose a superhuman burden. Parliamentary governments have evolved solutions to the problem of work load that are largely alien to this country. On the executive side, ministers do not actually administer their departments; that is left to a corps of permanent, senior civil servants of a type that the United States has never developed and would not easily tolerate. On the legislative side, ministers have duties of floor leadership, but the committee responsibilities that absorb members of Congress do not exist because committees on the U.S. model do not themselves exist; their work, for the most part, is done by executive departments under the ministers' direction. Ministers do not even have to devote much attention to getting reelected, because campaigns are short and senior members of the parliament usually enjoy safe seats. The ministers do not have constituent service duties either, because that tradition has not evolved in other countries.

Representative Reuss contends that much of U.S. legislators' constituency service is "make work and busy work" on the part of members who do not have enough genuine work to do.[8] But much of the work has come to be expected, and a member who neglected it would be open to attack by political opponents. Reuss proposed to relieve executive branch appointees from committee responsibilities. But that would appear to defeat the purpose of the scheme, for it would be through their committees—preferably as chairs—that executive officials would have the greatest opportunity to bring about collaboration between the branches. Without the participation of the dual officeholders, committees would have about as much inclination as they do now to go their own way in defiance of the executive branch.[9]

8. *Political Economy and Constitutional Reform*, Hearings, p. 334.
9. France has adopted a unique scheme for coping with the work load problem. Each member of the Chamber of Deputies has an alternate who, when the member assumes duties in the executive branch, takes the member's seat in the legislative

All these considerations weigh against the idea of prescribing a fixed set of positions to which members of Congress would be eligible for appointment. Yet there is merit in the objective of giving the president latitude to appoint one or more members of Congress to executive branch positions, entirely at his own discretion, without requiring the members to resign. Such an arrangement would broaden the range of talent available to a president when he assembles his administration. For every David Stockman or Dick Cheney or Edward Madigan willing to resign from Congress to accept an executive appointment, there might be several others who would enjoy tours of duty as administrative officials if they did not have to give up their careers in the legislature.[10] Such appointments could be made possible by a simple amendment that merely repealed the incompatibility clause and thus allowed presidents to experiment, as proposed by the CCS. They could appoint a chair of a small business subcommittee to head the Small Business Administration, or the chair of a veterans' affairs panel as secretary of veterans affairs and see what happened. A Secretary Cheney could keep his congressional seat and find out whether the work load was indeed insuperable. Authors of laws could be invited to take responsibility for their execution, for a time at least. Part-time jobs, including membership on advisory or supervisory boards and commissions, could be filled by legislators and even created for them. Congressional oversight of administration—one of the benefits of independent branches, when it is done well—would be sacrificed to some degree, but whether the gains from cooperation between the branches outweighed that loss would be tested. Each

---

body. If and when the member leaves his executive post and returns to the Chamber, the alternate steps down. The member serving in the executive branch loses his rights in the legislature but presumably retains his influence. If a proposal such as that of Representative Reuss were to be seriously considered, an adaptation of the French scheme would be worth exploring.

10. Stockman was a representative from Michigan appointed director of the Office of Management and Budget by President Reagan in 1981, Cheney a representative from Wyoming named secretary of defense by President Bush in 1989, and Madigan a representative from Illinois chosen secretary of agriculture by Bush in 1991. Four Democratic members of Congress resigned to join President Carter's administration: Representatives Brock Adams of Washington to be secretary of transportation, Bob Bergland to be secretary of agriculture, and Andrew Young to be ambassador to the United Nations, all in 1977; and Senator Edmund S. Muskie of Maine to be secretary of state, in 1980.

individual appointment would be reviewed through the normal process of Senate confirmation.

Once an executive post had been held by a legislator, and successfully, Congress might lay claim to it and advance its candidates,
much as would be the case under the Reuss amendment. But at the
outset at least, the initiative would lie with the president. Presidents
would undoubtedly proceed cautiously, and if a pattern evolved for
such appointments, it would be based on a series of effective trials.

Cabinet Members in Congress

Participation by executive branch officials in the deliberations of
Congress, as a means of linking the separate branches, would require
constitutional amendment only if the officials were in some sense
made members of the legislature, with some or all of the privileges
attendant on membership, such as voting. That would require not
only repeal of the incompatibility clause but also modification of those
sections of the Constitution that define the membership of the legislative body concerned. And the body concerned might be only the
House of Representatives, for to add to the Senate membership on
any basis other than one per state would run afoul of the clause
prohibiting any amendment that would deprive any state of its equal
suffrage in the Senate.

On balance, the advantages of actual membership in the House for
cabinet members would appear to be so limited that they would hardly
warrant the disruption that such a step would cause. To have two
classes of members, one elected in the usual manner and the other
appointed by the president to his cabinet and hence to the House,
would inevitably create divisions and jealousies that would threaten
the cohesion of that body. The appointed members would lack seniority and would therefore, under House tradition, occupy the most
junior positions on committees and subcommittees; they would lack
authority (and surely in many cases political skill) to lead the Congress, yet could hardly denigrate their own cabinet offices by submitting to someone else's leadership. The only workable solution
would appear to be the adoption of new rules that, revoking the
hallowed tradition of seniority, would give the presidential appointees instant and automatic chairmanships. Yet, unless the right to
chairmanships was somehow also fixed in the Constitution—a sug-

gestion that would defy draftsmanship—it is difficult to see how the sitting members of the House who had won and retained their seats through the ordeal of election could be persuaded to write and adopt rules yielding their prerogatives to neophyte members who had gained their positions through presidential patronage. Thus, to make executive branch officials leaders of Congress, they would have to be appointed from Congress in the first place, authorized by the constitutional amendment discussed in the preceding section.

Yet if interbranch collaboration is to be fostered through participation of executive officials in congressional activity, full membership for those officials—with all the complications that would follow— might not be crucial. Collaboration takes place not at the time that votes are taken but in the deliberations that precede the vote, and executive branch officials can be admitted to any stage of those deliberations under the Constitution as it stands. Each house can make its own rules in that regard, or, if the arrangement is to reflect a negotiated agreement between the president and the Congress, it can be formalized in organizational structures and written into law. All of the proposals seriously considered over the years to give the cabinet a legislative role, as reported in chapter 3, were in the form of statutes.

Yet all of those schemes foundered because they were recognized, by most presidents and all Congresses, to be either unnecessary or unworkable. When the two branches are disposed to cooperate, formal arrangements are not needed. But when they are not so disposed, any formal requirement for collaboration is likely to be ignored or negated.

When the president and the congressional majorities are of the same party, responding to the same popular mandate, and intent on carrying out a common program, the existing mechanisms for interbranch collaboration are quite sufficient—as they were in the brief periods of harmonious and fruitful cooperation in the early years of the administrations of Wilson, Franklin Roosevelt, and Lyndon Johnson. At such times, presidents, cabinet members, and other executive officials participated informally, at every stage, in deliberations of the Congress. Legislative agendas were established in meetings between the presidents and their Senate and House leaders. Legislation was drafted through give-and-take between administrators and legislators. In Wilson's day, the collaboration was formalized through executive participation in the House and Senate Democratic caucuses, but during the Roosevelt and Johnson years smaller, less formal meetings served the purpose equally well. Cabinet members were sometimes present during subcommittee and committee meetings, but if they were not within the room they or their representatives were just outside the door available for instant consultation. They were also just outside the House and Senate chambers during floor debate. When the political mood calls for collaborative effort, information flows freely between the branches, facilitated by the congressional liaison staffs of the White House and the executive departments; administrators and legislators influence the thinking of one another, and the final legislation is truly a joint product. Even when relations between a president and congressional majorities of his own party become strained, as they tend to do sooner or later, harmonious collaboration will continue in many areas of governmental activity, and nothing in the institutional structure stands in the way.

In other areas of activity, however—or in periods of divided government, in most or all areas—legislators and executive branch officials will find themselves in profound disagreement, each conscientiously intent on blocking the efforts of the other. In such circumstances, any requirement for collaboration that might be formalized in organizational structures and written into law—or into the Constitution—is certain to prove unavailing. Officials now may meet whenever they wish to; to compel any specified set of officials to hold meetings whether or not they may desire to confer, as in schemes for statutory joint councils or executive-legislative cabinets, would be to assure that the unwanted meetings would be brief, ill attended, and unproductive.[11] Administration bills that have substantial support in the Congress are always introduced and considered; executive officials need not be in the legislative process to assure that that happens.

11. For a review of proposals for joint councils, see James L. Sundquist, *The Decline and Resurgence of Congress* (Brookings, 1981) pp. 469–71. Among the proposals were those advanced in the 1940s and 1950s by Edward S. Corwin and Louis W. Koenig, and endorsed by Thomas K. Finletter, for a statutory cabinet made up of legislative leaders that would have no administrative responsibility (to avoid the constitutional prohibition against dual officeholding) but would be advisory to the president and department heads; the plan proposed by the joint Committee on the Organization of Congress in 1946 for majority policy committees in the two houses to meet regularly with the president, an idea that was killed by House Speaker Sam Rayburn; and more recent proposals by Francis O. Wilcox and Senator Hubert H. Humphrey for a joint executive-legislative committee on national security affairs.

Nor would any formal guarantee of the right to be heard in committee and floor proceedings be useful. Executive branch officials are now always given the courtesy of committee hearings whenever they desire to testify; to go further by guaranteeing the administrators access to committee rooms during deliberations when they are not wanted would not make them welcome or their advice more influential. Similarly, to give them the right of participation in floor debates would not bring them an audience they do not reach just as effectively through friendly members who expound the administration views or through participation in public debate outside the halls of Congress.

Proposals for participation of cabinet members in floor debates, as advocated during the nineteenth century and again in this century by Presidents Taft and Harding among others (see chapter 3), have not been revived in recent years. But the more limited idea of a question period, which Senator Estes Kefauver, Democrat of Tennessee, advanced in the 1940s, was given new life in a resolution introduced in 1991 by Representative Sam Gejdenson, Democrat of Connecticut, and forty cosponsors, all Democrats. The resolution took, however, the most cautious and tentative of forms. It would have been adopted only on a trial basis, for a single Congress. And it would have involved only one cabinet member per month, which would not even permit the House to cover the whole cabinet in the course of a normal congressional year.

In presenting his proposal, Gejdenson emphasized that his intention was "not to embarrass the Cabinet in any way," and his measure was carefully drafted to carry out that purpose. The officials would have been asked, not required, to appear for questioning, and the questions would be submitted in writing seven days in advance. The questioner would be given the opportunity for one follow-up question—which might conceivably be used to try to embarrass the cabinet member, but could, surely, with a minimum of skill, be evaded. The two party leaders would decide which questioners to recognize and would divide the time equally, which would assure the invited guest that at least half the questions would be friendly.[12]

Despite the fact that all of his forty initial cosponsors were Democrats, Gejdenson disclaimed any partisan intent. The purpose was

12. H. Res. 155, 102d Congress, 1st session, and statement by Representative Sam Gejdenson on introducing the resolution, *Congressional Record*, daily ed., May 16, 1991, p. E1816.

merely to "provide better communication," supplement the hearing
process by enabling persons not on the pertinent committees to query
cabinet members, and encourage interest in government by adding
"an element of drama" to the process. It may be doubted that much
information would be obtained through the question process that is
not now readily obtained or obtainable, either through hearings or
direct inquiry; cabinet members *do* pay attention to mail and telephone
calls from Capitol Hill, not just those from members of the committees
most important to the secretary. So the real justification would have
to lie in the benefit that might accrue from inaugurating a television
spectacular (on cable television, at least, and until the novelty wore
off). No doubt some viewers, particularly those who watch C-SPAN,
would find themselves better informed and, perhaps, favorably
impressed with the persons speaking for both branches, and any
innovation that improves public understanding of, and confidence
in, government should be welcomed.

It also may be doubted, however, that the question period would
not, in Gejdenson's words, "provoke partisanship." During a Republican administration, half the questioners—the Republican half—
would surely take pains to ask questions that would make the administration look good, and the Democrats could hardly be expected to
devote themselves to the same objective. Particularly in election
years—every second year, by the present calendar—they would
strive to score points for their own party against the administration
with whom they would be competing in November. But here the
advantage would lie clearly with the administration. A skilled secretary would have an unparalleled opportunity to present himself or
herself and the administration's policies and programs to the cable
and network television audiences—and promote the secretary's own
career in the process. With the questions submitted in advance, the
secretary would have ample time to prepare, and even if the follow-
up question were embarrassing, the secretary would have the last
word. The process would thus reverse the relationship that now exists
in committee hearings, where the legislators are in control, can catch
the witness off guard with unexpected questions, pursue their questioning at length, and have the final comment. One wonders why,
in 1991, the measure was sponsored by a partisan lineup of forty-one
Democrats rather than forty-one Republicans.

Strengthening Political Parties

"For government to function," wrote V. O. Key, Jr., "the obstructions of the constitutional mechanism must be overcome, and it is the party that casts a web, at times weak, at times strong, over the dispersed organs of government and gives them a semblance of unity."[13]

Accordingly, reformers who are daunted by the theoretical and practical obstacles to altering the constitutional mechanism itself have been attracted to the notion that strengthening the party web may be an alternative means for attaining governmental unity. For this purpose, it is the party-in-government that counts—the political level of the administration, headed by the president, and the majorities of the House and Senate, fewer than 500 people in all. (For the party-in-government to be effective, of course, it normally needs to control not only the presidency but also both houses of Congress, for a web that binds the presidency to a minority party in either house, or both, can hardly unite the organs of government.) Although the party-in-government has a life of its own, to some extent its strengths and weaknesses reflect those of the party organizations in the individual states and districts and in the nation at large, for that is the political training ground of the individuals who rise to national office. Anything that would strengthen the party outside the government would therefore help to unify the governmental party. But there are no ready means to achieving stronger party organizations. If there were, they would already have been adopted, for those who lead the Democratic and Republican parties assuredly desire to preside over more potent organizations. The barrier is that the American people have not wanted stronger parties. Quite the contrary, throughout this century—until the present time, at least—the people have distrusted party organizations and set out deliberately to weaken them.

The story of the decline of party was told in chapter 4—how the Progressive movement that crusaded against public corruption and governmental incompetence early in the century found the root of

13. V. O. Key, Jr., *Politics, Parties, and Pressure Groups*, 5th ed. (Crowell, 1964), p. 656. Key was expressing the consensus of political scientists, as noted in chapter 4. Other quotations appear briefly there and more fully in my "Needed: A Political Theory for the New Era of Coalition Government in the United States," *Political Science Quarterly*, vol. 103 (Winter 1988–89), pp. 613–35.

those evils in party organizations; and how the reformers struck at those organizations through professionalization of management, introduction or expansion of civil service systems, requirements for competitive bidding on purchases and contracts, and institution of nonpartisan elections for local offices and of direct primaries for nominations in partisan elections; and how a newly independent press and civic reform organizations of every stripe joined in lauding the concept of political independence. As the reforms and the attitudes spread, the old-style party organizations steadily withered. By now, they have all but vanished. In some places, they have been replaced by new-style party organizations that are open, democratic, and inclusive in their style and bound together by ideology and programmatic objectives rather than by patronage. In other places, the decline of the old-style machines has given way only to a politics of individualism, with candidates for office relying on themselves, their self-created personal organizations, and their skill in exploiting the mass media—especially television—to win their victories.

Members of Congress who arise from a political milieu of individualism carry their political style with them. Not accustomed to accepting party discipline at home, they are slow to recognize the need for it in Congress. If they had to defeat the remnants of old-style organizations in their initial races, they are likely to see merit in maintaining an independent, or at least semi-independent, stance on Capitol Hill. As one benefit, they can be sure of gaining more media attention by challenging the established leadership in Washington than by meekly following it.

Since the party machines were weakened, or destroyed, by deliberate actions taken in response to popular demand, to rebuild them in the old style would require a new popular demand, calling for reversal of a trend now nearly a century old. Yet, although an occasional voice is heard to suggest that such reforms as civil service be abolished in favor of a return to old-fashioned patronage, it is hardly conceivable that an attitudinal inversion on any significant scale could occur. More likely is the prospect that public sentiment may come to support the development and authority of the new-style party organizations, those that renounce the grosser forms of patronage and rely on ideology and programmatic goals as their unifying bond. There are signs that such organizations are indeed gaining strength, particularly in places where no old-style organization of consequence had to be displaced—for Republicans, in the once-solid Democratic South; for Democrats, in the formerly solid Republican northern tier of states. Yet the development and maintenance of such organizations cannot be legislated into being or otherwise created by anybody's act of will. Legal barriers to their activities can be removed—and this appears to be slowly happening, state by state and law by law—but otherwise their strengthening depends on their good behavior, by which they will earn and retain the public confidence.

Nevertheless, even if the new-style state and local parties gain in strength, that does not guarantee cohesive national party organizations, for the national parties are federations, and the organizations that compose them have always been diverse in composition and programmatic goals and even, sometimes, incompatible. The Democratic party in the 1920s, for example, was made up of locally powerful organizations in both North and South yet was never weaker as a national party, for its northern wing was urban, heavily Catholic, prolabor, more or less pro–civil rights, and wet, while its southern base was rural, overwhelmingly Protestant, proemployer, segregationist, and dry. The Republican party had a comparable East-West schism, with an agrarian bloc of progressives, or insurgents—indelibly dubbed "sons of the wild jackass" by a senatorial GOP opponent—pitted against a wing centered in the Atlantic seaboard cities that reflected the economic views of industrialists and financiers.

History may, however, be now on the side of more cohesive, more nearly ideologically homogeneous national parties, as the result of the realignment of the national party system that has been progressing for several decades, particularly in the South but also in the North. This point will be developed in the final section of this chapter. Meanwhile, as the country waits for party realignment to exert its unifying influence, and recognizing that some degree of ideological heterogeneity will always be found in both parties, the question is whether actions that might be designed to directly strengthen the web of the party-in-government hold promise both of effectiveness and of feasibility. Possibilities for such action fall into three categories—those that would alter the processes by which presidential candidates are selected, those that would strengthen the party organizations within the Congress, and those that would give national parties—and hence, in the case of the president's party, the president—stronger means for disciplining members of Congress.

The Presidential Nomination Process

The method by which the political parties choose their nominees for president has evolved through four stages. In each stage, the process that was employed had a profound effect on the relationship between the president and Congress.

As George Washington was completing his time in office, the Republican party that had taken form in the Congress under the leadership of James Madison sought a way to assure that the party's electors in 1796 would be mobilized to support the same candidates for president and vice president. They found the instrument, perhaps not unsurprisingly, in their own congressional caucus. The party members in the Senate and House met and proposed Thomas Jefferson and Aaron Burr. Jefferson finished second to John Adams that year, but four years later the party was so well organized that the caucus nominees—again Jefferson and Burr—received the same number of electoral votes, and the decision had to go to the House of Representatives, which chose Jefferson.[14] His successors, Madison and Monroe, gained the presidency as nominees of the Republican caucus. By then, however, it had become clear that this nominating process undermined the framers' concept of the separation of powers and the independent presidency. A president desiring reelection had to become the follower, even the creature, of his party's congressional wing; thus Madison, seeking renomination in 1812, had to acquiesce in the war with Britain that congressional jingoes, led by Speaker Henry Clay, were eagerly promoting. More important, the congressional caucus had earned the enmity of many state party leaders, who felt entitled to a role in the nominating process. Following the nomination of Monroe in 1816, therefore, it lapsed.

After a hiatus marked by the only other occasion in which the presidential choice was thrown into the House, in 1824, a far broader nominating institution was invented—the national convention that every party has since conducted each four years. How the delegates were to be selected has been left to the individual states, but throughout the nineteenth century they were chosen, in one manner or

14. Before adoption of the Twelfth Amendment, electors did not vote separately to fill the two offices but simply cast two votes, with the presidency going to the candidate with the most votes, providing he had a majority, and the vice presidency to the runner-up.

another, by the state party organizations. A successful presidential candidate therefore had to cultivate the party elite, including its office-holders and its bosses, and he had to construct his administration from persons acceptable to them and distribute patronage according to their dictates. The elite was not monolithic, of course, and presidents had to contend with rivalries among ambitious party leaders in the states, but the party-in-government was invariably led by a man who was bred on an ethic of party regularity and discipline, enforced by patronage. Members of the Senate, selected by state legislatures, were organization men—often the party bosses themselves—and House members arose from the same milieu. The traditions of party regularity and deference to leadership bred in the state and local organizations were bound to be reflected in highly disciplined congressional parties, dominated in the House before and after the turn of the century by the Republican "czar" Speakers, Thomas B. Reed of Maine and Joseph G. Cannon of Illinois, and in the Senate by a GOP oligarchy led by Nelson W. Aldrich of Rhode Island. Republican presidents had to deal with these powerful figures on equal terms, and relations were not invariably harmonious, but unity and decisiveness in government depended on the concurrence of only a few people who could easily be assembled in a small room.

Another invention—the presidential primary—carried the nominating process into a third phase, beginning in the first decade of this century and continuing through 1968. As the direct primary was introduced, state by state, in the selection of candidates for state office and for Congress, it was extended by some of those states to the choice of delegates to the national party nominating conventions. By 1920, twenty states had one or another form of presidential primary. After that, the number declined, fluctuating between fourteen and eighteen in the years from 1924 through 1968.[15]

Of these state primaries, however, some were preempted by favorite sons, whom serious national candidates usually did not risk challenging, and not all the candidates competed in all the others. In most campaign years, therefore, only a few states turned out to be true battlegrounds. In the 1960 Democratic contest, for example, Senators John F. Kennedy and Hubert H. Humphrey collided head on in only

---

15. Congressional Quarterly, *Guide to U.S. Elections*, 2d ed. (Washington: CQ, 1985), pp. 387–419.

two states—Wisconsin and West Virginia—and it was his triumphs there that clinched the nomination for Kennedy. In this kind of system, candidates had an opportunity to demonstrate their appeal to the voters, but the decision was finally made by a convention still composed predominantly of the party elite of professional politicians, officeholders, and leaders of interest groups allied with the party. All other things being equal, or nearly so, that elite preferred a candidate who was a proven vote-getter on a national scale, but if other things were not equal they were free to reject their most popular candidate— and often did. Thus Theodore Roosevelt in 1912 campaigned for the Republican nomination in all twelve of that year's primary states and won nine of them, but the convention renominated President Taft, who carried only one. In 1920 Warren G. Harding's name appeared on the ballot in only two Republican state primaries outside his own Ohio and he finished last in both of those, yet won the nomination. In the 1940 Republican primaries, Thomas E. Dewey won nearly 50 percent of all the votes but lost in the convention to Wendell L. Willkie, who tallied less than 1 percent. And in 1952 Senator Estes Kefauver of Tennessee swept the Democratic primaries, losing only two states, one to a favorite son. Yet the convention rejected him in favor of Governor Adlai E. Stevenson of Illinois, who had not even sought the nomination before the delegates met.[16]

After the tumultuous 1968 Democratic convention in Chicago, however, the presidential selection process was revolutionized. The party that defied the anti-Vietnam demonstrators in nominating Hubert Humphrey yielded to them on their demand for more open and democratic processes in the future. A reform commission headed first by Senator George S. McGovern of South Dakota and later by Representative Donald M. Fraser of Minnesota devised new party rules to ensure proportional representation of women, young people, and minorities in each state delegation whenever the delegates were chosen by caucus. The complexity and rigidity of these requirements, as well as the continuing demand from the underrepresented groups for more participatory processes, led state after state to shift from caucuses to primaries. The Republican party was swept along in the reform tide and joined, usually, in drafting state legislation that established primaries for both parties.

16. Ibid.

The number of primaries rose from fifteen in 1986 (fourteen states and the District of Columbia) to twenty in 1972, twenty-six in 1976, and thirty-five in 1980, then dropped back to twenty-nine in 1984, but rebounded to thirty-five in 1988 and forty in 1992. From a total of 11.7 million voters in the 1968 primaries (7.3 million Democratic, 4.4 million Republican), participation rose to 21.9 million in 1972 (16.0 million and 5.9 million), 26.4 million in 1976 (16.1 million and 10.4 million), and 31.4 million in 1980 (18.7 million and 12.7 million), then declined to 24.6 million in 1984 (18.0 million and 6.6 million) and rose again to 35.1 million in 1988 (23.0 million and 12.2 million).[17]

By the 1980s a large majority of convention delegates were selected in primaries, and even in the minority of states that still used caucuses, those meetings were required by party rules to be so open and well publicized that the party elite no longer controlled them either. The convention itself was reduced from a deliberative to a ratifying body, simply recording the decision made by the millions of party voters in primaries and caucuses. In an unusually close contest, the few delegates who were chosen uncommitted or who were committed to a candidate no longer in the race could, conceivably, wield the decisive influence, but since 1968 no contest in either party has been that close. Each four years, one candidate in each party has emerged from the delegate-selection season with enough votes to ensure his nomination. A candidate who dominates the primaries can no longer be jettisoned at the convention as was Roosevelt in 1912, Dewey in 1940, or Kefauver in 1952. The party elders no longer have the votes.

This has grave implications for the unity of the party-in-government. The party elite that includes the party's senators and representatives has lost the means to defend itself against the election of an outsider to the White House. The crucial qualifications of a presidential candidate now are an ability to raise money and to appeal to the public at large through television. Whether the candidate is accept-

17. Ibid., pp. 420–441; and Richard M. Scammon and Alice V. McGillivray, eds., *America Votes 19: A Handbook of Contemporary American Election Statistics* (Washington: Congressional Quarterly, 1991), pp. 50–59. The totals for states with primaries included a few where the primary was confined to only one of the two major parties; in 1992 two states fell into that category, Virginia holding only a Republican primary and Pennsylvania only a Democratic. The total also includes states that elected delegates in caucuses but still held "beauty contest" primaries; there were four such states on the Democratic side in 1992. The vote by parties may not add to the aggregate because of rounding.

able to, and capable of working effectively with, fellow party members in Congress and the other party leaders on whom a president must depend for support has not been a criterion that the voters deemed important—or would have the information to apply if they did. Indeed, independence from the party elite can be a source of strength with the party's voters. Thus Jimmy Carter could win the Democratic nomination by proclaiming himself an outsider and boasting of his lack of association with the party's Washington establishment. After his failure in the presidency—brought on in no small part by his inexperience in national affairs and his lack of rapport with the party leaders in and out of Congress—important elements of the party elite were determined not to make the same mistake in 1984. So they rallied around former Vice President Walter F. Mondale, only to find that another outsider—Senator Gary Hart of Colorado—could come within an inch of victory by using their endorsements of Mondale, particularly those by organized labor, as a club with which to bludgeon their favorite.

On the Republican side, Ronald Reagan rose as an outsider like Carter, even mounting a powerful and nearly successful primary assault on incumbent President Gerald Ford in 1976, but after his 1980 election he turned out to possess the political skills necessary to put together and lead a remarkably united Republican party-in-government. He was succeeded by the consummate political insider, George Bush, yet the Reagan 1980 challenge (though not the far weaker effort of Patrick J. Buchanan to defeat Bush in 1992) shows that the GOP may be as vulnerable as the Democrats to the threat that an outsider might reach the White House by defeating the party establishment. Indeed, for a time in 1992, an independent, Ross Perot, had enough popular support to suggest he had a chance to defeat both parties' candidates. And the next outsider who captures the presidency might turn out to lack the Reagan flair for leadership.

How, then, might the presidential nomination process be changed to assure the national party's leadership—and particularly its senators and representatives who with the president and his administration form, or would form, the party-in-government—sufficient influence to block the nomination of a candidate who is, in its view, unsuitable? At one extreme on the range of theoretical possibilities stands the 1796–1816 method of nomination by the party-in-Congress, but that was discarded as too cliquish and exclusionary even for that period and would surely be beyond the realm of possibility today. Yet if time cannot be rolled back that far, might it be carried back just twenty-five years? As late as 1968, the party elite had an effective veto power over the popular choice for president as expressed in the primaries, and unacceptable candidates could be, and often were, rejected. A working balance between democratic and elite influences protected the values of both. But that balance was struck by accident, not design. Responding to the reform spirit of the Progressive Era, some states introduced the presidential primary—but, as it happened, never more than a minority. Now, reacting to a new set of forces, an overwhelming majority of states has adopted that reform, and the balance has been destroyed.

The answer appears simple, then. Reduce the number of states with presidential primaries to something like the former level. But despite a modification of the rigid quota requirements that had been adopted by the Democratic party after 1968, the trend has been toward more, not fewer, primaries. The decision between primary and caucus methods is left, by tradition, to the individual state legislatures or state party organizations, and while the national parties have ample legal authority to intervene, it is hardly conceivable that they would do so to impose restrictions on democratic participation over the objections of the states. The trend from relatively closed to open delegate selection processes was set in motion, after all, by powerful political forces that are not likely to abate. The eruption at the 1968 Democratic convention released the pent-up frustration of many thousands of rank-and-file Democrats with their effective exclusion from the elite-controlled caucuses by which delegates had been selected. Women, blacks, and other minorities have been the beneficiaries of the new participatory processes, and so have antiestablishment Democratic candidates like Jimmy Carter, Gary Hart, Jesse Jackson, and Paul Tsongas. In the Republican party, new groups, notably those of the right wing mobilized in 1988 by the Reverend Pat Robertson and in 1992 by Buchanan, have likewise moved in force into party affairs. All the newcomers to political power have a stake in blocking any move toward restoration of the old elite control. Their influence in both parties will surely hinder the initiation of any headlong trend away from primaries and back to caucuses. Yet, even were such a movement to develop, the former outsiders would have strength enough to assure that caucuses were widely participatory, beyond recapture by any elite insider group.

If the balance of influence is not to be restored through a return to the pre-1968 model, the alternative must lie in altering the makeup of the convention itself. The Democratic party took a gingerly step in this direction after its 1980 defeat, by adopting a rule assigning 14 percent of its convention seats to unpledged delegates (who came to be known as superdelegates)—including 60 percent of the Democratic members of Congress, other elected officials, and party officers. The percentage of members of Congress was increased to 80 percent for the 1988 conclave, and in 1992 the superdelegates amounted to 18 percent of the full convention. Theoretically, in the event of a close convention contest, so large a bloc of uncommitted members of the party establishment could hold decisive power. But that prospect can easily be overestimated, because the superdelegates have not turned out to be either a bloc or uncommitted. They have tended to split along much the same lines as the convention as a whole, conforming to the decisions of the voters in their respective state primaries or caucuses. By convention time, most of them have become committed, either by choice or as the result of pressures they could not withstand. A small bias on the part of those who might manage to remain uncommitted among an 18 percent proportion of superdelegates would not often decide the nomination in a convention where virtually all the other participants were pledged to their candidates during the selection process.

If that proportion were significantly expanded, however, the chances would increase that the party establishment could exercise an effective veto over an unsuitable but popular candidate whose margin in the primaries and caucuses was less than overwhelming. Conceivably, in 1992, when many Democratic members of Congress and other party leaders were dissatisfied with the entire field of Democratic candidates and skeptical that any of them could defeat President Bush in November, enough superdelegates could have organized themselves as an uncommitted bloc—and combined forces with the relatively few delegates elected on uninstructed slates—to enable them to deadlock the convention and lead a movement to "draft" someone who had not been a candidate, just as the party's 1952 assemblage drafted a noncandidate, Governor Stevenson of Illinois.

In any case, a greater participation of leaders and officeholders would strengthen party organizations by forcing closer bonds between the elite and the rank and file of party activists. And, if the candidate were more dependent on the congressional wing of the party for nomination (and renomination for a second term), the ties between the president and the legislators would be stronger after the chief executive took office. To that end, the CCS recommended that all winners of nominations for House and Senate seats, plus the holdover senators, be named as delegates without having to compete in primaries or caucuses.[18] Hedrick Smith, concluding his massive analysis of the American political system, goes even further, suggesting that governors, big-city mayors, and other nominees for major offices be added to the superdelegate list, "perhaps giving them all double-weighted votes."[19]

Smith and other analysts and observers have suggested that a screening procedure used in several states might be adapted to the national scene.[20] In those states, the party organizations hold pre-primary conventions. To qualify to run in the primary, a candidate must receive the support of a "threshold" proportion of convention delegates. A candidate receiving more than a specified percentage of the vote may be declared the official party nominee.[21] Such a process at the national level would enable the party elite to exclude at the outset those candidates who lacked a significant base in the party

18. CCS, "A Bicentennial Analysis," p. 8.

19. Hedrick Smith, *The Power Game: How Washington Works* (Random House, 1988), p. 717.

20. Smith credits the idea of a national screening convention to Thomas E. Cronin, who with Robert Loevy wrote "The Case for a National Pre-Primary Convention Plan," *Public Opinion*, vol. 5 (December–January 1983), pp. 50–53. The proposal is also endorsed by Gary L. Rose, "Conclusion," in Rose, ed., *Controversial Issues in Presidential Selection* (State University of New York Press, 1991), pp. 287–89, and by several other political scientists cited therein. Gerald L. Baliles, former governor of Virginia, has proposed that a convention made up of "party people"—that is, elected officials, party leaders, grass-roots workers, and financial supporters—meet each June to nominate two slates (or only one, if two-thirds so voted). If two slates were nominated, they would compete in a national primary. Baliles, "A Better Way to Pick a President," *Washington Post*, April 19, 1992, p. C7.

21. In Colorado, a candidate must receive at least 20 percent of the convention vote in order to be eligible to run in the primary. In Connecticut, the convention is optional for the parties, but when one is held a candidate must receive a 30 percent vote to run later in the primary. New York holds party committee meetings rather than conventions, with 25 percent as the threshold. Council of State Governments, *Book of the States 1990–91* (Lexington, Ky., 1990), pp. 1234–35.

establishment. This proposal runs into the difficulty, however, that rules governing presidential primaries and caucuses have traditionally been set by state legislatures and state parties, and for the national party to attempt to exclude any potential candidates from running in individual states would centralize decisionmaking in a way that so far has been stoutly and successfully resisted by the state components of both parties.[22] Moreover, the national parties would be reluctant to adopt any such pre-primary screening process, for fear of alienating the supporters of any candidate that the procedure might exclude. The national Republican party was embarrassed in 1992 by the candidacy of David Duke, a former Louisiana state legislator with a background of Ku Klux Klan and Nazi affiliations, but many state Republican organizations found ways to keep him off their primary ballots and his candidacy quietly died; a ruckus at a national pre-primary screening convention, by contrast, might have given Duke a windfall of national publicity and a martyrdom that would have embarrassed the party even more.

Another approach to altering the makeup of the convention has been suggested by Lloyd N. Cutler, a cochair of the CCS. Let the regular delegates be selected through primaries and caucuses, as at present, Cutler has proposed, but let them compose one chamber of a bicameral convention, the other chamber to consist of the party's nominees for Senate and House seats and its incumbent carryover senators. The two bodies, meeting separately but simultaneously, would each nominate a candidate. In the event they chose different nominees, each chamber would hold a runoff ballot between the two

22. The right of the national parties to enforce rules for selection of delegates to their nominating conventions even when those rules contravene state law was affirmed by the Supreme Court in two cases, one arising in Illinois and one in Wisconsin, decided in 1975 and 1981, respectively, and both involving the Democratic party. Yet, as James W. Ceaser has pointed out, enforcement is difficult because the only sanction is for the national convention to refuse to seat improperly chosen delegates, which risks alienation of voters in the state involved. In the Wisconsin case, where the Democratic party tried to outlaw that state's anomalous "open" primary that permits Republicans to participate in choosing the Democratic nominee (and vice versa), the national Democratic party ultimately backed down. Those who likewise talked of action to establish a system of regional primaries—or at least to remove the self-asserted right of New Hampshire to always hold the initial primary—have become quiet in the face of the forceful position of the New Hampshire legislature. "The era of further national party efforts to dictate delegate selection procedures to the states seems to have come to an end," writes Ceaser. James W. Ceaser, "Improving the Nominating Process," in A. James Reichley, ed., *Elections American Style* (Brookings, 1987), p. 49.

victors, and the nominee would be the one with the highest combined percentage, the two chambers having equal weight. Each chamber would also adopt a platform, resolving disagreements through a conference committee.[23]

This plan has appeal, as the means of giving the party's legislators and legislative candidates an opportunity to veto the popular choice of the party's voters while preserving the party convention as now constituted (minus the delegates who would sit in the new congressional chamber). A candidate who had to survive the screening of his party in Congress would have to court the support of its members and make commitments about cooperation; Jimmy Carter, for one, would not have dared to run *against* the party establishment, including the party in Congress. And after taking office, a new president would have to continue to court his congressional party, lest it deny him renomination for a second term.

But a bicameral convention plan would encounter practical difficulties. It might place too much power in the congressional party, for the popular chamber might be narrowly divided while the congressional chamber would have a higher proportion of uncommitted delegates, some of whom would be receptive to leadership discipline to vote as a bloc. Since the 435 House candidates would outnumber the senators and Senate candidates in the congressional chamber by a ratio of six or seven to one,[24] the Speaker of the House would hold a power far exceeding that of any other individual in the nominating process, if he chose to promise rewards and punishments in order to influence even a small proportion of his House colleagues. He could become, conceivably, an individual kingmaker.

A party that adopted the bicameral convention scheme would, moreover, run the risk of crippling the candidacy of its nominee. If the two chambers agreed, of course, the candidate would be the beneficiary of two endorsements in two bursts of fanfare. But in the event they disagreed—and surely they would some of the time, if the change were worth making—the winner of the runoff election

23. Lloyd N. Cutler, "Getting Rid of Incoherent Government," *Washington Post*, March 27, 1983.

24. The number would probably be increased by those running for the five nonvoting House seats for the District of Columbia, Puerto Rico, Virgin Islands, Guam, and American Samoa, but minus a few districts that might have failed to nominate a candidate. Presumably, states whose nominees are now chosen in the autumn would advance their selection dates to the preconvention period.

would go before the country and be quickly branded by the opposition as a loser, one who had been rejected, either by the people's representatives in the popular chamber or by his party peers in the congressional chamber.

Given the practical difficulties and risks, the more promising approach would appear to be to proceed further along the road taken by the Democratic party in reserving seats for superdelegates at its quadrennial convention. The number could well be increased to include all of the incumbent senators and representatives and nominees for those offices. But the unicameral structure would be retained, so that tensions between popularly elected and ex officio delegates would be kept submerged and easily resolved through regular convention procedures.

Strengthening the Parties in Congress

Just as the party is the web that unites Senate, House, and presidency as the policymaking triad, it is also the institution that brings coherence to the separate activities of each chamber of the legislature. It is through the party mechanism that a house organizes to conduct its business, elects its leaders, constitutes its committees, develops a program insofar as it may have one, and schedules floor action. Whether the Senate or the House is efficient, productive, and creative depends on whether the majority party, which controls that body, itself possesses those attributes. That depends on whether it is unified enough to create strong internal institutions of leadership and disciplined enough to follow the leadership it has created.

But throughout the twentieth century, the unity and discipline of parties in Congress have been steadily breaking down. In both houses, the rise of the western Republican insurgents early in the century split the majority Republican party. The House GOP rebels joined with the Democrats in 1910 to strip Speaker Cannon of his dictatorial powers, while in the Senate the authority of the Aldrich oligarchy gradually dissipated as its members retired or died.

For a brief period, in 1913–14, the Democratic party used its caucuses in both houses as an instrument of discipline. The measures that made up Woodrow Wilson's New Freedom were forged in party meetings in which representatives of the administration participated. The House caucus then bound its members by two-thirds votes, and any member who violated the group's directive (unless an exception was made, which was possible under some circumstances) could be "read out of the party," with a loss of committee assignments and other perquisites. The Senate caucus was less authoritative but equally effective in enforcing discipline. But the procedure was vociferously denounced by the Republican opposition and by the reformist organizations and journals that flourished in the Progressive Era. Caucus coercion was undemocratic and tyrannous, they charged, destructive of the rights both of the Republican minorities as groups and of the Democratic members as individuals. The outcry contributed to the Democrats' decision to abandon caucus discipline after mid-1914, and except for a few measures in the early 1920s and the 1930s it has not been attempted again. The Republicans, having led the attack on King Caucus, even forsook the word, renaming their party meetings conferences. By Sam Rayburn's day, the Democratic caucus met only at the outset of each Congress to nominate its candidate for Speaker and elect the majority leadership; once installed, those officers saw nothing to be gained from further party meetings that could only attempt to restrict their freedom of action or otherwise embarrass them.[25]

When Czar Cannon was dethroned and authority slipped from the leadership group in the Senate, the repository of power came to be the chairmen of the Senate and House standing committees, who gained their posts not by party preferment but by simple longevity, as beneficiaries of rigid seniority systems adopted by both parties in both houses. A strong majority leader like Senator Lyndon B. Johnson, the Texas Democrat who held sway in the 1950s, could sense the limits of what his chairmen would accept, develop and announce a program within those limits, and then maneuver most of it to passage. But his contemporary, the strongest House Speaker of modern times, Sam Rayburn, could not do even that. Rayburn was at the mercy of a coterie of committee chairmen who gained and held their positions by seniority—in particular, Rules Committee Chairman Howard W. Smith, a Virginia Democrat who possessed the power, and used it, to block legislation emerging from Democrat-controlled committees that did not accord with his personal ultraconservative views.

25. Sundquist, *Decline and Resurgence*, pp. 168–76.

Eventually, the House Democratic party acted to destroy the arbitrary power of committee chairmen. The Rules Committee was enlarged in 1961, and, after Smith was defeated for renomination in his Virginia primary, the seniority system presently brought the first of a series of party loyalists to the chairmanship. The decisive actions, however, were those taken by the caucus to destroy the automaticity of the seniority system itself. When it deposed three veteran committee chairmen in 1975, it made clear that all chairmen held their posts at the sufferance of the party's House membership and must be responsive to it. But to make doubly sure, it adopted a "subcommittee bill of rights" that assured democratic procedures within committees.[26] Change in the Senate has paralleled that in the House. The majority Democrats in 1975 formally abandoned their rigid seniority system, and although no chairmen were dislodged, the rules change—and the example of the House—had its effect in democratizing committee operations. Once the Republicans gained control of the Senate in 1981, they adhered strictly to the seniority principle in assigning committee chairmanships, but no chairman gave evidence of relapsing toward the authoritarianism of earlier decades.[27]

The power held by autocratic committee chairmen was thus dispersed to subcommittee chairmen and to the individual members of the majority party, who not only could assert themselves more effectively at the subcommittee level but also had the power to choose,

26. House Republicans formally renounced seniority as an absolute principle even before the Democrats did, but in practice they have adhered to the tradition in designating the ranking minority members of committees and subcommittees. Since the Democrats have organized the House and held all chairmanships continuously since 1955, and for all but two Congresses since 1931, the story of redistribution of power in the House is necessarily a Democratic story. How a Republican majority party in the House would proceed in organizing the chamber and managing its business can only be speculated about, but the same attitudes and influences that have led the Democrats to introduce the institutional changes discussed in this section have been clearly apparent on the Republican side as well, and one may surmise that GOP institutions and practices would not differ fundamentally from those of the Democrats.

27. But the tradition became a matter of serious concern to the Reagan administration and the Senate Republican leadership. In 1985, Jesse Helms of North Carolina would have been entitled to the chairmanship of the Senate Foreign Relations Committee on the basis of seniority, had he claimed it, even though his policies would probably have been in conflict at times with those of the administration. Secretary of State George P. Shultz and other foreign policy officials were relieved when Helms chose to remain as chairman of the Agriculture Committee and allow an administration loyalist, Richard C. Lugar of Indiana, to take the Foreign Relations post.

and to unseat, subcommittee chairmen. Moreover, the steady growth in the number of subcommittees in the House from 119 in 1972 to 147 in 1991 introduced new opportunities for entrepreneurship, with groups inevitably competing for jurisdiction.[28] Accompanying these institutional changes—and, in the most fundamental sense, causing them—was what amounted to a cultural change in both the Senate and the House. A new breed of politicians had arisen from the individualistic politics that now flourished in the states and congressional districts where the old political machines had disintegrated, and they brought an ethic of individualism and egalitarianism to the legislative chambers that as late as the 1950s had been described as venerating seniority and experience. By the mid-1970s, Senate Majority Leader Mike Mansfield, Montana Democrat, was boasting that "nobody is telling anybody what to do" in the Senate, and House Majority Leader Thomas P. O'Neill, Jr., Massachusetts Democrat, was noting that since machine politics was "dead" in the country it was dead in the House as well, making that body "extremely difficult to coordinate."[29]

Nevertheless, the destruction of the power of independent committee chairmen opened new opportunities for the majority leaders to try to forge cohesive parties. Given the individualistic temper of the members, leaders had to move gingerly. Yet when they did move carefully, they met little resistance, for the members were in fact ambivalent. Each member valued his or her individual prerogatives, yet each was also concerned with the record of the legislative body as a whole, and members understood that if the legislature was to be productive, rampant individualism had to be restrained. The result has been a development of centralizing institutions that offsets to some degree the trend toward dispersion of power in the last two decades.

Most significant of these centralizing innovations has been the creation of a budget committee in each house with responsibility for

28. The House 1991 figure includes the task forces of the Budget Committee. The number of subcommittees has, however, stabilized. The 147 shown in the *Congressional Directory* for 1991–92 is only one more than the number in 1983. In the Senate, the number of subcommittees rose from 103 to 107 between 1972 and 1983 but declined to 87 in 1991–92. No fewer than nine Senate committees reduced the number of subcommittees; the Banking, Housing, and Urban Affairs committee cut its from nine to four.

29. Other members and journalistic observers made similar comments, summarized in Sundquist, *Decline and Resurgence*, pp. 395–402.

recommending spending and revenue levels, which as amended and adopted on the floor—and reconciled between the houses in conference committees—establish a general fiscal policy to which individual pieces of legislation are then supposed to conform. In admitting this new element into the legislature's power structure, the authorizing and appropriating committees yielded a significant share of their autonomy and their policymaking power. Tension has continued between the old committees and the new, and the resolutions presented by the Budget committees, and revised and adopted by the chambers, have not always been enforced. Yet in 1980 and especially in 1981, the budget process made possible the wholesale revision of laws that mandated expenditures, an achievement that would have been inconceivable under the former decentralized committee structure.

The Budget committees, as bipartisan bodies reporting to their respective houses, have had their effect on party cohesion only indirectly, but in both houses the majority party leadership has been linked more closely to the Budget Committee than it has ever been tied to the older authorizing and appropriating committees. In the House, the linkage is institutionalized. By tradition, the House majority leader does not serve on committees, but when the Budget Committee was established an exception was made. Majority Leader O'Neill was appointed to it, ranking just below the chairman, and the tradition has continued with subsequent majority leaders—Jim Wright, Thomas S. Foley, and Richard A. Gephardt. Similarly, the chairman of the Senate Budget Committee has usually been a key figure in the majority party's leadership structure.

The institutions that are designed explicitly to foster majority party unity are more important in the large, unwieldy House than in the more intimate Senate, and they have been gaining strength despite the rise of the culture of individualism. Since all of the instruments through which the party acts are created by, and responsible to, its caucus, the vitality of the instruments is likely to be no greater than the vitality of the caucus itself. No one in either party has suggested that a return to the binding caucuses of 1913 would be desirable or even conceivable, but the reformers who set out to democratize the House in the 1960s seized upon the caucus as their indispensable tool. They won an agreement from Speaker John W. McCormack, Rayburn's successor, that the caucus would meet not just biennially but every month. In those meetings, they carried out their successful attack on the entrenched seniority system, designed through a caucus committee the subcommittee bill of rights, and then inevitably plunged the caucus into discussion of party policy on legislative issues—particularly the Vietnam War. By the 1970s, the caucus was giving specific instructions to the Democratic members of committees on what they must do in those bodies as "agents of the caucus." But this presumed a greater degree of unity than the party had achieved. Dissenters from the positions taken by the caucus majority, including some senior and influential members, vehemently protested the attempts at party discipline; the leadership retreated, enough of the dissenters boycotted the meetings to reduce attendance below a quorum, and the caucus fell again for a time into disuse.

During the Reagan administration, however, the caucus was revived as a discussion forum, and late in 1984 Speaker O'Neill agreed that during the next two years regular meetings would be scheduled on a biweekly rather than a monthly basis. He also expressed an intent to use the party's steering and policy committee more systematically in the development of legislative strategy, and he agreed to formalize a smaller, representative consultative group to meet with him biweekly.[30] Speaker Jim Wright developed a more autocratic style of "go it alone" leadership but his successor, Thomas S. Foley, has returned to a more consultative—though sometimes criticized as less decisive—mode. In any event, the institutional mechanisms that undergird a potentially strong leadership guided by the will of the party majority remain in place. They were sufficient in both houses to enable the Congress, for example, to strike its budget deal with President Bush in 1990 and to forge a tax bill of its own that Bush vetoed in 1992.

That centralizing institutions have evolved at all in an environment of equality and individualism reveals House Democrats' acceptance of party unity as a necessary and desirable goal, but the slow and sporadic character of the institutional evolution also shows that the tolerance of the members has limits that are easily transgressed. Those who would seek to strengthen the congressional party can offer no panacea for instant party unity—not, at least, any panacea that

30. Diane Granat, "Junior Democrats Gain a Louder Voice . . . Leadership Panels Will Serve as a Forum," *National Journal*, December 8, 1984, pp. 3054–55.

today's individualistic members would find acceptable. Reformers can do no more than encourage steady experimentation with institutional devices by the majority party in each house and hope, perhaps, that the new generation of leaders emerging from the group that has demanded the revitalization of the caucus and of party committees may possess greater skill in using them to weld the disparate elements of the party into a more cohesive working body.

During the Reagan and Bush administrations, of course, greater unity and discipline among House Democrats has meant a lesser, rather than a greater, degree of unity in the government as a whole. Had the Democratic party been monolithic, the confrontations with the president and the Republican Senate would have been even more forceful, deadlocks more rigid, and negotiations to break them more arduous. The decisive governmental actions of 1981 were made possible by Democratic disunity that permitted a coalition of Republicans and southern Democratic "boll weevils" to make the essential decisions in the House. The early years of the Bush administration have produced fewer confrontations, because the president has proposed no radical program on the scale of Reagan's, but on some issues—the defeat of the nomination of former Senator John G. Tower to be secretary of defense, and the rejection of the president's proposed reduction in the capital gains tax, for instance—the Democratic legislators have displayed a remarkable degree of unity that portends a greater capacity not only for solid support of a Democratic president but also for solid opposition to a Republican one. Measures to strengthen parties within Congress will therefore tend to work against the unity of the government as a whole whenever party control of the branches is divided.

Money as a Means of Discipline

The ultimate disciplinary power that a political party can hold over legislators is the right to deny them the party's nomination for reelection or for advancement to a higher office. In other countries, parties commonly possess that right, whether or not they exercise it. The direct primary is unknown outside the United States, and nominations are effectively in the hands of the party elites at the national and district levels. Either the national party organization makes the choice, or it ratifies the selection of the party in the local electoral area—after, perhaps, having directly influenced the area nominating body in the first place. While it may be rare for a legislator to be read out of the party, the fact that an ultimate disciplinary power exists accounts in part for the power of the party whips to compel obedience on crucial votes in the legislature.

Before the invention of the direct primary, state and local party organizations in the United States exercised that kind of power, too. Although nominations might be made by conventions that were larger and involved wider citizen participation than those in other countries, they still were often tightly controlled by a boss or a small group of bosses who could deny renomination to a maverick legislator. And the results were reflected in the disciplined, party-line voting frequently recorded in state legislatures and city councils and the ready acceptance of party discipline as the norm in the Congress. Even after the primary replaced the convention as the nominating process in almost every state, the bosses in some places still retained a powerful influence, or even control, for a while, because their organizations could still dominate the relatively small turnouts in the party primaries. And, as mentioned earlier, a half dozen states have reintroduced the convention into the nominating process for senatorial (but not House) candidates, but usually as a pre-primary endorsing or screening mechanism rather than a nominating body. With the exception of these few states, then, and as a practical matter even in most of them, anyone self-identified as a Democrat or a Republican can enter the party's primary and, if successful—aided, perhaps, by the crossover votes of persons who are not even adherents of the party— carry its banner in the general election for Congress without the approval of that party's official governing body at the state level. And the national party organization has no ratifying authority whatever.

Thus Democrats and Republicans arrive in Congress with all the rights and privileges of party members even though they may be wholly opposed to the party's philosophy and program. They take their place on the seniority ladder and, until the abandonment of the rigid seniority system by the Democrats and House Republicans, they could rise automatically to the chairmanship of major committees. A party in Congress is able to deny preferment to a member, as House Democrats have shown. But it cannot deny a member the right to run for reelection on the party's slate.[31]

31. The national party headquarters of both parties have on rare occasions publicly repudiated nominees for Congress, because of their identification with racism or com-

In the absence of that ultimate sanction, however, the national parties—particularly the Republican party—have developed an alternative power that may turn out to be hardly less potent. That is the power of money. With television commercials now the dominant mode of communication from candidates to voters, campaigns have become, by any established standard, incredibly expensive. In 1990 a total of $229 million was spent in campaigns for House seats, or $525,000 per seat—double the total of a decade earlier. The average of the seriously contested seats was, of course, much higher, exceeding $1 million, or $500,000 per candidate. The corresponding total for thirty-five U.S. Senate races was $173 million—again more than double the level of a decade earlier.[32] However able and ambitious, a candidate without access to large sums of money will, in most states and districts, be left at the starting gate. And the power to influence, or even to dictate, nominations that was once held by the leaders of party organizations has now passed in large measure to informal networks of money raisers.

This shift in power may have contributed, in some unmeasurable degree, to the decline of party discipline in Congress. If the ultimate sanction—the capacity to grant or deny nomination and renomination—lies in money sources outside the party structure, it is they who have the power to impose discipline. To a great extent, the large blocs of outside money are in the hands of political action committees (PACs), which contributed about $145 million to 1990 Senate and House campaigns—more than six times the $24 million contributed by party organizations or spent by them on the candidates' behalf.[33] Legislators and PACs alike contend that campaign donations only buy the committees "access" to present their views on legislation, but journalistic exposés have produced solid evidence that money often

---

munism or because of personal scandal, but they have not been able to deny the use of the party name. Some have suggested that parties could gain proprietary rights to their names under the copyright laws, but the suggestion has not been followed.

32. Federal Election Commission data, compiled in Norman J. Ornstein, Thomas E. Mann, and Michael J. Malbin, *Vital Statistics on Congress, 1991–1992* (Washington: Congressional Quarterly, 1992), pp. 74–75, 78–79. The comparisons between 1980 and 1990 do not take account of inflation during the period. The expenditures for Senate races vary so widely, ranging as high as $21 million in North Carolina in 1990, that the average has little meaning and is omitted here.

33. Ibid., pp. 91–92.

directly sways votes. A quotation from Representative Mike Synar, Oklahoma Democrat, is typical of many: "I go out on the floor and say to a member, 'I need your help on this bill,' and often he will say, 'I can't do that, I got $5,000 from a special interest.' So I no longer lobby Congressmen. I lobby the lobbyists to lobby the Congressmen."[34]

The extent to which the power of money has flowed from the parties to the PACs may, however, be overemphasized, for the two are by no means divorced. Business PACs work closely with Republican party organizations, and labor PACs with Democratic, to determine where a concentration of campaign money is most likely to tip the balance in a close race. Spokespersons for both the Democratic and Republican national committees have described their function as "matchmaking" between their candidates and friendly PACS. Ronald Reagan himself made a plea in 1978 to business leaders for greater support to the Republican party from corporate PACs.[35] And Representative Tony Coelho, the Californian who became chairman of the Democratic Congressional Campaign Committee in 1980, built his solid reputation in that job partly on his success in persuading business PACs that since the Democrats were likely to control the House for the rest of the century, the committees would be well advised to divide their funds more equitably between Democratic and Republican candidates.[36]

Since party organizations can help or hinder a candidate's appeal to PACs for funds, both new candidates and sitting members have an incentive to maintain good relations with party leaders, inside and outside the Congress. Nevertheless, if the funds were actually at the disposal of the party itself rather than the independent PACs, the party's control—and with it, its disciplinary power—would be still greater. Accordingly, those who seek to strengthen the party as the

34. Quoted in Mark Green, "Political Pac-Man," *New Republic*, December 13, 1982, p. 19. Green assembles an array of such quotations and other evidence of PAC influence. More extensive treatments of the persuasive power of PACs are Larry J. Sabato, *PAC Power: Inside the World of Political Action Committees* (Norton, 1984), esp. chap. 4; Amitai Etzioni, *Capital Corruption: The New Attack on American Democracy* (Harcourt Brace Jovanovich, 1984), esp. chaps. 3, 4; and Elizabeth Drew, *Politics and Money: The New Road to Corruption* (Macmillan, 1983).

35. Sabato, *PAC Power*, pp. 141, 146.

36. Brooks Jackson, "How Money Matters: Democrats Credit Wins to Funding," *Wall Steet Journal*, November 12, 1984.

web that unifies the government have suggested reforms that would result in candidates' getting a greater proportion of their total campaign funds directly from party committees. This could be accomplished by (1) lifting the limits on the totals that party committees may contribute to candidates; (2) lifting the limits on contributions by individuals to party committees, as distinct from contributions to candidates; (3) adding from public funds to the total available to the parties for distribution to candidates; or (4) tightening the limits on PAC activity, thus increasing the relative importance of party organizations in campaign finance. These approaches are not mutually exclusive, and they would be most effective in combination.

The limits on PAC contributions were set in 1974 at $5,000 per House or Senate candidate in the general election (plus another $5,000 in the primary), and donations to House campaigns by a party's national committee or congressional campaign committee were treated as just another PAC contribution. The law permitted a $17,500 contribution by a party's senatorial campaign committee to each Senate race, plus direct expenditures of $8 million distributed among states by a formula based on voting-age population. Contributions to party committees were limited to $20,000 a year for individuals and $15,000 for PACs. The relative importance of party contributions would be enhanced if these ceilings on party contributions were raised or removed. They were, however, enacted by a Democrat-controlled Congress with the intent of preventing the Republicans from taking full advantage of their vastly superior capacity to raise campaign funds, and any proposal to remove them, or liberalize them significantly, would not be likely to attract bipartisan support.[37]

37. In the absence of bipartisan support in Congress for amendments to the campaign finance laws, it has been suggested that the Democratic party might unilaterally adopt party rules that imposed spending limits on candidates for national office, subject to acceptance by the Republicans of a challenge to do likewise. If the GOP declined to accept the limits, the Democrats presumably would gain politically from having issued the challenge, since the polls indicate the public favors limiting campaign expenditures. Proceeding by way of party rules would also circumvent that part of the Supreme Court's 1976 *Buckley* v. *Valeo* decision (424 U.S. 1) that invalidated those sections of the Federal Election Campaign Act that imposed limits on expenditures by candidates from their own resources. The Court held that those limits violated the free speech guarantees of the First Amendment, but that amendment applies only to statutes, not to party rules. No substantial support for this approach has yet developed, however, among Democratic party officials.

Public financing of congressional campaigns, with either a limitation or outright prohibition of private contributions, is an idea going
back to the Progressive era, but interest revived after the Watergate
scandal and after the Congress authorized public funds for presidential campaigns. A bill to extend public financing to congressional
campaigns passed the Senate in 1974 but failed by forty-one votes in
the House; a bill limited to House races, actively supported by the
House leadership and President Carter, died in a House committee
in 1979; and a provision for public funding contained in the campaign
finance reform bill passed by the Congress in 1992, after a partisan
struggle, was cited by President Bush as one of his principal reasons
for vetoing the bill.[38] None of these bills would have funneled the
money through the parties, however; the public funds would have
gone directly to the candidates on certification of their nomination
and as they raised the required matching funds from small contributors, and single-issue as well as major-party candidates would have
been eligible. Thus opponents argued on the House floor in 1974 that
the public financing provisions would actually weaken the parties.
The Committee for Party Renewal, an organization consisting mainly
of political scientists, urged in 1979 that any public financing bill
provide for channelling the funds through political parties, with "reasonable discretion" as to their allocation, and it restated that position
in 1992.[39]

Recognizing that television advertising now dominates campaign
expenditures, the CCS recommended creation of a congressional
broadcast fund similar to the existing publicly financed presidential
campaign fund. Half of each party's share would go directly to the
candidates and half would be distributed by the Senate and House
campaign committees, to be concentrated in whatever states or districts they might select. The party and its candidates would have to
agree to spend no other money for campaign broadcasts.[40] Larry

38. An account of the 1979 struggle is Gary W. Copeland, "The House Says 'No'
to Public Financing of Congressional Campaigns," *Legislative Studies Quarterly*, vol. 9
(August 1984), pp. 487–504.

39. "Statement on Public Financing," *Public Financing of Congressional Elections*,
Hearings before the House Committee on House Administration, 96 Cong. 1 sess.
(GPO, 1979), pp. 392–93; and *Party Line* (Committee for Party Renewal, Spring 1992),
p. 3.

40. CCS, "A Bicentennial Analysis," p. 9.

Sabato and others have suggested a more direct means of providing broadcast time: Simply require that television stations provide free time to the parties as a condition of their licenses, with the time to be distributed at the parties' discretion.[41] The latter proposal would, of course, be hotly resisted by the broadcast industry, and any proposal for public funding would fail to gain bipartisan support because the Republicans would find their fund-raising advantage reduced. Opponents, of course, center their arguments not on the public interest in maintaining their competitive advantage but on the nobler purpose of saving the taxpayers' money—and, in the present antigovernment public mood, it is easy to see how the voters would respond. "Take your political tin cup to the people on that one," Senate Republican Leader Bob Dole of Kansas challenged the Democrats in 1992, "and see what you come back with. My guess is, a black eye and a fat lip."[42]

One of the simplest ways to divert PAC resources to the parties would be to amend the tax law to encourage political contributions. Until it was abolished by the Tax Reform Act of 1986, a tax credit up to $50 per taxpayer was granted for contributions, but it included those made to PACs as well as to parties and candidates. If the credit were restored but restricted to contributions to parties, and especially if the limit were then raised, the parties would gain a significant advantage in the competition for campaign funds. To reduce PAC influence, proposals have been made to lower the $5,000 limit on a PAC's contribution to individual candidates or to put an aggregate limit on what a candidate may accept from all PACs. Such limits are vulnerable to criticism as favoring incumbents over challengers, as favoring wealthy candidates who under the Constitution can spend unlimited amounts of their own money, and as likely to prove ineffective because the PACs can turn to the alternative of spending the money directly to help their favored candidates.[43]

41. Sabato, "Real and Imagined Corruption in Campaign Financing," in Reichley, ed., *Elections American Style*, p. 168.

42. Quoted in Helen Dewar, "Accord Reached on Campaign Financing," *Washington Post*, April 4, 1992, p. A4.

43. Sabato, "Real and Imagined Corruption," pp. 164–67. Sabato makes these points under the heading "Reforms That Would Do More Harm Than Good." See also David B. Magleby and Candice J. Nelson, *The Money Chase: Congressional Campaign Finance Reform* (Brookings, 1990), pp. 203–05.

As the number of PACs and their total expenditures and aggregate influence continue to grow, the clamor for further reform of congressional campaign finance has continued to mount. The public interest group Common Cause has made that objective its central concern, editorial writers and cartoonists maintain a drumfire attack on PACs, and some candidates for Congress, including some incumbents, have sought political credit by refusing to accept PAC contributions. Yet the self-interest of the two parties, and of individual incumbent legislators, lies in such opposing directions on each of the main elements of a reform package that a compromise acceptable to both parties and a majority of incumbents has so far proved unattainable. A proposal by President Bush in 1989 that included elimination of PACs sponsored by corporations, trade unions, and trade associations was denounced by Democratic incumbents (who now garner the major share of contributions from such PACs) and by Democrats generally for failure to include spending limits. By the end of 1990, the two Democrat-controlled houses had each managed to pass a bill, but the divergences were so great and the controversy between the parties and within the Democratic majorities so intense that the House-Senate conference committee did not even meet.

In the next Congress, however, the Democratic majorities were able to agree on a bill, although, because President Bush had already announced his intention to veto it, the effort became little more than a partisan gesture. It would have imposed new limits on PACs, lowered the ceiling on the contributions of any individual PAC to a Senate candidate (though not to a House candidate) to $2,500 and set the aggregate limit at $200,000 for House candidates (with increases under specified circumstances) and limits of $375,000 to $825,000 for Senate candidates, depending on the state's population. It also set spending limits at $600,000 for House candidates (again with increases in certain cases) and from $950,000 to $5.5 million for Senate aspirants. (The upper figure was about half the cost of the 1990 Senate race in North Carolina.) Acceptance of the limits would have been voluntary, but compliance would have been encouraged through public subsidies. Senate candidates were to receive vouchers equal to 20 percent of the spending limit to be used to purchase television time, which broadcasters would have been required to make available at half the prevailing rate. House candidates would have received their public funds through matching of small contributions up to a maximum of $200,000. As promised, President Bush vetoed the bill, objecting to the spending limits, the public funding, and the difference in provisions applying to the House and the Senate.[44]

Yet under the bill the payments would have been made directly to the candidates and hence would not have served as a party-building mechanism. Indeed, party leaders contended that one provision of the bill would actually weaken party organizations, by placing limitations for the first time on "soft money"—that is, contributions by PACs and individuals to state parties made under state law but used in party campaigning for federal as well as state offices (thus circumventing the limits in federal law). Those whose object is to strengthen the cohesion and discipline of the parties-in-government continue to urge that when and if public financing is ever approved, or the campaign finance system otherwise reformed, the opportunity be seized to expand the share of congressional candidates' total campaign treasury that comes from their party, with discretion in the party to use cash as a means of discipline.

If money is to be so used by the party leaders, a further question remains: which leaders? In the case of privately contributed funds, of course, it will be whichever leaders succeed in attracting the contributions. But if public financing of congressional campaigns were instituted, a public choice would have to be made. If the funds were appropriated to a committee controlled by the president, his power to dominate Congress would clearly be enhanced. Congressional independence would be protected and even fortified, on the other hand, if the funds were appropriated to the Senate and House campaign committees made up of, and elected by, the parties' legislators. Then, assuming that those committees were granted the "reasonable discretion" suggested by the Committee for Party Renewal, the considerable increment of power would be gained instead by the leadership of Congress.

Even if one accepts today's prevailing judgment that authority in Congress is too diffused and stronger leadership is needed, would centralized control of the congressional campaign treasury strengthen

44. The bill's provisions are summarized in Beth Donovan, "Overhaul Plan Readied as Tool to Blunt Scandals' Effects," *Congressional Quarterly Weekly Report*, April 4, 1992, pp. 861–63; and the legislative struggle is also reviewed in Richard E. Cohen, "Congressional Chronicle," *National Journal*, May 2, 1992, p. 1072.

the leadership too much? Presumably, few would wish to recreate czar Speakers in the House or make the majority leader all-powerful in the Senate. Yet this seems but a faint possibility, whatever may happen in the realm of campaign finance. The authority to allocate campaign funds would be a step removed from the Speaker or majority leader, in the hands of a committee with its own chairman, chosen by the caucus by secret ballot and responsible to it. The culture of equality and individualism is so deeply embedded in the Congress that a campaign committee chairman could not discriminate blatantly without risking revolt within his own committee and eventually within the caucus itself.

Moreover, for campaign committees, the goal is victory. They are judged by the number of seats they win or lose in a given campaign year, not by whether they have successfully carried out ideological purges by denying funds to selected candidates. Traditionally, the committees have not used discretionary funds in that manner. A Republican candidate running a close contest as a moderate, or even a liberal, in a liberal district is therefore likely to be granted as much support as one who had regularly voted the party line, and Democratic committees likewise can be expected to give conservative candidates their share of party funds.[45] Nevertheless, a campaign committee chairman is in a strong position to help bring pressure to bear on wavering party members on crucial votes—even if only by hinting at the possibility of penalizing disloyalty when campaign funds are distributed at some future date. No one can say how much the power of money may have been influential in helping the Reagan administration obtain near-unanimous party support in 1981 for its tax and spending reduction measures, but most observers would probably concede that it had some influence.[46]

45. In 1980 the Republican National Committee did not distribute its money evenly among candidates, but "estimates of electability dominated the party choice," and a committee spokesman said "neither ideology nor issues entered into decisions." F. Christopher Arterton, "Political Money and Party Strength," in Joel L. Fleishman, ed., *The Future of American Political Parties: The Challenge of Governance* (New York: American Assembly, 1982), p. 129.

46. Paul C. Light reports that promises of financial support—or threats to withhold it—were effective in holding congressional Republicans in line in 1981. *The President's Agenda: Domestic Policy Choice from Kennedy to Carter* (Johns Hopkins University Press, 1983), p. xii. But President Reagan disavowed the use of presidential power to discipline members of Congress at his news conference of March 21, 1985. Asked whether he was satisfied with the loyalty of some Republican members of Congress, he responded:

On balance, a modest amount of public funds made available to the congressional campaign committees—perhaps, as has been suggested, in the form of a congressional broadcast fund—would probably be useful in promoting a greater degree of party unity without posing a serious threat that party leaders would once again attain the dictatorial power that the American people found intolerable nearly a century ago.

The Promise of Improved Collaboration

Whatever can be done to strengthen political party organizations will serve to improve cohesion between the executive branch and the president's party in Congress. The party is still the institution that infuses the organs of government with a sense of common purpose. But, as in the case of so many other of the reform ideas canvassed in this book, the end is easier stated than the means designed—assuming that one takes into account the problem of political acceptability of proposals for change.

The state of the party organizations is not essentially an independent variable, subject to manipulation, but a dependent one, the product of tradition and deep-seated public attitudes. The American people have been, in a real sense, antiparty since the framers in the 1787 convention and George Washington in his farewell address inveighed against "the spirit of faction." Distrust and hostility crested in the heyday of the corrupt political machines, but as patronage diminished and graft was rooted out, the public attitude changed but slowly. Moreover, the trend toward democratization within parties, epitomized by the direct primary as the means of choosing candidates for every office up to and including the presidency itself, has contributed to the decline of party organizations.

At the margin, party organizations can be strengthened through the judicious use of money for systematic institution building, as the Republican party in particular is now demonstrating. Yet ultimately,

---

"Well, I suppose this comes from the suggestion that I am supposed to penalize some members in the coming campaign. No, I've never done that. . . . I'm dedicated to doing my best to see if we can't maintain the majority we have in the Senate and someday get ourselves a majority in the House. . . . So, no, I'm not going to hold a grudge on anyone." *Public Papers of the Presidents, 1985,* vol. 1 (GPO, 1988), p. 331.

the organizations can exercise no more authority than the people are willing to confer on them. And from every indication, the public is not prepared yet to accept and trust political party organizations to exercise any real degree of discipline over elected officeholders. They expect their senators and representatives to be independent spirits, not cravens who allow party leaders or party majorities—or even the president as party leader—to tell them how to vote. Nor will the voters accept party discipline themselves. They will continue to prize their right to split their tickets and to put in place, if that is the outcome, divided government.

It is not the strength of party organizations, then, that is the all-important consideration bearing on unified and effective government, for strength as such will not be translated directly or immediately into greater party unity within the Congress. What is more significant is the internal homogeneity of the two parties, for to the extent that the parties consist of elements unified by a common philosophy and sense of the role and objectives of government, that unity will be reflected naturally and automatically by the party-in-government. And here, as suggested earlier in this chapter, is where the promise lies.

The trend toward homogeneity within both major parties, bridging the East-West and North-South cleavages that tended for so long to debilitate both, is the paramount political development of modern times, with a profound impact on every aspect of politics and government. Ever since the political realignment of the New Deal era, which created a new line of cleavage between a distinctly activist and liberal national Democratic party and a staunchly conservative national Republican party, ideology has been supplanting regional, religious, and ethnic group traditions as the basis for party attachment. The movement to the Democratic party of liberals who had been Republicans or who came from Republican families was largely completed by the 1960s; the once-considerable liberal wing of the GOP has all but died out, and although conservatism has its factions that will vie for supremacy, the party is no longer deeply divided, as it was from the time of Theodore Roosevelt to that of Nelson Rockefeller, over fundamental views about the role of government. The corresponding movement of conservative southerners into the Republican party has lagged, but in the last three decades has been proceeding at an accelerating pace. There is no reason to think this trend will be reversed. As the Democratic party is gradually stripped of the south-

ern conservative wing that once held sufficient power in the Congress
to thwart liberal Democratic presidents whenever it chose to do so,
the party grows stronger in ideological cohesion and hence in the
ability to concert its forces for legislative action.

That the realignment has already had its effects in improving the
cohesion of the congressional parties is evidenced in a sharp rise in
the "party unity scores" that *Congressional Quarterly* has been maintaining for the last several decades. Those scores measure the proportion of a party's members who support their party on votes where
a majority of Democrats and a majority of Republicans are on opposite
sides. The Democratic party unity scores (combining the votes in both
houses) rose from an average of 65 percent in the twenty-year period
1961–80, from Kennedy through Carter, to 73 percent in the first
Reagan term, 79 percent in his second, and 81 percent in each of the
first three years of Bush's tenure. The Republicans exhibited a somewhat higher degree of unity in the 1961–80 period (67.5 percent), but
rose to 73 percent in both Reagan terms and to 73 percent, 74 percent,
and 78 percent, respectively, in Bush's first three years.[47] With a few
exceptions, the congressional majority position of the party that holds
the White House coincides with the position of the administration,
so the higher party unity scores reflect not only greater cohesion
within the congressional parties but within the entire party-in-government. It would no doubt be overoptimistic to suggest that, in the
event the nation returns to unified party government, the need to
foster improved collaboration between the branches would no longer
be a problem at all. But certainly the Republican party-in-government
has been strikingly unified during the Republican era that began in
1981, and the prospect would be for a far more harmonious Democratic party-in-government if and when it is again entrusted with
control of both the executive and legislative branches.

Since 1981, then, it has not been party weakness as such but divided
government and the pressures of electoral politics that have rendered
the government impotent to cope with such problems as the mounting
deficit. To equip the governmental system to avert this partisan division of the government, to lessen the pressures of too-frequent elections, and to cope with governmental breakdown when and if it

47. The scores from 1961 through 1991 are tabulated in *Congressional Quarterly Weekly Report*, December 28, 1991, p. 3788.

occurs, one must look to the constitutional remedies suggested in the preceding chapters. Strengthening political party organizations, even if that could readily be done, as well as adopting any of the suggestions discussed above for formal institutional linkages between the branches, would have only a tardy, indirect, and limited effect.

CHAPTER EIGHT

Modifying the Checks and Balances

The shield against despotism, thought the framers, was the system of checks and balances they had artfully constructed for their new experiment in government. The executive and legislative branches would restrain each other through an interlocking mechanism of mutual vetoes, and an independent judicial branch would keep its watch on both.

The checks and balances have assuredly served their purpose. None of the three branches has been able to overreach itself and dominate the others—for any sustained period of time, at least. Ambition has indeed countered ambition, as Madison hoped and foresaw. Legislative excesses have been thwarted by the power of the presidential veto and by the authority successfully claimed by the judiciary to strike down acts of Congress that in their view exceeded constitutional limitations. Imperial presidencies have been curbed by congressional assertion of the power of the purse, by legislative investigations and oversight with their appeals to public opinion, by judicial enforcement of constitutional restraints, and in extremity by impeachment of the president or the threat to impeach. Judicial ambition and assertiveness have been controlled through the power of the Congress and the president to reconstitute the court system, including the Supreme Court, by statutory law, and through the authority vested in the president and the Senate to decide who shall wear the judicial robes.

It is a truism, however, that a government so constructed as to raise barriers to bad acts will also raise the same obstacles to good ones, however those two adjectives may be defined by any individual. The system of checks and balances that has been so secure a safeguard against tyranny has also given rise to the central problem with which this book deals. For government to function effectively, the legislative and executive branches that are so well endowed with veto powers to thwart each other must somehow be induced to rise above their conflicting political ambitions and move in concert on essential matters.[1]

Earlier chapters have considered how greater harmony between the two branches might be brought about without altering the basic structure of reciprocal vetoes. But to make it easier for the government to reach decisions and take forceful action, the weakening of one or more of the veto powers can be a direct and effective means. The disharmony that now so often saps the effectiveness of government is not overcome through this type of measure; it is simply circumvented, by making it more readily possible for one side of the controversy to override the other and impose its will. The risks of such a consequence must be weighed, obviously, against the advantages. A presidency can be too weak in relation to the Congress but it can also be too domineering; a Congress can be too subservient to the president but also too overbearing. The executive-legislative balance of power that has evolved over two centuries may not strike the happiest possible medium between the extremes, but each proposal to alter the constitutional structure of vetoes must be analyzed in terms of whether it keeps the balance close to that which the people have come to accept and expect, or whether it might lead to an unacceptable dominance of either branch over the other.

The most important of all the checks and balances is, of course, the presidential veto—the right of the president to reject legislation passed by Congress, subject to override by a two-thirds vote of both

1. Fifty years ago, the judicial checks on the executive and legislative branches would also have had to be discussed as a central constitutional problem. A series of Supreme Court decisions during President Franklin D. Roosevelt's first term invalidated major acts of Congress designed to cope with the crisis of the Great Depression, on the ground that the Congress had gone beyond its powers enumerated in the Constitution. The president's response was his famed court-packing plan. The proposal was rejected by the Congress, but whether partly because of the threat or wholly for other reasons the Court has ceased to be an obstacle to the policy aspirations of the other branches. Since the 1930s, no major legislative act has been declared unconstitutional on the ground that the Congress exceeded its constitutional powers.

houses. It is the possession of the veto that makes the executive branch a full partner in the legislative process. The president's views must be taken into account on every single measure, for the advocates of a policy know that if they flout the president's wishes, they are hardly likely to be able to prevail. From 1945 through 1990, only 41 of 413 presidential vetoes, or fewer than 10 percent, were overridden.[2] In President Bush's first three and a half years in office, not one of his 31 vetoes was overruled. To lower the override requirement from two-thirds to, say, 60 percent would certainly facilitate the enactment of legislation, but it would do so by reducing the bargaining power of the president and hence altering the executive-legislative balance in favor of the Congress. Conversely, to raise the two-thirds standard would shift the balance toward the president. While there would appear to be no theoretical reason that two-thirds should be the perfect standard for overriding the presidential veto, the undisputed acceptance of that figure by everyone concerned throughout the two centuries of national history suggests that it must come close to the ideal. No suggestion to alter the two-thirds requirement has ever been seriously advanced.

Five other issues relating to the checks and balances have, however, attracted attention in recent decades. One proposal would authorize the president to exercise his constitutional veto power not just over entire bills but, in the case of one or more types of spending bills, over individual items. A second would restore, in one form or another, the legislative veto that had come into widespread use but was declared unconstitutional by the Supreme Court in 1983. A third would seek to settle the constitutional division of responsibility between the branches in committing the United States to military action, which the Congress sought vainly to resolve in the War Powers Resolution of 1973. A fourth would lower the two-thirds requirement for approval by the Senate of treaties negotiated by the executive branch. The fifth would introduce a national referendum as a way of breaking legislative deadlocks. Constitutional amendments dealing with these questions would not necessarily have the effect in every

---

2. Congressional Quarterly, *Guide to Congress*, 3d ed. (Washington: CQ, 1982), p. 763; and Norman J. Ornstein, Thomas E. Mann, and Michael J. Malbin, eds., *Vital Statistics on Congress, 1991–1992* (Washington: Congressional Quarterly, 1992), p. 158.

case of aggrandizing one branch at the expense of another; some may have the potential of encouraging harmonious collaboration between the branches.

The Item Veto

In a time of mounting and seemingly uncontrollable federal budget deficits, a simple and logical—if only partial—remedy seems to many to lie in a proposal that has been advanced repeatedly for more than a century: giving the president the right to veto not just spending bills in their entirety but individual items within those bills. Scholars have traced the idea back to the constitution of the Confederate states and to President Ulysses S. Grant's State of the Union Message of 1873, which was followed by the first proposal for a constitutional amendment introduced in Congress on the subject. Since then, at least 150 amendment resolutions have been introduced, and among recent presidents, Franklin Roosevelt, Eisenhower, Ford, Carter, Reagan, and Bush have endorsed the concept. "Every year," said Bush in his 1992 State of the Union Message, "the press has a field day making fun of outrageous examples [of pork barrel appropriations]: A Lawrence Welk museum, research grants for Belgian endive. . . . Maybe you need someone to help you say no. I know how to say it, and I know what I need to make it stick. Give me the same thing 43 governors have: the line-item veto."[3] The idea appeals to the people, too; six Gallup polls between 1953 and 1983 produced a favorable response consistently in the 61–70 percent range, with only 19-26 percent opposed.[4]

3. "Address Before a Joint Session of the Congress on the State of the Union, January 28, 1992," *Weekly Compilation of Presidential Documents*, vol. 28 (February 3, 1992), p. 175.

4. Ronald C. Moe, "Prospects for the Item Veto at the Federal Level: Lessons from the States" (Washington: National Academy of Public Administration, 1988), p. 1; and Thomas E. Cronin and Jeffrey J. Weill, "An Item Veto for the American President," paper prepared for the 1985 annual meeting of the American Political Science Association, pp. 3–5, 13. The Gallup poll wording in 1981 and 1983, only slightly reworded from earlier surveys, was: "At the present time, when Congress passes a bill, the president cannot veto part of that bill but must accept it in full or veto it. Do you think this should be changed so that a president can veto some items in a bill without vetoing the entire bill?"

Occasionally, Congress has voluntarily conferred on the president the equivalent of an item veto (now usually called the line-item veto, through the ingestion of bureaucratic jargon), but only on a temporary and limited basis. Thus the legislators in 1968 directed the president to impound $6 billion of the funds they had appropriated for the ensuing fiscal year, which was an authority even stronger than an item veto because it was not subject to the right of Congress to override the president's action. President Johnson did not seek the authority and formally protested, calling it "most unwise" for Congress to "shift to the President the responsibility for making reductions in programs which the Congress itself is unwilling to do."[5] The directive, which was in the form of an expenditure ceiling for the fiscal year, carried over to President Nixon, who assumed office midway in that fiscal year. Nixon actually impounded a total of $8.2 billion, and the Democratic Congress gave the Republican president another grant of authority to cut $1 billion during the fiscal year that began in 1969.[6]

On occasion, too, presidents more eager than Johnson to seize the power of the purse have claimed an inherent right under the Constitution to impound appropriated funds. However, in the early 1970s, when President Nixon pushed this asserted power well beyond the limits of congressional tolerance—as well as that of the beneficiaries of public spending—he precipitated a constitutional struggle that ended in his defeat and settled the question. Of more than fifty court cases that challenged his right to impound funds, the president was sustained in fewer than half a dozen. And the Congress passed the Congressional Budget and Impoundment Control Act, which forbade impoundment without congressional concurrence. It became law when a humbled Nixon approved it a month before his resignation in 1974.[7]

With the president's lack of authority doubly confirmed, proponents of presidential power to cut spending had to fall back on pressuring Congress to confer the power, either by enacting general legislation or by initiating a constitutional amendment—the latter usually taking the form of simply extending the president's veto authority

5. "Statement of the President Upon Signing the Tax Bill," *Public Papers of the Presidents, 1968–69* (Government Printing Office, 1970), vol. 1, p. 756.

6. For a fuller account of these delegations of authority, see James L. Sundquist, *The Decline and Resurgence of Congress* (Brookings, 1981), pp. 85–86, 204–05.

7. Ibid., pp. 205–15.

over entire bills to parts of those bills (usually also limited to spending bills). As the outcry against the deficits of the first Reagan administration grew louder, editorial writers and members of Congress revived the proposal and the president quickly seized upon it, endorsing it as a constitutional amendment but willing to accept it in statutory form. In his 1985 State of the Union Message, he specifically endorsed a bill by Senator Mack Mattingly, Republican of Georgia, that had the cosponsorship of forty-six other senators—nearly half the membership of that body. The Mattingly bill would have granted the president the item veto on a two-year trial basis, simply providing that each appropriation bill be divided after passage into as many separate bills as the measure contained items, each then to be presented to the president for approval or veto.

Whatever the merits of the question, Reagan was credited with a smart political move, for he could paint himself as a fiscal conservative even while submitting to the Congress budgets with deficits enormous by peacetime standards and blame the legislators for not giving him all possible tools for bringing the budget into balance. In any case, he succeeded in raising the constitutional question to the level of a national debate, which reached the Senate floor in 1985 and won a 57-41 majority in favor of ending a filibuster and letting the question come to a vote. But sixty votes are required, under the rules, to close debate. So the minority—which included seven Republicans along with thirty-four Democrats—prevailed and the measure died. The fifty-seven votes may have overstated the bill's true strength, of course, because senators knew that they could take a popular position and gain favor with the Reagan administration without having to worry that the bill would ever become law. The Democratic House majority was certain to reject such a shift in the balance of power in favor of a Republican president.

After President Bush took office, two Republican senators—John S. McCain of Arizona and Daniel R. Coats of Indiana—resumed the crusade and managed to gain a Senate vote on three occasions. Unable to obtain committee hearings, they were obliged to offer their measure in the form of floor amendments to pending bills. But with a Democratic rather than a Republican majority in the Senate, they could not come close to mustering the degree of support that Mattingly won in 1985. They were defeated by a 51-40 vote in 1989, by 50-43 in 1990, and by 54-44 in February 1992. In the last of those tests, only seven Democrats supported the item veto (compared with twelve in 1985), while an equal number of Republicans crossed the party line to oppose it.

The Potential for Savings

The case for the item veto was buttressed during this period by what appeared to be a steady increase in the volume of "pork barrel" items—that is, appropriations earmarked for individual projects in the home districts of members of appropriating and authorizing committees (such as the Lawrence Welk museum in North Dakota that President Bush singled out), many of them added without any committee consideration, without the previous authorization required by normal procedure, and sometimes even in House-Senate conference committees after both houses had completed floor action on their separate bills.

Senator McCain said in the 1992 debate that $6.3 billion had been added in the preceding year for expenditures that had not been authorized.[8] His illustrations of waste came from the military budget: "a noncompetitive extension of a contract . . . worth over $1 billion . . . $20 million in gasoline truck engines to keep one firm alive at a time when the Army has more than a ten-year surplus of such engines . . . $356.5 million above the increase we made . . . for still more C-130s, a plane constantly being thrust on the National Guard without regard to the Guard's overall priorities . . . $114 million in university set-asides that subsidize certain schools without any competition . . . ," of which $10 million went to a small Pennsylvania school (equivalent to one-third of its annual budget) "to study stress in the military."[9] The highway bill was loaded with "demonstration" projects that amounted to no more than subsidies for particular highway construction projects that the states had not considered worthy of a place on their priority lists. The item veto, said Senator Coats, would "stop the pork barrel that has been held up to ridicule every year . . . that is the butt of talk show jokes that ridicule and denigrate this very institution."[10]

8. *Congressional Record*, daily ed., February 26, 1992, p. S2770.
9. Ibid., p. S2771.
10. Ibid., February 27, 1992, p. S2460.

Prodigious claims have been advanced as to the volume of "wasteful overspending" that the item veto would eliminate. Proclaimed the *Wall Street Journal* in 1983: "Resolution of the budget crisis clearly lies with the president, and we know of one proven mechanism for getting the job done. . . . Mr. Reagan should make the line-item veto the centerpiece of his reelection campaign, and he shouldn't flinch from claiming it as the Republican answer to the deficit issue."[11] Senator Mattingly was more modest. He termed the item veto "just one small step to fiscal sanity," not "a quick, total solution to the budget deficits."[12] McCain and Coats were equally modest in the later debates, conceding that the item veto was essentially a symbolic first step that would do more to restore the credibility of the government than to initiate a realistic attack on the deficit. For one thing, it applied to only the 40 percent of the budget that is controlled through the appropriations process—and the growth of the budget has been primarily in those parts of the budget not so controlled—"entitlement" programs such as social security, medicare, and medicaid, and interest on the national debt.[13] Finally, the item veto would not apply to tax expenditures—that is, subsidies of various kinds granted in the form of tax credits or deductions rather than through direct appropriations—which totaled $400 billion in the president's 1993 budget.[14]

A study by the General Accounting Office, introduced into the 1992 debate by Senator Coats, concluded that over a six-year period from fiscal year 1984 through fiscal year 1989, all of the items in appropriation bills to which the Reagan administration had raised objections amounted to $70 billion, and if the president had had the power to veto them—and had vetoed all of them—the deficits accu-

11. *Wall Street Journal* editorial, September 14, 1983.
12. Letter to editor, *Washington Post*, October 2, 1984.
13. The president has his opportunity to control the levels of entitlement payments through the use of his regular veto power when the bills that establish the entitlements are presented to him. Once he signs an entitlement bill into law, however, the expenditures are beyond the reach of the president and hence classified as "uncontrollable." The Congress can make some or all entitlements "controllable" by delegating authority to the president to reduce the payments at his discretion. But since these payments, once established by law, do not again appear as items in any bill presented to the president for approval, any such grant of authority would have to be made by a specific statute rather than encompassed in a general item veto authority.
14. Totaled from data in *Budget of the United States Government, Fiscal Year 1993*, pt. 2, pp. 39–40.

mulated during those years would have been reduced by only 6.7 percent.[15] Senator Robert C. Byrd, Democrat of West Virginia and chairman of the Appropriations Committee, who held the floor for seven hours in opposition to the proposal, disputed even those figures, on the ground that the administration had on occasion given mixed signals, with agencies favoring the appropriations but the Office of Management and Budget opposing them. During all this period, of course, President Reagan—and President Bush after him—had submitted budgets with deficits in the range of $200 billion to $399 billion. And Senator Byrd's figures showed that while the Congress had rearranged the priorities in the president's budget—mainly from defense to domestic programs—it had reduced the eight Reagan budgets, in the aggregate, by a total of $16 billion, or about one-third of 1 percent.[16]

Byrd defended many of the "pork barrel" items as entirely worthy, and contended that the judgment of the Congress was better than that of the Office of Management and Budget on the value of particular expenditures. His point would be stronger if it were true that the Congress as a whole had actually considered—or could consider—the items through its normal deliberative process, beginning with committee hearings and advice from program administrators, and had then applied some objective standard in approving individual projects. But this has not been the case. In the press of enacting measures involving the expenditure of huge sums of money, the Congress could hardly deliberate on the relatively small amounts that members holding key committee positions—among them most notoriously Senator Byrd himself as Appropriations chairman—had been able to quietly insert for local contracts, subsidies, or projects. Moreover, at such times the logrolling process takes over; an economy-minded member disposed to move to delete a "pork barrel" item would remember, or be reminded, that the day might come when he or she would desire a favor from the committee concerned. In any case, the effort would be futile because a solid majority of members are schooled in the advice that long-time Speaker Sam Rayburn used to offer new members: "To get along, go along."

15. *Congressional Record*, daily ed., February 26, 1992, p. S2272.
16. Ibid., p. S2302.

"The Real Issue Is Power"

But Senator Byrd's series of speeches centered not on a defense of pork barrel items on their merits but on the necessity for the legislature to possess the power of the purse. Tracing the history of that legendary power from the long struggles between king and Parliament in medieval England through the colonial period and the 1787 Constitutional Convention, Byrd contended that what the item veto "will do . . . and what it is meant to do is . . . shift the power over the purse from the legislative branch to the executive and thus destroy the delicate balance crafted by the framers of our Constitution." The power of the purse, he argued, is "the central pillar . . . upon which the Constitutional temple of checks and balances rests, and . . . if that pillar is shaken, the temple will fall."[17]

"The Real Issue Is Power" was the title of one of Byrd's series of speeches, and he could cite Budget Director Richard Darman's comments on a television show: "In and of itself, it [he item veto] isn't directly a significant way to cut the deficit. What it does do is it transfers a degree of power to the Executive branch and gives the President . . . a stronger position in negotiations. That stronger position could be used, for example, to get savings in other program areas."[18]

But the negotiations might just as readily have the opposite outcome. In the 1985 debate, Senator Charles McC. Mathias, Jr., Republican of Maryland and chairman of the Senate Rules and Administration Committee, quoted the then retiring director of the Office of Management and Budget, David A. Stockman, as saying what his successor Darman would repeat—that the item veto does not have to do with deficits but with power. Mathias agreed:

> For example, if President Reagan does not like my position on the issue of school prayer, and if he acquires the power to kill funds for the program that I have long supported to save the Chesapeake Bay without affecting his Pentagon program or any other administration request, then the President, whoever he may be, has a hostage. He can hold the Chesapeake for the ransom of my support for a major change, for my support for State-sponsored prayer in school, or any other subject that he might want my

17. Ibid., p. S2279.
18. Comments by Darman on "This Week with David Brinkley," American Broadcasting Company, May 13, 1990, quoted by Byrd, ibid., p. S2309.

support on. And it would be a major change in the relationship between the executive and the legislative branches.[19]

Senator Mark O. Hatfield, Republican chairman of the Appropriations Committee, who as governor of Oregon had "sparingly" used the power of item veto, concurred:

> I can visualize, with a line item veto in the hands of the President, reminding the President that there was a Bonneville lock project in the energy water appropriation bill that was very important to those of us in the Northwest. . . . I can imagine a President, whoever he might be, saying: "Well, I need your vote on nerve gas" or, "I want your vote on the MX missile" or, "I want your vote on Contra aid to overthrow the Government of Nicaragua"—all issues on which I have fought the President.[20]

The item veto would be essentially then, a bargaining chip in the hands of the president, to be used selectively and occasionally, and its importance would lie more in the threat of its use than in its actual use. In the Reagan-era battles over the MX missile, aid to the Nicaraguan contras, and increases in military spending in general, the president would have been given added leverage to win the votes of dissident legislators. To the dismay of those who saw the item veto as an expenditure-cutting device, the result would have been increases as well as decreases in spending—even an increase, conceivably, in total outlays. And the ramifications would have been felt in areas of executive-legislative relations far removed from budget policy. The president's bargaining power would be enhanced in putting through any policy resisted by the legislators or opposing any policy advanced by them.

Looking at the whole range of matters over which presidents have quarreled with Congresses in the last several decades, one may ask whether one truly wishes the president's authority to be materially strengthened. Should presidents have greater power to undertake military adventures that the legislators have resisted? To impose domestic spending cuts the legislators have rejected in order to support military expenditures they have thought excessive? To conduct foreign policy without congressional restraint and participation? Is the system now out of balance in favor of the legislature? Perhaps, on examination, one would conclude that it is, that the president needs a new accretion of power in his rivalry with the legislature. But

19. *Congressional Record*, July 17, 1985, p. 19293.
20. Ibid., p. 19302.

in any case, those are the criteria by which the desirability of the item veto should be measured. The general enhancement of presidential influence at the expense of the Congress would be the significant consequence of this innovation.

These views appear to be confirmed by experience in the forty-three states that President Bush (as well as Reagan before him) cited as examples for the federal government. Four separate studies concur that the principal consequence of the item veto at the state level has been not financial savings but a shift in the political balance of power. The veto "is first and foremost a political instrument and should be understood in this context," Ronald Moe of the Congressional Research Service concluded in a report originally prepared for the House Rules Committee: "It can be credited in a number of instances with altering the politics of the state budgetary process to the advantage of the executive. For many promoters, this was their real objective in the first place." [21] Based on questionnaire responses from legislative officials in forty-five states, Glenn Abney and Thomas Lauth wrote that a majority of the governors had used their veto power rarely—fewer than three times a year in the three-year period studied—and that it had been used most heavily when the governor and the legislative majorities were of opposing parties. State experience indicated that if the practice were adopted at the national level "it would enhance the president's ability to deal with the Congress on matters of a partisan nature, but it is not likely to have much impact on such fiscal matters as the size of the deficit." [22] Louis Fisher, also of the Congressional Research Service, wrote that the item veto in the states "may help resolve some disputes, but it can also heighten conflict among the branches" and generate a substantial amount of costly litigation. [23]

The studies also found evidence that the item veto encouraged legislative irresponsibility. Legislators, according to Thomas Cronin and Jeffrey Weill, "add certain funds to their budgets with the clear

21. Moe, "Prospects for the Item Veto," p. 20.
22. Glen Abney and Thomas P. Lauth, "The Line-Item Veto in the States: An Instrument for Fiscal Restraint or an Instrument for Partisanship?" *Public Administration Review*, vol. 45 (May–June 1985), pp. 372–77. Of thirty-three governors whose frequency of use of the veto was reported, twenty had used it fewer than three times a year.
23. Louis Fisher, "The Item Veto: The Risks of Emulating the States," paper prepared for the 1985 annual meeting of the American Political Science Association, p. 22.

expectation, and sometimes even the hope, that their governor will veto them."[24] Freed of having to bear final responsibility for their spending bills, legislators can gain credit with constituents for logrolling popular projects for their districts through the legislature, while leaving to the governor the onus of killing them.

Alternative Forms and Processes

Statutory item veto measures such as those offered by Mattingly and McCain have had to incorporate the constitutional "presentment" process, with its requirement of two-thirds majorities in both houses of Congress to override a presidential veto. But if the legislators chose to follow the route of constitutional amendment, they could reserve more power to themselves. Presumably that would make the concept more acceptable—though that proved not to be the case when such an amendment was proposed in 1983 by Senator Alan J. Dixon, Democrat of Illinois. The Reagan administration did not adopt the Dixon proposal as its vehicle, as it later adopted the Mattingly bill, and it was rejected by the Senate, 53-25.

Patterned on a provision of the Illinois constitution, the Dixon amendment would have authorized the president to eliminate or reduce appropriations items but allowed the Congress to override his actions by majorities of the membership of both houses, rather than by the usual two-thirds of members present and voting. Senator Dixon made the argument, not repeated in the later debates, that the item veto would unclog the machinery of government because, if the president and Congress were disputing only a few items in an appropriations bill, the entire bill would not, as at present, have to be held up by a presidential veto or the threat of one. The controverted items could be vetoed and the rest of the bill enacted. Thus would be averted the annual October 1 crisis, when the government enters a new fiscal year without operating funds for some departments because major appropriations bills are held up by disputes over a few programs. In 1983, Dixon noted, "Many programs not in dispute were either brought to a standstill or nearly so. Major parts of the government once again went to the brink. Social security checks were nearly not mailed, thousands of government employees were unnecessarily laid

24. Cronin and Weill, "An Item Veto," p. 44.

off, and many worthy and necessary government activities were curtailed."[25]

A reduced override requirement would certainly produce a less drastic shift of power to the president, because the Congress could easily prevail on the disputed items after the president had scored his political and public relations points. Yet this might not always be the case, for the Congress could override the veto only if it were still in session. More than 43 percent of presidential vetoes on public bills in the 1947–90 period were pocket vetoes—that is, disapproval of bills after adjournment of Congress, giving the legislators no opportunity to override.[26] In recent years, major appropriations bills have normally been among the last measures passed by Congress before adjournment. Even the seemingly innocuous Dixon amendment, then, would give the president the equivalent of an absolute veto over items in those bills—unless the Congress changed its ways and passed its appropriations before the final days of the session. An amendment making the item veto constitutional could, of course, be written so as to exclude pocket vetoes, but that would enable the Congress to circumvent the provision altogether by simply delaying final action on controversial spending items until just before adjournment.

If a constitutional amendment were adopted to require a balanced budget (which would have to be initiated by a constitutional convention called by the states, as has been pressed for more than a decade), the item veto question would undoubtedly arise again, because the Congress would have to determine a method for assuring that the intent of the amendment was carried out. The same arguments for shifting power to the president that were offered in support of the 1968 and 1969 actions and in opposition to the Congressional Budget and Impoundment Control Act of 1974—and have been reiterated throughout the item veto discussions—would again be heard. But the Congress in the 1974 act not only emphatically affirmed its determination to exercise final decision over the nation's fiscal program, both in general outline and in detail, but also created new congressional budget machinery and processes for that purpose. One can anticipate that if the present campaign for a constitutional convention comes close to success—which appears unlikely at this writing—the

25. Alan J. Dixon, "Restoring Veto Power," *Washington Post*, October 19, 1983.
26. Ornstein and others, *Vital Statistics*, p. 158.

Congress would act to sidetrack the movement by enacting some highly visible reinvigoration of the congressional budget process or by initiating a mild amendment of its own, perhaps along the lines of the Dixon proposal, in order to maintain essentially the present balance of power between the branches and forestall the loss of its cherished power of the purse.

Unable to obtain the item veto power he has sought, President Bush has chosen to challenge the Congress through two other approaches. First, he has made more extensive and systematic use than any other president of what has been called "constitutional excision." On signing various authorization and appropriation acts, he has announced his intention to regard as advisory rather than mandatory certain directives that he viewed as impairing various elements of his constitutional authority—such as his rights to supervise the executive branch, to conduct foreign policy, to deploy military forces, to protect sensitive national security information, and to interpret treaties—or as otherwise unconstitutional. Saying that Bush "threw down the gauntlet" when he signed nine bills on a single day— November 5, 1990—Gregory Sidak and Thomas Smith counted thirty-one provisions in those measures that the president called unconstitutional and therefore, either by direct assertion or by implication, enforceable only at the discretion of the executive.[27] Earlier, he had said he would "consider ignoring" at least nine provisions of the State Department authorization act.[28] President Bush was careful, however, not to excise any provisions on policy rather than constitutional grounds; that would amount to claiming the item veto power that the Congress has declined to give the president by statute and that the courts held in the 1970 cases are not his by constitutional right.

The president has also sought to make fuller use of a provision of the 1974 Congressional Budget and Impoundment Control Act that authorizes the president to propose to Congress rescissions of previously approved funds and to withhold the expenditures for up to forty-five days if the Congress does not act. But the forty-five-day period begins when the rescission message is sent to Capitol Hill and covers only days when Congress is in session. So if the administration

27. J. Gregory Sidak and Thomas A. Smith, "The Veto Power: How Free is the President's Hand?" *American Enterprise*, vol. 2 (March–April, 1991), pp. 59–64.

28. The act was signed on February 16. *Congressional Quarterly Almanac, 1990*, vol. 46 (1991), p. 20.

is slow in preparing its proposal, or if Congress is in adjournment or adjourns shortly thereafter, the forty-five days may stretch into a span of several months.

During the February 1992 debate, Senator McCain introduced data showing that the Congress had ignored nearly two-thirds of President Ford's rescission proposals (97 of 150), almost one-third of President Carter's (38 of 132), nearly two-thirds of President Reagan's (384 of 601), and all but two of President Bush's (45 of 47).[29] Shortly after McCain's amendment was defeated, Bush sent to Capitol Hill for rescission four "hit lists" of items totaling $7.9 billion. That amount far exceeded the total of all the rescissions he had proposed in his entire three previous years in office, but was still only 2 percent of the $399 billion deficit the administration had projected for the year, and even of that amount only a small part would have been spent on the type of projects that induced the ridicule on radio and television talk shows. Nearly 90 percent of the spending reduction would come from the defense budget, including items such as cancellation of the Seawolf submarine program originally supported by the White House, and most of the cuts—both defense and nondefense—could be more accurately ascribed to policy differences than to pork barrel waste.

Congressional Democrats were quick to point out that Bush himself in his primary campaigns had been endorsing local projects for inclusion in his next budget—such as a $34 million extension to the Concord, New Hampshire, courthouse and a $514 million reclamation project in Florida. In the end, the Congress accepted some of the Bush cuts (including funds for just one more Seawolf), rejected others, but added enough of its own (such as $1 billion for a B-2 bomber) to bring its rescission package to $8.2 billion, slightly more than the president's.[30] All the partisan wrangling could only produce fiscal savings negligible in relation to the total deficit.

And that would still be the case if the Congress were to relinquish to the president its power of the purse. To suggest that the item veto can be *the* answer to the deficit issue, or even *an* answer, is illusory, and to the extent that it diverts attention from the basic institutional

29. *Congressional Record*, daily ed., February 26, 1992, p. S2273.
30. Walter Pincus, "Parliamentary Fight Awaits Bush Cuts," *Washington Post*, March 22, 1992; and George Hager, "Recissions Top Bush's Target, Change What Will Get Cut," *Congressional Quarterly Weekly Report*, May 23, 1992, pp. 1433–35.

shortcoming—the inability of the government as now structured to muster the political will to increase revenues to the level of expenditures that both parties agree are necessary—the illusion is a dangerous one. The institutional changes that hold real promise of equipping the nation to grapple with its budgetary problem are the more fundamental ones discussed in the earlier chapters of this book.

The Legislative Veto

From the viewpoint of the Congress, the constitutional system of checks and balances has suffered from a glaring omission. All of the constitutional checks by which the legislators control the executive branch must be applied either before the fact or after the fact—not *during* the exercise by the administrators of the power the Congress has granted to them. But, in many areas of governmental activity, control must be exercised at the time the administrator acts, or prepares to act, if it is to be exercised effectively at all.

Before the fact, the legislature can write detailed instructions and restraints into the authorizing statutes, and the Senate has the power to confirm or reject the president's nominees for administrative office. The Congress is often criticized for writing broad, ambiguous statutes that give insufficient guidance to the administrative agencies, and there is truth in the complaint. But there is clearly a limit to what the Congress can hope to anticipate and resolve in advance; the most obvious illustrations arise in the field of foreign affairs, where the executive branch must have authority to deal with crises that flare up without notice in the middle of the night, Washington time, but unanticipated events may require immediate response in domestic affairs as well. As for controlling the administrators through the confirmation process, the Senate must almost always act on faith, for it cannot know in advance which executive officials will exceed or misuse the powers placed in their hands.

After the fact, the Congress can investigate, write clarifying legislation if it concludes that the law has been misinterpreted, chastise misbehaving officials and even drive them to resign or, as a last resort, impeach them. But by that time the administrative action to which the legislators object may have been fully accomplished. The damage will have been done.

Evolution of the Veto

It was to resolve this dilemma that the legislative veto was invented. By the use of that device, the Congress could authorize actions by the executive branch but require that before those actions took effect they would be subject to review and rejection by both houses, by one house, or even by a single committee of Congress. It would thus assert its control during the fact, which might be the only kind of control that could really count.

The oldest and longest-running series of legislative veto provisions—those contained in acts authorizing reorganization of executive agencies—well illustrates both the nature and utility of the mechanism. For more than half a century, the Congress has recognized that the legislative branch lacks both the capability and the interest to plan the restructuring of the executive branch that is necessary from time to time to accommodate its changing responsibilities. Yet it has been unwilling to give the president a completely free hand to organize and disband bureaus and departments and transfer functions among them, for on many such decisions a legislator's constituents may have strong views. In 1932 the Congress found a way out. It authorized President Hoover to reorganize the government by executive order, but each order had to be submitted to Congress and could be disapproved by either house within sixty days. That procedure was continued, with modifications from time to time, in a long series of reorganization acts spanning the subsequent decades.

After World War II, the Congress began incorporating the legislative veto in occasional other acts, usually in the form of a requirement that an executive agency "come into agreement" with designated congressional committees on particular types of actions. But after the historic constitutional clash between the Congress and President Nixon in 1973–74, the legislators began applying the veto on a broad scale, for a time attaching it almost routinely to new grants of power to the executive. In the period 1973–79, it was incorporated in more than sixty laws and sometimes in a dozen or more sections of a single law. By 1983, 122 statutes containing 207 legislative veto provisions were on the books.[31]

31. Department of Justice, Office of Legal Counsel, "Compilation of Currently Effective Statutes that Contain Legislative Veto Provisions" (July 15, 1983). The evolution of the legislative veto from 1932 to 1980 is sketched in Sundquist, *Decline and Resurgence*, pp. 344–54.

Since all of these laws were subject to a presidential veto in the first place, the legislative veto provisions had somehow obtained the chief executive's acceptance. But presidents did not always accept them gladly. Shortly after the 1932 reorganization act was signed, the Justice Department took a stand that the legislative veto was unconstitutional, and it maintained that position with unbroken consistency afterward. On its recommendation, several presidents disapproved bills containing veto provisions and so forced the Congress to delete them. But often the legislative vetoes were added as incidental and minor elements of major bills in the president's own program, or they were incorporated in the authorization bills required to continue essential governmental activities. The presidents might protest— Eisenhower, Nixon, and Carter all went so far as to announce that their administrations would not comply with certain of the vetoes, on the grounds that the Congress was acting unconstitutionally—but they had to sign the bills. One statute containing a legislative veto— the War Powers Resolution of 1973—was passed over President Nixon's veto.

But frequently the executive branch acquiesced happily in a veto provision, because it preferred a delegation of power under that limitation to the alternative, which would have been no delegation at all. Such was the case with the series of reorganization acts. In at least some instances, the executive branch initiated the suggestion for a legislative veto in order to win a grant of authority that the legislators were reluctant to approve. Even as he was denouncing legislative veto provisions as wholly unconstitutional, for example, President Carter publicly advocated inclusion of a veto procedure in a standby gasoline rationing bill; that provision broke the resistance to the measure, and the bill was passed. Inclusion of a similar provision was an essential compromise in enactment of the Congressional Budget and Impoundment Control Act of 1974, a statute that Nixon finally welcomed.

In its zeal to control the executive in the 1970s, however, the Congress overreached itself. Instead of acting selectively in cases where the administration might find the legislative veto grudgingly acceptable, legislators began enacting blanket veto provisions covering the entire range of regulations issued by particular agencies, such as the Federal Trade Commission and the new Department of Education. In 1976 almost two-thirds of the members of the House voted for a bill that would have subjected all rules and regulations issued by all agencies to a legislative veto, and the Senate passed a similar measure in 1982. Legal scholars began to condemn the legislative veto of agency regulations as a corruption of the rule-making processes that had been carefully designed and prescribed by law to protect the rights of affected parties; as permitting irresponsible, secretive, and inexpert meddling by congressional staff in what should be open and expert proceedings; and as conducive to delay and deadlock.[32] The Justice Department decided that the time had come for a judicial showdown on its long-argued contention that the legislative veto violated the Constitution.

Chadha *and Its Aftermath*

In June 1983 it won its case, in a sweeping Supreme Court decision that Associate Justice Byron R. White, in a dissent, said "strikes down in one fell swoop provisions in more laws enacted by Congress than the Court has cumulatively invalidated in its history."[33] The six-justice majority, through Chief Justice Warren E. Burger, took a simple, strict-constructionist approach. The Constitution in Article I, Section 7, specifies that every bill and every order, resolution, or vote requiring the concurrence of the Senate and the House of Representatives (except on a question of adjournment) "shall be presented to the President of the United States" for approval or disapproval and in the latter case, must be repassed by two-thirds of both houses. Legislative vetoes, being legislative acts, fall within the requirements of these "presentment" clauses. True, adhering to the strict language

32. The most influential study, conducted for the Administrative Conference of the United States by Harold H. Bruff and Ernest Gellhorn, is summarized by them in "Congressional Control of Administrative Regulation: A Study of Legislative Vetoes," *Harvard Law Review*, vol. 90 (May 1977), pp. 1369–1440. A treatise published in 1983 similarly condemned the use of the legislative veto to overturn regulatory policy decisions, warning that "if Congress continues to rely on the veto over the regulatory area, its utility may be undermined in other areas where it has served as a useful device of comity between the president and Congress, such as arms sales, reorganization, and war powers." Instead of using the legislative veto "as a means to avoid or postpone decisions," the author argued, the Congress "must be willing to endure the frustration and internal stress of moving slowly and incrementally" toward "more carefully thought out and more completely spelled out laws." Barbara Hinkson Craig, *The Legislative Veto: Congressional Control of Regulation* (Westview Press, 1983), pp. 135–36.
33. *Immigration and Naturalization Service* v. *Chada*, 103 U.S. 2764 (1983).

of the Constitution may "impose burdens on governmental processes
that often seem clumsy, inefficient, even unworkable," Burger
acknowledged, "but those hard choices were consciously made by
men who had lived under a form of government that permitted arbitrary governmental acts to go unpunished." One may question the
chief justice's reasoning: what prevents arbitrary governmental action
is not the independence of the legislative and executive branches that
Burger was upholding but their interdependence through checks and
balances. The legislative veto was an additional check and balance
that the framers did not think of. While it has no express sanction in
the Constitution, it did in fact serve the very constitutional principle
the chief justice chose to cite in striking it down.

A month after *Chadha*, Senator Dennis DeConcini, Democrat of
Arizona, and twenty-two cosponsors introduced a constitutional
amendment to authorize one-house or two-house legislative vetoes
as exceptions to the presentment clauses. DeConcini foresaw a
"tumultuous period of readjustment" as the Congress confronted the
old dilemma that led to invention of the veto: to rewrite the 120-odd
statutes with the specificity necessary to control administrative agencies was impossible, but to transfer wholesale the lawmaking function
was unacceptable.[34] Similar proposals were introduced in the House.
But the constitutional amendment process is time-consuming, the
Congress had to move immediately to decide what to do about all its
invalidated laws, and as Representative Elliott H. Levitas, Democrat
of Georgia, put it, "there are other ways to skin the cat." Levitas,
who had established himself as the House's leading advocate of the
legislative veto, expressed certainty that the Congress would "in some
way, or more likely in various ways, reassert the type of control"
required for accountability that the legislative veto had given it and
"the end result will be a much lesser delegation of power and much
more tightly drawn laws constraining the discretion and delegation
that had previously been given by Congress."[35] Since then the Congress has been proceeding slowly to reassert control, on a case-by-
case basis, procrastinating where possible in the absence of pressing
issues and, where delay was not possible, experimenting with various
approaches.

34. *Congressional Record*, July 27, 1983, pp. 21154–57.
35. Address to the American Bar Association, Atlanta, August 21, 1983.

At one extreme, the Congress has simply withheld delegations of power that in the pre-*Chadha* years it had granted contingent on the right of veto. Thus, predictably, the 1984 version of reorganization legislation simply authorized the president to recommend plans that Congress would then consider approving by joint resolution. (A joint resolution is subject to approval by the president and, when so approved, becomes a statute.) The only innovation was a "fast-track" provision, which required that each house bring a resolution of approval to the floor within ninety days. The new post-*Chadha* procedure was clearly disadvantageous to the executive. Where inertia was previously on the president's side—if neither house acted to disapprove the plan, it took effect—it was now on the side of whoever opposed the plan, for both houses had to act affirmatively, and do so within a relatively brief time period.

This approach—subjecting measures to approval by joint resolution—came to be widely adopted, with the executive branch similarly the loser in every case. Indeed, in those instances where a legislative veto had depended on disapproval of a proposal by *both* houses, the loss was greater, for the new requirement of concurrence by joint resolution meant that disapproval by *only one* house could block the proposed administrative action. This applied, for instance, to expenditures for the MX missile. Legislation before *Chadha* authorized certain of the expenditures to proceed unless both houses disapproved; after the Court decision, the administration was prohibited from proceeding unless both houses gave their concurrence. The president had to win his case in two arenas instead of one.[36]

If a fast-track procedure were not incorporated in the provision for approval of a proposed action by joint resolution, the delegation to the executive was nothing more than the authority to make recommendations—an authority it already possessed. But not every action previously subject to a veto could be put on a fast track, particularly the plethora of agency rules that had been so subjected, for the calendars of the committees and the two houses would be hopelessly clogged. The Congress has therefore been seeking to distinguish between major issues that warrant the fast-track procedure for rapid consideration—such as trade agreements and important regulatory

36. Louis Fisher, "Judicial Misjudgments about the Lawmaking Process: The Legislative Veto Case," *Public Administration Review*, vol. 45 (November 1985), pp. 709–10.

actions—and minor issues that do not.[37] In the latter case, a waiting period is specified, during which a joint resolution of disapproval by both houses can be passed. Under this procedure, the president is clearly advantaged, because not only is inertia on his side but a joint resolution of disapproval is subject to his veto and therefore, if he insists on his position, a two-thirds majority of both houses is required to overrule him. In one of its earliest post-*Chadha* applications, the joint resolution of disapproval was substituted for the legislative veto contained in the original War Powers Resolution (although this could hardly be classed as a minor issue). That provision declared that if the president engaged the military forces in hostilities, Congress by a vote of both houses could force him to withdraw them. Senate Majority Leader Robert C. Byrd, Democrat of West Virginia, who sponsored the new legislation after *Chadha*, admitted that two-thirds of both houses were hardly likely to oppose the president in a crisis but contended that a mechanism should be in place in the event of such "a very extreme difference in judgment between the President and the Congress."[38] The law incorporated a fast-track procedure, including a twenty-hour limitation on Senate debate to forestall a filibuster on a motion to override a presidential veto.

Intermediate between these extremes is the ever-popular appropriations rider, a means by which a majority of both houses could write the equivalent of a resolution of disapproval with normally no risk of presidential veto. By simply adding to an appropriation bill a sentence beginning "No part of any appropriation under this Act shall be available for . . . ," Congress can effectively prevent an administrative agency from developing or enforcing a particular rule or taking a specific action. Such limitations on executive discretion have been upheld by the courts as legitimate exercises of the legislature's power of the purse. When Secretary of the Interior James G. Watt announced in 1983 he would ignore a formal instruction from the House Interior Committee to postpone granting leases for coal mining on certain public lands, on the ground that the committee veto was unconstitutional, the committee simply got the moratorium included as a rider on the department's appropriation bill. Other

37. Ibid., p. 710.
38. *Congressional Record*, daily ed., October 19, 1983, p. S14164.

riders in that same bill prohibited the export of timber from the western states and halted oil leasing on designated sections of the continental shelf off both the Atlantic and Pacific coasts.

Finally, the Congress can continue to enact legislative vetoes, in the full knowledge that they are unconstitutional but in the equally full expectation that they will be adhered to anyway. Fisher estimates that about two hundred new legislative veto provisions were enacted in the seven years between *Chadha* and the end of 1990.[39] Many of these involved the reprogramming of expenditures, where a tradition had evolved that decisions involving more than a specified amount of money would be subject to the approval of the two Appropriations committees and sometimes the two authorizing committees as well. President Reagan, in signing bills containing these provisions, served notice in 1984, more than a year after *Chadha*, that he would treat them as invalid, and President Bush has included legislative vetoes among the unconstitutional provisions he has cited as not binding on the administration, as discussed above.[40]

Fisher, however, reviews an instance of what may happen subsequently in such a case. Before Reagan's 1984 pronouncement, the National Aeronautics and Space Administration had a workable arrangement with the Appropriations committees that ceilings would be placed on certain categories of expenditures, but funds could be shifted so as to exceed ceilings if the committees approved. After the president spoke, the House Appropriations Committee saw no alternative but to make the ceilings fixed rather than flexible. This, of course, would require both houses of Congress to enact legislation each time NASA desired to reprogram money, a restriction that the agency would find intolerable. NASA Administrator James M. Beggs therefore proposed an agreement that if the committees would set their ceilings by letter, rather than by statute, he would seek committee approval as before whenever he wished to reprogram funds. Thus the legislative veto was made informal rather than statutory, but no less effective, because the Appropriations committees always have the potential sanction of rigidifying the ceilings in law.

39. Louis Fisher, *Constitutional Conflicts between Congress and the President*, 3d ed. (University Press of Kansas, 1991), p. 150.

40. See, for instance, his comment on signing the Department of the Interior and Related Agencies appropriation bill, November 5, 1990, in *Weekly Compilation of Presidential Documents, 1990*, p. 1769.

This, as Fisher conjectures, may become the standard way of restoring the traditional legislative veto in cases where that power was lodged in committees.[41] Committees have often controlled administration by incorporating directives and instruction in committee reports and other communications, which the administrative agencies have voluntarily accepted as binding. Realism suggested that the agencies might as well do so—witness the appropriations rider that overrode Secretary Watt's rejection of such an order. The executive and legislative branches will continue to find ways to circumvent the *Chadha* ruling because, in Fisher's words, "The conditions that spawned the legislative veto a half century ago have not disappeared. Executive officials still want substantial latitude in administering delegated authority; legislators still insist on maintaining control without having to pass another law. . . . Forms will change but not power relationships or the need for a quid pro quo."[42]

While the committees responsible for individual statutes have been striving to perfect their individual solutions, those legislators who before *Chadha* were seeking to extend the legislative veto to all agency rules and regulations have transformed their efforts into a search for a uniform method of control that would be constitutionally permissible. Various bills introduced after *Chadha* would have required waiting periods before proposed rules could take effect and established uniform fast-track procedures for considering joint resolutions of disapproval or, in some cases, joint resolutions of approval, but no such general legislation has been approved by either house.

The question is whether a simple constitutional amendment that would restore the legitimacy of the legislative veto as it was employed before *Chadha* would be preferable to this panoply of statutory approaches. Events since that decision appear to be confirming Representative Levitas's prediction: whenever the Congress is intent on controlling administrative action, it can find a constitutional way to do so. That fact accounts, no doubt, for the lack of support on Capitol Hill for trying to resolve the problem by constitutional amendment. In the end, too, Levitas is likely to be proved right in predicting that the executive branch will be the loser, because some powers previously delegated to administrators on a contingent basis—such as reor-

41. Fisher, "Judicial Misjudgments," pp. 209–10. He provides other examples in *Constitutional Conflicts*, pp. 150–51.
42. Fisher, *Constitutional Conflicts*, p. 149.

ganization—will be withheld. But the legislature will be a loser, too, for the alternative ways of "skinning the cat" are less convenient and more burdensome and time-consuming, adding to the volume and complexity of matters that must be handled on the floors of the two houses.

If the executive branch is conceived, however, to be the winner in the *Chadha* decision—and Justice Department officials have boasted of their victory on behalf of the entire branch—then the opportunity exists for a tactical trade. Former Representative Melvin R. Laird, Wisconsin Republican who subsequently served as secretary of defense, has suggested that a single constitutional amendment might combine some form of item veto for the president with restoration of the legislative veto to the Congress. Legislators who now believe they are doing quite well in finding substitutes for their former vetoes might not consider that an even trade, but if they conclude at some point that public pressure is going to force them to accede to the item veto anyway, they might find it expedient to combine a relatively mild form of the item veto with a legalization of the legislative veto.

The War Power

On the war power, the Constitution is direct and seemingly clear: "The Congress shall have Power . . . To declare War . . . To raise and support Armies . . . To provide and maintain a Navy . . . To make Rules for the Government and Regulation of the land and naval Forces." And "The President shall be Commander in Chief of the Army and Navy of the United States." Waging war, then, was intended to fall into the same set of relationships that governed any other undertaking. Policy decisions and the power of the purse would be the legislature's responsibility; carrying out the policy would be the president's.[43]

43. Not all constitutional scholars, of course, agree with so categorical a conclusion. As noted below, throughout U.S. history, presidents have made unilateral policy decisions committing forces to hostilities, and a rationale had to be, and has been developed—particularly within the Justice and State Departments—for holding such actions to be in accord with the intent of the framers. For a convincing refutation of this expansionary, or "revisionist," view of the presidential power to make war, see David Gray Adler, "The Constitution and Presidential Warmaking: The Enduring Debate," *Political Science Quarterly*, vol. 103 (Spring 1988), pp. 1–36. The weight of disinterested

But that simple language was written in an age of sailing ships and horse-drawn cannons, at a time when the United States was a minor power with no global interests to defend. The same deliberative process that was suitable for regulating commerce or organizing the postal system might have been appropriate enough, in that day, for deciding questions of war and peace as well. Now, however, the United States has grown to the rank of superpower, with a vast structure of alliances supported by bases and military forces across the seas, and weapons move at supersonic speeds. The national interest may be threatened almost anywhere on the globe, at any time, and the decision to defend an interest, or repulse a threat, must be instantaneous—made in minutes and hours, not weeks and months—and the Congress may be out of session. Moreover, the Constitution did not define war. Is every use of military force a war requiring formal declaration, or are there "police actions," "punitive expeditions," defenses of U.S. lives and property that are less than war? And can they be carried out by the president as commander in chief wholly on his own authority, relying perhaps on his own interpretation of treaty obligations? As early as 1798, the country fought an undeclared naval war with France, and since that time it has entered into hostilities far more often without a formal declaration of war than with one. On many of those occasions, the legislative body had no part in the policy decision. The lawmakers were told about it after it was made.

In the twentieth century, the United States entered both world wars through congressional declarations. But it carried out other military operations, in Asia, in Mexico, in Central America and the Caribbean, and most recently in the Persian Gulf, without any such formality. Some of these interventions, even when the United States overthrew a foreign government and occupied its territory, have been called by other names than war. But two, at least, were wars in everybody's lexicon. Those were the Korean War, which was initiated by the president without explicit and prior sanction by the Congress, and the Vietnam War, authorized not by a declaration of war but by a congressional resolution that pledged support to the president if he chose to engage in military action.

authority is, I believe, on Adler's side of the debate (as is my own reading of the historical sources), but the purpose of this section is not to argue the case for restricting presidential authority but only to suggest that the boundaries of that authority are a recurring and potentially crucial issue that needs to be settled.

It was the latter experience that precipitated the War Powers Resolution of 1973. The congressional resolution of support had been whipped through Congress in 1964 in an atmosphere of crisis, after President Lyndon Johnson had told the legislators that two American destroyers had been fired on by North Vietnamese torpedo boats, without provocation, in the Gulf of Tonkin. The resolution was broad enough to authorize a full-scale war in alliance with South Vietnam, but Johnson had assured leading legislators that he had no such intention.[44] When, within three years, Johnson had cited the resolution as authority for plunging half a million American troops into Southeast Asia, many of those who had voted for the resolution felt betrayed, particularly J. William Fulbright, who as chairman of the Foreign Relations Committee had pushed the resolution through the Senate. And they felt doubly so when Fulbright's committee developed evidence that Johnson had misrepresented the facts about the Gulf of Tonkin incident, that perhaps the United States had actually provoked the encounter to provide grounds for seeking the congressional action.[45]

Yet whether President Johnson could have thrust the United States into the Vietnam War without the Tonkin Gulf resolution, on the ground that he was executing treaty obligations, was never settled. In ordering troops into Korea fifteen years before, President Truman had found legal justification in the country's duty under the United Nations Charter to oppose aggression, but the validity of that claim was never established either. Truman's Republican opponents challenged the president's right to unilaterally take the country into war, but Truman insisted that the Korean engagement was not a war but a "police action," and Democrats defended the president on various grounds. Senate Majority Leader Scott W. Lucas, Democrat of Illinois, contended that the president could dispatch military forces whenever he believed "that the safety, the security, and the honor of this country are involved." Paul H. Douglas, Lucas's Illinois Democratic colleague, invoked technology and hoary Senate rules: "The speed of modern war requires quick executive action . . . even the slightest delay may

44. Remarks of Senator Fulbright, during floor debate on the resolution, *Congressional Record*, August 6, 1964, pp. 18403–04, 18409–10.
45. Comments of Fulbright and other senators, ibid., March 7, 1968, p. 5645; and *Congressional Quarterly Almanac, 1968*, vol. 24 (1968), p. 714.

prove fatal," but the Senate did not even have a way to shut off filibusters. The ultimate defense came from Lucas: "Well, it [the commitment of troops] has been done."[46]

The debate on the Tonkin Gulf resolution found senators divided over whether Congress was delegating power to take military action to the president or whether he already possessed the power, and the wording of the measure carefully evaded the question.[47] In any event, those who believed they were delegating power did so willingly, under the pressure of the assumed crisis, and the president got what he wanted. Some years later, Fulbright could say that "the Congress has lost the power to declare war as it was written into the Constitution. It has not been so much usurped as given away."[48] And Under Secretary of State Nicholas Katzenbach, speaking for the Johnson administration, could tell Fulbright's committee that "the expression of declaring a war is one that has become outmoded."[49]

The War Powers Resolution of 1973

As senators in the late 1960s discovered that undeclared warfare had spread to Cambodia and Laos, supported by 45,000 troops in Thailand, the movement to bring presidential warmaking under control became irresistible. Senator Jacob K. Javits, Republican of New York, who led the movement, introduced a resolution that would delegate precise and limited powers to the president, specifying the circumstances under which he could order the armed forces into hostilities without prior approval by the Congress. The Senate approved the Javits measure by a big majority, but the House Foreign Affairs Committee would not accept the idea that all possible contingencies could be anticipated and the president's powers therefore "codified" in advance, and the House passed a resolution differing in that respect. The conference committee of the two houses found their compromise in that convenient—and then legal—device, the legislative veto. The Senate's proposed restrictions were made advisory. The president was required to consult with Congress before ordering the military into action and to report immediately thereafter, but oth-

46. Senate debate, June 28, 1950, summarized in Sundquist, *Decline and Resurgence,* pp. 108–09.
47. Ibid., pp. 120–23.
48. *Congressional Record,* July 31, 1967, pp. 20702–06.
49. Sundquist, *Decline and Resurgence,* pp. 245–46.

erwise was left free to act. If, however, both houses of Congress objected, they could by concurrent resolution compel the president to terminate hostilities. And in any case, if the Congress did not within sixty days give its affirmative approval to the president's course, he must abandon it.

The Congress thus conceded Senator Douglas's argument about the speed of modern war and Katzenbach's point that the constitutional provision for declaring war was indeed outmoded, but salvaged what it could. Presidential freedom and flexibility were assured and legitimated, but only for sixty days, and even within that time the Congress could step in to reverse the executive. The legislators felt they had once more brought the executive-legislative balance of power as close to the constitutional intent as today's technology permits. The trouble is, the executive did not agree then or later. President Nixon vetoed the resolution as an encroachment on his constitutional responsibilities, and the measure became law only when the Congress overrode his veto. Every subsequent president has upheld Nixon's constitutional position. Presidents Ford, Carter, Reagan, and Bush have complied with the reporting provisions of the resolution, but without (except in one instance) acknowledging any legal obligation to do so. Their reports were submitted not "pursuant to" the terms of the statute but "consistent with" or "taking note of" it.[50]

When Reagan sent marines to join a multinational force in Lebanon in 1983, the Congress hastened to authorize their presence there for eighteen months (they were withdrawn well before that time expired). When President Bush ordered a massive movement of forces to the Persian Gulf in November 1990, after the Congress had adjourned, he quelled the fierce reaction of a large segment of the two houses by sending a request when the Congress convened in January for authorization to use force—an authorization that was granted after a heated partisan debate. The president based his request not on any constitutional necessity but on the need to demonstrate to the Iraqi

50. The one exception was President Ford's report in 1975 on the seizure of the U.S. merchant vessel *Mayaguez* by Cambodian patrol boats and its subsequent recapture by U.S. forces. He referred to the section of the War Powers Resolution that starts the sixty-day clock, but by the time the report was transmitted the *Mayaguez* had been retaken and the incident was over. The twenty presidential reports made in accordance with the War Powers Resolution through 1989 are reviewed in Robert A. Katzmann, "War Powers: Toward a New Accommodation," in Thomas E. Mann, ed., *A Question of Balance: The President, the Congress, and Foreign Policy* (Brookings, 1990), pp. 57–61.

invaders of Kuwait that the United States possessed "the necessary unity to act decisively," and he made no reference to the War Powers Resolution; Congress, however, granted its authorization explicitly under the resolution's terms. The other actions reported were all terminated after a few days, so the power of Congress to impose the resolution's sixty-day time limit on the president's authority has not been tested.[51] Its power to exercise a legislative veto during the sixty days was, of course, stricken by the Supreme Court in the *Chadha* decision, but the rest of the statute is presumably unaffected.

The Issue Still Unsettled

So the basic constitutional question remains as unsettled as it was at the time of the Vietnam War or the Korean War or, for that matter, the Mexican War more than a century ago. The executive branch has carefully preserved its contention that it is not bound by the War Powers Resolution and any compliance with its terms is strictly voluntary. If a future president chooses to act as unilaterally as Truman did in Korea or Nixon in Cambodia and Laos, defying the Congress and taking it upon himself to declare the legislature's constitutional responsibility "outmoded," the Congress can fall back only on relatively ineffective checks—the power of the purse, which can be exercised only clumsily and late, and the impeachment power, which in addition to all its other difficulties would come into operation so late as to be almost surely useless.

If the constitutional design is indeed outmoded, as even the War Powers Resolution seems to concede, should a new design be written for the modern age? Is unrestrained presidential warmaking authority still a menace, as the Congress found it to be in Southeast Asia? If so, and if effective control is to be securely lodged in the legislative branch, some variant of the War Powers Resolution would have to be added to the Constitution. The notion that presidents know best and should be trusted has been severely undercut by the experience in Southeast Asia. One may argue that that debacle will forever chasten presidents, and no future leader, even one holding as expansive

---

51. In the case of the U.S. invasion of Grenada in 1983, a resolution limiting to ninety days the president's authority to use military forces, in the absence of further action of the Congress, passed the House but was not acted on in the Senate.

a view of presidential power as Truman, Johnson, or Nixon, will risk initiating a war without full popular support. If that argument seems dubious, perhaps a sounder one is that a new constitutional provision would not matter; in a crisis, the Congress would give the president whatever support and authority he requested—as happened in the recent cases of Lebanon and Operation Desert Storm.[52] But not all constitutional checks are designed for everyday use. A new war powers provision in the Constitution would be intended only as a safeguard in the event of another feud between the branches as rancorous and unrelenting as that of Richard Nixon's era, or Andrew Johnson's. Such constitutional collisions have occurred often enough in the nation's history, and have involved the war power frequently enough, that the question of whether the constitutional ambiguity needs to be resolved should not be lightly dismissed.

Leading members of the Congress have not dismissed the problem, but neither have they suggested constitutional amendment as the route to its solution. They have proposed, instead, various statutes that would, at the least, bring the War Powers Resolution into conformity with the *Chadha* ruling, and in some cases go further to establish a formal mechanism for the consultation prescribed by the resolution. Any constitutional amendment would be bound to contain language that would be subject to varying interpretation by presidents and Congresses—not as widely divergent as the interpretations of the present constitutional provisions, but still differing—and the result would be, in Robert Katzmann's words, to "require the courts to render judgments about military situations that they are not equipped to make."[53] At a time when powerful and determined forces are arrayed in diametrically opposed positions on the central question—the proper limits, if any, of presidential power—it is clear that the consensus necessary for settling the issue by constitutional amendment is beyond attainment. Only when a successful relationship is worked out in practice under the War Powers Resolution, as it may be amended and accepted by both branches, could that rela-

52. See comments of Senator Frank Church, Democrat of Idaho, later chair of the Foreign Relations Committee, quoted in Sundquist, *Decline and Resurgence*, p. 267.

53. Katzmann, "War Powers," p. 67. For two centuries, the courts have managed to avoid responsibility for rendering such judgments, often on the ground that war powers disputes involve policy rather than legal issues and therefore must be resolved by the government's political branches.

tionship be embedded in the Constitution—and were relations to become that harmonious, the long-term need to settle the war powers issue would surely be set aside.

Approval of Treaties

In the long struggle for control of U.S. foreign policy that marked the two decades between the First and Second World Wars, the internationalists had cause to complain that the Constitution was stacked against them. At the end of the first global conflict, the then-minority isolationists had succeeded in blocking the will of the internationalist majority that wanted to take the United States into a fully participatory role in world affairs. The thirty-five senators who voted against approval of the Treaty of Versailles had overridden the forty-nine who voted for it, who were backed by President Woodrow Wilson and, from all of the evidence, most of the country; and in doing so, the minority had blocked U.S. entry into the League of Nations. When that body proved ineffective as a guarantor of peace, its weakness could be blamed to some degree on the fateful minority decision that kept the world's strongest country from asserting the leadership that was its clear responsibility. Probably no League of Nations, however strong, would have been potent enough to check the ambitions of the dictators who brought on World War II, but it remains on the national conscience that the United States did not do everything it could. And the anomaly noted by James Wilson at the Constitutional Convention still prevails: a simple majority of both houses can vote to declare war, but a two-thirds majority of one body has to be attained for the presumably more worthy purpose of making peace.

Learning from the post–World War II experience, the country achieved a rare and overwhelming national consensus after World War II to approve full participation in the United Nations, which superseded the defunct league, and to sustain American leadership in erecting a series of regional alliances to check the spread of communism around the globe. As long as the consensus existed, the country's foreign policy could be truly bipartisan, and the two-thirds requirement for treaty approval was no barrier to any major foreign policy objective. But popular agreement and bipartisan harmony dissolved in the Vietnam War and have never been regained—witness the long and bitter conflict over aid to the Nicaragua contras—and that fact has given the provision renewed importance.

The most evident effect of the two-thirds requirement is, of course, the number of treaties rejected by the Senate. Probably none defeated since Versailles has been as important as that proposed pact, but following U.S. rejection of the League of Nations came a corresponding refusal to join the World Court. That refusal has continued to this day, despite support for adherence by a majority of the Senate when the issue came to a vote in 1935 and sponsorship by Republican and Democratic presidents, beginning with Warren G. Harding. The Committee on the Constitutional System counted forty treaties since World War II that were either spurned by the Senate or never came to a vote, including the second Strategic Arms Limitation Treaty (SALT II), treaties on underground nuclear tests, and a wide range of boundary, human rights, trade, tax, and environmental agreements.[54]

But probably more significant than the number of treaties formally rejected by the Senate is the uncounted number that were never negotiated at all or were written in a form different from what the president and a majority of the Senate would have found desirable, because of the power of the minority. The two-thirds requirement exerts a pervasive influence on the development and conduct of foreign policy at every stage. Every president and secretary of state know that they may go no further in any negotiation than the minority of the day will finally accept. In a very real sense, then, basic foreign policy decisions are controlled not by the governmental majority that is elected by the popular majority but by the governmental minority whose policies may have been soundly rejected in a whole series of elections—just as the minority determined the national position on the Treaty of Versailles.

In the era of the cold war that stretched from the 1940s through the 1980s, the critical foreign policy issue was arms control, and during all that period an irreconcilable minority could prevent any arms reduction agreement, however promising, from taking effect. The nation's leaders and negotiators had therefore to pay as much, or more, attention to the views and position of the opponents of arms control as to those of its supporters. Under such circumstances, the

---

54. Committee on the Constitutional System, "A Bicentennial Analysis of the American Political Structure" (Washington, January 1987), p. 3.

opponents gain a bargaining power that they can use in various ways, depending on the political climate at any given time. They can discourage negotiation altogether. They can discourage U.S. negotiators from proposing, or accepting, what the administration may conscientiously believe to be fair and reasonable concessions. In effect, the opponents rather than the responsible administration can define the treaty's ultimate terms. Benjamin S. Loeb, a former administration official, details how a proposed comprehensive nuclear test ban treaty in 1963 became the Partial Test Ban Treaty, filled with compromises and accompanied by policy concessions, because a vote count showed that while the comprehensive treaty would have had majority support in the Senate, it would have fallen short of two-thirds.[55] No one can be sure what would have happened to SALT II if President Carter had not withdrawn it, but it seems likely that it would have been defeated by a minority of senators. Yet the Reagan administration found it worthy of voluntary adherence.

It is sometimes difficult to distinguish, when treaties become controversial, how much of the opposition represents genuine policy objections and how much reflects the constant struggle in any democratic system for partisan advantage (or individual advantage, for senators may bargain their votes for concessions, perhaps wholly unrelated to the issue at hand, from the president). That "politics stops at the water's edge" is a myth; except in the rare periods of national consensus such as the one after World War II, politicians dispute foreign policy with the same intensity that they debate domestic policy, both within and between the parties. Politicians of the opposing party respond to public opinion, of course, and do not risk appearing to oppose a popular treaty just for the sake of opposition. But if a significant segment of public opinion has doubts about the treaty, the opposition's opportunity—and, many will say, its duty—lies in responding to the doubts, giving them a hearing, and exploiting them. The opposition view, after all, is entitled to an advocate. If it can be made to prevail, politicians reason, it probably deserves to. And if those who negotiated the treaty sink with it, that—in the inevitable perception of the partisan opposition—will be for the long-run greater good of the country anyway.

55. Benjamin S. Loeb, "Amend the Constitution's Treaty Clause," *Bulletin of the Atomic Scientists*, vol. 43 (October 1987), p. 40.

This being the necessary nature of democratic politics, the de facto requirement imposed by the two-thirds rule that every treaty have bipartisan support—since the president's party rarely commands two-thirds of the Senate—sets a standard of extreme severity. Defenders of the requirement contend that the standard should properly be severe; a treaty is binding not just on the administration and the party that negotiated it but on successor administrations of the other party too, and agreement by the opposition in advance of its responsibility is therefore not an unreasonable rule. The opposing argument is that the necessity for bipartisan agreement can render the country incapable of acting on any issue that is to any significant degree divisive and susceptible to partisan exploitation.

Even the most vigorous opponents of the two-thirds requirement would probably concede some merit to the view that a treaty, because of its binding character, should rest on a broader base than a simple—and perhaps transient—majority in popular opinion reflected in a bare majority, made up predominantly of one party, in the Congress. If supporters of the extraordinary majority would concede that the two-thirds requirement calls for a base so broad as to be in many reasonable circumstances unattainable, a solution might be found in the substitution of a lower percentage figure—60 percent, say (though that figure would not have saved the Treaty of Versailles, which garnered only 58.3 percent of those voting, unless the proponents had somehow mustered additional support).

All this leaves out of account the House of Representatives. The proposed constitutional amendment overwhelmingly approved by that body in 1945 would have authorized approval of treaties by a majority of the membership in both houses. There is good reason to involve the House as well as the Senate on treaty matters, for the implementing legislation and appropriations that most agreements require must win the approval of both bodies. The framers' concept of the Senate as a kind of privy council to the president, which was the origin of its special role in treaty approval, has long since given way. But because a constitutional amendment must win the approval of two-thirds of the Senate in order to be submitted to the states for ratification (assuming the normal method of initiating amendments by the Congress, rather than by a constitutional convention, is employed), any proposal to admit the House to equal responsibility stands little chance of passage. Perhaps a reduction of the Senate approval requirement for treaties to 55 or 60 percent could be combined with a provision for approval also by a simple majority of the House to form an acceptable, though awkward, solution.

What is difficult to justify, or even comprehend, is the view often encountered in the Senate that to reduce the two-thirds requirement would in itself denigrate that body and diminish its status and responsibility. True, the power of individual senators to defeat a treaty would be diminished, but their power to approve agreements would be enhanced. In the case of those treaties that would be affected by lowering the two-thirds standard—those with majority but not two-thirds support—more senators would always gain influence than would lose it; in the Versailles treaty instance, a requirement of 58 percent or less would have stripped thirty-five senators of their power to block the agreement but conferred on forty-nine the power to approve it. As is shown in other instances as well—notably in the case of the filibuster rule—senators appear to place greater value on their power to obstruct than on their power to concur. Senators willingly accept minority rule in order that they may rule, as part of a minority, on some future occasion and inflict defeat on some president—even though it can only be that, with minority rule, most members of the Senate will rule less often.

One way to escape the stringent two-thirds requirement for treaty approval while leaving the Constitution unchanged would be to expand even further the use, and the concept, of the executive agreement, which presidents have extensively employed in carrying out the terms of treaties and of statutes such as the trade agreements act that was renewed in 1991 to permit negotiation of a trade pact with Mexico. As in the case of trade, the Congress could authorize the president to negotiate international agreements covering particular subjects that would take effect if ratified by act of Congress or, as was provided in the original Reciprocal Trade Agreement Act of 1934, on the president's own authority. To the extent that becomes the practice, the purpose of modifying the treaty clause of the Constitution is largely achieved without altering the clause itself. But to legitimately remove any questions as to the legality and the propriety of using this approach on a broad scale, some constitutional language might be necessary and would certainly be useful. One approach would be to encompass international agreements in any amendment restoring the legislative veto. The Congress could then authorize the president to enter into agreements that would not require affirmative action but would be binding unless they were rejected by the legislators.

Breaking Deadlocks by Referenda

If the branches of government reach an impasse on a single crucial issue at a time when their relations are otherwise reasonably effective, a means of overcoming the checks and balances that produced the deadlock could be made available through constitutional amendment. That is the device of the referendum, by which the people themselves vote yes or no on a legislative proposition.

A comprehensive study of national referenda, published in 1978, counted more than five hundred such votes. A third of the countries belonging to the United Nations, including a majority of the European states, had employed the device at least once. Of the countries with an uninterrupted democratic history going back to the nineteenth century, only the United States and the Netherlands have never submitted a question to a direct popular vote. Most have used the device sparingly, but at the other extreme stands Switzerland, which has "accepted the principle that almost every major national decision could become the subject of a popular vote." Of the five hundred referenda, Switzerland accounted for 297, Australia 39, France 20, and Denmark 13.[56] The measures may be submitted for decision by the voters or simply for advice, as when the British Parliament in 1975 asked the electorate's view on withdrawal from the European Community. (It voted to retain membership, and the government followed its advice.) The questions are normally presented to referendum by the government, but in some countries a question can be placed on the ballot by petition, as when in Italy a national divorce law was appealed to referendum in 1974 and a law modifying cost-of-living wage increases was similarly taken to the people by the Communist party in 1985. (Both laws were upheld.)

The American states have used the referendum device extensively. In every state but Delaware, constitutional amendments must be approved by referendum. Changes in city charters usually require

56. David Butler and Austin Ranney, *Referendums: A Comparative Study of Practice and Theory* (Washington: American Enterprise Institute for Public Policy Research, 1978), pp. 5–7.

similar popular approval, and so do bond issues in many states and cities. In many states, constitutional amendments as well as statutory proposals may be placed on the ballot by petition—such as, most notably, California's tax limitation amendment (Proposition 13), adopted by referendum in 1978, and the limits on state legislative and (in one case) congressional terms approved in three states in 1990. Four public opinion polls taken between 1977 and 1981 reported margins of more than two to one in favor of a national initiative and referendum procedure. Another, in 1987, produced a more considered response by offering one sentence of argument on each side of the question, but the verdict was still favorable, 48 to 41 percent.[57]

Before, during, and after World War I, discussion of national referenda centered on proposals by pacificist and isolationist groups that a popular vote be required to authorize U.S. entry into war unless the country were attacked or invaded. The drive for the so-called peace referendum reached a vote on the House floor in 1938 (on a procedural motion to discharge the measure from further committee consideration), but the motion was defeated, 209 to 188, and with the outbreak of war in Europe the effort ended.[58]

Since the 1970s, the initiative and referendum idea has been revived for broader application to national issues. Advocates have included supporters of particular causes who seek to bypass a reluctant Congress, such as backers of legislation to balance the budget or to reduce or limit taxation on the pattern of California's Proposition 13. Other proponents have argued on principle that decision by popular vote is the purest expression of democracy and one that would arouse interest in the political process and encourage more citizens to participate.

While the initiative and referendum are commonly combined in the states (often with a third procedure, for recall of elected officials

57. American Institute of Public Opinion (Gallup) poll of 1977, reported in Austin Ranney, "What Constitutional Changes Do Americans Want?" *This Constitution: A Bicentennial Chronicle* (Winter 1984), reprinted in Donald L. Robinson, ed., *Reforming American Government: The Bicentennial Papers of the Committee on the Constitutional System* (Westview Press, 1985), p. 283. A 1977 poll by Cambridge Reports, Inc., and 1978 and 1981 Gallup surveys are reported in Thomas E. Cronin, *Direct Democracy: The Politics of Initiative, Referendum, and Recall* (Harvard University Press for Twentieth Century Fund, 1989), pp. 174–75. The 1987 poll was commissioned by Cronin and conducted by Gallup. Ibid., pp. 175–76.
58. Cronin, *Direct Democracy*, pp. 163–71.

by popular vote), the referendum can be instituted without the initiative. As noted earlier, every state but one requires a referendum on constitutional amendments, which are usually drafted and submitted by the legislatures. State bond issues follow a similar procedure, and legislators can elect to submit other measures for popular approval. In some states, the voters can, by petition, subject a measure enacted by the legislature to subsequent popular vote.

The experience of the states with the initiative has not been so successful as to suggest its application on a national scale. California represents the extreme case where the voters have been called upon to decide scores of issues placed on the ballot by initiative, many too complex to be readily understood by the voters, some poorly drafted, and a few even in conflict with one another. If the people could initiate national legislation, propositions with great popular appeal but also enormous complexity—budget and tax measures in particular— might well be placed on the ballot, and one need not be antidemocratic to question the capacity of the people to exercise soundly the responsibility that would be entrusted to them. The budget is made up of thousands of items on which the public could not hope to become educated. On any complex measure, enormous expenditures would be required to inform the whole national electorate, and that would tilt the scales toward the side with the greater financial resources.

If, for all these reasons, the idea of a national initiative procedure can be dismissed, the referendum on matters initiated by the legislators or the president, or both, remains a possibility. Measures so selected would involve issues that would normally have been the subject of mature consideration by both houses and by the administration. Also, those submitting the measures would presumably exercise a responsible judgment that the issues involved could be readily grasped by the voters and were of sufficient interest to stimulate voters to inform themselves. Perhaps useful legislation submitted to a national referendum would be beaten by confused voters who, in doubt, would choose to play safe by voting no. Since a defeat in referendum would weaken a measure in future Congresses, presidents and legislators would be inhibited from overusing the device. But as additional safeguards, the number of measures eligible for referendum could be limited, perhaps to two or three at the conclusion of each Congress, and official explanatory material could be distributed.

The question remains: Who would be empowered to select the measures for submission? Since the ostensible purpose of the referendum procedure (other than that of enabling legislators to evade altogether a delicate issue) would be to break deadlocks, the same questions arise that were discussed in chapter 6 in relation to calling special elections for that purpose. To make the referendum fully serviceable, either side in the controversy would have to be able to invoke the procedure over the opposition of the other. Any constitutional amendment, therefore, should authorize any two elements of the policymaking triad—president, Senate, and House—to ask the people to overrule the third. The Senate and House now have the power to impose their will on the president, of course, but to do so demands a two-thirds vote of both houses.

To incorporate a requirement for an extraordinary majority of the legislators would defeat the purpose of the referendum procedure. Impasses arise when the Congress (or one of its houses) rejects a presidential proposal, the president in turn vetoes any congressional alternative, and the Congress lacks the votes to override. Any requirement more stringent than a constitutional majority for a house to join in calling for a referendum would perpetuate the deadlock.

Some of the objections to a national initiative apply also to the referendum. In particular, the power of money could be decisive, and in any contest between the president and the Congress, the former would have the advantage, given the superior access of the executive to the media. The president and either house, particularly if they were allied with wealthy interests with a financial stake in the outcome, would be in a strong position to flood the country with advertising and overwhelm the other house.

The case for a referendum procedure would be stronger if unresolved issues could be identified that were simple enough to be easily presented to, and understood by, the voters. The central governmental stalemate at this time, concerning tax and spending policy, certainly fails the test of simplicity. Foreign policy issues are generally so subject to changing circumstances that they do not lend themselves to decisive resolution by popular vote. Abortion policy represents the kind of social issue that in other countries legislators have been eager to evade by putting the question to the people. But that policy does not yield easily to a yes-or-no vote. The issue is not simply between prohibition and permission; the debate has always revolved around a range of restrictions and deterrents, which are now being discussed one by one and state by state, each reviewed by the Supreme Court as it arises. A referendum could not overrule the Court's interpretation of the Constitution—unless the amendment authorizing the referendum procedure so provided, and that would open the entire Bill of Rights to demagogic attack. So even this hotly contested and delicate issue seems inappropriate for decision by popular vote.

In any case, deadlocks tend not to be confined to separable, easily definable, single issues but to be systemic across broad areas of public policy. If the Constitution needs to be amended to make their resolution easier, as has been suggested in preceding chapters, a referendum procedure would be a weak and limited instrument. The solution to the deadlock problem—for those who concede that it is a problem—must be sought in adoption of one or more of the further-reaching amendments discussed earlier.

Nothing in the Constitution, however, stands in the way of experimentation with the referendum as an advisory device. By statute, the Congress could submit a measure to the people for an expression of their collective opinion, which Cronin describes as allowing "the public-hearing stage of the legislative process to be opened up to the country as a whole for a national town meeting." Used in some states and local governments as well as in foreign countries (the British advisory referendum on participation in the European Community, for example), this approach was embodied in legislation introduced in 1980 by Representative Richard A. Gephardt, Democrat of Missouri, who later became House majority leader. His bill called for up to three issues to be placed on the ballot each two years, the questions to be selected following public hearings around the country and to be accompanied by a voters' guide containing explanatory material and arguments on both sides. With final responsibility still retained in the Congress, the procedure seems to have posed little risk in the states and appears worthy of encouragement—although, as Cronin notes, reliable information about public opinion (without benefit of the voters' guides, however) can be obtained more simply and quickly through sample surveys regularly conducted by polling organizations.[59]

Concluding his exhaustive and balanced review of the advantages and disadvantages of referenda, Cronin acknowledges they might on

59. Ibid., pp. 177–79.

occasion be helpful to national policymakers but finds the negative arguments more convincing.

> We must ask . . . whether we really want to make national laws based on taking the national popular temperature of the moment. Effective political leaders must shape public opinion, not just mirror it. They must also be willing to disregard current public opinion when situations call for vision. . . . Notable American leaders have sacrificed their personal and political popularity for what they knew was right. . . . Clearly, those who devised our national institutions . . . constructed a system that would allow representatives to concern themselves primarily with what ought to be done rather than with what the majority of the public might temporarily want or think was best.[60]

Preserving the Executive-Legislative Balance

Although they do not deal in any fundamental way with the central problem of executive-legislative stalemate to which this book is mainly addressed, all five of the proposed constitutional amendments discussed in this chapter are worth consideration on their merits as part of any broad effort to adapt the country's charter to the needs of modern government.

The item veto would give the president an additional means, although a relatively minor one, to bring the alarming national budget deficit under control. Restoring the legislative veto would give both the president and Congress a device that both branches have found useful in the past. Writing the essence of the War Powers Resolution into the Constitution would do as much as probably can be done to limit and control what some presidents have contended is their unilateral power to make war. Modifying the two-thirds requirement for treaty approval would give the president and the congressional majority, when they are in agreement, a greater opportunity, or even the absolute right, to determine the nation's foreign policy free of minority domination. And providing for a national referendum on disputed measures might make it possible to resolve some legislative impasses that now persist.

To make any of these changes, however, runs the risk of upsetting the present balance of power between the executive and legislative

60. Ibid., p. 188.

branches—a balance that has evolved over two centuries and that appears, on the whole, to satisfy both the country's political leadership and the public. If some modification of the existing system of checks and balances appears desirable, then, the objective should be to construct a combination of amendments that would grant roughly equal accretions of power to both branches. Quite apart from the intrinsic desirability of maintaining the present balance, if any set of proposals were seen as tilting the scales decisively in one direction or the other, the proposals would be doomed politically.

The most powerful of the proposals, in terms of potential disturbance of the executive-legislative balance, would be the item veto in any form that required a two-thirds majority of both houses to override the president. That would so enhance the president's bargaining power that no combination of other measures could offset it. But a milder form of the item veto, such as the Illinois variant that permits an override by an absolute majority of both houses, would pose nowhere near so great a threat—provided that the Congress remained in session long enough to consider the presidential vetoes. In that case, the president would have the opportunity to bring the offensive items to the attention of the country, but the legislators could still work their will if they were determined to do so.

In return for gaining a limited item veto, the president might be willing to support a restoration of the legislative veto. Again, a limitation might be in order, restricting the legislature's authority to two-house vetoes, and thus excluding the one-house and committee vetoes that were often enacted in the days before the *Chadha* decision. And international agreements could be encompassed in the legislative veto language, to encourage the Congress to authorize wider use of agreements as a substitute for treaties. A reduction of the two-thirds requirement for treaty ratification would still be desirable. Either, or both, of these would presumably be interpreted as a concession to the executive—although they should not be, for in fact either would enhance the power of the congressional majorities. But a war powers amendment could easily be added to the package as a step favoring Congress. In all of these measures, the opportunity to assemble a combination of amendments that would be both constructive and politically appealing seems clearly to exist.

CHAPTER NINE

The Prospects for Constitutional Reform

That there has been no powerful popular, or even elitist,
movement on behalf of fundamental alteration in the governmental
structure at any time in two hundred years testifies that the government has, most of the time, lived up to the expectations of the people.
When failures have occurred, they have proven to be temporary and
correctable. Yet some of the experienced leaders who are advocating
constitutional revision today are profoundly convinced that the
United States has been lucky in the past and that, in the future, the
deadlock and indecision built into the governmental structure will
sooner or later place the nation in peril. Perhaps the country's luck,
if that is what it has been, will continue. But there have been enough
periods of governmental failure in the nation's past to suggest the
imprudence of continuing to rely on providence if the weaknesses in
the governmental system can be identified and timely remedies can
be adopted.

In today's world, two dangers seem paramount. One is that the
division of power among the president, the Senate, and the House—
coupled with a partisan split between the branches—will render it
impossible to bring the national budget deficit under control, and the
accumulated weight of national debt will eventually produce a sudden, or a gradual, economic calamity. The other is that division of
power will produce a paralysis in foreign policy at a time of crisis,
leaving the president unable to conduct foreign relations in a coherent
and effective manner with the harmonious assured participation and
support of congressional majorities.

If one accepts the proposition that indecisive, stalemated government can place the nation in peril—and that those risks outweigh the danger that decisive government will make unwise decisions—the preceding chapters suggest a range of remedies. Without regard to the question of what may or may not be politically feasible, an ideal series of amendments to the U.S. Constitution would include these, roughly in order of importance (and in the order discussed in the earlier chapters).

1. *The team ticket*. The separation of powers is far more likely to lead to debilitating governmental deadlock when the organs of government are divided between the parties. Several measures give promise of discouraging the ticket splitting that produces divided government, but only one would prohibit it outright. That is the team ticket, which would combine each party's candidates for president, vice president, Senate, and House into a slate that would be voted for as a unit.

2. *Four-year House terms and eight-year Senate terms*. Even a united government is constantly distracted by the imminence of the next election, which is never more than two years away. The two-year life of the Congress—shortest of any national legislature in the world—normally limits an incoming president to barely a year as his "window of opportunity" to lead his party in enacting the program for which it sought its victory. To eliminate the midterm election and thereby lengthen the period of relative freedom from election pressure would require four-year House terms and either four-year or eight-year Senate terms, with the latter more in accord with the staggered-term tradition of the Senate. Presidents and Congresses alike would be better able to undertake short-term measures that might be unpopular, in order to achieve a greater long-run good, and the legislative process would benefit from a more deliberate tempo.

3. *A new or modified procedure for selecting the president*. The problem of the faithless elector, the danger of rejection by the electoral college of the popular vote winner, and the unfairness and disruptive nature of the contingency procedure for selection of the president by the House must all be dealt with. The national bonus plan proposed by a task force in 1978 appears to be the best approach to resolving all of these difficulties at the same time.

4. *A method for special elections to reconstitute a failed government*. Chapter 6 explores the almost infinite variations in form that a pro-

cedure for calling special elections might take. If the mechanism is to be suitable for use in all of the kinds of emergency circumstances that can produce governmental failure, the special election should be callable at any time, by the president or a majority of either house of Congress. All seats in both houses, as well as the presidency and vice presidency, should be filled at the election. Those elected should serve full terms (except half the senators would serve for only four years), and the terms could be adjusted by a few months so that the next regular election would fall on the customary November date.

5. *Removal of the prohibition against dual officeholding.* Permitting members of Congress to serve in the executive branch might turn out not to be practical, but removing the prohibition would permit constructive experimentation with that means of linking the executive and legislative branches.

6. *A limited item veto.* An item veto that could be overridden by absolute majorities of the two houses would give the president a means to publicize egregious "pork barrel" appropriations—and get at least some of them eliminated—yet not upset the executive-legislative balance of power.

7. *Restoration of the legislative veto.* This, too, might be limited, permitting only two-house vetoes.

8. *A war powers amendment.* Writing the essential terms of the War Powers Resolution of 1973 into the Constitution would clear up the unsettled question as to whether that resolution is valid and presidents are required to conform to its provisions.

9. *Approval of treaties by a majority of the membership of both houses.* This would remove the power to dominate critical foreign policy decisions from a minority of the Senate and restore it, like other governmental powers, to the majority.

These constitutional amendments could be supplemented by statutes and changes in party rules that would serve the same objectives, such as increasing the proportion of members of Congress, candidates for Congress, and other party leaders as delegates to presidential nominating conventions and providing for partial financing of congressional campaigns with public funds administered by party committees.

As observed in chapter 8, items 6 through 9 on this list of amendments all affect the balance of power between the executive and legislative branches and hence could best be combined in a single package that would include measures appealing to each branch and come as close as possible to preserving the present balance.

The Difficulty of Doing Anything

Even those most profoundly convinced that the U.S. government has serious structural weaknesses come to ask themselves and one another: Why even try to change the Constitution? Why not take for granted that it cannot be altered, and settle for whatever improvements can be made by lesser means—by passing laws, or changing party rules and structures, or concentrating on electing better officials to high office? The process of amending the country's 200-year-old charter is so formidable that reformers can be excused for being daunted at the outset, and theorists forgiven for devoting their analytical energies to other subjects. Not only may an amendment be blocked by 34 percent of the voting members of one house of Congress, but, if it passes that hurdle, it can still be defeated by the adverse vote, or simple inaction, of as few as thirteen of the ninety-nine state legislative houses, or fewer than 14 percent.[1]

No other country has a mechanism for constitutional amendment that requires so high a degree of consensus. Nor does any state of the United States. Of the fifty states, twenty permit legislatures to submit amendments to the people by simple majorities (in twelve of these, the legislature must act twice in separate sessions), one by a majority of total membership, one by a two-thirds vote in its Senate but only a majority in its House of Representatives, nine by a three-fifths vote in each house, eighteen by a two-thirds vote, and one by a two-thirds majority of the membership of each house. But while eighteen states make the initiation process as difficult as in the federal government and one makes it even more so, in forty-two of the states a simple majority approval by a popular referendum completes the

---

1. To make matters still more difficult, seven states have required extraordinary state legislative majorities for ratification of federal constitutional amendments: Arkansas, Colorado, Georgia, Idaho, and Kansas a two-thirds vote of both houses, Illinois three-fifths of both houses, and Alabama three-fifths of the lower chamber of the legislature. For an attack on these requirements as "unnecessary, undesirable, and unfair," see comments of Representative John J. LaFalce, Democrat of New York, *Congressional Record*, August 9, 1978, p. 25255.

process. One state does not require approval; five require approval
by a majority of the votes cast in the election (as distinct from votes
cast on the amendment itself), one requires that the majority be equivalent to the majority of votes cast for governor, and only one requires
a two-thirds vote of the electorate. Moreover, seventeen states permit
constitutional amendments to be placed on the ballot by initiative;
thirteen of these provide for their approval by simple majorities of
those voting, and none has a two-thirds requirement. Finally, the
states make it relatively easy to convene constitutional conventions;
in all, 233 such conclaves had been held through 1989, or more than
four per state.[2]

As the consequence of these comparatively workable amendment
procedures, the states had approved 5,807 amendments to their constitutions as of the end of 1989, or 116 per state, as compared with
26 for the federal government. Given that the states were then, on
the average, only 147 years old, that represents a frequency of constitutional change about six times that of the national government.[3]
The circumstances are not strictly comparable, of course, because state
constitutions have been more in need of amendment; in contrast to
the federal charter, they have incorporated much detail of types that
in the national government are left to statutory law, and many of the
amendments therefore accomplished purposes that in the federal system
could be, and have been, achieved by statute. Yet among the changes
were many that altered the basic structures of state governments, including lengthening the terms of governors and other officials, strengthening
the governor's power, shortening the ballot, and eliminating execu-

2. Janice C. May, "State Constitutions and Constitutional Revision: 1988–89 and
the 1980s," *The Book of the States, 1990–91* (Lexington, Ky.: Council of State Governments, 1990), pp. 22, 40–44. Of the twenty states listed as permitting submission of
amendments by simple legislative majorities and the forty-two allowing approval by
electoral majorities, one requires a three-fourths approval in each case for certain
specified matters. Of the seventeen states with initiative procedures, one limits the
procedure to amendments concerning the legislature; one requires approval by a majority of all voting in the election or 60 percent of those voting on the amendment; two
provide that the amendment majority must amount to 30 and 35 percent, respectively,
of all votes cast in the election; and one calls for approval by simple majorities at two
general elections.

3. Ibid., *1982–83*, p. 117, and *1990–91*, p. 21. The pace of state constitutional change
has quickened. Of the 5,807 amendments, 819 were adopted in the eight-year period
1982–89. This amounts to 14 percent of the total and about two per state per year. The
figures on amendments include those proposed by constitutional conventions.

tive councils. Whenever the people of the various states become aware of deficiencies in their governmental structures, the ease with which their constitutions can be modernized is impressive.

The question arises, then: Should the advocates of constitutional change in the interest of more effective government turn their attention first to modifying the amendment process itself—for instance, by providing that amendments be submitted for approval by a national popular vote rather than by three-fourths of the states? Probably not. A simplified amendment procedure would never be considered in the abstract, simply as a theoretical proposition in the interest of good government. To win any significant backing, it would have to be seen as making the course easier for one or more specific, popular amendments whose supporters could then be mobilized behind it. But arrayed against the change would be the opponents of not only those amendments but all the many other alterations in the Constitution that might be under public discussion at the time, including those that would modify the Bill of Rights. The proposal would be seen as a devious attempt to slip into the Constitution bad ideas that could not win approval otherwise, on their merits. It would simply carry too much baggage.

Variations in the Amendment Process

Reformers might find some slight promise, however, in two elements of the existing amendment process that have been little used. One is the option of state ratification by unicameral conventions rather than by bicameral legislatures, which would—in theory, at least—somewhat reduce the mathematical odds against approval of any proposition by three-fourths of the states. On the one occasion when that method was used—the Twenty-first Amendment repealing Prohibition—it was resoundingly successful. Ratification was completed in the course of barely nine months, between February 20 and December 5, 1933. As to why that expeditious procedure was not chosen by the Congress in any other instance, the historical record is blank; presumably the sponsors of the various amendments were confident that they could win approval by the legislatures readily enough, obviating the need for the expense and trouble of organizing state conventions. Or perhaps they feared that taking their case to the people, who would elect the convention delegates, would involve more risk than relying on the more experienced politicians who constitute the legislatures. If a proposed amendment is unpopular, the powerful lobbying organizations that support it are sometimes able to prevail on the legislators to approve it anyway, as the Senate debate of 1924 (discussed in chapter 3) brought out.

The second optional procedure is the initiation of amendments by constitutional convention rather than by Congress. A convention must be called, under the Constitution, on petition of the legislatures of two-thirds of the states. No such gathering has ever been held, but for any amendment that would be seen by a substantial bloc in the Congress as restricting in any way the powers of the legislative branch, the convention process would appear to be essential as the only way of bypassing the congressional opposition. Such was the case early in this century, when advocates of the direct election of senators began a drive for a convention in order to circumvent the Senate, which was stubbornly refusing to reform itself. When one legislature after another passed the necessary resolution and the move appeared headed for success, the Senate reluctantly yielded and joined the House in proposing the amendment to the states. Since then, the only significant attempt to call a convention has been the one that gathered force in the 1980s but seems to have lost momentum since, organized to support an amendment to require a balanced federal budget except in certain specified circumstances.

Constitutional lawyers dispute whether, if the Congress attempted to limit a convention to a single subject—such as a balanced budget amendment—the limitation would be binding. In the total absence of precedent, no one can be sure. It is unlikely that the delegates would choose to disregard any congressional limitation, because they would have been chosen to deal with only one subject and would not be prepared to cope with others. But if they did elect to broaden their agenda, it is clear that no one outside their body would have authority to prevent their doing so. The delegates of 1787, after all, had been assigned only to propose amendments to the Articles of Confederation but, once they met, they set their own agenda. Another such "runaway convention" is not beyond the realm of possibility, and the question would be what happened afterward. To the extent that the convention exceeded its mandate from the Congress, it would plunge itself into a public controversy that would create a negative presumption against all of its actions, and the accusation of illegality could be exploited in the state ratification process. But if, nevertheless, three-fourths of the states took cognizance of the challenged proposals and gave their approval, the amendments would no doubt ultimately become part of the Constitution—either because the Supreme Court validated the disputed amendments or because Congress took the initiative to resubmit them. Should the balanced budget movement succeed in compelling a convention, then, and that body decide to consider additional matters, critics of the governmental structure would have an opportunity to advance any proposals that, because of their effect on the Congress itself, would not be likely to be initiated by the legislators in the normal manner.

The Problem of Gainers and Losers

Still, ratification by three-fourths of the states would remain as formidable a barrier as ever. Institutional structure is not an issue likely to arouse popular fervor, in the absence of a patent breakdown in the functioning of government, and even then—as at the time of Watergate—most people would be inclined to place the blame on the failure of individual leaders rather than of institutions. Proposals for structural change may not arouse fervent opposition either, but in the absence of popular support any organized institutional opposition is likely to prevail. If either of the major parties sees its interests jeopardized by a proposal, or incumbent legislators discern a loss of power for their branch, or the president and defenders of presidential power foresee a weakening of the executive, the proposal is doomed. Any significant ideological bloc, also, would surely have enough strength in enough states to block an amendment; so no proposal has much chance of success if it arouses conservative concern that it hides a bias toward big government, or liberal concern that it fetters government, or elitist worry that it embodies an excess of democracy, or antiestablishment fear that it upsets the balance the other way.

But institutional changes are seldom neutral, and even if one (or a package of several) could be conceived that is truly neutral—and would be perceived that way—neutrality is not enough. Each of the elements of the institutional system, and each major ideological group as well, must see some benefit. Unless something is to be gained, why risk change at all? But gain for everyone is a logical impossibility. True, the government as a whole can accrue power, as it has been doing for most of two centuries, but the division among institutions and officeholders of the right to exercise any given aggregate of power becomes a zero-sum game. If one institution or one political party or one ideological group gains, another loses. That, at bottom, is why there has not been a single amendment in two hundred years that redistributed governmental power. The two amendments that can be classed as even affecting the institutional structure at all—the Seventeenth (direct election of senators) and the Twenty-second (the two-term limit on the presidency)—concerned only the selection of the individuals who would wield institutional power, not the scope of the institutional authority itself.

But the distribution of power among the elements of the governmental system is what all of the constitutional changes discussed in this book would, in one or another degree, affect. The scale of the benefit to governmental effectiveness to be derived from any measure or set of measures would depend on the magnitude of that effect. But so would the vigor of the opposition each measure would incite. It becomes an axiom of constitutional reform, then, that any structural amendment that would bring major benefits cannot be adopted—again, barring a governmental collapse that can be clearly attributed to the constitutional design—while any measure that stands a chance of passage is likely to be innocuous.

The strategy of reformers, in such a circumstance, must be to search for trade-offs, based on the possibility that institutions and groups affected may weigh gains and losses on different scales. If party A to a negotiation considers proposition X to be far more important than proposition Y, while party B perceives them in the opposite relation, then party A will gladly trade Y for X and party B will accept the trade. Constitutional amendments are, unfortunately, not easily combined in logical packages for trade-off purposes, nor can the parties involved be brought to a table for direct negotiations.

If one concludes, for instance, that much of the problem of governmental incapacity arises from divided government, as discussed in chapter 4, there appears to be no practicable remedy. The axiom applies: the only modifications that would come close to forestalling divided government—bonus seats and the team ticket—would encounter insurmountable opposition. Bonus seats would dilute the power and influence of every legislator elected through the normal process, thus solidifying the entire Congress as an opposition bloc. As for the team-ticket idea, only one of the two parties, at any given time, would see a possible gain, while the other would anticipate a certain loss. In the 1980s, the team ticket would have helped the Republicans. Ronald Reagan's strength in 1984 would surely have won GOP control of the House as well as the Senate. Even so, Republicans have not embraced or even discussed the idea, and were it to be seriously advanced it would no doubt be dismissed out of anticipation, among other reasons, that at some future date the situation might be reversed. Meanwhile, the Democrats would look at recent presidential elections and reflect on how many House and Senate seats they would have lost if their congressional candidates had been tied to George McGovern, Walter Mondale, and Michael Dukakis. All this would be opposition enough but, meanwhile ideological opponents would also appear. The right to split tickets would be touted as one of the inalienable rights of citizenship, not to be abridged for the politicians' gain.

The other two proposals discussed in chapter 4 would arouse less opposition simply because they would be potentially less effective, but at least one of the parties, at any given time, would find any measure that tended to promote united government against its short-run electoral interest. In the current period, when Republicans succeed in presidential elections while Democrats win more congressional contests, why would any Democrat wish to increase the chance that every time the Republicans won the White House they would sweep the House and Senate also?

Of all the proposals considered in this book, lengthening of congressional terms would seem to come closest to making everyone concerned a gainer, and none a loser—at least at first glance. House members should be expected to prefer terms of four years instead of two, Senate members ought to like eight-year terms better than six, and presidents should see benefit in electing members of Congress only in presidential years. But the rejection of Lyndon Johnson's 1966 proposal for four-year House terms coincident with the president's is instructive. Republican representatives saw their party placed at a disadvantage vis-à-vis the Democrats, and Democrats came to fear a loss of congressional independence vis-à-vis the president. Perhaps the latter worry could be shown to be ill founded—representatives would not have to run on a presidential ticket any oftener than they do at present—but the former concern is surely real, for one party or the other. In recent midterm elections, one of the parties would have been the gainer, and that party would be loath to see its opportunity for future gains eliminated. Only if recent midterm elections had been close to a dead heat would it appear possible to persuade members of both parties to assess the personal convenience of a longer term as outweighing any potential partisan loss.

As for the public reaction, the Johnson proposal met with some approbation, much indifference, but no mass cry of outrage. Perhaps that was because the amendment made so little progress on Capitol Hill. If a new proposal were to win serious consideration, a principled opposition would undoubtedly arise to contend that popular control over elected officials was being lessened. The public, it would be argued, should have the right to "throw the rascals out" at less than four-year intervals. The argument would be persuasive, even though the midterm election does not fully serve that purpose now because the president and two-thirds of the Senate cannot be touched. As argued in chapter 6, the country has always needed a truly effective mechanism for reconstituting failed governments, and lengthened terms would make the need more evident.

The prospect for winning longer terms might be enhanced, then, if that proposal were accompanied by a companion scheme to provide the people a genuine opportunity, in times of need, to redirect the course of government between presidential elections. But the exploration in chapter 6 of the range of remedies that would permit a complete reconstitution of the government between presidential elections confirms that no conceivable remedy is apt to be perceived as making all gainers and no losers. Presidents and legislators alike are sure to suspect that any proposed scheme for special intraterm elections would remove whatever advantages might be conferred by the lengthened terms. If the public gains control, the politicians lose it; that, too, is a zero-sum game. Perhaps it is not beyond reason that a combination of longer terms and special elections could be so designed that presidents, senators, and representatives would all see more benefit than loss. But the task for institutional architects is a forbidding one.

Finally, an opportunity for a trade-off may arise if the movement for limiting the number of terms a House member may serve continues to gather force. If those who favor the four-year term also see merit in term limitation (or if they see the latter proposition as likely to be adopted in any case), they could propose that the two changes be combined. Members of Congress, and the public generally, might see more gain than loss if the choice were between both measures or neither.

The proposal in chapter 7 for removing the prohibition against dual officeholding might encounter minimal opposition, for both branches might be seen to be the gainers. The president would gain the right to appoint legislators to executive office, yet without compulsion to do so; and legislators would gain at least a chance for broader responsibilities. Moreover, the amendment would require each specific use of the new authority to be approved by the Senate, and perhaps by the House too, as provided by law. The issue of gainers and losers would simply be deferred, and each particular appointment would have to worked out in such a way that both branches at that time were perceived to gain. The difficulty of achieving that objective would probably be great enough that, when the practical obstacles to combining executive and legislative work loads were also considered, the amendment would turn out to be inconsequential.

The proposals for strengthening political parties discussed in chapter 7, which do not require constitutional amendment, are clearly more feasible for that reason, but they nevertheless encounter the same problem of winners and losers. Passing laws usually requires some degree of bipartisan support, and any fundamental redesign of party institutions would have to be backed by all the major factions within a party. But changes in election laws, including controls over campaign finance, inevitably favor one party against another, some factions against others, incumbents against challengers or vice versa. Modifications in the presidential nomination process may also run afoul of state laws and of popular sentiment in favor of the broadest possible public participation and control. Changes in party and electoral institutions have occurred in the past, however, and reforms that enjoy broad though not overwhelming popular support can—unlike constitutional amendments with the same degree of public approval—eventually win adoption.

The possibility that the item veto and the legislative veto might be combined in a trade-off is noted in chapter 8. The president might find the item veto so appealing that he would concede the legislative

veto in exchange, in the knowledge that the Congress will find ways
of imposing its veto anyway and that the executive branch has often
gained, because of a veto provision, a delegation of power it would
not otherwise have received. The trade might not be seen by the
legislators as an even one, unless the president's item veto could be
overridden by a majority of the membership of both houses, as in
Illinois. In that case, of course, the president might lose his interest.
But the issue does appear to be one that lends itself to more or less
formal interbranch negotiation. The war power and the requirements
for treaty approval might be included in the bargaining as well.

All of the seemingly insurmountable obstacles to constitutional
change could be overcome, of course, if the government were indeed
to fail, palpably and for a sustained period. But the necessity to experience governmental failure, in order to prepare for it, is not a happy
prospect. This book must end, then, on a pessimistic note. Nothing
is likely to happen short of crisis—which is, of course, the case with
all fundamental constitutional reform, in every country of the world
and throughout history.

Nevertheless, nothing can be lost if, as the Constitution enters its
third century, the public can be brought to look hard at the weaknesses of the American governmental system and consider what, if
the worst comes to pass, the remedies might be. Even among those
who believe no constitutional crisis lies ahead, few argue that the
workings of governmental institutions are beyond improvement.
Whatever the future may hold, much is to be gained if politicians,
statesmen, and scholars carry forward the kind of analysis this book
has attempted to provide, trying to separate the workable modifications in the constitutional structure from the unworkable, the effective
from the ineffective, the possibly feasible from the wholly infeasible,
all in an uncharted area of institutional design where there are few
precedents to be evaluated and no one can be sure.

Index